Reproductive Realities in Modern China

Lasting from 1979 to 2015, China's One Child Policy is often remembered as one of the most ambitious social engineering projects to date and is considered emblematic of global efforts to regulate population growth during the twentieth century. Drawing on a rich combination of archival research and oral history, Sarah Mellors Rodriguez analyzes how ordinary people, particularly women, navigated China's shifting fertility policies before and during the One Child Policy era. She examines the implementation and reception of these policies and reveals that they were often contradictory and unevenly enforced, as men and women challenged, reworked, and co-opted state policies to suit their own needs. By situating the One Child Policy within the longer history of birth control and abortion in China, *Reproductive Realities in Modern China* exposes important historical continuities, such as the enduring reliance on abortion as contraception and the precariousness of state control over reproduction.

Sarah Mellors Rodriguez is Assistant Professor of History at Missouri State University.

CAMBRIDGE STUDIES IN THE HISTORY OF THE PEOPLE'S REPUBLIC OF CHINA

Series Editors

Jacob Eyferth, Daniel Leese, Michael Schoenhals

Cambridge Studies in the History of the People's Republic of China is a major series of ambitious works in the social, political, and cultural history of socialist China. Aided by a wealth of new sources, recent research pays close attention to regional differences, to perspectives from the social and geographical margins, and to the unintended consequences of Communist Party rule. Books in the series contribute to this historical re-evaluation by presenting the most stimulating and rigorously researched works in the field to a broad audience. The series invites submissions from a variety of disciplines and approaches, based on written, material or oral sources. Particularly welcome are those works that bridge the 1949 and 1978 divides, and those that seek to understand China in an international or global context.

Reproductive Realities in Modern China

Birth Control and Abortion, 1911–2021

Sarah Mellors Rodriguez
Missouri State University

Shaftesbury Road, Cambridge CB2 8EA, United Kingdom

One Liberty Plaza, 20th Floor, New York, NY 10006, USA

477 Williamstown Road, Port Melbourne, VIC 3207, Australia

314–321, 3rd Floor, Plot 3, Splendor Forum, Jasola District Centre, New Delhi – 110025, India

103 Penang Road, #05–06/07, Visioncrest Commercial, Singapore 238467

Cambridge University Press is part of Cambridge University Press & Assessment, a department of the University of Cambridge.

We share the University's mission to contribute to society through the pursuit of education, learning and research at the highest international levels of excellence.

www.cambridge.org
Information on this title: www.cambridge.org/9781009011570

DOI: 10.1017/9781009019880

First published 2023
First paperback edition 2024

A catalogue record for this publication is available from the British Library

Library of Congress Cataloging-in-Publication data
Names: Rodriguez, Sarah Mellors, author.
Title: Reproductive realities in modern China : birth control and abortion, 1911-2021 / Sarah Mellors Rodriguez, Missouri State University.
Description: Cambridge, United Kingdom ; New York, NY : Cambridge University Press, 2023. | Series: Cambridge studies in the hisjtory of the People's Republic of China | Includes bibliographical references and index.
Identifiers: LCCN 2022029404 | ISBN 9781316515310 (hardback)
Subjects: LCSH: Abortion–China–History. | Birth control–China–History. | China–Population policy.
Classification: LCC HQ767.5.C6 R64 2023 | DDC 363.9/60951–dc23/eng/20220628
LC record available at https://lccn.loc.gov/2022029404

ISBN 978-1-316-51531-0 Hardback
ISBN 978-1-009-01157-0 Paperback

Contents

Figures

Tables

Acknowledgments

This book would not have been possible without the support and guidance of countless individuals. My advisors at the University of California, Irvine (UC Irvine) – Emily Baum and Jeff Wasserstrom – have mentored me for nearly a decade, nurturing what began as an inchoate idea into a full-fledged research project and eventually a book. Kavita Philip and Laura Mitchell challenged me to approach my research through the lenses of science and technology studies and world history, while Harriet Evans, Jeremy Brown, and Wang Feng showed much-needed enthusiasm for my project from the beginning. Paul Pickowicz offered me precious opportunities to conduct research at Stanford University and East China Normal University (ECNU), experiences that proved critical in formulating my dissertation. Ling Ma, Mirela David, Bridie Andrews, Tina Phillips Johnson, Deborah Davis, Thomas Mullaney, and Frank Dikotter helped me to conceptualize my research in its early stages, while Justin McDaniel, Prakash Kumar, Howard Chiang, Mary Beth Norton, Mindy Smith, and John Chuchiak helped me navigate the process of reconfiguring my dissertation into a book.

I owe much to two well-timed workshops on medicine, science, and technology, sponsored by the Association for Asian Studies and the Social Science Research Council. Not only did I make lifelong friends, but I also received invaluable feedback on my research. A special thanks goes to my fellow scholars of birth control – Shoan Yin Cheung and Young Su Park – for their critiques and suggestions.

Gina Anne Tam, Jennifer Altehenger, Aaron Moore, John Kennedy, Hui Faye Xiao, Akiko Takeyama, and Gülnar Eziz offered me opportunities to share my research and graciously commented on my presentations. I am also grateful to UC Irvine's Research Librarian for Asian Studies, Ying Zhang; Yanjie Huang, who invited me to join the Columbia-Fudan primary source workshop "Revolutionary Routine: Grassroots Sources on Work, Family and Private Life in Maoist China" and introduced me to important contacts and sources in China; Zhang Letian and Li Tian at Fudan University's Contemporary

China Social Life Data and Research Center, who gave me early access to their collections; and Arunabh Ghosh, who shared research materials with me and made me aware of the collections at the University of Toledo. Participating in the UCLA Asia Institute-Shanghai Jiao Tong University Summer Workshop on Chinese Archival Texts in 2016 and the Thirteenth Annual Graduate Seminar on China at the Chinese University of Hong Kong in 2017 further enriched my research. I would remiss not to also thank Paul Jakov Smith, who introduced me to the possibilities of Chinese history as an undergraduate at Haverford College and enabled me to share my research with Haverford students as a junior faculty member.

While in China, I benefited from the sponsorship of Li Tiangang and Gao Xi at Fudan University, Yu Mingjing at ECNU, Cao Shuji and Liu Shigu at Shanghai Jiao Tong University, and Zhang Daqing at Peking University. Lin Li allowed me to interview her mother as well as stay in her home many times. Yupeng Jiao generously encouraged me to interview his parents and gave me a foot in the door at the Luoyang Municipal Archive. Librarians and archivists at the Hangzhou, Shanghai, Tianjin, Guangzhou, Luoyang, Qingdao, and Beijing Municipal Archives; the Guangdong and Zhejiang Provincial Archives; the Shanghai Library; the National Library of China; the Fudan University Contemporary China Social Life Data and Research Center; the Hoover Institution Archives; the Stanford University East Asia Library; the Chinese University of Hong Kong University Service Center for China Studies; the Wellcome Library; the Rockefeller Archive Center; Princeton University Rare Books and Special Collections; the Sripati Chandrasekhar Collection at the University of Toledo; the Columbia University C.V. Starr East Asian Library; and the Harvard-Yenching Library also assisted me during my research trips in China, the UK, and the US.

My research would not have been possible without grants from Fulbright-Hays, the Social Science Research Council, the Western Association of Women Historians, and the Hoover Institution Library and Archives. At UC Irvine, I also benefited from a School of Humanities Graduate Dean's Dissertation Fellowship, a Summer Dissertation Fellowship, a Humanities Commons Individual Graduate Research Grant, Charles and Ann Quilter Research Grants, and funding from the Center for Asian Studies and the Medical Humanities Initiative. At Missouri State University, a Summer Faculty Fellowship provided me with a summer off from teaching to devote to manuscript revisions.

A special thanks goes to my classmates – Marketus Presswood, Rachael De La Cruz, Clare Gordon Bettencourt, Olivia Hanninen,

Stephanie Narrow, Anandi Rao, Steve Pascoe, Daniella McCahey, Soodabeh Weaver, Yidi Wu, and Laurie Dickmeyer – who offered advice, emotional support, and humor through even the toughest of times. Yvon Wang, Jack Neubauer, Sandy Chang, and Jeff Guarneri generously read my drafts and offered insightful comments. In particular, I am indebted to my interviewees for welcoming me into their lives and for sharing some of their most personal memories with me.

Thank you to my manuscript reviewers for their thoughtful and meticulous feedback; to Lucy Rhymer and Emily Plater for shepherding me through the publication process; to the series editors for seeing value in my work; and to Victor Matthews, Kathleen Kennedy, and Glena Admire for their ongoing support at Missouri State.

A version of Chapter 3 appeared as "Less Reproduction, More Production: Birth Control in the Early People's Republic of China, 1949–1958," *East Asian Science, Technology and Society: An International Journal* 13, no. 3 (2019): 367–389. It is republished here with permission from Taylor & Francis. Sections of Chapters 2, 3, and 4 were also published as "The Trouble with Rubbers: A History of Condoms in Modern China," *Nan Nü: Men, Women and Gender in China* 22, no. 1 (2020): 150–178. They are reproduced here with permission from Brill.

Finally, I want to thank my family – my parents, Fern Bassow and Bob Gemmell; and my siblings, Kimberly Polishchuk and Rob Gemmell – for continuously supporting and encouraging me. My partner in all things, Luis Rodriguez, has been a constant source of love and inspiration from the beginning of my PhD to the present, even accompanying me on multiple extended research trips to China. I also want to thank my cat, Papi (may he rest in peace), who sat next to me through countless revisions, and my new kitties, Dewey and Chloe, for bringing me renewed joy.

Note on the Text

A Note on Terminology: Without denying the limits of biologically-based binary definitions of gender, for the sake of word variation, this book uses the terms "woman" and "female" interchangeably, as well as the terms "man" and "male." While in no way seeking to perpetuate the erasure of transgender or non-binary experiences, this semantic decision also reflects the fact that, in the eyes of historical power holders, the discourses and policies under discussion were primarily aimed at women and men assumed to be heterosexual and cisgender.

A Note on Chinese Characters: Citations of texts from the Republican period (1911–1949) are rendered in traditional characters, as was the norm during that period. The names of sources from the People's Republic of China (1949-present), however, are written in simplified characters, which became standard under the new regime. Because most of this book focuses on the period after 1949, the terms in the glossary are also written in simplified characters.

Table 1 *Timeline of Important Events*

1840–1842	First Opium War; establishment of foreign treaty ports in China
1856–1860	Second Opium War
1898	Failed Qing reforms
1911	Qing Dynasty overthrown and Republican Period begins
1916–1927	Warlord era
1910s–1920s	May Fourth / New Culture Movement
1921	Chinese Communist Party established
1927	Much of China unified under Nationalists; Communists retreat to the hinterland
1931	Japanese occupy Manchuria
1937	Japanese army invades northeastern China, starting World War II
1937–1945	World War II
1945–1949	Civil war between Communists and Nationalists
1949	Nationalists defeated; People's Republic of China established
1949–1953	Birth control, abortion, and sterilization tightly regulated; couples encouraged to have many children

Table 1 (*cont.*)

1954–1958	First "Birth Planning" Campaign; restrictions on birth control, abortion, and sterilization relaxed slightly
1956–1957	Hundred Flowers Movement; intellectuals criticize China's unfettered population growth
1957–1958	Anti-Rightist Campaign; critics of natalism silenced
1959–1961	Great Leap Forward and famine
1962–1965	Second "Birth Planning" Campaign; urban and rural couples encouraged to practice family planning
1966–1976	Cultural revolution
1968–1980	Sent-Down Youth Movement (this movement actually began in 1955, but the number of participants increased dramatically in 1968)
1968–1983	Barefoot doctors sent to the countryside
1971–1978	Birth planning work intensifies
1976	Mao Zedong dies
1978	Reform era begins
1979	One Child Policy enacted
1984	One Child Policy relaxed in some cases
2015	One Child Policy replaced with Two Child Policy
2021	Two Child Policy replaced with Three Child Policy

Source: The periodization of birth planning campaigns is taken from Masako Kohama, "Jihua shengyu de kaiduan – 1950–1960 niandai de Shanghai" (The Beginnings of Birth Planning in Shanghai in the 1950s and 1960s), *Zhongyang yanjiuyuan jindaishi yanjiusuo jikan* (Academia Sinica Institute of Modern History) 68 (2010): 99.

Introduction

Li Xiaoping was a credit officer at a small bank branch and a married woman. One day in 1956, Chen Xu, the director of a nearby military camp, visited the bank. Soon after meeting, the two began having an affair. However, when Chen professed his love to Li and asked her to leave her husband for him, she refused. Not long after, Li realized she was pregnant and that Chen was the father. Knowing that adultery was punishable by law and an out-of-wedlock pregnancy provided the most indicting evidence of infidelity, Li decided to abort the fetus using a method she had heard about that involved consuming quinine tablets. Today quinine is used to treat malaria, but for much of the twentieth century taking an overdose to deliberately terminate a pregnancy was relatively common in China and other parts of the world.[1] Though not technically banned at the national level, local authorities frequently charged and convicted people who underwent, performed, or facilitated home abortions.[2] Knowing this, Li had to convince her doctor to prescribe quinine for another illness. In the end, she successfully aborted the pregnancy, and the affair was not discovered for another two years.[3]

Li's account offers a rare glimpse of the diverse family planning strategies ordinary people employed during the early People's Republic of China (PRC; 1949–present). In 1949, the prolonged Chinese civil war ended when the Chinese Communist Party (CCP) defeated the ruling Nationalist Party and established a new government. For the Communists, eliminating class differences and colonial influences, forging a socialist citizenry, and improving the economy through

[1] Qingdao Municipal Archive (QMA), D0042-92-00079; QMA, D00011400034; Dorothy Dunbar Bromley, *Birth Control: Its Use and Misuse* (New York: Harper and Brothers Publishers, 1934), 103.

[2] Women who met certain conditions were permitted by law to have abortions; Wang et al., *Dangdai zhongguo de weisheng shiye* (Public Hygiene Undertakings in Modern China), vol. 2 (Beijing: Zhongguo shehui kexue chuban she, 1986), 233.

[3] Shanghai Jiao Tong University Archive (SJTUA), Z1-9-727.

agricultural collectivization and industrialization were central state objectives. In this context, women were encouraged to serve the state in terms of both productive power and reproductive labor: Women not only had to balance work inside and outside of the home, but they were also expected to have abundant children to grow the workforce. Indeed, women's social roles as wives and mothers were seen as essential for the maintenance of the nuclear family unit, the perceived basis for social stability in Chinese society. To protect those interests, the party policed out-of-wedlock pregnancies and dramatically restricted access to birth control and abortion. Set against the backdrop of resource scarcity, unpredictable political campaigns, and proscriptive social norms, Li Xiaoping underwent a dangerous covert abortion not merely out of self-interest but for self-preservation. Fear of being accused of social deviancy and facing untold judicial repercussions played an important role in her decision to abort the pregnancy.

This incident might seem unusual or anomalous, yet cases like this can be found throughout urban China, and in some instances in more rural areas, dating from at least the late imperial period.[4] In fact, the circumstances Li found herself in – seeking an abortion to cover up evidence of extramarital sex – were actually quite typical of abortion seekers, both in China and abroad.[5] Even the specter of state punitive power in the realm of private life was not new, as performing or facilitating an abortion to conceal infidelity had been punishable by law since the eighteenth century.[6]

Still, Li's experience is unique in that, set in 1956, it falls at the start of the period in which China's most sophisticated and elaborate mechanisms of reproductive surveillance were being honed. In the decades to come, the boundary between state, society, and women's bodies would become even blurrier.

⋆

Perhaps a more appropriate point of entry into a discussion of reproduction and contraception in modern China would be the One Child Policy

[4] Matthew H. Sommer, "Abortion in Late Imperial China: Routine Birth Control or Crisis Intervention?" *Late Imperial China* 31, no. 2 (2010): 97–165.

[5] Kate Fisher, *Birth Control, Sex, and Marriage in Britain, 1918–1960* (Oxford: Oxford University Press, 2006) and Leslie J. Reagan, *When Abortion Was a Crime: Women, Medicine, and the Law in the United States, 1867–1973* (Berkeley: University of California Press, 1998).

[6] Sommer, "Abortion in Late Imperial China," 119–123.

(1979–2015), one of the most ambitious social engineering projects of all time, which – at least in theory – restricted couples to one child.[7] Born out of heightened global concerns about resource shortages and overpopulation in the developing world, the policy aimed to accelerate China's economic growth and improve the standard of living.[8] Since the enactment of the One Child Policy, myriad academic studies and journalistic accounts have examined the policy's execution and its consequences. These publications range from news articles reporting the horrors of forced sterilization and abortion to demographic studies praising the efficiency with which the Chinese government lowered the country's birth rate. Yet, an obvious tension exists between the introductory anecdote, in which a young woman fears punishment for undergoing an abortion, and conventional narratives surrounding the One Child Policy. Through what process did undergoing an abortion or using birth control shift from a taboo, criminal offense in the early and mid-twentieth century to a state-mandated behavior under the One Child Policy? How was this epistemological change experienced in everyday life and manifested in women's bodies?

To answer these questions, this book approaches birth control and abortion from the perspective of lived experience. The existing research on population planning in China emphasizes the role of the social sciences in producing authoritative scientific knowledge and the ways in which government technocrats deployed certain narratives to justify top-down demographic change. By privileging the perspectives of officials and policymakers, most studies of population planning in modern China overlook how such policies were implemented and received. By contrast, *Reproductive Realities* draws on the oral histories of approximately eighty women and men and extensive archival research to investigate local enactment and reception of fertility policies since the founding of the Republic of China (1911–1949). In so doing, this research exposes the messy realities of local policy implementation and the ways in which

[7] Various exceptions to the policy were made beginning in 1984. See Chapter 6 for more on this topic.

[8] *The Population Bomb*, the 1968 book published by an influential American professor of population studies Paul Ehrlich, has come to represent the post–World War II preoccupation with limiting population growth in the developing world. Ehrlich deemed overpopulation "mankind's most pressing problem" and claimed that coercive population planning measures were necessary to prevent global poverty, food shortages, and environmental degradation; Paul R. Ehrlich, *The Population Bomb* (New York: Sierra Club/ Ballantine Books, 1968), 176.

officials, medical practitioners, and individuals (especially women) challenged, reworked, and coopted state policies to suit their own interests.

Consonant with state-building practices in other parts of the world, beginning in the early twentieth century disciplining the bodies of the citizenry played an increasingly central role in Chinese political governance.[9] In the mid-nineteenth century, the Qing dynasty (1644–1911) faced mounting internal and external threats to its rule. Dissatisfied with the state of trade relations with China, the British launched the Opium Wars (1839–1842, 1856–1860), which opened up China to more imperialist incursions and eventually led to the fall of the Qing dynasty in 1911. Against this backdrop, Chinese elites embraced scientific rationality as a means to transcend the nation's debased status as the "sick man of Asia."[10] In particular, the intelligentsia envisaged citizens' bodies to be microcosms of the nation, therefore creating a healthier citizenry would logically forge a stronger nation. During the Republican period (1911–1949), the preoccupation with modernity and the perceived link between science and national stature engendered increased attention to all aspects of citizens' bodies, including their reproductive functions. In theorizing this phenomenon, Michel Foucault coined the term "biopolitics" to articulate the ways in which the invasive and disciplinary nature of modernity brought bodily practices under the purview of governments and rendered human life a site of political concern.[11] In China and elsewhere, this new manifestation of state power normalized the surveillance of birth, sexuality, illness, and health.[12] In practice, as this book demonstrates, the intensifying focus on bodies disproportionately affected women because state surveillance of reproductive practices was intensely gendered.

[9] The body of literature exposing the centrality of health and bodies to modern state governance is too vast to cover in a footnote, but suffice it to say that this topic has been examined in countless colonial, national, and transnational contexts.

[10] Vera Schwarcz, *The Chinese Enlightenment: Intellectuals and the Legacy of the May Fourth Movement* (Berkeley: University of California, 1986); Ruth Rogaski, *Hygienic Modernity: Meanings of Health and Disease in Treaty-Port China* (Berkeley: University of California Press, 2004); Bridie Andrews, *The Making of Modern Chinese Medicine, 1850–1960* (Honolulu: University of Hawaii Press, 2014).

[11] Michel Foucault, *The History of Sexuality, Vol. 1: An Introduction* (New York: Pantheon Books, 1978), 140.

[12] The literature investigating how modernization and state-building efforts (and often, conditions of colonization or semi-colonization) led to increased government attention to health, sex, and reproduction around the world is too extensive to review in a footnote, but some examples can be found in Philippa Levine, *Prostitution, Race & Politics: Policing Venereal Disease in the British Empire*; Theodore Jun Yoo, *The Politics of Gender in Colonial Korea: Education, Labor, and Health, 1910–1945* (Berkeley: University of California Press, 2014); and Laura Briggs, *Reproducing Empire: Race, Sex, Science, and US Imperialism in Puerto Rico* (Berkeley: University of California Press, 2002).

Both of China's postimperial regimes, the Nationalist Party (1911–1949) and the Communist Party (1949–present), shared a commitment to policing the parameters of sexuality and reproduction and preserving the patriarchal family unit. Yet, they had conflicting and frequently changing policies toward fertility. Indeed, at various points both governments oscillated between banning and legalizing abortions, while contraceptives possessed a more ambiguous status ranging from being politically suspect to state mandated. Following in the footsteps of Western governments and late Qing reformers, the Nationalists initially imposed a blanket ban on abortion, but beginning in 1935 therapeutic abortions were permitted for women with life-threatening pregnancies.[13] During World War II and the Chinese civil war, the government again promoted natalism and sought to limit abortion and birth control use. As for the Communists, although the party at first adopted strict restrictions on access to birth control and abortion, these policies were relaxed in the mid-1950s due to fears of unsustainable population growth. Despite two short-lived attempts at systematically promoting family planning – the first in 1954 and the second in 1962 – government efforts to limit family size were erratic and uneven through the 1970s.[14]

Building on historian Gail Hershatter's observation that "the working out of state policies was everywhere contingent upon geography, prior social arrangements, and local personalities," this book examines birth control and abortion in three cities of differing sizes with divergent levels of economic development – Shanghai, Tianjin, and Luoyang – as well as other locations in China.[15] Inconsistent local policies and a weak medical infrastructure meant that throughout the twentieth century, contraceptive practices differed radically according to demographic factors, such as

[13] Ling Ma, "Gender, Law, and Society: Abortion in Early Twentieth Century China" (PhD diss., State University of New York, Buffalo, 2016), 1.

[14] The PRC's first organized birth planning campaign technically dates to 1954 with the repeal of the ban on contraceptives, yet I have noted that official efforts to actively promote the campaign did not pick up until 1956. As for the second birth planning campaign, Masako Kohama periodizes it as running from 1962 to 1970, but the campaign was most active between 1962 and the start of the Cultural Revolution in 1966. Masako Kohama, "Zhongguo nongcun jihua shengyu de puji – yi 1960–1970 niandai Q cun wei li" (The Popularization of Birth Planning in Rural China – The Case of Q Village, 1960s–1970s), *Jindai zhongguo funü shi yanjiu* 19 (2011): 178; Masako Kohama, "Cong 'feifa duotai' dao 'jihua shengyu': jianguo qianhou xing he shengzhi zhi yanlun kongjian de bianqian" (From "Criminal Abortion" to "Birth Planning:" The Changes of Discursive Space with Regard to Sex and Reproduction Before and After 1949), in *Jindai zhongguo chengshi yu dazhong wenhua*, eds. Jiang Jin and Li Deying (Beijing: Xinxing chubanshe, 2008), 331.

[15] Gail Hershatter, *The Gender of Memory: Rural Women and China's Collective Past* (Berkeley: University of California Press, 2011), 12.

location, class, and education level. Acting first and foremost out of necessity, women bore the primary burden of family planning and thus drew on a diverse array of indigenous and imported contraceptive methods. At the same time, technologies ostensibly designed to "liberate" women from the burdens of motherhood actually re-inscribed existing gender hierarchies. Approaching sexuality and contraception from a grassroots perspective highlights the role that ordinary people played in shaping their own reproductive futures and the diversity of their experiences with reproduction.

In seeking to unravel the history of the One Child Policy, this book also situates contraceptive practices during that period within long-term trends. Far from being a linear, top-down movement, the enactment of "birth planning" – as state-led family planning efforts are still referred to in the PRC – was a circuitous, convoluted, and contested process. In the Mao era – and to a degree in the Republican period – debates in the upper echelons of government over the relationship between population size and economic development, as well as disagreements over the efficacy of various family planning options, resulted in repeated condemnation and endorsement of abortion and different types of birth control. Perhaps due to these contradictory messages, even as birth planning became the cornerstone of the modern Chinese public health regime, individual and familial considerations continued to play a central role in shaping reproductive practices. Moreover, despite repeated articulations of the importance of family planning to gender equality, women continued to be defined by their biological roles as mothers. Examining reproduction and contraception beyond official rhetoric demonstrates not only the growing depth and breadth of state intervention but also the precariousness of state biopolitical control.

Moving Beyond the One Child Policy

In charting the history of reproduction and contraception in China, scholars have analyzed in great detail the mechanics, as well as the short and long-term consequences, of the One Child Policy. Yet, even the most comprehensive works seeking to situate the policy historically and politically approach this topic almost exclusively through the analysis of policy documents and give short shrift to the decades preceding the policy's enactment.[16]

[16] One exception is sociologist Cecilia Nathansen Milwertz's book *Accepting Population Control: Urban Women and the One-Child Family Policy*, which focuses on mothers' experiences negotiating the implementation of the One Child Policy. Drawing on

Offering the most comprehensive analysis of the One Child Policy to date, in *China's Longest Campaign: Birth Planning in the People's Republic, 1949–2005,* political scientist Tyrene White locates the historical roots of the One Child Policy in earlier PRC birth planning policies. She argues that the new limits on birth control enacted in 1979, though apparently drastic, only represented an "incremental tightening of a birth limitation program that had been in place for some time."[17] Considering this topic from the perspectives of regime capacity and Foucauldian biopolitics, in *Governing China's Population: From Leninist to Neoliberal Biopolitics* anthropologist Susan Greenhalgh and political scientist Edwin Winckler highlight the centrality of population issues to post-Mao politics and power.[18] Greenhalgh and Winckler argue that population planning in the Mao era (1949–1976) was "soft" and only became bureaucratically enforced in the era following Chairman Mao Zedong's death.

Despite their important contributions, none of these works investigates how local contingencies and circumstances might have shaped individual reproductive experiences. In seeking to better understand the lives of ordinary women, two pioneering feminist historians, Masako Kohama and Gail Hershatter, have analyzed women's experiences in the Mao era from a grassroots perspective.[19] Although Kohama focuses narrowly on reproduction and Hershatter addresses women's experiences in general, both scholars combine archival research with oral interviews to uncover the perspectives of non-elite women. Yet, neither scholar's work crosses the 1949 historical divide, which makes it difficult to situate these findings within a longer historical trajectory. Positioning women's reproductive experiences during the Mao era within the macro-narrative of modern Chinese demographic history necessitates taking an even longer view of history.

What can be gained from studying the history of birth control and abortion in the *longue durée*? Many social scientific analyses of the years surrounding the One Child Policy have painted this period as one of seismic shifts: the shift from pro-natalism to anti-natalism, the dramatic

extensive interviews, Milwertz attributes urban mothers' acceptance of the policy to factors beyond mere coercion; Cecilia Nathansen Milwertz, *Accepting Population Control: Urban Women and the One-Child Family Policy* (London: Curzon Press, 1997).

17 Tyrene White, *China's Longest Campaign: Birth Planning in the People's Republic, 1949–2005* (Ithaca: Cornell University Press, 2006), 5.

18 Susan Greenhalgh and Edwin A. Winckler, *Governing China's Population: From Leninist to Neoliberal Biopolitics* (Stanford: Stanford University Press, 2005), 4.

19 Kohama, "Cong 'feifa duotai' dao 'jihua shengyu'," 330–355; Hershatter, *The Gender of Memory.*

increase in state policing of sexuality and reproduction, and the move from nonexistent or nonscientific reproductive medicine to ubiquitous contraceptive devices and surgeries. Moreover, the One Child Policy's implementation is often viewed, along with Deng Xiaoping's launching of economic reforms in 1978, as denoting the start of the post-Mao reform era, in which the Communist Party sought to reposition itself as the source of citizens' socioeconomic prosperity, rather than Communist ideology.[20] Because the years 1978 and 1949 marked significant power changes that drew global attention, these two years are also viewed as historic milestones and often treated as the cut-off or starting points for research on demography in China.[21]

While these observations about rupture and change are valid to a degree, they obscure important historical continuities. A closer look at the Nationalists' and Communists' evolving stances on science and reproduction reveals that each was the product of China's ongoing engagement with global modernizing discourses. In other words, global debates about what a modern nation should look like and the extent of government intervention in society; women's rights and normative gender roles; and how best to improve the health and productivity of the population continually informed state population policies in each chapter of China's modern demographic history. These discourses were not merely imported wholesale, but rather, were repeatedly adapted to specific political contexts and local circumstances. Still, not all of these ideas carried equal weight, and socioeconomic and political factors continually played a more central role in determining policies toward birth control and abortion than did concerns about women's welfare.

In the realm of everyday life, changes in reproductive attitudes and contraceptive practices across the twentieth century were also not nearly as stark as they appear on the surface. As population policies evolved, individual and familial attitudes toward family life, childbearing, and contraceptive technologies continued to reflect both old and new ideas. There have long been couples who desired small families and who actively sought out ways to regulate fertility. By contrast, others have consistently resisted using contraception or undergoing abortion for a

[20] Wang Feng, Yong Cai, and Baochang Gu, "Population, Policy, and Politics: How Will History Judge China's One-Child Policy?" *Population and Development Review* 38 (2012): 118.

[21] Thomas Scharping, for example, begins his study of population policy in China in 1949 in *Birth Control in China, 1949–2000: Population Policy and Demographic Development*. Similarly, in *Governing China's Population*, Greenhalgh and Winckler periodize the Mao era as a distinct unit within the demographic trajectory of modern China.

variety of reasons. In light of the high cost of raising and educating a child in contemporary China, some couples, particularly those who enjoy a middle-class, urban lifestyle, have adopted the attitude that smaller families are more feasible and that sons and daughters are equally valuable in the context of only child families. Yet, this view has not entirely displaced existing ideas about family structure and normative gender roles. Among a certain contingent, son preference and the desire for more children, regardless of state policies, have endured. What can be observed is that between the early twentieth century and the present, the dynamics of sex and childbearing have continually been of great social and political significance. In addition, official policies and cultural norms have perpetuated the focus on women's bodies and the gendered burden of family planning.

Birth Control and Medical Modernity

The story of birth control and abortion in twentieth-century China mirrors the trajectory of medicine in China as whole during that same period and speaks to the intimate relationship between medicine and modernity. In the early twentieth century, Western medicine came to be seen as a panacea for China's problems – domestic weakness and corruption, foreign imperialism, and disintegrating faith among elites in traditional Confucian cosmology. Chinese medicine, conversely, became emblematic of national impotence.[22] In reality, though, the categories of "Western" and "Chinese" medicine were relatively porous. Just as scholars have demonstrated of colonial medicine in other non-Western contexts, interactions between indigenous and Western medicine did not eviscerate either but yielded clearer distinctions between the two as well as medical synthesis.[23] Bridie Andrews has shown that the institutionalized form of traditional medicine in China today does not reflect a timeless and unchanging tradition. Rather, Traditional Chinese Medicine (TCM), as it is now referred to, involved the deliberate reconfiguration of older practices into a unified and distinct medical system in the early twentieth century.[24] Faced with government threats to abandon

[22] Rogaski, *Hygienic Modernity*, 2–3.

[23] See, for example, David Arnold, *Colonizing the Body: State Medicine and Epidemic Disease in Nineteenth Century India* (Berkeley: University of California Press, 1993).

[24] Andrews, *The Making of Modern Chinese Medicine,* 11; From 1928 to 1929, reformers who viewed Chinese and Western medicine as adversarial and incommensurable sought to terminate traditional medicine altogether, but traditional medicine ultimately endured as a state-sanctioned medical system. Ralph Croizier accounts for this phenomenon in the 1968 classic *Traditional Medicine in Modern China*, which posits that Chinese

Chinese medicine, Sean Hsiang-lin Lei contends that practitioners of Chinese medicine scientized Chinese medicine, positioning it as a viable and empirical alternative to biomedicine and one that warranted state support.[25] Writing about the early Mao period, Kim Taylor argues that the state endorsed Chinese medicine not because it was believed to have superior therapeutic value but because it met certain political ends.[26] Although official policies toward TCM repeatedly changed course, in both the Republican and Mao eras the government played an active role in regulating the field of medicine.[27]

The notion that Western and Chinese medicine coevolved in response to particular political, epistemological, and practical challenges is also useful for interpreting the history of birth control. During the Mao era, tensions repeatedly emerged between the desire to affirm TCM's validity and the inability of some traditional birth control methods to withstand empirical scrutiny. For political reasons, the state continued to differentiate between Chinese and Western medicine even while synthesizing traditional and biomedical abortion techniques. At the level of practice, however, these distinctions were often insignificant. Whereas some women perceived Western birth control and abortion methods to be more sophisticated, hygienic, and "scientific" than their indigenous counterparts, others privileged abortifacients or prophylactics made from more familiar Chinese herbal recipes. Yet, for the average woman, whether a birth control technique or abortifacient was categorized as Western or traditional was far less important than its efficacy and availability. Indeed, women and couples arbitrarily combined contraceptive and abortion techniques from TCM, Western medicine, and folk traditions.[28]

medicine only survived its encounter with biomedicine because conservative elites embraced it as a critical part of China's cultural legacy. In so doing, Croizier reinforces the binary between Western and Chinese medicine, a construction that other scholars have more recently challenged. Ralph Croizier, *Traditional Medicine in Modern China: Science, Nationalism, and the Tensions of Culture* (Cambridge: Harvard University Press, 1968), 106.

[25] Sean Hsiang-lin Lei, *Neither Donkey nor Horse: Medicine in the Struggle over China's Modernity* (Chicago: University of Chicago Press, 2014), 8.

[26] Kim Taylor, *Chinese Medicine in Early Communist China, 1945–1963: A Medicine of Revolution* (Abingdon: Routledge, 2005), 151.

[27] Volker Scheid and Sean Hsiang-lin Lei, "The Institutionalization of Chinese Medicine," in *Medical Transitions in Twentieth-Century China*, eds. Bridie Andrews and Mary Brown Bullock (Bloomington: University of Indiana Press, 2014), 245.

[28] While other research on birth control and abortion in China largely focuses on biomedicine, this book also takes into account practices derived from TCM and folk traditions.

Going to the Source(s)

To establish the foundation for this project, I conducted archival research at more than ten university, municipal, and provincial archives in eastern and central China. Due to the increasingly limited access to materials in state archives, in many ways I was forced to cobble together incomplete and fragmented materials, including county, municipal, provincial, and national birth planning reports; condom and oral contraceptive production records; legal accounts; and internal reference (*Neibu cankao*) documents. I also drew on articles in regional newspapers and women's magazines, as well as medical texts available in the Shanghai Library and used book markets.

I supplemented my textual research with oral histories to contextualize published documents and gain insight into those experiences "official" narratives elide. Between 2015 and 2019, I interviewed eighty women and men who came of age after 1949. Except for one Uyghur woman, the interviewees were all ethnically Han and ranged in age from thirty-nine to ninety, with the majority being in their sixties and seventies. My interviewees were socioeconomically diverse, from factory workers with little formal education to white-collar employees, such as professors and doctors. Without denying the unique biological and social implications of motherhood, I elected to interview men, in addition to women, because men are typically overlooked in studies of family planning. Moreover, given the predominance of biological essentialism in Chinese sexual discourses, this methodology allowed me to assess gendered perceptions of reproduction and contraception, as well as evolving constructions of femininity and masculinity.[29]

When I mention my interviews to anyone inside or outside of academia, the first question raised is always about how I gained access to interviewees. Finding individuals willing to share some of the most personal acts of their lives with me was a challenge but a rewarding one. The vast majority of my interviewees were people I met in public spaces. Every morning just as the sun came up and in the evening before

[29] In her exploration of the dominant discourses of sexuality in China between 1949 and the 1990s, Harriet Evans finds that in the 1950s, as well as in the 1980s, the prevailing discourse on sexuality was that of biological essentialism, whereby "nature dictated an unchanging set of gendered attributes and expectations." This discourse of essential difference, which conflates biological sex and gender behavior, was (and continues to be) used to justify state intervention into private life, particularly with respect to women, and to define so-called normative and deviant sexual behavior; Harriet Evans, *Women and Sexuality in China: Dominant Discourses of Female Sexuality and Gender Since 1949* (Cambridge: Polity Press, 1997), 34.

sunset, I would visit a local park where dozens of retirees would be practicing tai chi, playing Chinese chess, dancing, or simply sitting and gossiping. I would sit in the park day after day until regulars had come to recognize me. I ballroom danced, I joined a senior citizens' group (the organizers gave out free eggs to participants, which I offered to prospective interviewees in exchange for conversations), I took belly dancing classes, and I chatted with people everywhere I went. I found that if I was able to strike up a conversation with one retiree, other individuals – either bored or intrigued – would want to talk to me. As I became closer to these older people, they would ask me about my research and introduce me to their friends and family. While some laughed at the strange and taboo nature of my research, others were more than happy to tell me about their experiences with birth control, sex education, and even abortion. Differences in attitudes toward these topics emerged along generational lines, with people in their eighties and above being much less willing to answer the questions that people in their sixties found routine. I observed that it was easiest to talk about these subjects in single-sex groups, as almost no one felt comfortable talking about sex in co-ed environments. For that reason, I rarely conducted interviews with a man and a woman unless the two were married and comfortable discussing their shared history. As I became more accustomed to conducting interviews, I started bringing props with me, usually sex guides from the 1950s. Anyone who had previously dismissed me was now eager to talk to me about my stash, either to ask where I had gotten such materials or to tell me that I had odd hobbies. These memories bring me continual joy.

However, conducting interviews about events that took place six decades ago proved challenging for a number of reasons. At times, I struggled to understand my interviewees because they did not speak Mandarin. In such cases, other people fluent in both Mandarin and the local dialect would help translate the conversation. I was also fortunate to interview the parents of friends, who not only helped mediate the discussions but also conveyed the nature of my research to their parents so it would seem less alien. The limits of memory, particularly among the very elderly, also presented significant obstacles. While remaining cognizant of the ways in which contemporary politics shape recollections of the past, I encouraged my interviewees to move backward through time from the present to the 2000s to the 1990s and so on. Bringing sex guides and objects from earlier periods also helped trigger memories in interviewees. Still, my survey sample may seem random because I selected interviewees based on their proximity and willingness to participate in the study. Sometimes if I had a question after an interview, I would schedule another meeting or message the interviewees on WeChat, a popular Chinese messaging service.[30] A final point worth mentioning is my own identity. Although I am not an anthropologist, the realities of privileged positionality are not lost on me. As a white American woman in my late twenties (and later, in my early thirties), I am convinced that conducting oral histories would have been much more challenging had my outward appearance – with respect to age, skin color, gender, sexual orientation, or even body type – been different. My research findings, then, need to be understood in the context of my own inherited biases and particular positionality, as well as those of my interviewees.

While neither the source base nor the interviewer is perfect, the interviews are valuable in their ability to provide diverse perspectives on reproduction and serve as a counterweight to the political agendas of official sources. Analyzing the correspondences and tensions between the oral and archival sources revealed instances in which everyday life intersected with or diverged from official narratives. My hope is that the benefits of using oral histories to gain nuanced perspectives on reproduction and birth control, coupled with the use of more official sources, will outweigh the limitations of this methodology.

Birth Control Case Studies: Shanghai, Tianjin, and Luoyang

Why focus on Shanghai, Tianjin, and Luoyang? The heightened restrictions on archival access since at least 2015, when I began investigating this topic in China, made choosing research sites as much about intellectual merit as feasibility. I settled on these three cities, in part because they all had rather extensive post-1949 state archives with a greater degree of openness than I had experienced elsewhere. A friend's introduction to an archivist at the Luoyang Municipal Archive proved critical in enabling me to obtain exclusive access to local materials, most of which had never received scholarly attention. The ease with which I was able to recruit interviewees for the study was also a crucial factor in my decision to focus on these locales.

Shanghai, Tianjin, and Luoyang vary greatly in terms of location and demographics. Shanghai is located in the lush eastern part of China, abutting the East China Sea, and is directly administered by the central government. Positioned near the mouth of the Yangtze River in Jiangnan, a historically wealthy region boasting high levels of literacy,

[30] The study had IRB approval and all participants consented to participate. To ensure privacy, pseudonyms have been used in place of real names.

Shanghai served as a regional trade hub during the late imperial and Republican periods.[31] Tianjin, also under direct federal administration, is located southeast of the capital, Beijing, and borders on the Bohai Sea. This city was the site of early industrialization and modernization projects in the late Qing dynasty. In contrast to these larger cities, Luoyang is a provincial-level city located in the populous but landlocked province of Henan in central China's Yellow River Valley. Situated south of the Yellow River, Henan has long been an agricultural region and Luoyang became an industrial center during the Mao period. According to the first census of the People's Republic of China, in 1953 Shanghai had a population of 6.2 million and Tianjin 2.69 million.[32] Due to limited recordkeeping, the first recorded population statistic for Luoyang was 601,250 in 1964.[33] By the early 1980s (1981–1982), all three cities had grown significantly: Shanghai's population had reached 11,810,000; Tianjin, 7,780,000; and Luoyang, 963,718.[34] As of 2018, following a massive influx of rural migrant workers and state-led urbanization programs, the cities' populations stood at 24.23 million (Shanghai), 15.60 million (Tianjin), and 7.10 million (Luoyang).

Aside from their population densities, these cities also differ significantly with respect to their historical contact with foreigners. Mimicking the "semicolonial" status of the late Qing territory as a whole, Shanghai and Tianjin were under partial foreign occupation from the end of the First Opium War to the late Republican period.[35] In Shanghai, the British and Americans carved out the International Settlement while the French established the French Concession, producing unique styles of architecture and governance. The city's foreign residents hailed from more than twenty European nations, Japan, India, Vietnam, and Korea,

[31] Frederic Wakeman Jr. and Yeh Wen-hsin, eds., *Shanghai Sojourners* (Berkeley: University of California Press, 1992), 6.

[32] Guojia jihua shengyu weiyuanhui zonghe jihua si (National Birth Planning Committee Integrated Planning Division), Quanguo jihua shengyu tongji ziliao huibian (*Chinese Birth Planning Statistical Yearbook*) (N.p.: n.p., 1983), 2.

[33] Office of the Luoyang Population Survey Leading Small Group, *Di sanci renkou pucha shougong huizong ziliao huibao* (The Compiled Materials of the Third Manual Population Survey) (Luoyang: Office of the Luoyang Population Census Leading Small Group, 1982), 11.

[34] National Birth Planning Committee Integrated Planning Division, *Chinese Birth Planning Statistical Yearbook*, 2; Luoyang shi renkou pucha lingdao xiaozu bangongshe (Office of the Luoyang Population Survey Leading Small Group), *Henan sheng Luoyang shi di sanci renkou pucha shougong huizong ziliao huibian* (The Compiled Materials of the Third Manual Population Survey of Luoyang, Henan) (Luoyang: Luoyang shi renkou pucha lingdao xiaozu bangongshe, 1982), 9.

[35] Rogaski, *Hygienic Modernity*, 10.

as well as nations of the Middle East and Latin America.[36] Similarly, Tianjin was, in the words of Ruth Rogaski, a "hypercolony." Between 1860 and 1943, alongside a Chinese-administered district, the city contained as many as eight foreign concessions – Japanese, French, British, German, Belgian, Russian, Austro-Hungarian, and Italian.[37] As treaty ports, Shanghai and Tianjin played critical roles in facilitating cultural, commercial, and medical exchanges with foreigners. Nestled in China's hinterlands, Luoyang stands in sharp contrast to these major port cities. Situated along the Silk Road trade routes, Luoyang had enjoyed a prominent status from the Eastern Han Dynasty (25–220) through the Jin Dynasty (1115–1234) when the city intermittently served as one of China's ancient capitals. However, during the late imperial period when Luoyang was no longer the capital and the Silk Road trade had fizzled out, the city's limited economy and distance from the coast ensured that it never had a significant Western presence. Even after Deng Xiaoping opened up China's economy in 1978, economic development was slow to reach Luoyang and other parts of Henan province.

As a result of their differing histories, Shanghai and Tianjin boasted flourishing economies and multilingual public spheres in the early twentieth century, whereas Luoyang had little in the way of economic development or published media. As one of China's most economically developed cities during the Republican period, Shanghai was home to a robust network of publishing houses producing hundreds of thousands of books, newspapers, and magazines.[38] Tianjin's economy lagged behind Shanghai's during the same period, but the city was still home to numerous Chinese and foreign-language newspapers and related publications. In contrast, Luoyang was relatively undeveloped and only published one periodical at any point in the Republican era. These differential trajectories make for interesting points of comparison but also posed challenges to conducting research, particularly because Luoyang's municipal archives do not contain records from the Republican period. The fact that it is nearly impossible to interview people who lived in Republican Luoyang further exacerbated this issue. Nevertheless, drawing on information from places for which records are available has allowed me to make educated inferences about Republican-era Luoyang and draw cross-regional parallels.

[36] Hanchao Lu, *Beyond the Neon Lights: Everyday Shanghai in the Early Twentieth Century* (Berkeley: University of California Press, 1999), 38.
[37] Rogaski, *Hygienic Modernity*, 13.
[38] Leo Ou-Fan Lee, *Shanghai Modern: The Flowering of a New Urban Culture, 1930–1945* (Cambridge: Harvard University Press, 1999), 82.

Given China's vastness and heterogeneity, my findings about these three cities are not representative of China as a whole. Yet, this book sheds light on broader trends in Chinese history while engaging themes of global and interdisciplinary relevance: the centrality of gender and reproduction to modernity and state-building, the fragility of biopolitical power, and the role of individuals in redirecting state policies to produce unforeseen consequences.

Chapter Outline

This book moves chronologically from the founding of the Republic of China to the present, and the periodization reflects the turning points I have identified in the history of reproduction and contraception. Chapters 1 and 2 focus on the theory and praxis of birth control and abortion in Republican China (1911–1949). Chapter 1 demonstrates the interplay between domestic and international ideas about fertility. Eugenic discourses linking individual health to national strength and modernity gained currency in the early Republican period, and the visit of birth control pioneer Margaret Sanger to China in 1922 further fueled elite preoccupation with using contraception to improve the "quality" of the population. Unlike sterilization and abortion, which were prohibited, contraception was neither explicitly endorsed nor banned at the national level. In interrogating quotidian birth control and abortion practices, Chapter 2 reveals that a wide range of contraceptive and abortive techniques were available to women in urban China, with abortion being the most prevalent form of fertility regulation that appeared in the historical record. *Tiaojingyao* – patent drugs and homemade herbal decoctions that blurred the line between abortifacients and emmenagogues designed to induce regular menses – were also particularly common, and by their nature, difficult to police.

Taking a more overtly natalist approach to fertility than their predecessors, Communist officials initially placed strict restrictions on birth control and abortion, encouraging high birth rates. Focusing on the early years of the People's Republic of China (PRC) from 1949 to 1958, Chapter 3 shows that even in this constrained environment, literature on sex and birth control continued to be published, promoting a gendered focus on women's sexuality and fostering diverse local contraceptive practices. The need to more fully mobilize women's labor led to a gradual loosening of birth control limitations, but the availability of birth control and information about it varied greatly.

Demonstrating the state's shift away from natalism, Chapters 4 and 5 explore the establishment of local family planning programs. As

Chapter 4 shows, in the wake of the failed Great Leap Forward (1959–1961), officials taking up the call for "birth planning" sought to weave birth control into the local cultural fabric through plays, exhibitions, and focus groups. Yet, resource shortages, contradictory messages from the state about the efficacy of traditional medicine, and individual distrust or dislike of birth control continually undermined efforts to more systematically monitor and control reproduction. Focusing on the period from 1966 until the establishment of the One Child Policy in 1979, Chapter 5 investigates birth planning during two of modern China's most disruptive mass movements, the Cultural Revolution (1966–1976) and the Sent-Down Youth Movement (1955–1980). Although the deployment of minimally trained "barefoot doctors" helped integrate state-led family planning into the rural healthcare system, local authorities used the court system to arbitrarily police abortions. By creating unprecedented opportunities for sex among unmarried youth with limited access to prophylactics, the state paved the way for the contemporary reliance on abortion as a primary tool for family planning.

Chapter 6 and the epilogue situate the One Child Policy within the macro-history of reproduction in modern China. In tracing the One Child Policy's lifespan from its introduction in 1979 until its dissolution in 2015, Chapter 6 reveals that there is no one representative narrative of life under the policy. Instead, the extent to which the One Child Policy was actually enforced and the ways in which it was received differed significantly in Shanghai, Tianjin, and Luoyang. This chapter also interrogates the renewed interest in eugenics among parents wishing to "optimize" the qualities of their one and only child, as well as the limited scale and scope of sex education. The epilogue addresses the question of what can be ascertained from studying sex and reproduction in the *longue durée*. As demonstrated by the ongoing substitution of abortion for birth control, family planning remains deeply gendered, with women shouldering much of this burden. The persistence of eugenic ideas and the state's intrusive but uneven policing of sexuality have also been features of Chinese history since the early twentieth century. Despite drastic changes in fertility policies and attempts to promote a particular construction of normative sexuality, though, attitudes toward contraception and perceptions of what constitutes the ideal family remain heterogeneous.

1 Building a Fitter Nation: Eugenics, Birth Control, and Abortion in Public Discourse, 1911–1949

In 1918, modern China's most famous author, Lu Xun, wrote, "Chinese children, so long as they are born, it does not matter if they are good or bad; so long as they are many, it does not matter if they have talent" (*Zhongguo de haizi, zhiyao sheng, buguan ta hao bu hao, zhiyao duo, buguan ta cai bu cai*).[1] For the iconoclast Lu Xun, the traditional emphasis on having many children for the purpose of serving their parents, regardless of the quality of the children's lives, epitomized the deficiency of Chinese culture. Only by throwing off the shackles of Confucianism – including filial piety, reverence for the past, and traditional fertility culture – would China be able to endure in a rapidly changing world.

This assessment stemmed from China's particular circumstances in the early twentieth century. In the wake of the Qing dynasty's collapse, Chinese elites like Lu Xun anxiously debated the path the newly established republic should take to modernize and strengthen itself. With memories of the Opium Wars – and the resultant semi-colonization of China by European powers – still fresh, participants in the New Culture Movement of the 1910s and 1920s considered to what extent China should retain "traditional" Chinese culture or adopt foreign scientific knowledge and models of governance.

China's identity crisis also coincided with a wider global discussion about the status of women. Debates about free love and marriage, sexuality and reproduction, and women's suffrage and economic labor were coming to the fore all over the world. But for Chinese male elites, the political stakes of women's rights were particularly high: Bringing Chinese women's subjectivity and bodies into the fold of modernity was a precondition for saving the nation and restoring its global reputation. Writing in the early twentieth century, one of China's earliest modern feminists, He-Yin Zhen (1886–1920), argued just this: that men supported calls for women's liberation so that China – and the men leading

[1] Lu Xun, "Suigan lu ershiwu" (Collection of Random Thoughts 25), *Xin qingnian* (New Youth) 5, no. 3 (1918): 291.

it – would be welcomed into "the ranks of civilized nations."[2] The act of "liberating" Chinese women, she warned, was viewed as a means to achieve nationalist goals rather than an end in itself.

The concurrent search for new ontological truths to replace Confucian cosmology, a process begun in the late Qing, also involved reevaluating traditional ideas about society, knowledge, and sexuality.[3] As a result, this period experienced a number of related epistemic shifts and an explosion of competing discourses. Chinese elites began viewing the people within China's borders as a "population" and social facts (namely, statistics) as sources of truth.[4] In this context, publications discussing population-related issues proliferated, reaching their height between the late 1920s and the mid-1930s, the period of relative peace between the two world wars.[5] At the same time, in dialogue with foreign ideas, Chinese definitions of sexuality and ethnic difference became bound up with anatomy and biology, marking a critical break with traditional understandings of gender and identity.[6]

Efforts to delimit and fortify the nation, make Chinese society statistically legible, and construct normative sexual behavior converged in debates over abortion and birth control. Whereas explicit discussions of abortion appeared in Chinese newspaper articles throughout the Republican era (and even earlier), contraception became a topic of

[2] Lydia Liu, Rebecca Karl, and Dorothy Ko, eds., *The Birth of Chinese Feminism: Essential Texts in Transnational Theory* (New York: Columbia University Press, 2013), 2.

[3] During the New Culture Movement, the family unit also emerged as a site of reformist debate. In her study of the May Fourth ideal of the "small family" (*xiao jiating*, the nuclear family as opposed to the traditional extended family), Susan Glosser argues that the "revolutionary" family reforms adopted by the Communists in the 1950s actually had their origins in the debates of the 1920s. Susan Glosser, *Chinese Visions of Family and State, 1915–1953* (Berkeley: University of California Press, 2003), 13.

[4] Tong Lam, *A Passion for Facts: Social Surveys and the Construction of the Chinese Nation State, 1900–1949* (Berkeley: University of California Press, 2011), 3–4.

[5] Between 1911 and 1949, more than 750 articles relating to population issues were published in newspapers and periodicals, whose focus spanned society, politics, finance, commerce, agriculture, public health, and women. During the same period, 194 books devoted solely to population – and an additional 350 books with at least one chapter on population – were published. In total, these books accounted for about 0.4 percent of the estimated 100,000 books published in the Republican period. Gu Jiantang, "Minguo shiqi renkou yanjiu tanwei" (An Exploration of Population Studies during the Republican Era), *Beijing University Journal: Philosophy Society Edition* (2001), http://www.szrmf.com/paper/48916.html.

[6] Malcolm Thompson dates the emergence of the concept of "population" in China to the 1920s, a period in which modes of governance and the family were reconceptualized; Malcolm Thompson, "Foucault, Fields of Governability, and the Population-Family-Economy Nexus in China," *History and Theory* 51 (2012), 51; Howard Chiang, *After Eunuchs: Science, Medicine, and the Transformation of Sex in Modern China* (New York: Columbia University Press, 2018), 6; Frank Dikotter, *The Discourse of Race in Modern China* (London: C Hurst & Co, 1992), 3.

public interest only in the 1920s after Margaret Sanger, the world-renowned birth control advocate and founder of the American Birth Control League (later the Planned Parenthood Foundation of America), first visited East Asia.[7] Mirroring the trend among population-related publications as a whole, publications debating the value of birth control were particularly abundant between the early 1920s and the late 1930s, the period historian Yu Lianshi refers to as the "golden age" of the birth control movement in China.[8] Yet, as with debates about "the Woman Question" in general, discussions of birth control also became increasingly politicized as tensions mounted between the Communists and the Nationalists.[9] In the late 1930s, though, World War II – and later, the Chinese civil war – circumscribed the national dialogue about birth control.

This chapter traces the emergence of Republican-era discourses on birth control and abortion. The first section analyzes the synthesis of domestic and international ideas about reproduction and eugenics in the early twentieth century, showing how Western and Japanese scientific terminology gave birth to a new Chinese-language vocabulary for discussing birth control. Situating birth control in the context of debates over infanticide, child abandonment, and abortion, the second section argues that birth control emerged as a compromise solution that could satisfy both the modern impulse to engineer the population and the moral imperative to limit social ills. The final section shows that Chinese elites mobilized debates about women's roles in society as a way to promote their own political agendas. Examining debates about abortion and birth control in light of competing gender paradigms reveals the centrality of women's sexuality and reproduction to Republican visions of modernity.

Translating Modernity: Eugenics and Birth Control

Records from the late imperial period explicitly mention abortion, crudely referred to as *datai* (literally, hitting the fetus), *duotai*, or *zhuitai*

[7] In her analysis of text frequency in several key Republican newspapers, Kohama Masako finds that references to abortion (*duotai*) eclipsed discussions of birth control (*biyun*); Kohama, "Cong 'feifa duotai' dao 'jihua shengyu,'" 332–333; "Zhang Xiaocun han" (Zhang Xiaocun's Case), *Shenbao*, May 28, 1913; "Yuzhang jinshi" (Recent Events in Yuzhang), *Shenbao*, November 13, 1885.

[8] Yu Lianshi, "Minguo shiqi chengshi shengyu jiezhi yundong de yanjiu: Yi Beijing, Shanghai, Nanjing wei zhongdian" (The Birth Control Movement in Republican Cities: A Focus on Beijing, Shanghai and Nanjing) (Unpublished PhD diss., Fudan University, 2008), 88.

[9] Louise Edwards, *Gender, Politics, and Democracy: Women's Suffrage in China* (Stanford: Stanford University Press, 2008), 167.

(the last two refer to a falling or dropping fetus). However, the terms *shengyu kongzhi* and *shengyu jiezhi*, the literal translations of "birth control," only came into use in China in the 1920s. Other shorter expressions for birth control, such as *jieyu* (literally "to conserve births"), and the alternative terms, *biren* and *biyun* (both meaning "to prevent pregnancy"), also emerged in this period. While the former term (*biren*) is rarely used today, the latter (*biyun*) has remained in common usage up to the present.

The etymology of these terms is best understood in the context of new discourses about modernity and the natural world that emerged in China in the early twentieth century. As Leon Rocha has demonstrated, prior to the twentieth century, the Chinese character *xing* referred to human nature. In the late 1910s and early 1920s, however, it came to mean "sex," in addition to its original meaning.[10] As part of the New Culture Movement's iconoclasm, reformers argued that – somewhat like the "Repressive Hypothesis" of sexuality in the West that Michel Foucault criticized – Confucian morality suppressed sexuality, a universal, natural condition and one that could be understood only through modern science.[11] In an effort to modernize, scientize, and liberate China, May Fourth reformers replaced the euphemistic language once used to refer to sex with an explicit and broader term: *xing*.[12]

The path to the contemporary meaning of *xing* followed a course similar to those of many Chinese neologisms and loanwords in the late nineteenth and early twentieth centuries. As Lydia Liu observes, "the Japanese used *kanji* (Chinese characters) to translate European terms, and the neologisms were then imported back into the Chinese language" in one of three forms: (1) two-character compounds consisting of Chinese characters only found in premodern Japanese but not in Classical Chinese; (2) Classical Chinese expressions used by the Japanese to translate Western terms that were then reincorporated into Chinese but with a changed meaning – expressions termed "return graphic loans"; and (3) modern Japanese compounds with no Classical Chinese equivalent.[13] Within this framework, *xing* falls into the second category as a return graphic loan, a word

[10] Leon Antonio Rocha, "Xing: The Discourse of Sex and Human Nature in Modern China," *Gender and History* 22, no. 3 (2010): 606.

[11] Foucault argues that, rather than being repressed, discourses on sexuality exploded with the rise of capitalism and bourgeois society between the seventeenth and mid-twentieth centuries; Michel Foucault, *The History of Sexuality, Vol. 1: An Introduction* (New York: Pantheon Books, 1978), 8.

[12] Rocha, "Xing," 603.

[13] Lydia H. Liu, *Translingual Practice: Literature, National Culture, and Translated Modernity – China, 1900–1937* (Stanford: Stanford University Press, 1995), 32–34.

first borrowed from Classical Chinese by Japanese scholars and then imported back into China with a different meaning.[14]

What, then, are the origins of Chinese expressions for birth control? As Ruth Rogaski has demonstrated with *weisheng* (hygienic practices or "hygienic modernity"), Japan played a critical role in shaping elite Chinese attitudes toward health and modernity in the early twentieth century.[15] More specifically, many eugenic discourses were introduced to China vis-à-vis Japan.[16] The Republican-era terms for birth control (*shengyu kongzhi*, *shengyu jiezhi*, *jieyu*, *biren*, and *biyun*) that first appeared in the Chinese press in the 1920s likely originated from Japanese translations of English words. *Shengyu kongzhi* and *shengyu jiezhi* – which typically refer to broad social categories as opposed to specific technologies – are likely translations of a Japanese expression meaning birth control or birth limitation, *sanji seigen*. Similarly, *biren* and *biyun* could come from the Japanese word *hinin*, which also translates as birth control or the avoidance of pregnancy. The fact that the formulation of the characters in *hinin* appears earlier in Japan than in China confirms the theory that *biren* comes from Japanese.[17] As for *sanji seigen* and the Chinese equivalents, Japanese works prior to the 1920s do not make reference to this expression, so it is possible that the terms *sanji seigen* in Japan and *shengyu kongzhi*/*shengyu jiezhi* in China emerged more or less simultaneously when Sanger visited these two countries in 1922.[18] Tiana Norgren notes in her study of birth control and abortion in modern Japan that "indeed in the 1940s and early 1950s, abortion and contraception were popularly understood to be two different forms of 'birth control' (*sanji seigen*): only later did the term come to be used exclusively to refer to contraception, as was intended by the Western family planning advocate [Margaret Sanger] who coined the phrase."[19]

In China, as well, a fuzzy linguistic distinction existed between abortion (which was illegal) and prophylactics; the two were often assumed

[14] Rocha, "Xing," 617. [15] Rogaski, *Hygienic Modernity*, 2–3.

[16] Yuehtsen Juliette Chung, *Struggle for National Survival: Eugenics in Sino-Japanese Contexts, 1896–1945* (London: Routledge, 2002), 13–14.

[17] Japan Center for Asian Historical Records (JACAR), Ref. A05032148900; Karen Lee Callahan, "Dangerous Devices, Mysterious Times: Men, Women, and Birth Control in Early Twentieth-Century Japan" (PhD diss., University of California, Berkeley, 2004), 53.

[18] It is also possible that *shengyu kongzhi* evolved from the Japanese term "*ninshin seigen*," which appears in Japanese texts at least as early as 1902 but later fell out of common usage; Callahan, "Dangerous Devices, Mysterious Times," 53.

[19] Tiana A. E. Norgren, *Abortion Before Birth Control: The Politics of Reproduction in Postwar Japan* (Princeton: Princeton University Press, 2001), 83.

to be the same thing.[20] This slippage is particularly important when considering public debates about birth control and its position under the law. Even much later, in the 1960s, state-issued health guides continued to remind readers that birth control was in fact distinct from abortion.[21] As for the term *jieyu*, there is no equivalent expression in premodern or modern Japanese, which likely means that this term is not a product of translingual borrowing but a term unique to Chinese in the twentieth century. Regardless of its origin, *jieyu*, more so than the other terms (except for *biyun*, which remains in conventional use) continues to be used in contemporary Chinese. From this analysis, it is evident that the lexicon of birth control in China and the semantic shifts it involved cannot be disentangled from global intellectual and linguistic flows. Moreover, these terms are not simply neutral or static translations of foreign words; the expressions framing birth control that emerged in China reflect the particular historical and cultural nuances of early twentieth-century Japanese and Chinese.

Indeed, the story of birth control and eugenics in China is inseparable from global debates on these topics. Eugenic tracts were likely first translated from Japanese into Chinese at the turn of the century.[22] Between 1885 and 1890, having read Japanese translations of the work of Francis Galton, who coined the term "eugenics," as well as the writings of Japanese eugenicists, Chinese reformer Kang Youwei first recommended prenatal care, women's education, and sterilization as methods to improve human selection (although these ideas would not be published until 1935).[23] As early as 1902, Kang Youwei's student, Liang Qichao, also advocated banning early marriage on the grounds that it is harmful to offspring (leading to "immature physical condition" and "feeblemindedness") and that it prevents parents from completing their studies and contributing to the national economy.[24] These same concerns would be reiterated almost verbatim by Nationalist and Communist lawmakers and intellectuals in debates spanning the next 100 years.

Yet, eugenic thinking – and discussions of birth control in particular – did not become part of mainstream intellectual discourse until Sanger

[20] Masako Kohama, "Jihua shengyu de kaiduan – 1950–1960 niandai de Shanghai" (The Beginnings of Birth Planning in Shanghai in the 1950s and 1960s), *Zhongyang yanjiuyuan jindaishi yanjiusuo jikan* (Academia Sinica Institute of Modern History) 68 (2010): 127.

[21] Hebei sheng weisheng ting, *Jiezhi shengyu wenda* (Questions and Answers about Birth Control) (Tianjin: Hebei renmin chubanshe, 1962), 46–47.

[22] Yuehtsen Juliette Chung, *Struggle for National Survival: Eugenics in Sino-Japanese Contexts, 1896–1945* (London: Routledge, 2002), 13.

[23] Chung, *Struggle for National Survival*, 13. [24] Ibid., 14.

visited China.[25] In the political climate of the New Culture Movement, influential reformers, such as Hu Shi and Cai Yuanpei, enthusiastically welcomed Sanger to China. Hu even personally translated her initial speech at Beijing National University, which stressed the importance of birth control.[26] Sanger's visit resulted in countless newspaper articles debating the merits and shortcomings of birth control.[27] Her works, as well as those of her British colleague Marie Stopes, were promptly translated into Chinese, and Sanger's speech from Beijing National University was reprinted in full in *The Ladies' Journal* and *The Women's Review*.[28] In 1924, Pan Guangdan, one of China's most-distinguished Republican-era sociologists and eugenicists and a political conservative, first translated the Japanese term for eugenics, *yusei*, into Chinese (*yousheng*) and founded the Chinese Eugenics Association.[29]

Following Sanger's historic visit, a broad range of materials on population and birth control, often foreign texts from Japan, the Soviet Union, the United States, Britain, and Germany, were translated into Chinese and circulated in the popular press.[30] Newspapers and women's magazines also helped disseminate the writings of prominent foreign eugenicists, physicians, and sexologists.[31] Of note were the writings of

[25] Sanger had initially planned to visit China again in 1935, but the trip was cancelled due to illness; Mirela David, "Female Gynecologists and Their Birth Control Clinics: Eugenics in Practice in 1920s–1930s China," *Canadian Bulletin of Medical History* 35, no. 1 (2018): 11; Masako, "Cong 'Feifa duotai' dao 'jihua shengyu," 335.

[26] Mirela David, "The Task is Hers:" Going Global, Margaret Sanger's Visit to China in 1922," Asian Pacific Perspectives 14, no. 1 (Fall 2016): 78; Margaret Sanger, "Shengyu zhicai de shenme yu zenyang" (Birth control's what and how), translated by Hu Shi, transcribed by Xiao Feng and Mao Chen, *The Ladies' Journal* 8, no. 6 (1922): 129.

[27] Zhou Jianren, "Chan'er zhidu gaishu" (A Summary of Childbirth Limitation), *Dongfang Zazhi* (East Asian Miscellany) 19, no. 7 (1922): n.p.; "Shengyu zhicai de shenme yu zenyang" (The What and How of Fertility Sanctions), *Ladies' Journal* (Funü zazhi) 8, no. 6 (1922): 126; and Michelle T. King, "Margaret Sanger in Translation: Gender, Class, and Birth Control in 1920s China," *Journal of Women's History* 29, no. 3 (2017): 61.

[28] Mirela David, "Free Love, Marriage, and Eugenics: Global and Local Debates on Sex, Birth Control, Venereal Disease and Population in 1920s–1930s China" (Unpublished doctoral diss., New York University, 2014), 171; Marie Stopes, *Ertong Ai* (Wise Parenthood) (Shanghai: Guanghua shuju, 1926); Margaret Sanger, "Jieyu zhuyi" (Birth Control Doctrine), Chen Haicheng, trans., Shanghai: Shanghai shangwuban, 1928.

[29] Pan Guangdan, "Zhongguo zhi yousheng wenti" (The Problem of Eugenics in China), *Dongfang zazhi* (East Asian Miscellany) 21, no. 22 (1924): 15; Chung, *Struggle for National Survival*, 14.

[30] Dong Pingmei, "Shengyu jiezhi de lilun he shiji" (The Theory and Practice of Birth Control), *Dongfang zazhi* (East Asian Miscellany) 33, no. 7 (1936): 55–61.

[31] Sex first emerged as a site of empirical inquiry in nineteenth-century Europe, and sexology – the "scientific study of sex" – was subsequently established as a field of specialization. Claiming that sex could only be understood through modern science, sexologists used their new-found authority to identify normative sexual behaviors as well as sexual pathologies; Chiang, *After Eunuchs*, 4.

Annie Besant and Charles Bradlaugh, both early supporters of birth control in Britain and colonial India; Ernst Grafenberg, the inventor of the intrauterine device (IUD); and Havelock Ellis, a eugenicist and one of the founders of the sexology movement.[32] Chinese eugenicists took particular interest in the Soviet Union, where abortion was made legal and offered virtually free of charge between 1920 and 1936 to encourage women's involvement in the labor force and prevent dangerous home abortions.[33] The Soviet case therefore was referenced frequently in publications weighing the benefits of legalizing abortion versus promoting birth control use.[34]

The explosion of literature on birth control also contributed to the existing domestic discussion about eugenics and the fate of the Chinese "race," an incipient concept in the late nineteenth and early twentieth centuries positing that biological similarities more than socio-cultural ties bound together the people within China's borders.[35] As Frank Dikotter has shown, eugenic thinking in China was not merely imported wholesale from abroad. Rather, the scientific language of biological determinism served to further legitimize eugenic ideas that had long been present in China.[36] China's foremost sexologists, Ye Dehui and Zhang Jingsheng, saw eugenics as a means through which "to produce a new nation inhabited by a stronger and more intelligent Chinese race, more able to defend itself against foreign powers."[37] On the one hand, Ye Dehui drew on Han dynasty religious and medical texts to argue that China had long had an "indigenous" field of sexology, known as *taijiao*, that predated Western science and was superior to it. *Taijiao* – literally, fetal education – is the idea that a fetus can be educated in utero to optimize its intelligence and health and ensure that it will not be born prematurely or with birth defects. In the Republican period, the language of science and

[32] "Zui xin biyunfa" (The Newest Birth Control Methods) (Shanghai: Zhongguo yousheng jiezhi xiehui, 1948), 1; Sun, *Jieyu yi yousheng*, 7; and Yan Yukuan, *Jieyu de lilun yu fangfa* (Birth Control Theory and Methods) (Shanghai: Dadong Shuju, 1933), 10.

[33] Abortion was banned again in 1936. The new edition of the constitution promulgated that year emphasized improving maternal and child welfare through state subsidies and increased access to childcare; Alexandre Avdeev, Alain Blum, and Irina Troitskaya, "The History of Abortion Statistics in Russia and the USSR from 1900 to 1991," *Population* (English Edition) 7 (1995): 41.

[34] Sun Yanyu, *Jieyu yu yousheng* (From Birth Control to Eugenics) (Shanghai: Meilingdeng & Co., 1949), 1; Zhen Ni, "Duotai he biyun" (Abortion and Birth Control), *Xin funü yuekan* (New Women's Monthly) 4 (1946): 20–21.

[35] Frank Dikotter, *The Discourse of Race in Modern China* (London: C Hurst & Co, 1992), 3 and Gu, "Weekly Comment: Early Marriage and Birth Control" (Yizhou jianping: zaoyun yu jieyu), *Shanghai dangsheng* 1 (1935): 22.

[36] Dikotter, *Imperfect Conceptions*, 8.

[37] Leon Antonio Rocha, "Translation and Two 'Chinese Sexologies': *Double Plum* and Sex Histories," in *Sexology and Translation: Cultural and Scientific Encounters across the Modern World*, ed. Heike Bauer (Philadelphia, PA: Temple University Press, 2015), 154–155.

eugenics lent further credence to *taijiao* practices.[38] On the other hand, inspired by the disparate writings of Jean-Jacques Rousseau, Havelock Ellis, and Marie Stopes, Zhang Jingsheng argued that foreign sexological discourses needed to be imported immediately in order to produce a strong and emancipated China free from traditional Confucian sexual repression.[39] Despite their nearly diametrically opposing perspectives with regard to sexology in China, both men's work had eugenic undertones and sought answers to the intertwined problems of perceived national and racial weakness.

Like Ye and Zhang, the writings of Margaret Sanger and Marie Stopes also conveyed the urgency of racial regeneration. However, Sanger and Stopes were primarily focused on the fate of the white race. They favored "purifying" and "improving" the white race by decreasing the prevalence of genetic disabilities, mental illness, and sexually transmitted diseases. This concern dovetailed with anxieties about "race suicide," a eugenic theory positing that higher birth rates among the poor and people of color would outstrip birth rates among Caucasians, leading to non-white people outnumbering whites. For these reasons, Sanger, Stopes, and other advocates of negative eugenics (the eugenic camp concerned with restricting reproduction among the "unfit" rather than promoting reproduction among those with "superior" genes) supported reducing the birth rate among the poor, the colonized, and those with "undesirable" traits.[40]

Modern Chinese discourses on race emerged in the context of the struggle against Western colonial domination and Otherization. At the turn of the century, Kang Youwei and Liang Qichao reconfigured Chinese lineage discourses into a racial hierarchy of biological groups with dark-skinned people at the bottom, whom Kang and Liang argued should be eliminated.[41] Building on this foundation, the construction of modern Chinese identity that emerged during this period was predicated as much on the notion of Chinese being non-white as on the racial proximity between whites and Asians relative to the "darker races."[42] The particular position of Chinese people as both "non-white" (and

[38] Tina Phillips Johnson, *Childbirth in Republican China: Delivering Modernity* (Lanham: Lexington Books, 2011), 39.
[39] Rocha, "Translation and Two 'Chinese Sexologies,'" 155.
[40] Dikotter, *Imperfect Conceptions*, 105.
[41] Frank Dikotter, *Imperfect Conceptions: Medical Knowledge, Birth Defects, and Eugenics in China* (New York: Columbia University Press, 1998), 61.
[42] Emma Teng, *Eurasian: Mixed Identities in the United States, China, and Hong Kong, 1842–1943* (Berkeley: University of California Press, 2013), 12.

therefore part of the Other) and "like-white" shaped domestic eugenic debates about how to strengthen the Chinese race.[43]

In part due to these tensions, Chinese reformers did not unanimously support Sanger's and Stopes' views on birth control and eugenics, and elite opinions on these topics reflected a diversity of perspectives across the political spectrum. Pan Guangdan, for one, shared Sanger's contention that sterilization of the lower classes could aid in racial regeneration by preventing the so-called unfit from reproducing. However, he also feared that birth control use among the "quality" classes would lead to race suicide with the weak continuing to have large families and consequently overtaking the strong.[44] In contrast, Zhou Jianren, another distinguished Chinese eugenicist, supported eugenics and birth control as a means to alleviate overpopulation, contending that birth control use would not lead to the end of the Chinese race.[45] Rather than emphasizing sterilization of "undesirable" groups, however, he envisioned enhancing the physical strength and health of the Chinese race as a way to prevent the racial extinction of Chinese vis-à-vis whites.[46] Meanwhile, other vocal elites argued that birth control was unnatural, abortion was tantamount to murder, and coercive eugenics was unethical.[47] One article in *Dongfang zazhi* (East Asian Miscellany) even took issue with the claim that certain traits could be inherited, arguing that the Nazis' coercive sterilization of the handicapped, the Jews, and other "deviants" was fundamentally wrong since disabled or unintelligent people do not necessarily produce children with the same characteristics.[48] These vociferous debates reveal that even the fundamentals of eugenic thinking were not uniformly agreed upon or universally endorsed.

Other arguments for and against birth control were framed less explicitly with respect to race and more in terms of the related issue of national stature. Building on the work of neo-Malthusians, who feared that overpopulation would lead to global resource shortages, Chinese eugenicist Yan Yukuan argued that a lower birthrate was necessary for the country to accumulate wealth, avert war, and prevent overuse of the land.[49] As Chapter 6 explains, in the period following World War II,

[43] Teng, *Eurasian*, 12. [44] David, "Free Love, Marriage, and Eugenics," 200.
[45] Ibid., 27. [46] Dikotter, *Imperfect Conceptions*, 61.
[47] Gu Nan, "Changshi tanhua: biyun yu duotai" (Common Sense Conversation: Birth Control and Abortion), *Tielu zhigong* (Railway Worker) 43, no. 133 (1930): 2–4.
[48] Gong Jin, "Guanyu deguo de qiangpo jueyu lu (ouzhou tongxun)" (About the Law of Forced Sterilization in Germany (European Communication)) *East Asian Miscellany* 31, no. 9 (1934): 7–10.
[49] Supporters of neo-Malthusianism revived the ideas of the late eighteenth-century scholar, Thomas Malthus, who argued that overpopulation would lead to famine and ecological disaster. To avert this crisis, rather than advising sexual self-restraint as

these ideas would become the basis for dominant demographic theories about achieving economic growth among developing nations. Pan Guangdan similarly argued that Chinese children – and therefore the nation – were falling behind due to insufficient education, poverty, and biological deficiency. Only through birth control use, he argued, could the Chinese stock be improved.[50] Like many of his peers, Yan Yukuan also felt that birth control efforts should focus on those who are poor, mentally ill, disabled, or have sexually transmitted diseases, while encouraging healthy "quality" births over sheer quantity.[51] Other intellectuals argued that birth control was necessary to prevent the births of unwanted "bastards," who were significantly more likely to turn to crime, begging, and bachelorhood, phenomena that contribute to societal disorder.[52] Although these debates petered out in the 1940s, texts reflecting various eugenic principles continued to be published here and there through the end of the Republican period.[53]

The debates about eugenics and birth control also attracted the attention of Chinese feminists, many of whom were inspired by Sanger and Stopes. A key tenet of Sanger's and Stopes' writings was their commitment to a liberal feminist vision of female sexual independence. Although Sanger once admitted that "birth control is practically identical in ideal with the final aims of eugenics," she viewed empowering women as a central goal of the international birth control movement.[54] Sanger and Stopes both felt that the ability to have an active and healthy sex life without the constant risk of pregnancy was not only essential for a happy marriage but would also liberate women from the physical burden of constantly being pregnant.[55] Moreover, sexual independence, the right to choose when to procreate, and freedom from successive pregnancies

Malthus had, neo-Malthusians advocated population control, particularly in non-Western countries, in communities of color, and among the world's poor and uneducated.

[50] Pan Guangdan, "Yousheng fukan: shengyu jiezhi de jige biaozhun" (Eugenics Supplement: Several Criteria for Birth Control), *Huanian* 4, no. 22 (1935): 431–435.

[51] Yan, *Jieyu*, 78.

[52] Wu Zelin, "Yazhou de jieyu wenti" (Asia's Birth Control Problem), *Tushu pinglun* (Book Reviews) 2, no. 6 (1934): 94 and Gu, "Changshi," 2–4.

[53] Sun, *Jieyu*, 7. [54] David, "The Task Is Hers," 79.

[55] Stopes, *Ertong Ai*, 37; Some scholars have argued that Margaret Sanger strategically aligned herself with eugenicists to garner broader support for birth control. Although this alliance required her to endorse racist ideas, she felt it was the only way to overcome opposition to expanding access to birth control, and therefore, granting women reproductive independence. Her original supporters, however, disagreed with the idea that, on the grounds of race, birth control should be thrust upon the non-white peoples of the world. Rather, they viewed birth control as a universal tool for female empowerment; Dorothy Roberts, *Killing the Black Body: Race, Reproduction, and the Meaning of Liberty* (New York: Vintage Books, 1997), 116–121; Aiko Takeuchi-

would ensure that women could improve their economic and social status in relation to men. Inspired by Stopes' and Sangers' contemporaries – the Swedish feminist Ellen Key and the British philosopher Bertrand Russell – vocal liberal writers Zhang Xichen and Zhou Jianren also argued that eugenics was a kind of new sexual morality, which could mobilize the liberal discourses of free love and women's liberation in the service of social and racial betterment.[56] Yet, their pursuit of sexual independence for women and their simultaneous endorsement of coerced sterilization for certain individuals, including the mentally ill, reveal a fundamental contradiction in their thinking.[57] Likewise, Sanger's and Stopes' desire to empower the world's poor women conflicted with their elitist conviction that white, upper-class, Euro-American women should prevent other women from having children.[58] Although ostensibly fighting for universal women's rights and therefore access to ways to improve the socioeconomic status of all women through control over fertility, in reality Sanger's and Stopes' commitment to female empowerment cannot be divorced from its eugenic origins.

Some Chinese reformers initially embraced these feminist ideals, but in the long-term feminist concerns were subordinated to the larger goal of strengthening the nation. For example, Yan Yukuan felt that the women of China needed to be saved from the burdens of large families. He argued that healthier and stronger mothers and children are more productive and enjoy a higher standard of living – lines of thinking endorsed, at least rhetorically, by the Chinese Communist Party beginning in the late 1950s.[59] Still, more often than not, in China as elsewhere, feminism as it related to women's agency and sexual liberation was simply the handmaiden of nationalism.[60] The next two sections will show that despite the sidelining of feminism, women's reproductive behavior

Demirci, *Contraceptive Diplomacy: Reproductive Politics and Imperial Ambitions in the United States and Japan* (Stanford: Stanford University Press, 2018), 11.

56 Mirela David, "Bertrand Russell and Ellen Key in China: Individualism, Free Love, and Eugenics in the May Fourth Era," in *Sexuality in China: Histories of Power and Pleasure*, ed. Howard Chiang (Seattle: University of Washington Press, 2018), 78.

57 David, "Free Love, Marriage, and Eugenics," 179.

58 Takeuchi-Demirci, *Contraceptive Diplomacy*, 5.

59 Yan, *Jieyu*, 78.

60 Christina Gilmartin elaborates on this point in *Engendering the Chinese Revolution: Radical Women, Communist Politics, and Mass Movements in the 1920s* (Berkeley: University of California Press, 1995), which examines the precarious partnership between feminism and Marxist visions of the Chinese nation in the early years of the Chinese Communist Party. Aiko Takeuchi-Demirci argues that the birth control movements in Japan and the United States also became disassociated from their original feminist missions and eventually became tools of state power; Takeuchi-Demirci, *Contraceptive Diplomacy*, 5.

remained central to arguments about how best to build a powerful, modern nation.

In sum, Chinese elites supported eugenics and birth control to varying degrees and for a number of different reasons that intersected with questions of racial strength, national identity, and gender roles. Adding to the cacophony of voices were calls to end child neglect and poverty, issues that birth control had the potential to resolve.

Infanticide, Abandonment, and Abortion in Public Discourse

Eugenic debates in China emerged from the ashes of late Qing tracts decrying the immorality of infanticide, infant abandonment, and abortion. Since the nineteenth century, Chinese reformers and foreign missionaries had devoted reams of paper to condemning Chinese women for sustaining such practices. These Orientalizing and self-Orientalizing texts, which affirmed Western stereotypes about China as a place of debased morality and unrestrained sexuality, accused Chinese mothers of neglect and sinful behavior. The proliferation of these writings, in turn, put pressure on Chinese elites to dispel rumors about the prevalence of these issues – issues that threatened China's claims to modernity.

In the late nineteenth and early twentieth centuries, the French Holy Childhood Association, a transnational religious philanthropic organization originally based in France, was also propagating this image of widespread child abuse and abandonment in China. The association even solicited donations among French Catholics to "save" orphaned Chinese children, both physically and spiritually. Henrietta Harrison speculates that the reason that this call for funds was so appealing to middle-class French families was that it spoke to contemporaneous issues of infanticide and child abandonment in France.[61] Michelle T. King has shown that at the turn of the century, infanticide was a common phenomenon worldwide, rather than an issue specific to China. Indeed, more than 20 percent of children were put into foundling homes in Paris, Milan, and other major cities in Europe at this time.[62] Countering Western assumptions of moral superiority and accusations that the barbaric sexism inherent in Chinese culture led to the widespread abandonment or death of daughters, King highlights the diversity

[61] Henrietta Harrison, "'A Penny for the Little Chinese': The French Holy Childhood Association in China, 1843–1951," *The American Historical Review* 113, no. 4 (2008): 76.
[62] Harrison, "'A Penny for the Little Chinese,'" 76.

of perspectives with respect to this topic. Her work reveals that moralizing Chinese texts condemning infanticide predated the arrival of Westerners in China by many centuries. King convincingly argues that the Western imperialism and Orientalism of the nineteenth century reframed what was in fact a global problem as a uniquely Chinese cultural issue of international concern.[63]

Discussions of infanticide in China often occurred in tandem with debates about the morality of abortions. Even though Margaret Sanger denounced infanticide and abortion as methods of controlling population growth, she openly criticized missionaries who sought to prevent infanticide, including female infanticide, because she claimed those lives would not be worth living and would only further contribute to social ills like prostitution.[64] Debates about infanticide, abortion, and child abandonment predated Sanger's visit to China and continued long afterward. Many intellectuals both in China and abroad were in favor of population control but against abortion. In fact, they advocated birth control use as a way to *decrease* rates of abortion and infanticide.[65] With the introduction of birth control, the discourses framing infanticide, abandonment, and abortion gradually shifted from questions of morality to the need for modernization grounded in science.

Some humanitarians also endorsed birth control as the solution to widespread poverty, economic inequality, and child abandonment in China. During the late Qing and Republican eras, a robust child welfare network of Chinese and foreign activists, was established in Shanghai to deal with child welfare issues.[66] In the eyes of Chinese and foreign reformers, religious and secular, children were the blameless victims of capitalist inequality and unethical social practices.

The play *Qi'er* (Abandoned Child), published in 1937 by a New Culture Movement playwright, highlights the ongoing debate over the issue of abandoned children in China and the ways in which gendered narratives betrayed anxieties about national weakness. The play is set in a soup kitchen somewhere in urban China where a young mother has recently abandoned her son because she cannot afford to feed him.

63 Michelle T. King, *Between Birth and Death: Female Infanticide in Nineteenth-Century China* (Stanford: Stanford University Press, 2014), 8.

64 David, "Free Love, Marriage, and Eugenics," 178; Margaret Sanger, "Birth Control in China and Japan," October 31, 1922, https://www.nyu.edu/projects/sanger/webedition/app/documents/show.php?sangerDoc=101865.xml.

65 Sun, *From Birth Control to Eugenics*, 7; "Jieyu yu duotai shaying" (Birth Control and Abortion as Baby Killing), *Yongsheng* (1936): 80.

66 Maura Elizabeth Cunningham, "Shanghai's Wandering Ones: Child Welfare in a Global City, 1900–1953" (PhD diss., University of California, Irvine, 2014), 18–19.

Although starving children huddle like ghosts on street corners, she hopes that someone with more money will take in her son and raise him. Despite the mother's misgivings, the abandoned child's grandmother repeatedly tells her daughter that she made the right decision. The grandmother laments that she could not bear "listening to his (the boy's) calls of hunger, watching him get thinner day by day, living to starve to death."[67] The daughter argues that it is better to die together, but her mother counsels, "We can barely survive. Why on earth would we want a child to follow us to death?"

When other men and women enter the scene, some argue that abandoning one's own flesh and blood is unthinkably cruel and that mothers who do so are like monsters. One woman says that she had had several children and all of them died young – not one survived. She brazenly declares, "Poor people really should not have children." The play concludes with the young mother returning to look for her abandoned son. Upon reuniting, the grandmother pulls the two apart, forcing the child to leave on his own and the young mother to go home in tears.[68] For the grandmother, allowing the child to starve to death early on is preferable to a life of poverty on the brink of starvation.

This play illustrates in deliberately heart-wrenching language the dilemmas that impoverished mothers faced. In this context, it makes sense why an abortion, when available, might be more appealing than abandoning or even killing one's own child in the face of hunger and destitution. The fact that this play was written by an elite male reformer reveals that women's bodies, maternal morality, and the care of children were indeed central to wider debates about modernity and nation building. The woman's conclusion that poor people should not have children can be interpreted as evidence of eugenic logic or a genuine commitment to the welfare of mothers and children, or both. Regardless, by projecting his own argument onto poor female characters, the author seems to imply that what is good for the nation also benefits poor women. In addition, the characters' repeated blaming of mothers for abandoning their children affirms the notion that children are the sole responsibility of mothers and therefore anything bad that befalls them is the fault of their mothers, rather than their fathers or society as a whole. Plays like this, while designed to shock and educate the masses (as the director's forward to the play suggests), also reinforced stereotypes about China as a place with rampant child abuse and provided fertile ground for birth control advocates.

Relatedly, at various times in late imperial and Republican history, due to the high mortality rates associated with them, charitable organizations

[67] Zhang Min, *Qi'er* (Abandoned Child) (Shanghai: Xin yanju she 1937), 4.
[68] Zhang, *Qi'er*, 18.

and orphanages were accused of abusing and even murdering the children they were charged with caring for.[69] These concerns stemmed in part from media reports of orphans who died from disease or poor living conditions, as well as the desire to rid China of imperialist influences embodied in foreign philanthropic – typically Christian – organizations.[70]

Such elite anxieties linking the abuse of children to national decline endured into the early People's Republic. Tu Peilin, for example, was a reporter for the newspaper *Shenbao* in the late Republican period and became a journalist with the *Jiefang ribao* (*Liberation Daily*) after the Communist victory.[71] Carrying on the tradition of exposing unethical behavior at charitable institutions, in 1952, Tu published a report called "Infanticide Hall" (*Shaying tang*) chronicling the abuse of children in a foundling home called Ren'ai Hall in Shanghai. Ren'ai Hall was established in 1892 by a French clergyman. According to Tu, this philanthropic organization had separate quarters for babies, orphans, the elderly, and the disabled and also cared for the unwanted daughters of impoverished families.[72] Tu said that at first Shanghai locals thought Ren'ai was a place of kindness and good deeds; they observed foreign priests in black robes and nannies (*mama*) in big white hats singing songs and praying for the salvation of irreverent people's souls. However, local residents noticed that each day the dead bodies of children were being placed outside the backdoor of the "Nanny Hall" (*mama tang*) for infants. In addition, locals heard crying within the hall and observed that children entered but never left. Yet, no outsiders were permitted to enter the grounds to confirm these stories.[73] While it is likely that these observations were at least partly accurate, the deaths of so many children were probably the result of the chronic malnutrition, unsanitary living conditions, and illness that plagued underfunded philanthropic institutions, rather than a product of malicious and deliberate abuse, starvation, and murder, as the report charged.[74] Nonetheless, incidents like these

[69] Angela Ki Che Leung, "Relief Institutions for Children in Nineteenth-Century China," in *Chinese Views of Childhood*, ed. Anne Behnke Kinney (Honolulu: University of Hawai'i Press, 1995), 251–252.

[70] Cunningham, "Shanghai's Wandering Ones," 180.

[71] "Tu Peilin," *Shanghai Local History Office*, accessed February 28, 2018, http://www.shtong.gov.cn/node2/node2245/node4522/node10080/node10084/node63755/userobject1ai54188.html.

[72] Tu Peilin, *Shaying tang* (Infanticide Hall) (Shanghai: Huadong renmin chubanshe, 1952), 2.

[73] Tu, *Shaying tang*, 5; These anxieties were not new. Fears that missionary-run orphanages were kidnapping small children to convert them to Christianity had also fueled popular antipathy toward foreigners during the late Qing dynasty.

[74] Tu, *Shaying tang*,10–11; Harrison, "'A Penny for the Little Chinese,'" 91.

ensured that the fate of China's unwanted or less privileged children remained in the public focus, where these issues were widely discussed and debated in the Republican and early Communist periods. Fears of child abuse in orphanages no doubt influenced the decisions of women unable to care for their babies to resort to abortion or infanticide. Moreover, even most opponents of birth control would have to agree that compared to the alternatives, contraception was a more ethical course of action for a poor young woman seeking to prevent pregnancy.

In addition to plays and journalistic exposés, debates about abortion, infanticide, and child abandonment also filled newspaper and magazine articles. An opinion piece "Birth Control, Abortion, and Childcare" and a subsequent series of letters to the editor published in *East Asian Miscellany* encompass many of the prevailing debates surrounding birth control. The magazine's editor and the author of the article, Ke, argued that neither birth control nor abortion could solve China's social problems, and as a result, a reader extensively debated with Ke the value of birth control to China.[75] Wu, the reader writing to the editor, stated that:

> In fact, in many isolated villages in our country, abortion and infanticide are still common due to poverty, backward culture, and bad habits … In Changshu, regardless of whether a baby is male or female, if a woman gets pregnant with a fourth child, she will suffocate it in the toilet even if the family is relatively well off … Abortion and infanticide are not small problems in our society. They are cruel, despicable, and absolutely should not exist in the twentieth-century world.[76]

Wu continued by saying he felt that although people had fundamentally no idea what either birth control or abstinence were, they should be taught modern birth control methods to prevent further atrocities. Furthermore, he explicitly stated that birth control was not related to population or eugenics but was instead a means to fight barbaric practices. Ke, agreeing with Wu that abortion and infanticide were common in the countryside, maintained that although he did not "oppose the adoption of birth control methods by the poor," in reality Chinese people were too destitute and uneducated to understand how to practice contraception. He clarified that even if these methods were made simpler, they would likely be ineffective due to the limits of birth control technology.[77] Such elitist perspectives and assumptions that abortion and infanticide were primarily rural practices were prevalent in the public sphere.

[75] Ke Shi, "*Shengyu jiezhi datai he ertong gongyu*" (Birth Control, Abortion, and Childcare), *Dongfang zazhi* (East Asian Miscellany) 31, no. 21 (1934): 5–6.
[76] SMA, D2-0-625-24. [77] SMA, D2–0-625-24.

Using a rhetorical strategy common among Communist sympathizers, other publications from this period linked the issue of abortion to Republican China's corruption and moral bankruptcy. One famous Chinese doctor, Lu Shifu, blamed Chinese druggists and doctors for irresponsibly convincing innocent young girls whose periods did not arrive on time or who accidentally became pregnant to take illegal abortifacient pills. According to the article, young women were told that these pills would clear up the entire problem, but in reality these medications were not always effective and could lead to severe vaginal inflammation or even death.[78]

Like Lu, a female author, Zhen Ni, blamed the commercialization of medicine and doctors' greed for the ubiquity of abortion. In an article she published in *New Women's Monthly* in 1946, she put forth a number of intriguing and at times contradictory ideas. Zhen argues – in an implicit critique of capitalism and Nationalist rule – that doctors mainly perform abortions because it is an easy way to earn a relatively large sum of money. Zhen commented that this phenomenon was also common in "civilized" countries like Japan and Germany. According to Zhen, many women in China desire birth control so they can pursue study, careers, or economic security, but they rarely are knowledgeable about Western birth control methods. Therefore, they resort to dangerous indigenous methods (*tufa*) of contraception and abortion or pay for expensive surgical abortions. Zhen counseled, "According to the medical point of view, the most appropriate time to abort a fetus is during the sixth month of pregnancy or later. The mother's health will be the safest if she has an abortion during the sixth month."[79] Zhen noted that most doctors prefer to perform abortions in the first three months of pregnancy because it is much easier to dispose of the evidence that way and therefore not get caught violating the law. She also warned that if the abortion is not performed in a sanitary environment, the mother can contract a dangerous infection. Like many other outspoken social critics, Zhen appropriated the language of science to substantiate her sometimes questionable claims. Her overarching point was that in more equitable and scientifically modern societies, women have access to birth control and therefore do not need to rely on back-alley abortions performed by extortionate black-market practitioners.

[78] Lu Shifu, "Feifa zhidao jieyu de chawu he weixian" (The Errors and Dangers of Illegally Advising on Birth Control), *Shengming yu jiankang* (Life and Health), 6 (1928): n.p.

[79] Zhen Ni, "Duotai he biyun" (Abortion and Birth Control), *Xin funü yuekan* (New Women's Monthly) 4 (1946): 20–21.

Despite their differing thrusts, many of the arguments intellectuals put forth against abortion, infanticide, and abandonment would prove valuable for promoting birth control. It would seem that birth control, although not a perfect solution, at least could simultaneously resolve the issues of unchecked population growth and "undesirable" births, phenomena eugenicists saw as antithetical to nation-building goals. Furthermore, birth control had the potential to limit "barbaric" practices like infanticide and child abandonment. From the perspective of some feminists, too, access to birth control promised to protect vulnerable women from the underground abortion market while granting them paths to economic independence. Birth control, then, could address myriad different concerns. Still, in relation to Chinese society as a whole, these discourses remained marginal and confined to elite circles.

Many of the most prolific scholars debating the value of birth control and abortion in the Republican-era public sphere were elite men. In one of the previously mentioned articles, a magazine editor named Ke accused a reader, Wu, of being ignorant about the masses of China and only focusing on the elite perspectives of China's handful of intellectuals. This charge could be made against many of China's most vocal Republican elites – Pan Guangdan, Zhou Jianren, and others – most of whom were highly educated with training abroad and teaching positions at elite universities. Pan Guangdan, for example, was educated at Tsinghua University in China, as well as Dartmouth College and Columbia University in the United States. Similarly, Zhou Jianren was the younger brother of the acclaimed writer Lu Xun and a professor of human biology in China.[80] Evidently, the perspectives of male intellectuals dominated discussions of birth control and related issues in the urban press. And, as in the case of the author of *Qi'er* (Abandoned Child), such men sought to inject their eugenic arguments into the national discussion by framing their views as being beneficial for the nation's poor and marginalized.

Chastity, Birth Control, and the Ideal Woman

Not so differently from debates over the childbearing practices of China's poorest women, the intelligentsia was also deeply preoccupied with the ideal reproductive behavior of modern, cosmopolitan women. In the Republican period, two archetypes of the modern woman, representing

[80] Frank Dikotter, *Sex, Culture and Modernity in China: Medical Science and the Construction of Sexual Identities in the Early Republican Period* (Hong Kong: Hong Kong University Press, 1995), 38.

contradictory views of modernity, emerged in response to the conservative Confucian ideal of women as "good wives" and "wise mothers" (*liangqi xianmu*): the "New Woman" and the "Modern Girl."[81] On the one hand, the New Woman presented the positive aspects of modernity. She was depicted as well educated, politically active, and nationalistic, willing to forego marriage to advance and modernize the nation. On the other hand, the Modern Girl symbolized the fears associated with modernity, such as danger, alienation, and cultural loss. Sarah Stevens argues that in female-authored works, the Modern Girl was typically disillusioned with modernity and represented the struggle women faced in finding their voices in a changing China. In male-authored works, however, the Modern Girl was a *femme fatale* or *flaneuse*, who embraced bodily pleasure and consumerism while rejecting chastity and monogamy. In this case, the Modern Girl represented male fears about female subjectivity.[82] These two archetypes at times can be difficult to distinguish, and indeed they overlap and diverge in interesting ways in Republican discourses on abortion and birth control.

Writers – male and female – utilized the New Woman/Modern Girl dichotomy to further their arguments in support of birth control or abortion. While in many instances men's voices seem to have dominated the public discussion of eugenics, abortion, and birth control in China, women in fact also contributed to this public discourse. Ling Ma shows that some feminist writers in fact reinforced certain fixed understandings of the correct societal roles of women by representing urban women undergoing abortions as pure and hardworking, closer to the nationalistic New Woman than the hedonistic Modern Girl. For example, fiction writers often painted young urban abortion seekers as victims seeking to liberate themselves from marriage and economic dependence.[83] In these works, though, the reader still shares the male gaze, wherein the women under discussion are depicted from a heterosexual male perspective.[84]

As with abortion, writers also used the New Woman/Modern Girl binary to various extents to support their arguments about birth control. Take, for example, a book called *Zai gei nürenmen* (Again to the Women)

[81] Sarah E. Stevens, "Figuring Modernity: The New Woman and the Modern Girl in Republican China," *NWSA Journal* 15, no. 3 (Fall 2003): 83.

[82] Stevens, "Figuring Modernity": 83; Sometimes women who rejected marriage and children were also portrayed in the popular press as incomplete women or a "third sex." This suggests that fears about the New Woman and Modern Girl were in essence fears about threats to reproduction.

[83] Ma, "Gender, Law, and Society," 162–163.

[84] A. W. Eaton, "Feminist Philosophy of Art," *Philosophy Compass* 3 (2008): 873.

published in 1933 by Ma Guoliang, a member of the China Democratic League, an editor for the influential Shanghai pictorial company and eponymous pictorial, *Liangyou*, and the editor-in-chief of the women's magazine *Jindai funü* (Modern Woman). In his lengthy plea for birth control use, first Ma declares, "The new Modern Girl is knowledgeable, empowered, and independent. She is not controlled by men."[85] Here, he seems to be praising the Modern Girl's self-reliance. However, in a long passage on the importance of birth control, his portrayal of her also takes on some of the characteristics of the self-sacrificing, patriotic New Woman:

Children, many people have praised them, said they are the little angels of the family, that they are the Cupid who makes the love between a husband and wife even more profound.

This is good if you can provide for them, as can some people who take more than one wife and raise a dozen or more children, for what they have is money.

But you cannot imitate them, and if your ability to support yourself and your spouse is too limited, then you should not even have one child of your own.

Many in our society are thieves and prostitutes, and there are many, many people who do not have food in their stomachs and shelter. But weren't they all born from a mother's womb?

They were abandoned because their parents could not support them, and society did not hold the parents accountable for their children's upbringing. As a result, they will be left as bandits despised by all!...

Of course, sexual fulfillment is necessary, and it is one of the key elements of a prosperous marriage. Children are the result of the fulfillment of sexual desire.

We need sexual fulfillment, but at the same time we have to have birth control, or completely avoid childbearing! Lying ahead of us is this kind of society!

People who fully understand their own power and adopt birth control are worthy of praise. This is first for society – not only will we ourselves benefit substantially, but also the whole of society will reap the benefits.

If you do not have the ability to raise a child on your own, you not only bring greater hardship upon yourself, but you also make your innocent child suffer...

Unless you are a rich capitalist, your child will become the heir to the flesh and blood-eating devil you created!

So, you do not need to practice abstinence; [instead] use contraceptive methods to control your fertility...

You [will] not have to worry about being unable to afford parenthood and that your child will be useless to society.

[85] Ma Guoliang, *Zai gei nürenmen* (Again to the Women) (Shanghai: Shanghai Liangyou Book Printing Company, 1933), 8.

Discard the selfish prejudices of individualism, and give your energy for the happiness of all mankind...
You should practice birth control![86]

In this passage, Ma conflates the Modern Girl and New Woman motifs, yet he does not actually show genuine concern for women's wellbeing. On the one hand, he praises the strength and independence of the Modern Girl and liberally acknowledges that sexual fulfillment is necessary for a happy, healthy marriage. On the other hand, he repeatedly invokes the image of the nation and mankind in general to justify birth control use, arguing that it can save lives, diminish suffering, and improve the country. Ironically, even as he implores the reader to "discard the selfish prejudices of individualism" – behavior associated with the Modern Girl – he invokes individualistic arguments to persuade readers that it is in their personal best interest not to have too many children. From the perspective of class, Ma's use of the term "rich capitalist" in a Marxist sense would seem to imply a disdain for the wealthy and yet Ma contends that only affluent people should be having a lot of children, a borderline eugenic argument. In this case, he is not affirming the importance of individual morality (i.e., chastity) with respect to sexual satisfaction and instead is more focused on ethical childrearing and national reform. Ma capitalizes on certain aspects of the Modern Girl and New Woman archetypes to support his call for birth control but remains more focused on what women represent than on the needs and desires of women themselves.

Overt discussions of birth control and sexual liberation sat uneasily alongside contemporaneous discourses arguing that the ideal woman was pure and chaste (something akin to the New Woman). The trope of the ideal woman as one lacking or repressing sexual desire has a long history in China.[87] In the Republican and Mao eras, the state still sought to

[86] Ma, *Zai gei nürenmen*, 151–166.

[87] Mark Elvin, Matthew Sommer, Janet Theiss, and others have illustrated the ways in which control over female sexuality served as a source of state and cultural authority in the late imperial period. While the cult of chastity was primarily an elite practice in the Ming dynasty, Sommer argues that the Qing state expanded the expectation of chastity to commoners. The state's objectives were to create legally enforced, uniform sexual expectations and to ensure that all males, regardless of class, could share the same monopoly over their wives' sexuality. Theiss complicates Sommer's claims by illustrating the limits of attempted state control over sexuality; she argues that the conflicting agendas of ordinary people and contradictory constructions of female sexual morality undermined state hegemony in this area. Matthew H. Sommer, *Sex, Law and Society in Late Imperial China* (Stanford: Stanford University Press, 2000), 7–8; Janet Theiss, *Disgraceful Matters: The Politics of Chastity in Eighteenth-Century China* (Berkeley: University of California Press, 2004), 211.

affirm this particular vision of sexual morality through various legal, social, and political mechanisms. But unlike in the past, the Nationalist and Maoist regimes were armed with the rhetoric of science.

Articles from women's magazines in the 1930s and 1940s used arguments couched in terms of morality as well as science to affirm the importance of premarital virginity. An article from *Funü zazhi* (Ladies' Journal) published in 1941, argues that there are two types of chastity – not engaging in sex before marriage and not engaging in extramarital sexual relations – both of which are essential to maintaining individual purity.[88] Similarly, an article in *Yixun* (Medical News) argues that chastity is critical because an unmarried woman who has lost her virginity will never find a husband.[89] Other authors took a different approach to chastity, using the legitimating language of science to argue against premarital sex. For example, one article shifts the issue of premarital sex from a primarily moral one, as it was in imperial times, to a physiological issue. The author argues that premarital sex can expose couples to dangerous diseases and harm.[90]

Even as progressive writers upheld the ideal of premarital chastity, they frequently decried the outdated expectation that women commit suicide if sexually violated or remain chaste if widowed. A feminist article in *Xiandai funü* (Modern Woman) cautions, "Often a boy will forcibly take an inexperienced girl's virginity. Other people will look down on her and the girl of course will be hurt. For the sake of her honor, she will be forced to marry someone she barely knows and does not love."[91] The article describes a well-known story in which a young college student is raped by a married taxi driver. When the young woman discovers that she is pregnant, she commits suicide out of shame. The author condemns this situation in favor of sexual reform. Yet, as Harriet Evans argues, even in the 1950s many of the narratives on sex were moralizing tales seeking to protect young women's virginity while implicitly exonerating men from blame for indulging in sexual behavior.[92]

With respect to birth control or abortion, the enduring importance of premarital chastity and marital fidelity caused anxiety among some vocal

[88] Hong Li, "Zhencao wenti" (The Chastity Problem), *Funü zazhi* (Ladies' Journal) 2.2 (1941): 29.
[89] Xie Yunshou, "Duotai zui" (The Crime of Abortion), *Yixun* (Medical News) 2, no. 1 (1948): 3.
[90] Ren Jin, "Weihun fufu de xingxingwei" (Unmarried Couples' Sexual Behavior), *Funü yuekan* (Women's Monthly) 6, no. 6 (1948): 59.
[91] Zuo Songfen, "Zhencao, aiqing, hunyin" (Chastity, Love, Marriage), *Xiandai Funü* (Modern Woman) 13 (1949): 11–12.
[92] Harriet Evans, *Women and Sexuality in China: Dominant Discourses of Female Sexuality and Gender Since 1949* (Cambridge: Polity Press, 1997), 105–107.

elites; they felt that endorsement of birth control and decriminalization of abortion would enable and even encourage premarital sex and adultery.[93] In the late imperial and Republican periods, extramarital intercourse and fornication (typically premarital sex) were illegal for women, and perpetrators of these crimes could be tried in court. In 1935, this law was extended to male adulterers, though prosecutors continued to focus primarily on female offenders.[94] Condoning birth control use or abortion would seem, then, to be subtly undermining the legal and moral commitment to female chastity and marital fidelity. Patriarchal fears about the legalization of birth control and abortion were not completely unfounded. In fact, despite the criminalization of abortion, women continued to have abortions to hide evidence undermining the façade of chaste widowhood or premarital abstinence.[95]

Because of the controversy surrounding female sexuality, feminists did not universally demand the legalization of abortion and instead focused on improving the status of women as a whole in relation to men. Some felt that seeking the decriminalization of abortion – a practice opposed by social conservatives concerned with preserving women's roles as wives and mothers – would undermine larger efforts to acquire support for the cause of gender equality.[96] Vocal Japanese feminist, Yashioka Yayoi, opposed birth control in Japan for similar reasons.[97] In an effort to appeal to a broader swath of society, some Chinese feminist groups chose to maintain a moderate position with respect to the divisive topic of abortion.[98]

To an extent, the debates of the 1920s and 1930s were curtailed by the exigencies of World War II and the return to conservative views of women as the nation's reproducers. A longtime supporter of natalism and eugenic ideals, Sun Yat-sen had once argued that China was only able to endure Western invasions and colonial rule because of its large population, and for that reason he opposed birth control. At the same time, he had supported the adoption of premarital health examinations, sterilization of the "unfit," and other programs designed to socially

[93] L. D. Weatherhead, *Controlling Sexual Life* (*xingshenghuo de kongzhi*) (Shanghai: Youth Association Books (qingnian xiehui shuju), 1936), 58.

[94] Alison Sau-Chu Yeung, "Fornication in the Late Qing Legal Reforms Moral Teachings and Legal Principles," *Modern China* 29, no. 3 (July 2003): 303; Lisa Tran, "Sex and Equality in Republican China: The Debate over the Adultery Law," *Modern China* 35, no. 2 (March 2009): 214.

[95] Ma, "Gender, Law, and Society," 218–219. [96] Ibid., 150–152.

[97] Chung, *Struggle for National Survival*, 136.

[98] Ma, "Gender, Law, and Society," 150–152.

engineer the Chinese population.[99] During the Anti-Japanese War (1937–1945), abortion laws became more stringent because China's most prominent eugenicists, such as Pan Guangdan, viewed the war with Japan as a contest of population that would allow only the strongest to survive.[100] Following this logic, during the Chinese civil war, particularly in the second half of the 1940s, abortion laws continued to be restricted.[101] In 1945, Sun's successor, Chiang Kai-shek, also adopted a eugenic population policy, although it was never put into practice due to the civil war. Enthralled with the promise of "hybrid vigor" – the idea that racial mixing improves the gene pool – Chiang's policy prohibited abortion but encouraged intermarriage between Chinese people and members of the "white" race, a combination he purported would marry the desirable fair skin of Europeans with the superior intelligence of the Chinese.[102] As with abortions themselves, references to abortions in newspaper articles during this period were also limited, and where they did exist, they emphasized the negative consequences of doctors facilitating illegal abortions.[103] In this way, the Nationalist government pursued a policy of controlled natalism that combined eugenic ideals with the desire for population growth.

Conclusion

During the Republican period, birth control, population growth, and the "quality" of births became critical social issues, as Chinese elites linked individual health and reproduction to national unity and strength. As a result of domestic and global intellectual exchanges, reformers melded Chinese and foreign ideas about sex and reproduction. In addition, semantic blending took place between the language of Western and Japanese science and traditional Chinese medical discourses. Within the vibrant Republican public sphere, feminists, birth controllers, and eugenicists held a broad and heterogeneous range of opinions with respect to overpopulation, state authority, family structure, and gender roles. The tension between the idea of women as desired objects – embodying virtue and "Chineseness" – and women as economic

[99] Chung, *Struggle for National Survival*, 158–159; Emily Baum, "Healthy Minds, Compliant Citizens: The Politics of 'Mental Hygiene' in Republican China, 1928–1937," *Twentieth-Century China* 42, no. 3 (2017): 229.
[100] Chung, *Struggle for National Survival*, 142.
[101] Kohama, "Cong 'Feifa duotai' dao 'jihua shengyu,'" 338.
[102] Matthew Connelly, *Fatal Misconception: The Struggle to Control World Population* (Cambridge: Harvard University Press, 2008), 142; Teng, *Eurasian*, 120–121.
[103] Masako, "Cong 'Feifa duotai' dao 'jihua shengyu,'" 338.

producers, consumers, and desiring subjects was central to elite debates about birth control. Yet, the majority of these debates focused more on what women signified for the modern nation than on what women themselves wanted and needed. As Chapter 2 will demonstrate, although some intellectuals argued that birth control offered solutions to China's social problems, in reality these debates had little effect on Chinese society as a whole.

2 Birth Control in Practice

Emmenagogues, Contraceptives, and Abortions, 1911–1949

Li Shenhua, a nineteen-year-old woman from Beijing, was working at the Third Branch Clothing Factory in Tianjin. When Li, who was not married, discovered that she was six months pregnant, she sought help from a doctor. The doctor refused to help her abort the pregnancy, so Li reached out to a colleague, Guo Bao, a thirty-nine-year-old married woman working at the same factory. Guo agreed to help Li induce an abortion through massage, but during the procedure, Guo noticed that Li was vomiting white foam and called the factory doctor for help. He gave Li an injection and administered oral medication, but she died soon after. Later when investigators found Li, her vagina was dilated and bleeding. The umbilical cord still connected her belly with that of a small lifeless baby boy. Moreover, Li's lower abdomen was red and swollen and had the marks of repeated hand-rubbing. Guo was charged with committing an abortion that led to death.[1] Were situations like this common in urban China in the early twentieth century, or was this simply an anomaly? If the former, what kinds of women were undergoing abortions or using birth control and in what contexts? What motivations drove them to employ birth control or resort to abortion?

This chapter broadly examines birth control and abortion in practice during the Republican period, an era when these topics garnered considerable attention worldwide. As Chapter 1 argues, questions of morality, modernity, women's rights, and national stature all undergirded these discussions. At the level of individual practice, though, the circumstances in which women employed birth control or underwent abortion were most often connected to patriarchal social pressures and financial challenges.

While the rest of this book takes birth control and abortion in Shanghai, Tianjin, and Luoyang as its focus, this chapter investigates Beijing rather than Luoyang because the latter was small and

[1] Tianjin Municipal Archive (TMA), J0044-2-038811.

underdeveloped during this period, leaving little in the form of written records.[2] Moreover, Luoyang and Beijing shared some important similarities. Although Republican Beijing was much more populous than Luoyang, both cities had relatively little industrial development. Like Luoyang, Beijing was also never divided into separate Chinese and foreign administrative domains, allowing it to retain a greater degree of autonomy than port cities like Shanghai and Tianjin.[3]

In Shanghai, Tianjin, and Beijing, abortions were the most prevalent forms of contraception that appeared in historical records. Using court records and advertisements, this chapter demonstrates that abortion seekers and practitioners of abortion drew on techniques taken from folk traditions, traditional Chinese healing, and Western medicine. Some women, for example, used patented pills or herbal decoctions available in pharmacies and through midwives to induce abortion, while others used acupuncture needles or surgery to terminate their pregnancies. Whereas sterilization and abortion were criminalized at the national level, birth control was neither explicitly endorsed nor banned for married couples.[4] Therefore, when available, some women relied on contraceptives or medicines with contraceptive properties. Yet, most evidence of fertility regulation comes from court records charging women with surgical or medicinal abortions.

This chapter also reveals that some of the most common rationales for undergoing abortion – adultery, premarital intercourse, and sex among "chaste" widows – cut across class and geographic lines and had little to do with elite concerns about improving population quality or fortifying the nation. Nonetheless, poor, uneducated women and women at the margins of society bore the brunt of laws regulating abortion and were the primary target of public censure. In contrast to wealthier women, whose abortions were largely shielded from public scrutiny, lower-class women were singled out for being "loose" and "backward," traits believed to threaten the prevailing social order.

[2] Although Luoyang has no official archival records and only one periodical from this period, I located two articles reiterating the fact that infanticide and abortion were banned (and these public statements were likely released in response to particular instances of infanticide or abortion); "Yusheng fu chongshen qianling chedi chajin niying" (Henan Provincial Government Reiterates Order Completely Prohibiting Infanticide through Drowning), *Xingdu ribao*, August 11, 1939; "Qieshi baoyu ertong" (Earnestly Protect Children), *Xingdu ribao*, September 13, 1941.

[3] Emily Baum, *The Invention of Madness: State, Society, and the Insane in Modern China* (Chicago: University of Chicago Press, 2018), 12–13.

[4] Tyrene White, *China's Longest Campaign: Birth Planning in the People's Republic, 1949–2005* (Ithaca: Cornell University Press, 2006), 22.

Abortion or Menstrual Regulation?

What types of birth control products and methods for inducing abortion were available in urban China at this time, and who was using them? The medical marketplace in China's largest cities, particularly in port cities with large migrant populations, thrived from the late Qing era onward, introducing the populace to an assortment of medicines at several different price points. In this way, consumers of different statuses and class backgrounds could draw on a panoply of products and procedures for their medical needs. Practitioners with varying degrees of expertise – from licensed Chinese and foreign doctors of Western medicine to itinerant peddlers, unlicensed Chinese medicine healers, and druggists selling contraceptive and abortifacient drugs – also coexisted within this marketplace.[5]

China's first clinics dedicated exclusively to Western birth control emerged in the 1920s. Inspired by the work of Margaret Sanger, a female gynecologist named Yang Chao Buwei established a birth control clinic in Beijing in 1925, where she distributed contraception and information about it.[6] However, the police raided and shut down the clinic.[7] In 1930, Yang Chongrui (Marion Yang), a leader in the Chinese birth control and midwifery modernization movements, established another birth control clinic in Beijing. She was responsible for training a generation of midwives to administer birth control, and although the clinic closed in 1933, Yang's students would go on to serve in medical institutions across China.[8] Yang Chongrui had primarily hoped to alleviate the burdens of working-class women, but she reported that most of her patients belonged to the middle and upper classes.[9] Given her goal of empowering women, the most common birth control products offered in Yang's clinic were diaphragms, sponges, and "vaginal plugs" (*yindaosai*).[10] Following these models, during the 1930s, other small birth control clinics were established (albeit for short periods of time) in major cities

[5] "Caoyao datai laoyu beidai" (Herbal Abortion, Old Woman Arrested), *Libao* (1947): n. p.; "Shaonü pinren huaiyun, pinfu jianqing danfu" (Young Mistress Gets Pregnant, Poor Woman Eases Her Burden), *Fu'er mosi* (Sherlock Holmes) (1937): 2; "British Women Found Guilty: Jury Deliberates Three and a Half Hours in Tientsin Abortion Case: Strong Recommendation for Mercy," *North China Daily News*, March 29, 1937; TMA, J0043-2-010192.

[6] Mirela David, "Female Gynecologists and Their Birth Control Clinics: Eugenics in Practice in 1920s–1930s China," *Canadian Bulletin of Medical History* 35, no. 1 (2018): 5.

[7] David, "Female Gynecologists," 17. [8] Ibid., 18.

[9] Chung, *Struggle for National Survival*, 123–125.

[10] David, "Female Gynecologists," 19.

like Shanghai and Nanjing to circulate information about sexual hygiene and distribute contraceptives.[11]

Unlike using or selling contraception, performing an abortion was illegal according to all versions of the Republican criminal code. That policy only changed when therapeutic abortion was legalized in 1935, allowing for abortion if a woman was too sick to carry the pregnancy to term. According to the 1928 draft of the Republican criminal code, the advertising of abortion services was also strictly prohibited.[12] As part of efforts to regulate and professionalize the medical industry, the Nationalist government ordered that advertising the abortifacient properties of drugs would result in a pharmaceutical company or pharmacy losing its license to sell medicine.[13] Building on the framework set forth at the national level, in 1929 the Shanghai and Beijing governments banned the promotion and dissemination of drugs with contraceptive, abortifacient, or aphrodisiac properties.[14] In 1935, the Tianjin municipal government followed suit.[15]

Enforcement of the new mandates varied by location but was often sporadic.[16] In Shanghai, the municipal police conducted a few searches of drugstores, confiscated suspicious drugs and books, and charged certain newspaper owners with disseminating illegal material. In one case from 1937, Shanghai police investigators disguised themselves as customers and exposed two pharmacies selling "obscene" products. The owners of the two pharmacies were charged with selling a variety of aphrodisiacs, contraceptives, and sexual aids, including 8 eight-pack boxes of condoms, 22 boxes of disease-preventing contraceptives, 7 bottles of *gujing* pills to fight nocturnal emissions, 483 sex guides,

[11] You Ji, "Gulou yiyuan zhishi jieyu" (Gulou Hospital Provides Birth Control Instruction), *Guangji yikan* (Guangji Medical Journal) 12, no. 2 (1935): 10–11; Mao Xian, "*Yiyao wenda: da di 365 hao: beiliuxian guan xizhang jun wen jieyu*" (Medical Q&A: Answer Number 365: Beiliu County Government's Sa Zhangjun Asks about Birth Control), *Guangxi weisheng xunkan* (Guangxi Hygiene Journal) 3, no. 2 (1935): 18.

[12] Ma, "Gender, Law, and Society," 243.

[13] "Shanghai tebie shi qudi yinwei wuyao xuanchuan pin zanxing guiding" (Temporary Rules for the Prohibition of Publicizing Obscene Drugs in Shanghai), *Shenbao*, May 4, 1929; Emily Baum, "Health by the Bottle: The Dr. Williams' Medicine Company and the Commodification of Well-Being," in *Liangyou, Kaleidoscopic Modernity and the Shanghai Global Metropolis, 1926–1945*, eds. Paul G. Pickowicz, Kuiyi Shen, and Yingjin Zhang (Leiden: Brill, 2013), 87.

[14] "Shanghai tebie shi qudi yinwei wuyao xuanchuan pin zanxing guiding" (Temporary Rules for the Prohibition of Publicizing Obscene Drugs in Shanghai), *Shenbao*, May 4, 1929.

[15] "Qudi yiyao guanggao guize, jin shi fu tuoding houri zuo zhengshi gongbu" (Yesterday the Tianjin Municipal Government Finalized and Officially Announced the Regulations Banning Medicine Advertisements), *Xin Tianjin* (New Tianjin) 5 (1935): 5.

[16] Ma, "Sex, Law, and Society," 175.

and 5 vaginal warmers (believed to aid female arousal).[17] All of the offending products were seized. The pharmacies were also charged with advertising these products in print.[18] In a similar case from 1930, a Shanghai pharmacy was charged 900 *yuan* for selling aphrodisiacs (*chunyao*) and *Baoyulin*-brand contraceptive tablets.[19] Likewise, in 1935, the owner of the Yongde Pharmacy in Tianjin's Japanese settlement was charged with advertising and selling forbidden patent medicines, including those that purportedly enabled the user to quit smoking and drugs, with implied abortifacient properties. The pharmacy owner was arrested and charged 400 *yuan*, and his goods were confiscated.[20] Despite the risk of being charged fines and having their property seized, individual pharmacists, pharmacies, and medicine companies continued to advertise and sell these types of products.

Police also occasionally raided medical clinics suspected of offering abortions or advertising abortion services. In Tianjin, for example, under pressure from a Catholic home for children, the municipal government ordered the Ministry of Health to crack down on practitioners of abortion, arguing that abortions were harmful to society.[21] Police similarly penalized abortion clinics that illegally advertised their services in periodicals, as in the case of the Tianjin Ming Medical Clinic (*Ming zhenliao*), which openly advertised that it offered abortions.[22]

Contraceptives, although rarely the sole focus of police crackdowns and never the cause for sentencing in court cases, occupied a tenuous legal and social position. In many parts of the world in the late nineteenth and early twentieth centuries, contraception was denounced on the grounds that it promoted immoral behavior.[23] Similarly, the

[17] Leon Rocha, "A Small Business of Sexual Enlightenment: Zhang Jingsheng's 'Beauty Bookshop,' Shanghai 1927–1929," *British Journal of Chinese Studies* 9, no. 2 (2019): 19.

[18] "Liang yaofang chaohuo yinju chunyao" (Two Pharmacies Were Searched – Obscene Products and Aphrodisiacs Were Seized), *Shenbao*, March 4, 1937; Charlotte Furth, *A Flourishing Yin: Gender in China's Medical History: 960–1665* (Berkeley: University of California Press, 1999), 292.

[19] "Chunyao an jieshu qifeng" (Aphrodisiac Case Closed), *Shenbao*, July 28, 1930.

[20] "Gongdu: weisheng: gonghan: di sisanwu hao (ershisi nian shiyi yue jiu ri): han xingzheng yuan weisheng shu han wei ben shiyong de yaofang wangdechen shoumai weijin ji duotai deng yaopin jingben fuling chi gong'an ju chachao ji fa ban ge qingxing fu qing chazhao wen" (Official Document: Hygiene: Public Letter: Number 435 [November 9, 1935]: Letter to the Department of Public Health Regarding the Punishment of Yongde Pharmacy's Wang Dechen for Selling of Banned Drugs and Abortifacients), *Tianjin shi zhengfu gongbao* (Tianjin Municipal Government Gazette) 82, nos. 151–153 (1935): 74–76.

[21] TMA, J0025-2-003626-030; TMA, J0116-1-000615.

[22] TMA, J0116-1-000616-064.

[23] Susanne M. Klausen, *Race, Maternity, and the Politics of Birth Control in South Africa, 1910–39* (London: Palgrave Macmillan, 2004), 13; Claire L. Jones, *The Business of Birth*

Guomindang authorities viewed contraception as encouraging abortion, extramarital sex, or both and therefore policed the sale of prophylactics. Moreover, as in the United States in the nineteenth century, the association of contraception with "pornography" – texts and images deemed harmful for public consumption – made it vulnerable to further censure.[24] In addition to issues of morality, the lack of clarity about the difference between contraception and abortion further tarnished birth control's reputation, and as a result, contraceptives at times drew suspicion from the authorities.

The fuzzy line between legal medicines that happened to prevent pregnancy (emmenagogues) and illegal ones that prevented carrying a pregnancy to term (abortifacients) made policing abortion and contraception even more difficult. Charlotte Furth and Francesca Bray argue that in Traditional Chinese Medicine (TCM), a regular menstrual period was believed to indicate health and balanced *qi*, "a vapor taken to constitute the essence of matter." If amenorrhea occurred due to either pregnancy or illness, this indicated the existence of a menstrual blockage – the result of imbalanced levels of *yin* and *yang*, the complementary types of *qi*.[25] Therefore, during the eighteenth and nineteenth centuries, if a woman's menses were irregular, this might lead her to consume *tiaojingyao* or *tongjingyao*, medicines that induced menstruation, which in turn would prevent pregnancy.[26] While a doctor might be reluctant to

Control: Contraception and Commerce in Britain before the Sexual Revolution (Manchester: Manchester University Press, 2020), 14.

[24] Y. Yvon Wang, "Whorish Representation: Pornography, Media, and Modernity in Fin-de-siècle Beijing," *Modern China* 40, no. 4 (2014): 368; Tone, "Making Room for Rubbers," 57.

[25] T. J. Hinrichs and Linda L. Barnes, eds., *Chinese Medicine and Healing: An Illustrated History* (Cambridge, MA: Harvard University Press, 2012), 7–11; Francesca Bray, *Technology and Gender: Fabrics of Power in Late Imperial China* (Berkeley: University of California Press, 1997), 334.

[26] Charlotte Furth and Francesca Bray have shown that the practice of women avoiding pregnancy to preserve their health and independence is hardly new. Bray argues that, in imperial times, some women avoided intercourse with their husbands or used abortifacients to put off pregnancy as long as possible because giving birth could mean a loss of autonomy and a break with their natal family. Scholars in sociology, history, and anthropology have built on and pushed back against these claims. According to anthropologist Arthur Wolf and historian Theo Engelen, "The received view of Chinese fertility is that most couples made no effort to control their fertility because they wanted as many sons as possible." Demographers James Z. Lee, Wang Feng, and Li Bozhong have argued that unlike the West, China did not experience a Malthusian population crisis, nor did it struggle to undergo a modern demographic transition, in part because abortion had been widely practiced for centuries. Matthew Sommer rebuts this claim, arguing instead that traditional abortifacients were unreliable, dangerous, expensive, and difficult to use. Therefore, they were neither mechanisms for female empowerment nor tools of routine family planning. Sommer further contends that

help a woman arbitrarily terminate a pregnancy, medicines for inducing menses could be purchased from private sellers and apothecaries.[27]

Scholars of medicine note that emmenagogues bring on (delayed) menstruation regardless of whether a woman is pregnant. Abortifacients destroy the fertilized ovum and/or cause the uterine lining in which the embryo is implanted to be expelled. In the early stages of pregnancy, embryos and fertilized ova simply look like menstrual blood.[28] Therefore, there has always been a fine line between emmenagogues and abortifacients. Records show that, at various points in history, women in Europe, the Americas, Africa, and Asia all experimented with these techniques, but the degree to which abortifacients and emmenagogues were viewed as unique technologies differed across cultural contexts.[29] In China and parts of the West, marketers specifically advertised abortifacients as emmenagogues or "patent medicines" to make them more palatable to the public.[30]

Yet, the blurry distinction between emmenagogues and abortifacients was no secret. In 1938, the Shanghai newspaper *Huamei wanbao chenkan* (Chinese-American Evening News Morning Edition) published a political cartoon titled "Treating Life as Trifling Matter" (*ba xingming dang zuo erxi*) decrying the use of abortifacients. In the cartoon, a man explains

abortifacients were an emergency response either to a medical crisis, such as a pregnancy that was dangerous to a woman's health, or to a social crisis, like an extramarital affair that resulted in pregnancy. Furth, *A Flourishing Yin*, 76; Bray, *Technology and Gender*, 325; Arthur P. Wolf and Theo Engelen, "Fertility and Fertility Control in Pre-Revolutionary China," *Journal of Interdisciplinary History* 38, no. 3 (2008): 103; James Z. Lee and Wang Feng, *One Quarter of Humanity: Malthusian Mythology and Chinese Realities, 1700–2000* (Cambridge, MA: Harvard University Press, 1999), 7–8; Matthew H. Sommer, "Abortion in Late Imperial China: Routine Birth Control or Crisis Intervention?" *Late Imperial China* 31, no. 2 (2010): 99.

[27] Li Bozhong, "Duotai, biyun, yu jueyu: Song Yuan Ming Qing shiqi Jiang-Zhe diqu de jieyu fangfa ji qi yunyong yu chuanbo" (Abortion, Contraception, and Sterilization: Fertility Control and Its Dissemination in Jiangsu and Zhejiang during the Song, Yuan, Ming, and Qing Dynasties), in *Hunyin jiating yu renkou xingwei* (Marriage, Family, and Population Behavior), eds. Li Zhongqing, Guo Songyi, and Ding Yizhuang (Beijing: Beijing daxue chubanshe, 2000), 172–196.

[28] Anne Hibner Koblitz, *Sex and Herbs and Birth Control* (Seattle: Kovalevskaia Fund, 2014), 11.

[29] Klausen, *Race, Maternity, and the Politics of Birth Control*, 14; Gigi Santow, "Emmenagogues and Abortifacients in the Twentieth Century: An Issue of Ambiguity," in *Regulating Menstruation: Beliefs, Practices, Interpretations*, ed. Etienne van de Walle (Chicago: University of Chicago Press, 2001), 78; Heidi Tinsman, *Partners in Conflict: The Politics of Gender, Sexuality, and Labor in the Chilean Agrarian Reform, 1950–1973* (Durham: Duke University Press, 2002), 58–59; Nancy Scheper-Hughes, *Death without Weeping: The Violence of Everyday Life in Brazil* (Berkeley: University of California Press, 1993), 333–335; Koblitz, *Sex and Herbs and Birth Control*, 21.

[30] Koblitz, *Sex and Herbs and Birth Control*, 43–44.

to a grieving woman: "Even if you are sick, do not take abortifacients! Now we need to perform a memorial service!" The man is referring to the death of a young woman, mentioned in an accompanying article, who consumed an abortifacient (*dataiyao*) to simultaneously treat her blood stasis and terminate an unwanted pregnancy.[31] The article contains religious undertones but does not explicitly mention the sanctity of fetal life in a Christian sense. Instead, the overarching message is that abortifacients and emmenagogues are dangerous.

The use of emmenagogues as abortifacients took on a new form in the globalizing and modernizing context of the Republican period, in which many areas of life, particularly medicine, became commercialized and commodified. Much as science came to be seen as a panacea for China's problems as a nation, health products became the cure for individual ailments, so that the individual body could be strengthened along with the nation as a whole. Newspapers began advertising commodities to be bought as part of a modern health regimen, products that denoted a modern, consumerist lifestyle.[32] Convenience was part and parcel of the commodification of health, and customers increasingly demanded affordable drugs that could be purchased easily without having to consult a potentially costly medical practitioner.[33]

Relatedly, so-called wonder drugs and health-boosting cure-alls (*buyao*), which have a long history in China, gained new authority in the era of mass media and commercialization. As Eugenia Lean has argued, in the early 1900s, doctors, pharmacy houses, and apothecaries advertised wonder drugs or elixirs claiming to cure a wide range of health problems – from loss of energy and nocturnal emissions to opium addiction and even death.[34] The language of Western biomedical science and flashy advertisements lent an air of legitimacy and expertise to druggists' and drug companies' claims. However, Western medicine was also viewed as lacking the personal engagement between doctor and patient that is common with traditional practitioners. The fact that Western medicine depicted health and illness in terms of dissected organs within a physical body, rather than as an immaterial system of interacting meridians, further contributed to this sense of medical alienation.[35] To overcome this stigma, advertisements utilized the holistic language associated with TCM – a vocabulary more familiar to consumers than the

[31] "Fu dataiyao hou" (After Consuming an Abortifacient), *Huamei wanbao chenkan* (Chinese-American Evening News Morning Edition), May 21, 1938, n.p.
[32] Eugenia Lean, "The Modern Elixir: Medicine as a Consumer Item in the Early Twentieth-Century Chinese Press," *UCLA History Journal* 15 (1995): 66–67.
[33] Baum, "Health by the Bottle," 80. [34] Lean, "The Modern Elixir," 69.
[35] Ibid., 71.

alienating and impersonal language of Western medicine – to sell their products.[36]

If one opens a Chinese women's magazine or newspaper from the 1920s or 1930s, the likelihood of encountering advertisements for various products marketed as emmenagogues is particularly high (although these advertisements can be found in the late Qing period as well). The notion of emmenagogue pills that ensured menstrual harmony merged nicely with the idea of cost-effective, premade tablets as cures for everything – including unwanted pregnancy. More specifically, these advertisements couched the utility of *tiaojingyao* and *tongjingyao* in terms of TCM – they enabled menstrual regularity or harmony, which fit within and appealed to a particular conceptualization of menstruation as signifying wellness. While framed in terms of *qi* and bodily balance, the drugs themselves were premade, packaged, and marketed in a highly impersonal way.[37]

Advertisements conveyed to varying degrees the link between regular menstruation, health, and pregnancy: While some used more veiled language about promoting menstrual regularity, others explicitly claimed to prevent or terminate pregnancy. Examining advertisements for *tiaojingyao* and *tongjingyao* from the 1920s and 1930s provides concrete examples of these different advertising techniques. Take, for example, a 1931 edition of the magazine *Funü shijie* (Women's World), which advertised a product called *Yue yue hong*. The product name might refer to the flower China Rose (which can be used to regulate menses), or *Yue yue hong* can be translated as "monthly red," a possible euphemism for menstruation. The fine print of the advertisement reads:

> Women's medicine = fixing menstrual blockages and improving blood circulation
>
> This is an extremely effective formula for improving blood circulation. The Western name of this medicine is "emmenagogue pills" and it is suitable for women's systems.
>
> It melts easily in the body, so the treatment is very safe and fast.
>
> Effectiveness: Good for treating women with blood deficiency in blocked or astringent meridians, blood stasis, post-partum discharge, or other unclear symptoms.

The advertisement was published by Wuzhou Pharmacy Publishing, the head office of which was located in Shanghai with branches in various provinces and port cities. The pills sold for 1 *yuan* per bottle, or a dozen

[36] Sherman Cochran, "Marketing Medicine and Advertising Dreams in China, 1900–1950," in *Becoming Chinese: Passages to Modernity and Beyond*, ed. Wen-hsin Yeh (Berkeley: University of California Press, 2000), 67.

[37] Lean, "The Modern Elixir," 78.

bottles for 10 *yuan*.[38] By invoking the term "emmenagogue" in English (prominently written in all capital letters), the company wanted to appear foreign and cutting-edge. Yet, the text merged the notions of "improved circulation" and "blood stasis" in TCM with the Western medical concept of "amenorrhea." In keeping with the language of modern advertising, the product is framed as effective, fast, and safe – features critical to the modern female consumer. The strategic marrying of the familiar language of TCM with Western product design and visual motifs was not unique to birth control advertisements but could be found in advertisements for all sorts of patented medicine (marketed as "new medicines" or *xinyao*) during the Republican period.[39]

Advertisements for *Yue yue hong*, like an increasing number of advertisements in early twentieth-century China, took young women, rather than male heads of households, as their target consumers.[40] Perhaps this was a tacit acknowledgment that mobilizing female consumers was a necessary condition for capitalist profit. The *Yue yue hong* advertisement even defined "women's medicine" to educate potential consumers about which products they should desire and the ways in which consumption is central to modern subjectivity. The sketch of a woman on the bottle (Figure 2.1) was also part of attempts to project modernity; adding visual representations of products and silhouettes of beautiful women to advertisements was a popular marketing strategy that emerged in the 1910s and remained popular through the 1930s.[41] In this context, women and their bodies became overtly central to consumerist modernity.

As for emmenagogues and contraceptives, other advertisers were more explicit about the fact that the products they were selling were intended to prevent pregnancy, rather than only emphasizing the medicines' therapeutic functions. An advertisement for a drug called "Speton: Ideales Anticoncipiens," featured in a 1931 edition of the magazine *Funü shijie* (Women's World), sought to market fertility regulation to the mobile, assertive, and busy modern woman (Figure 2.2). The advertisement prominently displayed the product's Latin name, which literally translates as "Ideal Anti-Pregnant." This was meant to denote foreign status and reliability, as well as the allure of Western medicine. The advertisement also featured the image of the bird wrapped in rope – an ensnared version of a stork, known for delivering newborn babies. As in certain parts of the West, storks appear in some Chinese stories about fertility, so

[38] "Yue yue hong," *Funü shijie* (Women's World) 17, no. 7 (1931): n.p.
[39] Cochran, "Marketing Medicine," 64. [40] Lean, "The Modern Elixir," 80.
[41] Cochran, "Marketing Medicine," 74.

Figure 2.1 Advertisement for *"Yue yue hong"* emmenagogues, 1931.
Source: "Yue yue hong," *Funü shijie* (Women's World) 17, no. 7 (1931): n.p.

the imagery would have been meaningful to both Chinese and foreign consumers. The advertisement reads:

> Preeminent birth control medicine
> Absolutely no oil; common, pure, and effective
> For leucorrhea (vaginal discharge) and neighboring tissues
> Inflammation, corrosion, and other illnesses in the body cavities
> Disinfectant is effective like something miraculous
> Various pharmacies sell it.

According to the advertisement, the drug was produced by a foreign-owned company, manufactured at the Taylor Chemical Factory, and sold exclusively in China by the manager's office in Shanghai. While "Speton" was first and foremost a birth control medicine, like many other miracle drugs or "new medicines" of the time, it served a number of other functions. Not only could it supposedly prevent conception

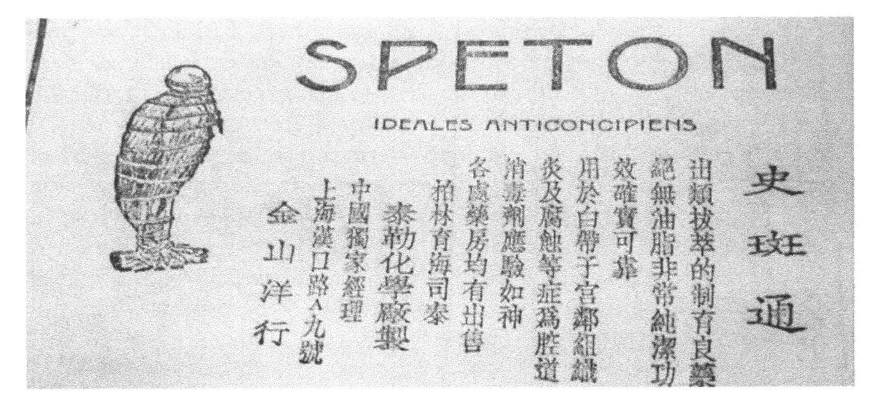

Figure 2.2 Advertisement for "Speton" contraceptives, 1931.
Source: Funü shijie (Women's World) 17, no. 7 (1931): n.p.

without the use of oil (which many vaginal inserts used to trap sperm during intercourse), it also cured several vaginal and abdominal illnesses and even boasted "miraculous" disinfectant properties.[42]

Other related products, which have received greater scholarly attention, were "Birth Control Friend" (*Zhiyu liangyou*) and "Lady's Friend" (*Ta de you*). Michelle King dates advertisements for Birth Control Friend to less than a year after Margaret Sanger's first visit to China in 1922, and one advertisement for Birth Control Friend even claimed local demands for birth control in the aftermath of Sanger's visit created the impetus to produce these types of products. Birth Control Friend was purported to be able to prevent pregnancy, alleviate feminine discharge problems, and even prevent men from contracting venereal disease.[43] While this product was advertised as being "for external use only," King posits that it was almost certainly a vaginal suppository because of its claims to prevent transmission of venereal disease, a topic that is rarely mentioned in advertisements for products labeled as either emmenagogues or contraceptives. In this gendered scenario, the woman was presumed to have a venereal disease that her relatively pure male lover was afraid of contracting – a motif present in many writings on sexually transmitted diseases from the Republican period to the present. This suggests that not only were the target customers for Birth Control Friend middle-class men, rather than so-called modern women, but that advertisers also appropriated women's bodies to assuage male concerns about unrestrained

[42] "Speton," advertisement, *Funü shijie* (Women's World) 17, no. 7 (1931): n.p.
[43] King, "Margaret Sanger in Translation," 73–74.

female sexual desire. According to King and others, Chinese men preferred vaginal suppositories over other contraceptives because they were easy to use and did not diminish the male sexual experience, a trend the advertisers of Birth Control Friend undoubtedly recognized.[44]

Advertisements for Lady's Friend were similar to those for Birth Control Friend in many ways. However, the former highlighted the drug's contraceptive properties by featuring the Chinese word *jieyu* in large, prominent letters on the left side of the advertisement. Like Birth Control Friend, the use of the word "friend" in the name evokes a kind of modern intimacy and trust between the user and the product. The full advertisement reads:

> "Lady's Friend" topical pills are the most effective medicine for contraception.
>
> It is generally recognized that this medicine is used by women with frail bodies and blood deficiency who are not suited for childbearing and are familiar with modern living and economic circumstances.
>
> (Introduced by a world-famous Western doctor).
>
> Tested by the Central Health Laboratory and proven non-toxic.
>
> Each box is one *yuan* two *jiao* and comes with Chinese-language instructions available on request by letter.[45]

As with the other products, this one was sold by a company headquartered in Shanghai and was retailed at all major pharmacies. While the focus was on the drug's ability to prevent pregnancy, the language suggests that the target consumers were women who should not conceive for health reasons, rather than women who solely wanted to have sex for pleasure. The reference to modern living and economic circumstances alludes to the fact that raising children was costly and time consuming, factors modern consumers and independent women took into consideration.

Yet, Lady's Friend still sought to position itself as a product for women with some means and an eye to Western-influenced consumer culture. The claim linking Lady's Friend to a world-famous Western doctor, for example, lent an air of worldliness and legitimacy to the product. Furthermore, the fact that the product did not come with Chinese-language instructions was likely an attempt to feign foreign origins or to target foreign and bilingual consumers. At its price point of 1.2 *renminbi* per dozen, Lady's Friend would also have been more costly than

[44] King, "Margaret Sanger in Translation," 74.

[45] "Ta de you" (Lady's Friend), *Funü shijie* (Women's World) 19, no. 11 (1931): n.p.; Other advertisements for Lady's Friend can be found in the magazines *Funü zazhi* (Ladies' Journal) 1, no. 2 (1931): 14 and *Nü qingnian* (Young Women) 17, no. 1 (1931): 136.

comparable domestically produced old-style products like *qipao yaofen*, an inexpensive foaming spermicide popular among the urban poor.[46] Despite efforts to appeal to the allure of Western medicine, though, one article in the Shanghai newspaper *Shenbao* proclaimed that contraception like Lady's Friend would save the nation and allow China to be reborn as a nation free from foreign subjugation.[47] Such a claim reveals the simultaneous appeal of foreign medicines and the distrust of their imperialist origins.

Advertisements for products like Birth Control Friend and Lady's Friend were not limited to Shanghai. For example, throughout the 1930s and 1940s, the periodical *Xin Tianjin Huabao* (New Tianjin Pictorial) continually featured advertisements for *Tingyundan* (literally, stop pregnancy pill). At the cost of 5 *yuan* for a two-year supply, this medicine was marketed as a simple way to protect women from dangerous pregnancies that, if not prevented, might need to be aborted. Advertisements for *Tingyundan* could be found alongside those for venereal disease clinics, *tongjingyao*, and medicine that treats gonorrhea. According to the advertisements, *Tingyundan* could be purchased at pharmacies in both Tianjin's Japanese and French settlements.[48]

Not all emmenagogues were mass manufactured and as prominently advertised as those just mentioned; some were clandestinely made and sold by local druggists, peddlers, and even midwives.[49] In a case from Beijing in 1932, the police looked into a series of crimes – bribery, heroin trafficking, and the outbreak of a fight over the price of a rickshaw ride. This led the police to discover that a man named Hu Shoushan was manufacturing emmenagogues (*tongjingdan*). The police report alleged that "[a] very large the number of people were purchasing this medicine for use as an abortifacient" while claiming to not know the true effect of the drug. As a result, Hu was charged with disseminating illegal medicines.[50] In another case from Beijing, a young woman surnamed Jian, who was four months pregnant, sought an abortion. Fearing that her father and brother would find out about the pregnancy and her sexual relationship, Jian allegedly purchased an abortifacient (*dataiyao*) at a

[46] Typically, domestically produced products of this sort (or at least products openly advertising their domestic origins) sold for approximately 1 *renminbi* per dozen, slightly less than the Western-style equivalent; Shanghai jieyu yanjiushe (Shanghai Birth Control Research Society), *Shanghai yishi zhoukan* (Shanghai Medical Weekly) 6, no. 41 (1940): n.p.

[47] Long Sao, "Dushi de feng" (The Urban Scene), *Shenbao*, May 15, 1933.

[48] "Tingyundan," *Xin Tianjin Huabao* (New Tianjin Pictorial) 3 (1940): n.p.; "Tingyundan," *Xin Tianjin Huabao* (New Tianjin Pictorial) 5, no. 10 (1940): n.p.

[49] Zi Nan, "Guafu duotai" (Widow Abortion), *Shenbao*, March 10, 1935.

[50] Beijing Municipal Archive (BMA), J181–020-09957.

local drug store owned by a woman surnamed Yang. Suspicious investigators soon uncovered a stash of illegal abortifacients in the shop, and Yang was charged with selling illicit drugs.[51] As these and many other cases illustrate, emmenagogues and abortifacients were not difficult to purchase in China's major cities.

Western drugs with abortifacient properties were also available for purchase in urban China. In some instances, these medicines were marketed explicitly in terms of biomedical family planning, whereas in other cases they were sold to treat other illnesses and misused to induce abortion. Carbizone (*jiabuxi*) tablets, a type of American birth control pill introduced to China by Margaret Sanger, were available for purchase in Shanghai as early as March 1923.[52] Similarly, the Shanghai Bai'er Pharmaceutical Company – a subsidiary of the German multinational pharmaceutical company, Bayer – published a booklet in 1938 advertising a variety of products including Rivanol, a potent abortifacient used in China from the Republican era to the present in second-trimester and late-term abortions.[53]

Quinine (a medicine used to treat malaria) could also be purchased in pharmacies in large cities and could induce abortion. Cinchona, the active ingredient in quinine, was mainly imported from the Dutch East Indies, but to meet the overwhelming domestic demand for this malaria medicine, in the 1930s farms in Yunnan began experimenting with cinchona cultivation.[54] In fact, quinine was even endorsed in Republican and Mao-era sex guides and appears in a wide range of abortion cases from the Republican period through the Mao era.[55] Take for example the 1947 case of a young couple living on Nanjing Road in Shanghai. The husband was an employee of the China National Goods Corporation, where he earned a humble salary. In the seven years

[51] BMA, J181–019-56986.

[52] Yu, "The Birth Control Movement in Republican Cities," 277.

[53] Shanghai bai'er yaopin wuxian gongsi (Shanghai Bayer Pharmaceutical Company, Ltd.), "Bai'er yiliao xinbao" (Bayer Medical News), 12, no. 2 (1938): n.p.; K. H. Tien, "Intraamniotic injection of ethacridine for second-trimester induction of labor," *Obstetrics and Gynecology* 61, no. 6 (1983): 733–736.

[54] Chinese cinchona cultivation escalated during the Second Sino-Japanese War in an effort to achieve independence from global cinchona networks; Yubin Shen, "Cultivating China's Cinchona: The Local Developmental State, Global Botanic Networks and Cinchona Cultivation in Yunnan, 1930s–1940s," *Social History of Medicine* (2019): 5–6.

[55] "Zui xin biyunfa," 1; Jane Achan et al. "Quinine, an Old Anti-Malarial Drug in a Modern World: Role in the Treatment of Malaria," *Malaria Journal* 10, no. 144 (2011): 1–12; SJTUA, Z1–9-727; Tianjin Municipal Archive (TMA), X0191-C-000058.

the couple had been married, the 22-year-old wife had given birth to five children, of which three had survived. When the young woman became pregnant again, she feared that the family could not afford to take care of another child. First, she tried consuming some type of acid to abort the fetus, but it simply made her throw up. She knew that quinine was used to treat specific illnesses but that it could trigger a miscarriage when taken in large quantities. For this reason, she overdosed on it. The toxicity of the medicine caused her uterus to contract and release the fetus, but she bled continuously until her face turned blue and her heart gave out.[56] Other cases suggest that this was a fairly common last resort for poor women without access to other types of contraceptives or abortifacients.[57]

Some women even formulated emmenagogues and abortifacients from scratch at home. In one case from Beijing in 1945, a 36-year-old unemployed married woman named Jiang Liu was having an affair with a 20-year-old unemployed man named Zhou Shulin, who lived in a nearby alleyway (*hutong*). Eventually, Jiang's abdomen became swollen and hard, and soon after, became soft. Jiang was charged with colluding with Zhou to abort the pregnancy and cover up evidence of the affair. The method of abortion used was a concoction made from black soybeans taken orally.[58] Jiang was sentenced to seven months in prison for committing adultery and having an abortion, while Zhou was fined and sentenced to four months in jail for committing adultery and harming Jiang.[59]

Other women utilized a variety of abortion techniques associated with traditional medicine. These included consuming herb mixtures orally in tea or inserting a blend of toxic insects, as well "ox knee" (*tu niuxi*), musk, and monkshod root, into the cervix.[60] References to these types of abortion appear in a wide variety of sources from the imperial period through the present. In fact, Matthew Sommer uses court records and works of fiction to chronicle the use of these methods since the late Qing

56 "Xinshui jieji de bei'ai, xian er'nu duo datai jian fudan, chi kuining wan buxing zhongdu si" (Sorrow of the Working Class, Feared Having Too Many Children So Had an Abortion to Reduce the Burden, Consumed Quinine and Died of Poisoning), *Daminbao*, December 17, 1947.

57 Qingdao Municipal Archive (QMA), D00429200079.

58 As mentioned in Chapter 5, a sent-down youth claims that a similar concoction can prevent pregnancy, perhaps alluding to the fuzzy distinction between preventing a pregnancy and aborting it in its early stages.

59 BMA, J191-002-09401.

60 Matthew Sommer, "Abortion in Late Imperial China: Routine Birth Control or Crisis Intervention?" *Late Imperial China* 31, no. 2 (2010): 100.

dynasty. The type of herbs used, however, differed by region according to local flora and medicinal practices. The insertion of ox knee root into the cervix was a common abortive technique used by native healers in Shanghai and southern China during the Republican period.[61] In one case from 1940, Zhou, a 25-year-old married woman working as a live-in maid in Shanghai, became pregnant. Fearing she would lose her job due to the pregnancy, she paid a traditional Chinese healer, Yao, and his wife to perform an abortion on her. Yao inserted a "daikon-shaped item" (*luobo zhuang de dongxi*) into Zhou's cervix, which induced abortion. Unfortunately, Zhou could not stop bleeding and after she died in the hospital, Yao was sentenced to three and a half years in jail and a fine of 300 *yuan*.[62] In another case from Shanghai, a 33-year-old woman named Gui Xu who was several months pregnant sought out an elderly local healer to help her undergo an abortion. The healer inserted herbs roots into Gui's uterus. After successfully aborting the pregnancy, Gui threw the body of the male fetus into the toilet. Her crime was only discovered when Gui admitted herself to a hospital because she was suffering from poisoning (from the herbs). In Gui's case, she survived the abortion and the aftereffects.[63] Many women who used such herbal methods consequently suffered from sterility, as depicted in the novel *The Obsessed*, by Liu Heng, which director Zhang Yimou later adapted into the film, *Ju Dou*. Herbal abortifacients were definitely one of the most common forms of fertility control that entered the historical record, and in later chapters we will see that similar methods were practiced in various parts of China in the Mao era and beyond.

Acupuncture was another method used to induce abortion, but it was more common in northern China, where acupuncture was popular.[64] Traditional healers inserted one or more needles just under 3 inches long through the abdominal wall to stimulate uterine contractions and premature delivery.[65] Like many other abortion techniques from this period, needling (*dazhen* or *zhazhen duotai*) did not always successfully induce abortion, and at times it could be dangerous or even fatal. In one case from 1921, a young woman paid 5 silver dollars (*wu kuai da yang*) to the middle-aged owner of a local shop for abortion through needling. When the pregnancy failed to terminate, the young woman consumed an abortifacient. The case sparked public criticism of back-alley abortion clinics,

[61] Ma, "Gender, Law, and Society," 33.
[62] SMA, Q180-2-4464; Ma, "Gender, Law, and Society," 179.
[63] SMA, Q180-2-2460. [64] Ma, "Gender, Law, and Society," 31.
[65] Susan M. Rigdon, "Abortion Law and Practice in China: An Overview with Comparisons to the United States," *Social Science Medicine* 42, no. 4 (1996): 548.

where healers preyed on the poor and ignorant.[66] A British medical missionary living in Beijing and working at Peking Union Medical College in 1928 observed cases of needling with even more catastrophic consequences. In two cases, the needle broke off or got lost in the abdomen and had to be removed surgically. In a third case, a 43-year-old woman, who had become pregnant through adultery and wanted to hide the evidence from her husband, attempted abortion through needling. After being needled four times, the fetus emerged, but the woman died of abdominal inflammation (peritonitis).[67] Like other abortion methods, abortion through needling was extremely risky.

In addition to medicinal abortions and those performed through massage or needling, surgical abortions were also somewhat common in urban China and they often took place in privately run health clinics or in STD clinics that offered abortions on the side.[68] A number of foreign and Chinese-run public hospitals and clinics simply refused to treat women seeking abortions or treatment for postabortion health problems (excessive bleeding, infection, etc.) because the hospital did not want to be associated with illegal abortions.[69] In some cases, Western philanthropic hospitals in Shanghai even reported abortion seekers to the local police and helped with community surveillance.[70] Given these realities, women who could afford more expensive treatment in Shanghai (and to a lesser degree in other cities) sought out private clinics, staffed by both foreign and Chinese practitioners of Western medicine. In these types of establishments, services were many times more expensive than self-administering abortifacients or seeing a native healer, but the chances of getting caught were also much lower and the facilities more sanitary.[71]

In fact, some of the same doctors who held legitimate positions at hospitals or health clinics secretly performed abortions on the side to make extra money, not least because a single abortion could cost several hundred *yuan* at a Western-style clinic.[72] One court case, for example, alleged that the director of Panlin Hospital in Shanghai, Pan Jiahe, earned an additional 1,000 to 2,000 thousand *yuan* per month performing clandestine abortions. He was accused of throwing the fetuses into a

[66] "Zhazhen datai ye suan yingye me, kongpa jingting bu hui pizhun" (Does Abortion Through Needling Count as a Business? The Police Cannot Approve It), *Xin shehui bao* 4 (1921): n.p.

[67] Sommer, "Abortion in Late Imperial China," 140–141.

[68] "Sheyan: duotai yu jieyu" (Community Statement: Abortion and Birth Control), *Xinghua* 27, no. 31 (1930): 1; "Xingbingyuan mimi weiren duotai" (STD Hospital Secretly Performs Abortions), *Shenbao*, August 10, 1930.

[69] Ma, "Gender, Law, and Society," 174. [70] Ibid., 157. [71] Ibid., 160.

[72] SMA, Q186-2-21165; "Xingbingyuan mimi weiren duotai" (STD Hospital Secretly Performs Abortions), *Shenbao*, August 10, 1930.

nearby river at night or cremating and burying the remains, evidence that was used to convict Pan.[73] Similarly, in a case from 1931, the director of Huifen Medical Clinic, a health clinic located in one of Beijing's *hutongs*, was charged with regularly performing illegal surgical abortions. Police investigators found that the director, Wang Guoqing, was not only selling heroin but also burying fetuses in a small grave at the base of the western wall of his courtyard. Wang was a 30-year-old pharmacist from Wuqiang county in Hebei province with a wife and three children. According to Wang, the abortions he was charged with performing were done to save the lives of pregnant women who were sick and experiencing difficult pregnancies. Wang maintained that he did not perform abortions for healthy women but that occasionally women who had undergone an abortion (elsewhere) brought the corpses to him to be buried nearby. The police uncovered the remains of several babies, as well as heroin, and Wang was convicted on both accounts.[74] Had the case been brought to trial after 1935 when therapeutic abortion was legalized, Wang may have been able to evade punishment if he could convincingly argue that the pregnancies were life threatening.

As these cases illustrate, numerous methods for inducing abortion were available to urban women, though they all involved some degree of risk. Some women ingested *tiaojingyao* or *tongjingyao*, which could regularize menstruation and abort unwanted pregnancies but could also prove dangerous. Other women, often in dire circumstances brought on by poverty or patriarchal social norms, resorted to medicinal or surgical abortions. For its part, the public press oscillated between demonizing these women and painting them as the hapless victims of avarice and oppressive Confucian values.

The Trouble with Rubbers

It is worth noting that despite the ubiquity of abortion and abortifacients, contraceptives like condoms still had a limited presence in Chinese cities. Reports from pharmacy raids, like those mentioned earlier, and other records also reveal that throughout the Republican period, imported condoms (*baoxiantao* or *guitoutao*) were sold in drugstores. To prevent the transmission of syphilis, condoms were distributed at hospital-sponsored birth control clinics in major urban centers, particularly in port cities with their thriving prostitution industries.[75] Sexual hygiene

[73] SMA, Q186-2-21165. [74] BMA, J181-031-03649.
[75] Xu Wancheng, *Zuixin shiyan nannü biyunfa* (The Newest Experimental Birth Control Methods for Men and Women) (Shanghai: Guoguang shudian, 1941), n.p.; "Gulou

guides and news articles explaining how to procure and use products like the "French Letter" condom (*ruyidai*) were also common in urban areas.[76] But, perhaps because of the association of condoms with prostitution and infidelity, condoms were never very popular. Historian Yuehtsen Juliette Chung observes that although foreign-funded condoms were available at Peking Union Medical College in the 1920s, "the idea of using condoms did not seep into Chinese men's mentality."[77] Indeed, men's dislike of condoms globally, as well as in China, was and remains one of the key reasons for the gendered bias of much of the literature on contraception. When asked why they did not use condoms, many men cited the fact that they diminish the male sexual experience.[78]

The limited popularity of condoms can be attributed in part to certain assumptions about medicine and the body. As discussed earlier, in TCM, the balance of *yin* and *yang* governs bodily health. Daoist teachings argued that men needed a certain amount of female *yin* to balance out their abundant *yang*. Excessive sex could drain a man of his *yang*, but an appropriate amount of sex would benefit him by replenishing his *yin*. A man could receive *yin* from female orgasms, but he himself should try to limit emission of his seminal essence (*jing*) so as to avoid depleting his finite *qi* and causing illness.[79] Hence, the practice of "cultivating life" (*yangsheng*) – preserving *jing* through proper sleep, diet, temperature regulation, and even engaging in intercourse without releasing semen – arose.[80] Following this logic, using condoms would enable a man to have more intercourse, thus depleting his *jing* while not allowing him to gain any of the complementary advantages of women's *yin*. Writing in 1941, sexologist Yao Lingxi raised this concern with respect to condom use.[81]

yiyuan zhishi jieyu: yi you sanshi ren" (Gulou Hospital Provides Birth Control Instruction: Already Served 30 Patients)," *Guangxi yikan* (Guangxi Medical Journal) 12, no. 2 (1935): 10–11.

[76] Xu, Zuixin, n.p.; Hui Mingzeng, "Cong Luo Guifang de duotai shuoqi" (Talking about Luo Guifang's abortion), *Wufeng banyue qikan* (Dance Bimonthly Periodical) 2, no. 3 (1938): 15; Xue Deyu, *Chan'er tiaojie zhi lilun yu shiji* (The Theory and Practice of Birth Control) (Shanghai: Shanghai xinya shudian, 1933), 37.

[77] Yuehtsen Juliette Chung, *Struggle for National Survival: Chinese Eugenics in a Transnational Context, 1896–1945* (New York: Routledge, 2002), 119.

[78] Yu, "The Birth Control Movement in Republican Cities," 347.

[79] Hugh Shapiro, "The Puzzle of Spermatorrhea in Republican China," *Positions* 6 (1998): 553–554; Everett Yuehong Zhang argues that *jing* was originally translated as seminal essence because it signified more than just semen. Since the Republican period, however, the term has become synonymous with semen; Everett Yuehong Zhang, *The Impotence Epidemic: Men's Medicine and Sexual Desire in Contemporary China* (Durham: Duke University Press, 2015), 137–138.

[80] Zhang, *The Impotence Epidemic*, 149.

[81] Yao Lingxi, *Si wu xie xiao ji* (A Short Record of Thoughts Without Depravity) (Tianjin: Tianjin shuju, 1941), 34.

Condoms were also associated with other health risks for men. When Margaret Sanger visited China in 1922, she argued that frequent use of the withdrawal method or condoms could cause men to suffer from nervous disorders (*shenjing shuairuo de bing*).[82] For this reason, she encouraged female contraception instead.[83] Similarly, in 1946, one vocal female advocate of birth control, Zhen Ni, published an article in *Xin funü yuekan* (New Women's Monthly) warning that using a condom too often can lead to neurasthenic disorders among men, an argument that draws on the language of Western biomedicine and speaks to the ubiquity of misinformation masquerading as scientific advice.[84] Taken together, concerns about the negative side effects of using condoms may have served to deter potential customers. This may also account for advertisements promoting condoms as a tool for male sexual enhancement, a marketing ploy meant to circumvent the issue of condoms' perceived health risks.[85]

Condoms rarely appear in legal records because they were not explicitly banned. When they are mentioned in the archive, it is often not in connection with birth control. Instead, condoms were often used to transport illegal drugs. In 1932, for example, a husband and wife in Shanghai were charged with illegally transporting more than ninety condoms full of morphine as part of a large-scale crime syndicate.[86] Similarly, in 1948, the Tianjin Municipal Bureau of Health investigated a case in which a woman was caught trafficking morphine and opium in rubber condoms.[87] This suggests that, at the very least, people were aware of the existence of condoms but were not necessarily using them as prophylactics.

Perhaps yet another reason why condoms were not a popular form of contraception was their high failure rate and the fact that they were not very comfortable. Despite advertisements with slogans like "Flexible and Comfortable, Won't Break Easily" (*Rouren shuchang buyi pohuai*) and

[82] Hugh Shapiro investigates at length the historical reconceptualization of *yijing* (spermatorrhea) as the disease of neurasthenia (debilitated nerves) in Hugh Shapiro, "The Puzzle of Spermatorrhea in Republican China," *Positions* 6 (1998): 554–554. Sexual hygiene literature from the 1950s also claimed that excessive masturbation among boys and men could cause neurasthenia and even infertility; Evans, *Women and Sexuality*, 71–72.

[83] Michelle T. King, "Margaret Sanger in Translation: Gender, Class, and Birth Control in 1920s China," *Journal of Women's History* 29, no. 3 (2017): 61–83.

[84] Zhen Ni, "Duotai he biyun" (Abortion and Birth Control), Xin funü yuekan (New Women's Monthly) 4 (1946): 20–21.

[85] Hershatter, *Dangerous Pleasures*, 462.

[86] "Yibing yanzao jiekai mimi: huanbei nanlu pohuo mafei jiguan (Secret Revealed: South Huangbei Road Morphine Stratagem Uncovered), *Shenbao* 6, no. 25052 (1947): n.p.

[87] TMA, J0116–1-000707-107; TMA, J0116–1-000707-108.

"Soft Texture and Durability" (*Zhidi meiruan jingjiu naiyong*), according to a 1942 clinical study at Shanghai Women's and Children's hospital, condoms had a failure rate of 42.8 percent.[88] Before the 1850s, most condoms in the United States and Britain were made from intestines. Rubber condoms were first developed in the nineteenth century when Charles Goodyear invented vulcanized rubber. By the 1920s, latex condoms, which were more pliable, less combustible, and better suited for mass production on the assembly line, had begun replacing rubber condoms in the West.[89] In China, however, rigid rubber condoms remained standard until the 1960s, and their limited elasticity made them uncomfortable to use. They also came in restricted sizes and could break easily. Fish-skin condoms, said to be more comfortable, could sometimes be procured, but these were even more difficult to obtain.[90] For these reasons, condoms seem to have been a less used contraceptive option in the Republican period despite their popularity elsewhere.

During the late Republican period, access to condoms grew in some places and became more restricted in others. In the wake of the Anti-Japanese War, American army surplus goods, including large quantities of condoms, became available for purchase in street markets and pharmacies in Shanghai and other major cities.[91] In fact, American condoms – said to look like "milk grapes" (*niunai putao*) – were so prevalent, people used them to make balloons bearing slogans like "Long Live the Republic of China" (*zhonghua minguo wan sui*).[92] Seeking to corner the condom market, one woman allegedly purchased 960 boxes of condoms (three condoms per box) from the army surplus store to resell.[93]

In theory, condoms were also plentiful in Japanese-occupied Manchuria. During the war, the Japanese army distributed millions of "Attack No. 1"-brand condoms, which soldiers were required to use

88 Yu "The Birth Control Movement in Republican Cities," 258, 288.

89 Tone, "Making Room for Rubbers," 70–71; Ross McKibbin, *Classes and Cultures: England, 1918–1950* (Oxford: Oxford University Press, 1998), 305.

90 Yu, "Minguo shiqi," 205

91 Jiu Jiu, "Ruyidai junshi shang de gongxian" (The Military's Contribution of Condoms), *Yizhou jian* 13 (1946): 9.

92 Gong Mu, "Ruyidai bian yang paopao" (Condoms Become Foreign Balloons), *Guoji xinwen huabao* (International News Pictorial) 52 (1946): 11; Cheng Hu, "Jingju qudi shaonü kouchui ruyidai" (Authorities Prohibit Young Girls from Inflating Condoms," *Jipu* 36 (1946): n.p.

93 Ju You, "Wang Wenlan tunji ruyidai" (Wang Wenlan Hoards Condoms), *Yefeng* (Wild Wind) 2 (1946): n.p.

when having sex with "comfort women." [94] Likely in response to the soldiers' refusal to use condoms, Manchuria Medical University published guidelines for preventing the spread of venereal disease, encouraging readers to use condoms.[95] In reality, though, Chinese comfort women reported that condoms were scant at temporary comfort stations on the front line. Comfort women and local laborers, in fact, were tasked with washing and recycling used condoms.[96] Moreover, given the power dynamics and brutal circumstances underlying the comfort women system, male soldiers refused to use condoms and comfort women had no way to resist them.[97]

In regions of China where fighting was taking place between the Nationalists and the Communists, condom supplies were also very limited. According to one anecdote from the 1940s, a young man and woman, both of whom were serving in the People's Liberation Army, were given permission to get married. On their wedding night, their commanding officer gifted them some condoms that had been taken from the Nationalist army because the couple was not allowed to have children immediately. In less than a month the condoms were used up, but when the couple asked for more, they were told that condoms were in shorter supply than tanks.[98] Indeed, access to condoms varied greatly during the 1940s.

In addition to condoms, sexual hygiene guides during the Republican period also recommended the use of the withdrawal method, abstinence, and washing after sex to prevent conception. One guide advised that women wash out their vaginas to drown the sperm (*nichu jingfa*) "the way that prostitutes do."[99] Other recommended birth control strategies included inserting *foam powder*, a foaming spermicide applied to a sponge (later proven to be dangerous), cervical caps, and concoctions of cocoa butter and acetic acid, into the vagina prior to sex.[100] Gail

[94] The term "comfort women" was a euphemism for the system of institutionalized sexual slavery employed by the Japanese military during World War II. Allegedly intended to prevent the wanton raping of civilian women during war and occupation, the "comfort women" – women from across the Japanese empire who were forced into sexual slavery – were mobilized to satisfy the Japanese soldiers' sexual urges; Peipei Qiu, *Chinese Comfort Women: Testimonies from Imperial Japan's Sex Slaves* (Oxford: Oxford University Press, 2014), 12.

[95] "Hualiubing yufang xuzhi" (Notice on the Prevention of Venereal Disease), *Manzhou yike daxue* (Manchuria Medical University) (n.d.): n.p.

[96] Qiu, *Chinese Comfort Women*, 48. [97] Ibid., 105.

[98] Nanfang Wang, "1950 niandai zhongguo jietou lugu de biyun guanggao" (Explicit Contraceptive Advertisements on the Streets of China in the 1950s), *Sina* (blog), September 7, 2015, http://blog.sina.com.cn/s/blog_4ac5b19f0102vzxm.html?tj=2.

[99] Xu, *Zuixin shiyan nannü biyunfa*, n.p and Mao, "*Yiyao wenda*," 18.

[100] Xu, *Zuixin*, n.p and Connelly, *Fatal Misconception*, 101.

Hershatter even speculates that infertility caused by acute sexual transmitted diseases such as syphilis may have prevented higher rates of pregnancy among Republican-era prostitutes, an argument that could be applied to the population at large since venereal disease seems to have been widespread in major cities.[101]

In short, written records suggest that condoms were not a very popular form of birth control during the Republican period. Although it is impossible to venture a guess as to how frequently they were used since their sales were not uniformly monitored, it would seem that public perceptions about health worked against the popularization of condoms. Moreover, difficulties accessing condoms, which needed to be imported and were often costly, meant that they were not available to the majority of people.

Abortion in the Records

In contrast to condoms, because performing an abortion was illegal during the Republican period, most evidence of abortions comes from court records. Therefore, in theory, one could use those records to estimate the number of prosecuted abortions in certain Republican cities. Still, enforcement of the abortion law was both uneven and unsystematic, further complicating efforts to estimate contraception and abortion rates.[102] Abortion records in the archives of major Chinese cities make up only a fraction of the total crimes on record. Beginning in 1910, when the national criminal code was restructured, crimes such as abortion were re-categorized as police contraventions.[103] Therefore, as part of the expanding role of the police in urban governance, police were permitted to settle abortion cases outside of the standard legal process, a practice that remained more or less unchanged until 1949. As a result, crimes such as abortion were not reflected in local crime statistics, making it even more challenging to estimate to what extent abortion was practiced and policed.[104] In addition, criminal records – particularly in Shanghai – tended to highlight the offenses of lower-class women, who often first saw inexpensive native healers. If these abortions resulted in serious aftereffects, the abortion seekers would be forced to go to the hospital, where they might be turned in to the authorities.[105]

[101] Gail Hershatter, *Dangerous Pleasures: Prostitution and Modernity in Twentieth-Century Shanghai* (Berkeley: University of California Press, 1997), 175.
[102] Rigdon, "Abortion Law and Practice in China," 544.
[103] Michael H. K. Ng, *Legal Transplantation in Early Twentieth Century China: Practicing Law in Republican Beijing* (Abingdon, Oxon: Routledge, 2014), 95–96.
[104] Ma, "Gender, Law, and Society," 76–82. [105] Ibid., 176–177.

Women who underwent abortions in more hygienic settings with trained medical practitioners likely would have no need to visit the hospital and risk being caught. Based on this skewed evidence, the primary form of birth control in urban China seems to have been abortion via the consumption of *tiaojingyao*, or *tongjingyao*, application of herbal concoctions, or related methods. What were the most common rationales for undergoing abortion? Adultery (*tongjian*) and premarital sex as the impetus for consuming *tongjingyao* or inducing abortion is a recurring theme in Republican abortion records (and those from later periods). Although infidelity was eventually decriminalized for unmarried women and widows in the late Republican period, numerous records cite fear of evidence of an affair as the reason for a woman in an extramarital relationship seeking to prevent or terminate her pregnancy.[106] Cases of premarital sex resulting in abortion were also fairly frequent, as young women or their family members sought to cover up the shameful evidence of intercourse before marriage, an act that could make those young women unmarriageable.[107] In one case, two young women even traveled from their rural villages to Shanghai to undergo abortions after premarital sex.[108]

Quite a few abortion cases also involved widows who had intercourse after the deaths of their husbands.[109] Though no longer married, so to speak, the widows were expected to preserve their chastity out of loyalty to their husbands and husbands' families. Appearing unchaste not only was shameful but also made the widows ineligible to receive pensions from their deceased husbands' families, which could leave the widows penniless.[110] In other circumstances, the widow's lover – who was often already married – arranged for her to have an abortion without her permission, probably to protect himself from charges of adultery. This happened in the case of a 34-year-old Jiangbei widow, Shen Xu, whose married lover, Xiang Shijun, paid a Chinese medicine healer 30 *yuan* to insert herb roots into Shen's womb and induce abortion.[111] Many such

[106] SMA, Q180–2-15037; TMA, J0044–2-023274; TMA, J0043–2-010192; TMA, J0044–2-029693; BMA, J183–002-21722; Ma, "Gender, Law, and Society," 235.

[107] "Youjian weichengnian nüzi bufang fangmian tiqi gongsu" (Court Prosecution for Luring an Underaged Girl), *Shenbao* 15, no. 22335 (1935): n.p.; TMA, J0044–2-038811; SMA, Q180–2-2348.

[108] "Nongcun pochan shengzhong, lai Hu duotai rizhong" (Amid Rural Bankruptcy, Many Come to Shanghai for Abortion), *Shenbao*, September 25, 1936.

[109] SMA Q180–2-14737; Zi Nan, "Guafu duotai" (Widow Abortion), *Shenbao,* March 10, 1935.

[110] SMA, Q180–2-14737. [111] SMA, Q180–2-14379.

cases ended in death, legal penalties, or both.[112] Evidently, abortion seekers, such as those who had committed adultery, engaged in premarital sex, or violated their vows of chastity, often were left with few options aside from abortion if they did not want to face legal and social backlash.

While court records suggest that abortion in Republican cities transcended socioeconomic boundaries, I offer two brief observations with respect to the class and occupational dimensions of urban abortion. First, according to the records I viewed, the majority of abortion seekers caught by the police were factory workers, domestic servants, or other working-class individuals, who likely had little education.[113] This is not particularly surprising, given that in Republican cities, factory work, entertainment, domestic servitude, and prostitution constituted some of the primary forms of female employment.[114] This finding also fits with Susan Rigdon's and Ling Ma's conclusions that middle- and upper-class women who underwent abortions did so in more hygienic and expensive clinics.[115] Such clinics offered greater privacy and protected abortion seekers from the law, and thus few of these cases can be found in court records.[116]

Second, abortions among actresses, courtesans, prostitutes, and other female entertainers were also fairly common, but the media tended to play up the link between these professions and voluntary or coerced abortion.[117] Numerous articles discussed the hardships singers, prostitutes, and famous actresses faced, criticized their occupations and individual morality, and decried the practice of undergoing one or more

[112] Legal penalties for performing an abortion ranged from fines to imprisonment and penal servitude. For detailed information about the legal processes and penalties associated with providing abortions during this period, see Ma, "Gender, Law, and Society," 111–232.

[113] SMA, Q180-2-2348; BMA, J181-021-32692, SMA, Q180-2-15037; SMA, Q180-2-14379; Christian Henriot, *Prostitution and Sexuality in Shanghai: A Social History, 1849–1949*, trans. Noel Castelino (Cambridge: Cambridge University Press, 2001), 125.

[114] Emily Honig, *Sisters and Strangers: Women in the Shanghai Cotton Mills, 1919–1949* (Stanford: Stanford University Press, 1992), 21; Gail Hershatter, "Regulating Sex in Shanghai: The Reform of Prostitution in 1920 and 1951," in *Shanghai Sojourners*, eds. Frederic Wakeman Jr and Yeh Wen-hsin (Berkeley: University of California Press, 1992), 145.

[115] Rigdon, "Abortion Law and Practice in China," 544.

[116] Ma, "Gender, Law, and Society," 205.

[117] J181–023 – 07469; J181–021-32692; "Huoshan baofa (liu yuefen de wunü zhang: liu yue san ri (ponü datai))" (Volcanic Eruption: June Dancer's Account: June 3 (A Girl's Forced Abortion)), *Wuchang texie* (Dance Scene) 2 (1939): n.p.; "Kelian jinü duotai zhiming" (Pitiful Prostitute Dies from Abortion), *Shenbao*, September 1, 1933.

abortions.[118] The fact that prostitution was legal for most of the Republican era and that differences in status among entertainers, courtesans, and prostitutes diminished over that period undoubtedly contributed to this trend.[119] Public denouncement of entertainers and prostitutes betrayed elite male anxieties about national stature and reflected the growing association of these professions with social disorder and cultural backwardness, rather than with the cultivated courtesans of the nineteenth century.[120] In this way, abortion became a tool through which to criticize modernity, capitalism, and women in the public sphere.

Returning to the case in the chapter's introduction, this background knowledge provides useful context for interpreting the case of Li, the 19-year-old migrant factory worker in Tianjin. Li likely resorted to abortion for both social and financial reasons: to hide evidence of premarital sex and to retain her job at the factory. Like many other young women in similar situations, Li solicited the help of a woman, Guo, with some amount of training in traditional abortion practices. When the abortion took a deadly turn, Guo turned to a trained physician for help but to no avail. As a working-class woman who sought the help of a traditional woman healer, Li's and Guo's circumstances were precisely the type that the authorities cracked down on.

Birth Control and Abortion: Theory versus Practice

What can be ascertained from investigating birth control and abortion practices and the debates surrounding them? On the one hand, there was indeed a disconnect between the lofty notions of modern nationhood mentioned in Chapter 1 and the concerns of ordinary women presented in this chapter. While intellectuals had the privilege to reflect on the fate of society, the meanings of modernity, and the intelligentsia's collective role in ensuring healthier babies, in reality, women who used birth control or underwent abortion did so for practical reasons framed by individual or familial concerns – not wanting an affair to be discovered, fearing the loss of a job due to pregnancy, or concern about the

118 "Wei jinü datai, beigao fa juban" (Abortion for a Prostitute, the Accused was Detained and Dealt With), *Shenbao*, January 19, 1949; Hui Mingzeng, "Cong Luo Guifang de duotai shuoqi" (Talking about Luo Guifang's abortion), *Wufeng banyue qikan* (Dance Bimonthly Periodical), 2, no. 3 (1938): 15; "Mou hongxing duotai sici" (A Certain Celebrity had Four Abortions), *Yingwu xinwen* (Film and Dance News) 1, no. 12 (1935): 5.

119 Hershatter, *Dangerous Pleasures*, 20.

120 Gail Hershatter, *Women in China's Long Twentieth Century* (Berkeley: University of California Press, 2007), 38.

detrimental social implications of premarital sex. Moreover, elite discourses, consumer culture, the law, and medical hierarchies worked together to position affluent, educated women as the face of modernity, leaving lower-class, uneducated women as the socially undesirable residue in need of reform. Indeed, the languages spoken by vocal intellectuals and birth control users/abortion seekers barely overlapped. Rarely if ever did working-class women articulate birth control or abortion in terms of eugenic progress or individual sexual rights. For these women, the need to control births was more than a theoretical or existential issue.

On the other hand, debates in the public sphere may very well have shaped access to and policing of emmenagogues and abortifacients. Advertisements for medicines with abortifacient properties, as we have seen, were fairly ubiquitous, tacitly endorsing female agency at least in the realm of individual consumption and subtly promoting the notion that one's body was one's own domain. Although abortifacient use could still result in legal sanction, by not policing contraception and at times laxly enforcing abortion laws, national and local authorities created a space in which women could make some of their own reproductive decisions without state intrusion. Ling Ma, for example, argues that sometimes judges lessened sentences for abortion seekers because they acknowledged that abortion was often a product of poverty, coercion, or dire circumstances.[121] This selective policing of reproduction might suggest that powerholders were engaging to a degree with ideas about individual rights and modern subjectivity. However, the link between elite eugenic concerns and individual contraceptive or abortion practices is more tenuous.

Conclusion

Exploring the range of contraceptive and abortive techniques available to women and those they chose to employ demonstrates that abortion was the most common form of fertility control that made it into the historical record. Yet, abortion – particularly as it relates to emmenagogues with their questionable function – took on many forms derived from folk practices, traditional Chinese healing, and Western medicine. Although less popular, contraceptives similarly consisted of a broad and elusive assortment of medicines ranging from patent medicines to technologies endorsed by trained medical specialists. Regardless of one's demographic background, three of the main reasons for seeking abortion were

[121] Ma, "Gender, Law, and Society," 209.

adultery, premarital sex, and intercourse among "chaste" widows. Yet, lower-class women dominated both the court records and the media reports on abortion.

As Chapter 2 will show, these trends, concerns, and priorities with respect to birth control and reproduction did not simply disappear with the founding of the People's Republic. Rather, certain practices were temporarily suppressed or reconfigured to fit within a Communist framework and deployed as part of the party's modernizing agenda, with its emphasis on economic growth.

3 Reaping the Fruits of Women's Labor: Birth Control in the Early PRC, 1949–1958

In 1949, after years of civil war, the Communists finally defeated the Nationalists and founded the People's Republic of China (PRC). Whereas it might be said that the Nationalists subscribed to a population policy of haphazard natalism – a policy marked by uneven enforcement of laws regulating abortion and limited attention to contraceptives – shortly after the Communist victory, the Chinese Communist Party (CCP) adopted a blanket pro-natalist stance.[1] Faced with the mounting social costs of semi-colonization and prolonged war during the Republican era, the conviction that more workers would produce a stronger economy and greater national self-sufficiency led the CCP to severely restrict access to birth control, abortions, and sterilization surgeries.

Nevertheless, as this chapter demonstrates, the first efforts to loosen constraints on birth control and abortion were enacted only a few years later. In fact, the CCP even adopted a new linguistic framework for discussing state-endorsed birth control and abortion practices, many of which were carryovers from the Republican period that had been rebranded to fit with the party's political agenda. Internal conflicts within the CCP over the political implications of birth control, however, stymied efforts to enact more comprehensive changes. The rocky start to PRC-era population planning foretold the long-term challenges the state would face in consolidating its control over fertility.

By comparing circumstances in Shanghai, Tianjin, and Luoyang, this chapter shows that throughout the 1950s, access to information about sex, as well as access to birth control, differed dramatically according to demographic factors, such as location, class, and education level. Educated urbanites were not only more likely to have knowledge about birth control, but they were also some of the first people to gain access to legal contraception and abortion. Although state media sought to promulgate ideas about normative sexuality and childbearing that supported

[1] White, *China's Longest Campaign*, 23.

broader national goals, the ambiguous positions of abortion and birth control in public policy and discourse inadvertently created some space for individual maneuvering in the realm of reproduction. This uncertain environment, in turn, fostered heterogenous approaches to fertility control.

"More Sons, More Happiness"

In what context did the shift from state-endorsed natalism to birth planning emerge, and how did this change initially manifest itself?

According to two elderly men I interviewed in Shanghai, the traditional Chinese adage "more sons, more happiness" (*duozi duofu*) best illustrates China's early fertility policy.[2] Indeed, in the early years of the People's Republic, most efforts at fertility control, because of their association with Malthusianism, were deemed "bourgeois" and "capitalist" and therefore in opposition to the goals of the party-state.[3] Official attitudes toward birth control gradually began to change when the results of the first national census in 1953 revealed that the population had grown by nearly 60 million people in just four years.[4] In 1957, during the brief window of political openness known as the Hundred Flowers Movement (1956–1957), prominent intellectuals openly criticized the state's natalist policies, yet they were thoroughly punished during the subsequent crackdown on "anti-rightists."[5]

In terms of daily life, limited access to contraceptives, due to both resource scarcity and bans on contraceptive sales, as well as a lack of information about birth control use, were the most effective means of

[2] Interview with author, Shanghai June 8, 2016.

[3] The English economist Thomas Malthus (1766–1834), for whom the term "Malthusianism" is named, had warned that unmitigated population growth would exhaust the food supply, leading to widespread famine and poverty. In contrast to Malthus, Karl Marx, the "intellectual father" of Communism, argued that population issues were unique to the capitalist mode of production; Greenhalgh, *Just One Child,* 45; Shi Chengli, "Jianguo yilai jihua shengyu gongzuo gaikuang" (Summary of Birth Planning Work After the Founding of the PRC), *Xibei renkou* (Northwest Population) (1980): 35.

[4] Masako Kohama, "Cong 'Feifa duotai' dao 'jihua shengyu:' jianguo qianhou xing he shengzhi zhi yanlun kongjian de bianqian" (From "criminal abortion" to "birth planning:" The changes of discursive space as regards to sex and reproduction before and after 1949), in *Jindai zhongguo chengshi yu dazhong wenhua*, ed. Jiang Jin and Li Deying (Beijing, Xinxing chubanshe, 2008), 344; National Birth Planning Committee Integrated Planning Division (*Guojia jihua shengyu weiyuanhui zonghe jihua si*), *Chinese Birth Planning Statistical Yearbook* (Quanguo jihua shengyu tongji ziliao huibian) (N.p.: n. p., 1983), 1.

[5] Judith Shapiro, *Mao's War Against Nature: Politics and the Environment in Revolutionary China* (Cambridge: Cambridge University Press, 1999), 22.

promoting natalism.[6] Instances in which the government took a hard stance against those attempting to regulate their fertility were typically cases of abortion, in which those responsible were caught and tried.[7] Indeed, in later justifying access to safe and legal abortions, national, provincial, and municipal-level directives even acknowledged the prevalence of dangerous home abortions in the early People's Republic.[8] Yet, in its first decade of rule, the CCP played a much less invasive role in the reproductive lives of its citizens than it would in the future.

In the long term, party leaders determined that birth control facilitated state modernizing efforts and could offer a solution to lagging grain production and the resulting grain shortages, both pressing problems that peaked in the crisis of the Great Leap Forward (1959–1961), a campaign to shift China from an agrarian economy to a socialist planned economy through industrialization and collectivization. Chairman Mao had initially adopted the philosophy that "many hands make light work" (*ren duo liliang da*), meaning that China's large population was an asset. However, the belief that slowing population growth to align with bleaker agricultural realities began to gain credence over the prevailing notion that a larger population could produce higher outputs. Rather than openly acknowledging the impending food shortage, the issue was often framed in terms of improving maternal and infant health, expanding childhood education, and reducing household burdens.[9]

Elite female cadres also played a part in pushing for greater access to abortion and sterilization, arguing that women could not "hold up half the sky" and continue their revolutionary work with too many children.[10] In fact, when the Women's Federation magazine, *Xin Zhongguo funü* (New Women of China), conducted a reader poll in 1955 about demand for birth control and abortions, urban cadres, followed by university professors, secondary school teachers, students, and factory workers, most desired birth control to limit family size.[11] The poll

[6] Shanghai Municipal Archive (SMA), B242–1-585. [7] ECNUA, En 0351-150-012.
[8] LMA, 14–16. [9] White, *China's Longest Campaign*, 35, 52.
[10] Chinese University of Hong Kong Archives (CUHKA), "Beijing you bushao jiguan ganbu yaoqiu biyun he rengong liuchan" (Many Government Officials in Beijing Demand Birth Control and Abortion), *Neibu cankao* (Internal Reference) (1955); White, *China's Longest Campaign*, 21.
[11] The All-China Women's Federation, an organization established to represent the interests of women in the CCP, began publishing the magazine *Zhongguo funü* (Women of China) in Yan'an in 1939. In 1941, publication of the magazine ceased due to challenges associated with the war against Japan. In 1949, the Women's Federation renewed publication of the magazine but this time under the name *New Women of China*. In 1956, the magazine's name was changed back to *Women of China*. Beginning in 1967, publication was disrupted again when the magazine came under

results – 226 written responses penned by urban individuals from much of eastern and central China who either supported or opposed birth control – were so significant that they were even secretly circulated among the highest echelons of the Communist Party.[12]

Because the Communist Party sought to shift women's productive energies away from the demands of family and kin toward the interests of the collective, concerns about maternal health and postpartum productivity – at least rhetorically – dominated the conversation about birth control.[13] High rates of miscarriage and premature delivery among pregnant women workers, who then required sick leave, was viewed as an impediment to meeting factory quotas.[14] Relatedly, even as cities like Shanghai pushed greater numbers of women into the workforce, worker shortages – caused by too many workers becoming pregnant and taking sick leave during the same period – also curtailed production.[15] Therefore, the Ministry of Health called on local governments to

attack during the Cultural Revolution. However, in 1978, the Women's Federation began publishing *Zhongguo funü* once more; "'Zhongguo funü' zazhe she" (*Women of China* Magazine Publisher), Zhonghua quanguo funü lianhe hui (All-China Women's Federation), May 18, 2021, http://www.women.org.cn/zhuanti/www.women.org.cn/quanguofulian/zhishudanwei/funvzazhishe.htm.

12 CUHKA, "Duzhe dui 'Xin Zhongguo funü' kandai 'Biyun fangfa' yiwen de fangying" (Readers' Responses to the Article 'Birth Control Methods' in *New Women of China* Magazine).

13 Kimberly Ens Manning argues that during the 1950s, and even earlier, the CCP adopted the principle of "Marxist maternalist equality" to address women's liberation. "Marxist maternalist equality" combined the Marxist ideal of gender equality with the notion that the conjugal family unit and women's capacities as mothers were foundational to the nation. Manning contends that, despite state policies ostensibly designed to protect women's bodies and compensate women for their labor outside of the home, underlying social inequalities meant that only women with certain privileges, such as family or party connections, enjoyed these benefits and that men's work was valued more highly than women's. Moreover, of the rural women Manning interviewed about their experiences during the Great Leap Forward, many said they felt betrayed by the party because of its inability to live up to its own promises to women. Whereas state propaganda painted mass mobilization as a way to uplift women, many women – especially mothers with several children – said that these policies forced them to bear an even greater labor burden, which in turn negatively impacted their health and wellbeing. These conclusions align with many of Gail Hershatter's findings about rural women's experiences during collectivization, as described in *The Gender of Memory*. Kimberly Ens Manning, "Marxist Maternalism, Memory, and the Mobilization of Women in the Great Leap Forward," *The China Review* 5, no. 1 (2005), 87–97.

14 CUHKA, "Xicheng gong siying mian chang huaiyun nügong liuchan xianxian yanzhong" (The Miscarriages of Pregnant Women Workers in Xicheng Public and Private Cotton Factories are a Serious Phenomenon); CUHKA, "Xibei fangzhi gonghui shangwu baohu huaiyun nügong de juti banfa" (The Northwest Textile Trade Union has No Specific Measures for Protecting Pregnant Women Workers).

15 Fudan University Contemporary China Social Life Data and Research Center (CCSL), SA201700000409; Kohama, "Jihua shengyu de kaiduan," 117.

"address the masses' demands for birth control, enabling them to plan their births and adjust their birth density,"[16] In short, it was thought that women should carry out their biological duties as mothers; however, they should not give birth so frequently that they could not remain useful contributors to the workforce.[17]

Beginning in the early 1950s, couples were also encouraged to have children when their bodies had fully matured and at a pace that was healthy for the mother. This was not, however, an effort to limit population growth but rather a plan to improve the quality of the population: Healthier mothers meant healthier children and a healthier labor force.[18] As later chapters will demonstrate, campaigns promoting delayed marriage (*wanhun*), rather than dying out with increased access to contraceptives, escalated throughout the 1960s and 1970s.

At the same time, the CCP gradually adopted a new linguistic framework for discussing state-endorsed birth control and abortion practices. This deliberate refashioning demonstrates well the CCP's changing attitude toward birth control and its efforts to reframe the discourses surrounding family planning. One of the most common terms for abortion in Republican China was *duotai* (literally, dropping the fetus). Other frequently used terms were *zhuitai*, which has the same literal meaning as *duotai*, and *datai* (hitting the fetus). Seeking to draw a sharp break with the past, reformers in the early People's Republic deliberately ceased referring to abortion as *duotai* and instead adopted the expression *rengong liuchan* (man-made miscarriage). Although technically referring to the same procedure, the two terms had very different connotations. While *duotai* was associated with the backward, illegal, and dangerous abortions common in capitalist Old China, *rengong liuchan* purported to be a product of scientific advancement and socialist modernity.[19] In the years to come, the central government would argue that the ability to regulate one's fertility vis-à-vis *rengong liuchan* was evidence of the party's progressive thinking and sensitivity to the needs of the masses.

A similar linguistic shift occurred with regard to the expression for birth control. In the Republican period, the most common terms for contraception were *shengyu kongzhi* and *shengyu jiezhi*, direct translations of the English phrase "birth control" (see Chapter 2 for more on this topic). Although these terms were never considered antithetical to

[16] Luoyang Municipal Archive (LMA), 14–16.
[17] Guangdong Provincial Archive (GPA), 233-2-267-33-39.
[18] LMA, 14–16.
[19] Kohama, "Cong 'Feifa duotai' dao 'jihua shengyu,'" 354.

science to the extent that the term *duotai* was (perhaps because of birth control's association with Western modernity), the CCP still replaced the expressions *shengyu kongzhi* and *shengyu jiezhi* with ones more specific to its reproductive vision. Phrases like *jihua shengyu* (literally, planned birth) and *biyun* (pregnancy prevention) came into more frequent use and marked an indigenization of what was originally a largely foreign or at least international discourse. This linguistic transition was indeed a significant one, marking a conceptual shift from *shengyu kongzhi* (literally, birth control), a kind of passive and reactive response to overpopulation, to *jihua shengyu* (planned birth), a proactive and strategic engineering of the population.[20] The intention was to gradually change the primary form of birth control from abortion, the most prevalent method for fertility control in the Republican period, to other methods of birth prevention, namely condoms and cervical caps during this period.

This linguistic transformation was part of the larger post–World War II international move away from overtly eugenic terminology toward the subtler language of family planning.[21] While eugenics had emphasized racial fitness, family planning was primarily concerned with alleviating poverty through smaller families and improved healthcare. Building on Republican-era initiatives to modernize midwifery and increase access to health services, the party's medical agenda emphasized limiting infant and child mortality and preventing the spread of illness. The first access to birth control, abortion, and sterilization would be granted on the basis that it would help "ensure safe childbearing (for mothers with health conditions) and protect the health of mothers and babies" (*baozhang funü shengyu de anquan, bing baohu muqin he ying'er de jiankang*).[22]

In the early 1950s, China also modeled itself in many respects after its closest ally, the Soviet Union. China borrowed heavily from its neighbor's fertility policies, which incentivized large families and prohibited contraception to promote collective consciousness.[23] As in the Soviet Union, Chinese women who had many children were honored as "glory

[20] Tyrene White translates *jihua shengyu* as birth planning; White, *China's Longest Campaign*, 39.
[21] Matthew Connelly, *Fatal Misconception: The Struggle to Control World* Population (Cambridge: Harvard University Press, 2008), 114.
[22] SMA, B242-1-560
[23] Ekaterina Selezneva, "Struggling for New Lives: Family and Fertility Policies in the Soviet Union and Modern Russia," *Ideas*, https://ideas.repec.org/p/hit/hitcei/2015-8.html, 8.

mothers" (*muqin yingxiong*).[24] When the Soviet Union legalized abortion in 1955, this policy change similarly gained support in China.[25] In the late 1950s and early 1960s, though, as relations with the Soviet Union began to sour, the literature in China on contraception stopped relying so heavily on information translated from foreign languages – Russian, Japanese, English, German, and French – and domestic research came to dominate the field of Chinese birth control.[26] The Sino-Soviet split hastened along the process of China developing its own unique approach to population management.

Reflecting this awkward transition from natalism to limited population control, in 1953 the central government published a preliminary declaration ordering local governments to loosen restrictions on access to abortions and sterilizations (a policy that would be made permanent in 1955), yet at the same time, importation of contraceptives was banned.[27] Local policy changes, however, occurred at different rates. For example, in 1953, Beijing first permitted noncadre women over thirty-five with at least six children or a serious illness to undergo these procedures but only with both their husband's and their work unit's consent.[28] That same year, Shanghai enacted a similar policy change allowing chronically ill married women over thirty-five to undergo sterilization and sick women who had undergone more than two miscarriages or caesarian sections to have abortions.[29] In 1956, Luoyang's government began allowing women with debilitating illnesses to have abortions and women over thirty with at least four children to undergo sterilization surgery.[30] In 1957, Tianjin implemented a comparable policy with provisions for work

[24] Chongyi Wang et al., *Dangdai zhongguo de weisheng shiye* (Public Hygiene Undertakings in Modern China), vol. 2 (Beijing: Zhongguo shehui kexue chuban she, 1986), 230 and Anchee Min, *Red Azalea* (New York: Anchor Books, 1994), 77.

[25] Kohama, "Cong 'Feifa duotai' dao 'jihua shengyu,'" 344.

[26] Established in the early 1950s, the Population Research Center (*shehui yu renkou xueyuan*) at Renmin University in Beijing became the central hub for demographic research in the PRC. In 1957, East China Normal University also established the "Population Research Room" (*renkou yinjiu shi*) to study the population question. Although the Population Research Room was closed a year later due to the changing political climate, its work was renewed again after the Cultural Revolution. Yang Faxiang, "Dangdai zhongguo jihua shengyu shi yanjiu" (Research on the History of Family Planning in Contemporary China), (PhD dissertation, Zhejiang University, 2003), 44.

[27] Wang et al., *Dangdai zhongguo de weisheng shiye* (Public Hygiene Undertakings in Modern China), 230–233; Yang, "Dangdai zhongguo jihua shengyu shi yanjiu" (Research on the History of Family Planning in Contemporary China), 44.

[28] Thomas Scharping, *Birth Control in China, 1949–2000: Population Policy and Demographic Development* (London: RoutledgeCurzon, 2003), 45; Beijing Municipal Archive (BMA), 135-001-00226; BMA, 002-002-00213.

[29] SMA, B242–1-560. [30] Luoyang Municipal Archive (LMA), 48–301.

unit subsidization of medical fees and paid leave for recovering patients.[31] Such policies and the reproductive options they entailed, however, did not extend to the rural population. For instance, the Ministry of Health published a directive in 1957 permitting women with the desire for sterilization, who had undergone a professional medical examination and had no medical contraindications, to have this procedure and women not wishing to carry a pregnancy to term to undergo abortion.[32] Yet, local governments continued to police these practices, likely due to the widespread belief that women had a "natural duty" (*tianran yiwu*) to become mothers.[33]

Moreover, initially there were no provisions for male sterilization, even though vasectomies would have been equally effective in preventing further births and were less invasive than tubal ligations. When I asked a seventy-year-old interviewee why women were encouraged to have sterilizations rather than men, she argued that men worked more efficiently than women and that their work was often more important than women's work, so it made sense for them to continue working while their wives underwent surgery.[34] Other female interviewees in their sixties and eighties expressed similar views, arguing that as the primary breadwinners, men could not afford to be temporarily incapacitated from surgery, so therefore women must instead bear the physical burden of sterilization.[35] To counteract this line of thinking and assuage male fears about sterilization, in the early 1960s *New Women of China* even published several articles attempting to convince readers that vasectomies were in the best interest of couples with many children.[36] As with childbearing, though, sterilization in China would become another form of gendered labor. In the 1950s, the law and common assumptions about proper gender roles worked in concert to ensure that women carried more than their share of the burden of reducing fertility.

Did Sex Education Exist in 1950s China?

Some scholars have argued that Communism's focus on the state and society, rather than on the individual, and Marxist denial of gender

[31] Tianjin Municipal Archive (TMA), X0044-Y-000378-013.
[32] Wang et al., *Dangdai zhongguo de weisheng shiye* (Public Hygiene Undertakings in Modern China), 233.
[33] Evans, *Women and Sexuality in China*, 122.
[34] Interview with the author, Ningde, June 12, 2016.
[35] Interview with author, Shanghai, December 20, 2016; interview with author, Luoyang, January 12, 2017.
[36] Song Hongjian, "Jieza shujing guan hui yingxiang jiankang ma" (Can Undergoing a Vasectomy Influence One's Health?), *Zhongguo funü* (New Women of China) 4 (1963): 10; Lu Dachuan, "Wo jieza shujing guan de qianqian houhou" (Before and After My Vasectomy), *Zhongguo funü* (New Women of China) 4 (1963): 11.

difference, meant that sexuality and reproduction were rarely discussed in Maoist China.[37] It is true that the CCP's media monopoly far surpassed that of its predecessors with repeated campaigns to identify and destroy titillating "yellow" media (commodified sexual representations).[38] Despite attempts to regulate materials deemed obscene, some erotic media still continued to circulate underground.[39]

As for state-endorsed publications, Harriet Evans has demonstrated that writings discussing various aspects of sexuality were published throughout the 1950s.[40] Taking the form of news articles, magazines, and books, these publications used biology to define gender difference, condemn pre- and extramarital sex, and promote heterosexual monogamy.[41] Moreover, the authors of these texts often assumed that readers were educated, urban, and had contact with the opposite sex.[42] Although they were technically official publications, books on sexuality and reproduction occupied a liminal position at the boundary of the "perverse" and the "scientific," categories that were vaguely defined and evolved along with the changing political context.[43] Their graphic images, overt discussions of the mechanics of sex and birth control, and similarity to "yellow" Republican-era texts left such books in a precarious political position, as one interviewee suggested when he characterized 1950s sexual hygiene guides as "yellow."[44]

Indeed, support for overt discussions of sex and contraception was certainly not unanimous within the party, as simultaneous efforts to promote natalism evince. During a nationwide campaign to purge erotic media, in November 1951, the Ministry of Propaganda banned publication and distribution of four major publications on birth control: two texts entitled *Guide to Married Life* and *Women's General Physiological Knowledge*, as well as two contraceptive guidebooks, *Commonly Used Birth Control Methods* and *Practical Birth Control.* The CCP condemned them for spreading knowledge about birth control that might undermine

[37] Joanna McMillan, *Sex, Science and Morality in China* (Abingdon-on-Thames: Taylor and Francis, 2006); Fang Fu Ruan, *Sex in China: Studies in Sexology in Chinese Culture* (New York: Spring Science and Business Media, 1991); À la Foucault in *The History of Sexuality*, Y. Yvon Wang refers to the assumption that the Maoist state stifled sexuality as China's "repressive hypothesis"; Y. Yvon Wang, "Yellow Books in Red China: A Preliminary Examination of Sex in Print in the Early People's Republic," *Twentieth-Century China* 44, no. 1 (2019): 77.

[38] What constituted "yellow" media, however, was open to debate; Wang, "Yellow Books in Red China," 82.

[39] Wang, "Yellow Books in Red China," 91.

[40] Harriet Evans, *Women and Sexuality*, 2.

[41] Evans, *Women and Sexuality*, 34.

[42] Evans, *Women and Sexuality in China*, 24.

[43] Wang, "Yellow Books in Red China," 91.

[44] Interview with author, Luoyang, November 11, 2016.

the "spirit of increasing the population."[45] These publications, which contain detailed descriptions of the sex organs and diagrams demonstrating birth control methods, read much like the eugenic treatises of the Republican period. Books promoting a healthy sex life, such as *Arts of the Bedchamber*, were also banned.[46]

Despite the initial ban, information on sex and birth control continued to circulate. Indeed, the limited scope of the ban offers some of the strongest evidence that government leaders were ambivalent toward natalism. In addition, long before sterilization and abortion became widespread, guides detailing these procedures were being mass produced.[47] The showcasing of contraceptives at exhibitions in Shanghai and other cities, as well advertisements for contraceptives in newspapers and on billboards, further highlights the relative prominence of birth control in public discourse.[48]

When I asked my interviewees what, if anything, they were reading about sex and birth control in the 1950s, they had a variety of responses. Some, like a group of men in their late seventies who I interviewed in Luoyang, said there was little information on birth control at that time and noted that even if there had been written information about sex, only the city's small literate population could have taken advantage of it.[49] While a limited number of urban residents had access to health classes that covered sex (Figure 3.1), my other interviewees – all of whom were literate – said they learned about sex primarily through reading books.[50] One man, who told me to refer to him as Old Wang, was born in Shanghai in 1946. He was one of nine children raised in a wealthy Guomindang household. Of the nine children, only six lived to adulthood. Shanghai is a city of immigrants and Wang's parents were no

[45] SMA, B1–2-3622-152; Guo Quanqing, *Shiyong biyunfa* (Practical Birth Control Methods), Shanghai: Jia zazhi she, 1950; Wang, "Yellow Books in Red China," 82.

[46] SMA, B1-2-3622-152.

[47] Wang Yanrui, *Shuluanguan jueyushu* (Fallopian Tube Sterilization Surgery) (Beijing: Renmin weisheng chubanshe, 1959); Zhonghua renmin gongheguo weisheng bu weisheng jiaoyu suo (Bureau of Hygiene Education of the People's Republic of China Ministry of Health), *Jiezhi shengyu xuanchuan shouce* (Birth Control Propaganda Handbook) (Beijing: kexue puji chubanshe, 1958).

[48] "Chulemi Contraceptive Cream." Inside Red China; "Jiajiale biyun pian" (Happy Family Birth Control Pills), 1959. *Hangzhou ribao*: n.p.; Deng Liqun, Ma Hong, and Wu Heng, eds. *Dangdai zhongguo de jihua shengyu shiye* (The Contemporary Chinese Birth Planning Project) (Beijing: Contemporary China Publishers, 1992), 78–79; UOT, "China Trip, 1958," June 1, 2018, http://radfilms.com/China_1957_Birth_Control_Vaginal_Foam.html.

[49] Interview with author, Shanghai, August 10, 2016; interview with author, Shanghai August 11, 2016; and interview with author, Luoyang, November 11, 2016.

[50] "A Women's Health Class in 1955," *Everyday Life in Mao's China*, https://everydaylifeinmaoschina.wordpress.com/2015/10/02/a-womens-health-class-in-1955/.

Figure 3.1 A women's health class in 1955.
Source: "A Women's Health Class in 1955," *Everyday Life in Mao's China*, https://everydaylifeinmaoschina.wordpress.com/2015/10/02/a-womens-health-class-in-1955/.

different – his mother originally came from Shandong and his father from Jiangsu. When Wang was a child, his family had eight nurses and house-keepers, a big house, plentiful food, a car, and beautiful clothes. His parents were well educated, but he only received a high school education under the Communists. According to Wang, urban people learned about sex from books like *Knowledge about Sex*.[51]

Knowledge about Sex was first published in the People's Republic in 1956 to spread awareness about sexual hygiene and to help young people

[51] Harriet Evans translates *Xing de zhishi* this way in *Women and Sexuality in China.*

with sex-related illnesses treat themselves.[52] The book was loosely based on a eugenic treatise of the same name published first in 1926 and then again in March 1949 as part of a series on "women's problems" (*funü wenti*). Although the Republican and Communist-era books contained similar information, because the original book was a translation of an American text associated with capitalism and the period before "liberation," the PRC edition did not acknowledge its Republican antecedent or its foreign origins.[53] In choosing what material to publish for the PRC edition, readers submitted questions to the authors (two gynecologists and a neurologist), who responded in subsequent editions of the book. *Knowledge about Sex* was so popular that several more editions were printed in 1957 and 1958 in Beijing, Guangxi, Chongqing, and Shanghai.[54] Altogether, more than 3.6 million copies of this book were sold, and copies of these books are still fairly common in used book markets and bookstores in China today. The fact that a new edition of *Knowledge about Sex* was published in 1981 as part of the post-Mao reforms is a testament to the enduring value attributed to this text.[55]

Knowledge about Sex, like other books about sexual hygiene from the 1950s, equated gender with sex, defining women by their reproductive functions, rather than their gender performance. Categories like "woman" and "female" were treated as fixed and stable, even though they varied over time and across cultures.[56] This formulation of gender affirmed the idea that women were passive, lacking in sexual desire, and innately designed to be wives and mothers.[57] As Harriet Evans argues, the discourse of essential difference between the sexes was used to reinforce the existing gender hierarchy.[58] In this environment, there was little room for alternative gender identities, and discussions of sex and sexuality were confined to static gender roles and the fundamentals of reproduction.

According to three interviewees – Old Wang, a shop owner in her fifties surnamed Liu, and Zhao, a seventy-two-year-old gynecologist

[52] Wang, Wenbin, Zhao Zhiyi, and Tan Mingxun, *Xing de zhishi* (Knowledge about Sex) (Beijing: Renmin weisheng chubanshe, 1956), introduction.

[53] W.J. Robinson, *Xing de zhishi* (Knowledge about Sex), trans. Fang Ke (Shanghai: Kaiming shudian, 1949).

[54] *Knowledge about Sex* was even translated into Korean and Vietnamese. Wang, Wenbin, Zhao Zhiyi, and Tan Mingxun, *Xing de zhishi* (Knowledge about Sex) (Beijing: Renmin weisheng chubanshe, 1957).

[55] Wang, Wenbin, Zhao Zhiyi, and Tan Mingxun, *Xing de zhishi* (Knowledge about Sex) (Beijing: Renmin weisheng chubanshe, 1981).

[56] Judith Butler, *Gender Trouble: Feminism and the Subversion of Identity* (New York: Routledge, 1990), 1.

[57] Evans, *Women and Sexuality in China,* 27. [58] Ibid., 27.

from rural Fujian province – in the 1950s and even in the 1960s, most people were not comfortable talking about sex or birth control. Wang, Liu, and Zhao, who were all interviewed separately, agreed that most mothers wanted to share information about sex and sexual hygiene with their daughters but did not want to do so outright because it was vulgar.[59] Therefore, people with culture (*you wenhua de ren*) or a good upbringing purchased books like *Knowledge about Sex* as wedding gifts for their daughters to help them prepare for sex on their wedding night. Also, grooms might give books like this to their new brides to educate them about sex and pregnancy.[60] Zhao said that in the 1950s and 1960s, most information about sex and birth control, if not learned through personal experience, was conveyed through reading books rather than speaking with friends or family. The introduction to *Knowledge about Sex* echoes this sentiment, lamenting that too many young people and even married couples lack an accurate understanding of sexual hygiene and that this can destabilize marriages. Both the authors of *Knowledge about Sex* and Old Wang blamed "feudalism" (*fengjian zhuyi*) and the "old society" for widespread ignorance about sex.

All three editions of *Knowledge about Sex* featured sections on both sexes' reproductive systems, masturbation, menstruation, pregnancy, and birth control. These books also contained detailed diagrams of male and female genitals, as well as charts on the ideal timing of male and female orgasms during sex. *Knowledge about Sex* claimed that intercourse typically lasted between two to three minutes and ten minutes, but that women usually take between ten and thirty minutes to orgasm and that a lack of knowledge about timing could lead to an "unharmonious" sex life.[61] The books' authors attempted to make sex into a science that could be studied and mastered, and writers of medical guides such as *Knowledge about Sex* drew on the authority of science to reinforce culturally constructed notions of gender difference.[62] In this way, the rhetoric of science helped lend credence to ideas and practices intended to preserve social stability and safeguard the existing gender order.[63]

As for birth control, *Knowledge about Sex* recommended contraception for the benefit of both parents' and children's health. It claimed that in the old society, couples used methods such as practicing sexual

[59] Interview with author, Ningde, June 12, 2016; interview with author, Shanghai, August 11, 2016.
[60] Interview with author, Shanghai, August 10, 2016.
[61] Wang, Zhao, and Tan, *Knowledge*, 38–39.
[62] Harriet Evans, "Defining Difference: The 'Scientific' Construction of Sexuality and Gender in the People's Republic of China," *Signs* 20, no. 2 (1995): 387.
[63] Evans, "Defining Difference," 387.

self-control and taking abortifacients to terminate unwanted pregnancies but that neither approach was ideal. The book introduced three methods for regulating fertility. The first involved inserting a contraceptive suppository covered in spermicidal jelly or another substance with spermicidal properties into the vagina before intercourse to kill sperm that attempt to enter the uterus. The authors conceded that although this method was simple and convenient, it was largely ineffective. The second approach involved using contraceptive devices: for men, condoms, called *yinjingtao* or *baoxiantao* (literally, insurance sheath), and for women, diaphragms or cervical caps. The authors stressed that using a diaphragm with contraceptive jelly is effective 98 percent of the time while condoms are effective in preventing conception in 95 percent of cases. Finally, *Knowledge about Sex* recommended using the "rhythm method" or "safe period method" (*anquanqi biyunfa*) – planning sexual intercourse based on the woman's menstrual schedule to prevent pregnancies.[64] Each month was broken up into three periods: the "easy conception period," the "safe period," and the "menstruation period." It was believed that if a couple kept to a schedule of intercourse dictated by the woman's period, chances of unwanted conception could be reduced (Figure 3.2).[65] My interviewee, Zhao, said that the most common and effective form of birth control in the 1950s and 1960s was the rhythm method. She said that couples, especially women, began using this approach when they felt they could not handle having any more children.[66] Other sources also indicate that the rhythm method was being practiced in China at this time, particularly in rural areas with little access to mass-produced contraceptives.[67]

The rhythm method, still used today worldwide, was entirely compatible with Chinese beliefs about fertility and health. As mentioned in Chapter 2, according to the Chinese medical canon, a woman's body was ruled by blood and therefore regular menses indicated harmony and health within a woman. Therefore, if amenorrhea occurred due to either pregnancy or illness, this indicated that the woman's *yin* and *yang* levels were imbalanced.[68] A couple not wanting to conceive would adhere to the rhythm method to ensure that the woman's menses were regular. Alternatively, as in the Republican period, a woman might consume

[64] Matthew Connelly, *Fatal Misconception: The Struggle to Control World Population* (Cambridge: Harvard University Press, 2008), 101.
[65] Shandong sheng jihua shengyu gongzuo weiyuan hui, Shandong sheng weisheng ting, "Anquanqi biyunfa" (Safe Period Birth Control Method), poster, 1966.
[66] Interview with author, Ningde, June 12, 2016.
[67] East China Normal University Archive (ECNUA), B 0357-001-018.
[68] Francesca Bray, *Technology and Gender: Fabrics of Power in Late Imperial China* (Berkeley: University of California Press, 1997), 334.

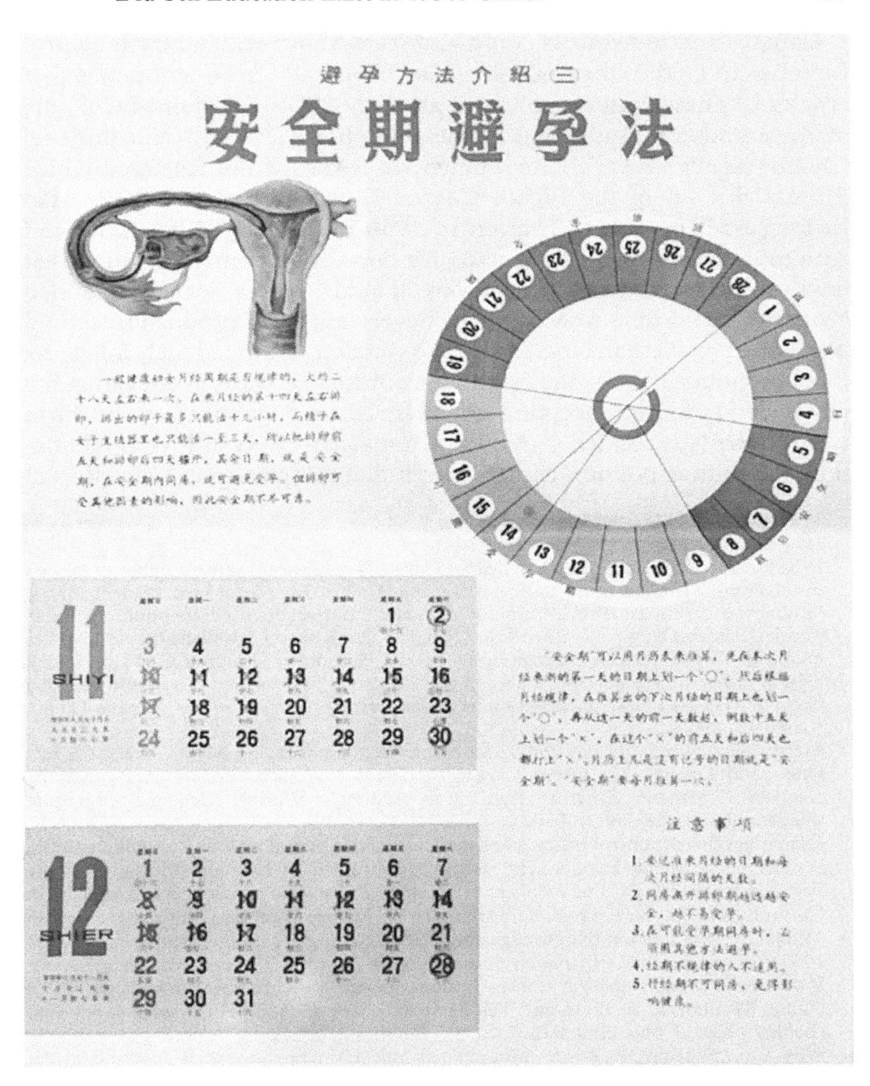

Figure 3.2 Rhythm method reference calendar and instructions, 1966.
Source: Shandong sheng jihua shengyu gongzuo weiyuan hui, Shandong sheng weisheng ting, "Anquanqi biyunfa" (Safe Period Birth Control Method), 1966.

tiaojingyao, or medicines that induced menstruation, to prevent pregnancy.[69] Indeed, such practices endured in the PRC.

[69] Bray, *Technology and Gender*, 325.

Couples and individuals could also learn about sex and birth control from health guides, the magazine *New Women of China*, and newspaper articles.[70] These materials blended aspects of Western biomedicine, the many strands of Traditional Chinese Medicine (TCM), and imperial Chinese ideals about chaste women. In 1957, at the Enlarged Third Plenary Session of the Eighth Central Committee of the CCP, Mao Zedong built on a speech given in 1956 by Premier Zhou Enlai and tentatively acknowledged the need for population control, arguing that unmitigated population growth was at odds with a socialist planned economy. According to Mao's logic, every aspect of production should be planned by the state, including reproduction.[71] Immediately following these pronouncements, the first state-coordinated effort at educating the populace about contraception commenced, and publications on birth control briefly expanded.[72] While such materials were always in circulation, the shifting political climate meant that this particular state effort at

[70] In 1956 and 1957, for example, Qingdao Daily (*Qingdao ribao*) ran a number of articles discussing the fundamentals of birth control and advertising local birth control clinics; "Zhongyao biyun danfang" (Chinese Medicine Contraceptive Perscription), *Qingdao ribao* (Qingdao Daily), July 22, 1956; "Xingjiao zhongduan – tiwai shejing de biyun fa haobu hao" (Intercourse Interruption – Is the Withdrawal Method Good or Bad?), *Qingdao ribao* (Qingdao Daily), December 22, 1957; "Fei budeyi buyao zuo rengong liuchan" (Do Not Have an Abortion as a Last Resort), *Qingdao ribao* (Qingdao Daily), March 12, 1957.

[71] Martin King Whyte, Wang Feng, and Yong Cai, "Challenging Myths About China's One-Child Policy," *The China Journal* 74 (2015): 147; *Mao Zedong zhuzuo zhuanti zhaibian* (Thematic Excerpts from Mao Zedong's Works) (Beijing: Zhongyang wenxian chubanshe, 2003), 970.

[72] Examples of birth control guides published during this period include Zhonghua renmin gongheguo weisheng bu weisheng jiaoyu suo (Bureau of Hygiene Education of the People's Republic of China Ministry of Health), *Biyun qianhou* (Before and after Birth Control) (Tianjin: Kexue puji chubanshe, 1957); Wang, Wenbin, Zhao Zhiyi, and Tan Mingxun, *Xing de zhishi* (Knowledge about Sex) (Beijing: Renmin weisheng chubanshe, 1957); Zhang Ruolin, ed., *Funü weisheng ji biyun changshi* (General Knowledge about Women's Hygiene and Birth Control) (Shijiazhuang: Hebei renmin chubanshe, 1957); (Wang, Wenbin, Zhao Zhiyi, and Tan Mingxun, *Xing de zhishi* (Knowledge about Sex) (Beijing: Kexue puji chubanshe, 1958); Beijingshi gonggong weishengju weisheng jiaoyusuo yu beijingshi kexue jishu puji xiehui (Hygiene Education Institute of the Beijing Public Hygiene Bureau and Beijing Science and Technology Popularization Association), *Nongcun jihua shengyu huace* (Rural Birth Planning Album) (Beijing: Beijing Publishers, 1958); Shandong weisheng ting (Shandong Department of Hygiene), *Jieyu xuanchuan shouce* (Birth Control Propaganda Handbook) (Jinan: Shandong People's Publishing House, 1958); Shanghai di er yixue yuan fu chan ke jiaoyanzu (Obstetrics and Gynecology Teaching and Research Group of Shanghai Number Two Medical College), *Qingnian hunyin weisheng* (Youth Marital Hygiene) (Shanghai: Shanghai kexue jishu chubanshe, 1958); Zhonghua renmin gongheguo weisheng bu weisheng jiaoyu suo (Bureau of Hygiene Education of the People's Republic of China Ministry of Health), *Jiezhi shengyu xuanchuan shouce* (Birth Control Propaganda Handbook) (Beijing: kexue puji chubanshe, 1958).

promoting birth control only lasted until the end of 1958.[73] A second surge in birth planning promotion took place between 1962 and 1963, but as with the previous wave, this effort suffered from lack of organization and manpower. Like *Knowledge about Sex,* guides to sexual hygiene produced in the 1950s contained detailed images and diagrams of the reproductive organs. While in theory these books would have been intelligible to people with varying degrees of education, the guides were largely designed for an urban audience with access to contraceptives.

In 1958, for example, the Shandong People's Publishing House printed a booklet generically titled *Birth Control Propaganda Handbook* explaining how to practice birth control. The booklet recommended several strategies for controlling births, some of which are still advocated today and some of which are of questionable utility. *Birth Control Propaganda Handbook* explained how to wash out contraceptive devices such as condoms and cervical caps for reuse, presumably because such items were relatively rare. Condoms were to be treated with talcum powder to ensure that they dried correctly and inflated or filled with water to check for punctures (this strategy was also practiced in Europe and the United States in the early twentieth century). These methods were echoed in other guides to sex from the 1930s and 1940s as well as in contemporaneous books, and health publications continued to recommend washing and reusing condoms through the 1970s.[74] At least one interviewee, an eighty-one-year-old woman who was a retired factory worker from Tianjin, told me that she and her husband used condoms briefly in the early 1960s after giving birth to their two children but switched to an intrauterine device (IUD) soon after because they felt that reusing condoms was unsanitary.[75]

Birth Control Propaganda Handbook also discussed how to make birth control products from scratch in the event that standard, ready-made options were unattainable. The authors offered three recipes for making homemade suppositories that could be inserted into the vagina before intercourse. The recipes involved rolling cotton into a ball (leaving a dangling 8-inch string, something like a contemporary tampon) and soaking it in diluted vinegar, hot soapy water, or wheat flour boiled with salt.[76] According to similar sources, one cotton ball could be used

[73] H. Yuan Tien, "Sterilization, Oral Contraception, and Population Control in China," *Population Studies* 18.3, 233.

[74] Xu, *Zuixin,* n.p. [75] Interview with author, Tianjin, July 2, 2019.

[76] Shandong weisheng ting (Shandong Department of Hygiene), *Jieyu xuanchuan shouce* (Birth Control Propaganda Handbook) (Jinan: Shandong People's Publishing House, 1958), 25–26.

repeatedly and would prevent sperm from entering the uterus.[77] The authors also recommended using the withdrawal method because it did not require any medicine or contraceptive devices, did not negatively impact a couple's sex life, and was easy to put into practice.

This guidebook included another method of birth control derived from Daoist practices: the "Urinary Tract Compression Method" or the "Acupuncture Point Method." The book explained that, like the withdrawal method, this approach had been in use since ancient times and did not require any medicines or birth control devices. During intercourse, when a man feels he is ready to orgasm, he should use his right hand to apply pressure for three minutes to the area between the anus and the base of the penis. After he has climaxed, he can release his hand. The pressure will have allowed him to orgasm without releasing any sperm, thus vastly decreasing the risk of pregnancy. The book's authors stated that if performed correctly, this method was very effective and aligned with traditional Chinese ideas about health and healing.

Other guides to birth control suggested alternative ways of reducing the risk of pregnancy but also argued that nonbiomedical birth control methods generally failed. For example, *General Knowledge about Birth Control*, published first in 1955 and then again in 1957 by the Shanghai Hygiene Press, conceded that many birth control methods were troublesome, unreliable, and potentially dangerous. Yet, the authors claimed that some of these methods have been practiced widely in China. One category of birth control methods was *jieyu biyunfa,* literally birth control methods that limit desire; by curbing the desire for sex, they could reduce the risk of pregnancy.[78] However, *General Knowledge* also cautioned that these methods were unreliable and could occasionally result in unintended pregnancy, which might disrupt a happy marriage. Other contraceptive methods included the withdrawal method (*tiwai paijingfa,* literally ejaculating outside the body), the rhythm method, and prolonging breastfeeding (because a woman is physiologically less likely to get pregnant while nursing). The book argued that, since time immemorial, rural couples wishing to have fewer children or to at least lengthen the intervals between pregnancies have deliberately prolonged nursing.[79]

[77] Shengmin Wang, "Tan anquanqi ji shiyanhu shuansai biyunfa" (Discussing the Safe Period and Salt Paste Suppository Birth Control Methods), *Hangzhou ribao* (Hangzhou Daily), April 19, 1957.

[78] Bray, *Technology and Gender*, 17.

[79] Today, however, it is known that this method is not equally effective for all women and that prolonging nursing for too long can cause a child to develop malnutrition; Song Hongjian and Zhao Zhiyi, *Biyun changshi* (General Knowledge about Birth Control) (Shanghai: Shanghai weisheng chubanshe, 1957), 18–19.

General Knowledge about Birth Control argued that in contrast to "unscientific" birth control methods of the past, new, scientific methods were entirely safe and much more effective. This was not in fact the case. Instead, as Masako Kohama has shown, the language and legitimacy of science were deployed to shift public opinion in favor of birth control.[80] In many ways, birth control medicines and devices in 1950s China were just as unreliable as earlier ones but appeared more trustworthy under the guise of scientific-sounding names and explanations. These so-called scientific approaches to contraception involved inserting acetic acid, soap, quinine, or mercury into the vagina before sex to dissolve sperm during intercourse.[81] While such approaches may have acted as effective spermicides, these substances – especially mercury – could cause long-term harm to a woman's body. The book suggested combining these homemade spermicides with other methods such as cervical caps and contraceptive jellies, cautioning that when used alone spermicides are not entirely effective. An alternative technique involved washing out the vagina after sex with water, soap, and vinegar to kill any leftover sperm. Similar birth control advice also appeared in Chinese and foreign contraceptive guides from the 1930s and 1940s.[82]

These types of contraceptive methods were held in such high regard that, as of 1955, the Chinese central government was domestically manufacturing boric acid and importing tannic acid, cocoa butter, lactic acid, gelatin, and quinine for use as birth control. According to contraceptive guides from the 1930s and 1940s, as well as internal CCP directives from the 1950s, fatty substances like cocoa butter or acidic materials like tannic or boric acid, could be inserted into the vagina before sex, thus serving as spermicides.[83] Historically, similar approaches had been used in Europe, the United States, and the premodern Muslim world to some effect.[84] High-profile Western birth control advocates like Margaret Sanger and Marie Stopes had even espoused these techniques

[80] Kohama, "Cong 'Feifa duotai' dao 'jihua shengyu,'" 348.
[81] Song and Zhao, *Biyun*, 24.
[82] Xu Wancheng, *Zuixin shiyan nannü biyunfa* (The Newest Experimental Birth Control Methods for Men and Women) (Shanghai: Guoguang shudian, 1941), n.p.
[83] Xu, *Zuixin*, n.p; Yan Yukuan, "Jieyu de lilun yu fangfa" (The Theory and Method of Birth Control) (Shanghai: Dadong Shuju, 1933), 110–111; TMA, X0191-C-000058.
[84] Daniel Winder, *Reproductive Control or a Rational Guide to Matrimonial Happiness* (Cincinnati: n.p., 1855), 48; Musallam, *Sex and Society in Islam*, 62–63; Andrea Tone, "Making Room for Rubbers: Gender, Technology, and Birth Control Before the Pill," *History and Technology* 18.1 (2010), 67.

in the 1920s and 1930s, though by the 1950s condoms and douches had largely supplanted these birth control methods in the West.[85]

Another less well-known form of birth control was also being produced en masse in China in the 1950s: Lysol.[86] Beginning in the 1920s, the company known for its powerful cleaning agents produced inexpensive feminine hygiene products. It was recommended that women douche with Lysol after sex to disinfect the vagina and kill any lingering sperm. Though largely ineffective and potentially life-threatening, douching with acerbic Lysol was a popular birth control method in the United States during the Great Depression up until the invention of oral birth control in the 1960s.[87] Douching was later discredited because it caused vaginal inflammation, destroyed the vagina's healthy flora, and failed to prevent pregnancy. Historian Andrea Tone attributes the success of Lysol in the United States to the collaboration between the scientific community and advertisers in endorsing the product.[88] As with other "scientific" methods of birth control, Lysol was appealing because it offered the promise of Western science, and therefore China sought to manufacture it with costly imported materials.

No example better demonstrates the varied approaches to birth control in 1950s China than the case of the tadpoles. Between 1956 and 1958, the Chinese government set about "scientifically" testing the folk practice of tadpole consumption as a form of contraception. The study concluded decisively that mice that consumed a daily diet of tadpoles and mated still became pregnant.[89] Likewise, fertile women who consumed a tadpole regimen also became pregnant under similar conditions.[90] The fact that women in Hangzhou and other parts of Zhejiang province were consuming live tadpoles a few days after menstruation to prevent conception inspired this study. Multiple folk remedies recommended this procedure, which had been in use since imperial times and allegedly proven successful for prostitutes in the Republican period.[91] The "cold element" in

[85] B. F. Musallam, *Sex and Society in Islam: Birth Control before the Nineteenth Century* (Cambridge: Cambridge University Press, 1983), 62–63; Connelly, *Fatal Misconception*, 101; Tone, "Making Room," 70.

[86] TMA, X0279-C-000312-004.

[87] Andrea Tone, *Devices and Desires: A History of Contraceptives in America* (New York: Hill and Wang), 170.

[88] Tone, *Devices*, 160.

[89] Xiao Feng, "Fu kedou buneng biyun" (Tadpoles Are Not Birth Control), *Hangzhou ribao* (Hangzhou Daily), July 7, 1957.

[90] Xiao, "Fu kedou buneng biyun" (Tadpoles Are Not Birth Control).

[91] "Qiqu shihua: gudai biyun kao tun kedou gan he tu?" (Unusual History: Ancient Birth Control Relied on Swallowing Tadpoles?" *Apple Daily*, November 20, 2013, https://hk.news.appledaily.com/china/realtime/article/20131120/51920129

tadpoles was believed to counteract the "heat" of pregnancy."[92] It was also said that these birth control methods were so powerful that if a woman consumed fourteen tadpoles on the first day and ten on the second, then she would become sterile.[93] Other similar methods for preventing pregnancy involved consuming snails, fish eggs, or bird eggs to induce abortion.[94] Newspaper articles in the late 1950s warned against "blindly consuming tadpoles as a form of birth control" and argued that not only were such methods ineffective but they also could cause infection.[95] Ironically, according to one anecdote from the 1950s, a young woman in rural China hoping to avoid pregnancy was actually inspired to try this birth control method when she read an article condemning it in the newspaper.[96] If anything, the debate over the efficacy of consuming tadpoles as birth control reveals that some women were attempting to regulate their own fertility and that biomedical ideas about reproduction were not neccesarily dominant.

The late imperial ideal of chastity was yet another important thread in the mix of information about sexuality and birth control.[97] Harriet Evans rightly argues that many of the narratives on sex in the 1950s were intended to safeguard the chastity of young women.[98] Though some reformers sought to put an end to the centuries-old trope of the loyal widow and the chaste bride, these ideals continued to shape narratives on female sexuality.[99] For example, women were frequently stigmatized for

[92] Zheng Tiantian, *Ethnographies of Prostitution in Contemporary China: Gender Relations, HIV/AIDS, and Nationalism* (New York: Palgrave MacMillan, 2009), 34.

[93] Shao Lizi, "Wo dui jieyu wenti de yidian yijian" (My Opinion on Birth Control), *Renmin ribao* (People's Daily), June 26, 1956; Xiao, "Fu kedou buneng biyun" (Tadpoles Are Not Birth Control).

[94] Sommer, "Abortion in Late Imperial China," 105.

[95] Xiao, "Fu kedou buneng biyun" (Tadpoles Are Not Birth Control); "Kedou biyun danfang wuxiao" (Tadpole Birth Control Home Remedy Is Not Effective), *Zhejiang ribao* (Zhejiang Daily), April 16, 1958; "Kedou biyun zhengzai shiyan, xianzai bu yao mangmu fuyong" (Using Tadpoles As Birth Control Is Currently Being Tested, For Now Do Not Blindly Consume Them), *Zhejiang ribao* (Zhejiang Daily), March 31, 1957.

[96] Nanfang Wang, "1950 niandai zhongguo jietou lugu de biyun guanggao" (Explicit Contraceptive Advertisements on the Streets of China in the 1950s), *Sina* (blog), September 7, 2015, http://blog.sina.com.cn/s/blog_4ac5b19f0102vzxm.html?tj=2.

[97] Siyen Fei, "Writing for Justice: An Activist Beginning of the Cult of Female Chastity in Late Imperial China" *Journal of Asian Studies* 71 (2012): 991–1012.

[98] Evans, *Women and Sexuality,* 107.

[99] Shanghai di er yixue yuan fu chan ke jiaoyanzu (Obstetrics and Gynecology Teaching and Research Group of Shanghai Number Two Medical College), *Qingnian hunyin weisheng* (Youth Marital Hygiene) (Shanghai: Shanghai kexue jishu chubanshe, 1958), 30–31.

losing their virginity before marriage, even if it occurred as a result of rape or sexual assault.[100]

An article published in 1951 in *Zhejiang ribao* (Zhejiang Daily) blamed premarital or extramarital sex for the ubiquity of infanticide. It charged that too many couples were having affairs that resulted in pregnancy. Afraid that their affairs would be discovered, women either secretly aborted their fetuses or drowned the babies after birth, fearing that their "bastards" (*si shengzi*) would face abuse for the rest of their lives. The article's author argued that abortion was not only dangerous, but like infanticide, it also amounted to murder. Publications like this, reminiscent of the type of antiabortion propaganda missionaries and reformers produced during the Republican period, were particularly prevalent during the early years of the PRC. Like much of the state-sponsored literature on sexual hygiene, these writings affirmed the centrality of marriage and women's roles as wives and mothers to the social order.

Class, Location, and Birth Control

Socioeconomic status and location-shaped birth control practices in important ways. For much of the 1950s, for example, the cost of contraceptives differed radically in different regions. For this reason, in 1957, the Ministry of Health ordered that regional price differences be eliminated through the creation of blanket national prices for the four primary types of birth control available within China: condoms, cervical caps, contraceptive ointments, and suppositories.[101] The Ministry of Health also sought to increase access to condoms by expanding the types of establishments where birth control products could be bought from a handful of hospitals to smaller health clinics, delivery stations, rural midwives, and even street vendors. Since 1954, some contraceptives – cervical caps, condoms, ointments, and suppositories – were being produced domestically while others were being imported to meet the rising demand for such products. As of 1957, imported contraceptives in Tianjin were more than twice the price of domestically produced ones, and this disparity continued to grow as the Ministry of Health repeatedly reduced the cost of contraceptives. According to the newly mandated national contraceptive prices, condoms imported from Japan would cost

[100] Jiang Liu, "Yi ge bei nüedai de nüxing" (An Abused Girl), *Xiandai Funü* (Modern Woman) 13 (1949): 28.

[101] TMA, X0092-Y-000123-007; The Ministry of Health's decision to eliminate regional differences was likely also related to the nationalization of commerce and business ownership in 1956.

0.12 *yuan* whereas condoms produced domestically at the Tianjin Rubber Products Factory and other places cost only 0.05 *yuan*. In 1955, the magazine *New Women of China* published an interview with a female cadre named Liu Yunqian. According to Liu, two of her colleagues – also elite women – had sent someone to Shanghai and Beijing to buy condoms on their behalf and had paid the exorbitant sum of 10 to 20 *yuan* per condom.[102] It is difficult to obtain accurate income statistics for this period, but two years later in 1957 the average urban couple in China had an annual expenditure of 220 *yuan*.[103] At 10 to 20 *yuan* each, condoms would have been a major expense, one only conceivable for wealthy elites. Liu, however, argued that if used correctly and washed after each use with soap, a condom should last one to two years if used once or twice a month (apparently she felt that having intercourse once or twice a month was representative of a "normal" sex life). The same article also stated that cervical caps cost only 3 *yuan* each and could be used repeatedly.[104] This price contrasted with the new cost of domestically produced caps, which were less than half as expensive as imported ones.[105]

Not only did the price of contraceptives differ by region and proximity to major urban centers, but the types of devices that were available also varied with location. The party center mandated that in medium- to large-sized cities preference be given to selling cervical caps, whereas in small cities condoms should primarily be sold.[106] A circular published in 1957 by the China National Pharmaceutical Company of Tianjin lamented that it was difficult to enforce national prices for contraceptives as this required physically visiting each place where contraceptives were being sold and checking for discrepancies. Because the company was understaffed, it struggled to undertake all of the necessary local inspections.[107] Anecdotes like this reveal the practical challenges associated with implementing uniform contraceptive prices on such a large scale.

A particularly surprising example of variation across class lines can be found in the case of what could be called "upscale" contraceptives. In 1957, lamenting that birth control products appeared "drab" (*dandiao*) and "old-fashioned" (*chenjiu*), the Chinese National Medical Company recommended that the styles of these products be updated to make them more appealing. Specifically, condoms and diaphragms would be sold in

[102] Zhou, "Biyun," 26.
[103] "Per Capita Annual Income and Expenditure Urban and Rural Households," All China Data Center, chinadataonline.org.
[104] Zhou, "Biyun," 26. [105] TMA, X0092-Y-000123-007. [106] Ibid.
[107] TMA, X0092-Y-000123-026.

cute boxes made of plastic or Bakelite (an early form of plastic) with accompanying perfumed sachets of talcum powder.[108] This marketing strategy tacitly acknowledged the materialistic consumer tendencies still apparent in 1950s China. More stylish birth control products could have been an effort to appeal to wealthier elites or style-conscious newlyweds.

Class and location even shaped the kind of customer service customers could expect with regard to birth control. In the cities, it was mandated that establishments selling birth control products have a male sales associate for selling male contraceptives and a female one for female products to make customers, especially shy young women, feel more at ease.[109] The staff members would be trained in the practice of birth control and able to provide instructions for use to customers. At this time, however, there was no such provision for sales of contraceptives in the countryside. Businesses selling contraceptives in rural China were few, under-stocked, and generally offered "poor" customer service.[110] In fact, the Tianjin government scolded local business for allowing their staff to make vulgar remarks about birth control during sales rather than taking the issue seriously.[111]

Even for those who did have access to businesses selling birth control, there were still many other obstacles to overcome. One issue was quality. While it is unclear whether the quality of contraceptives differed according to location, what is certain is that birth control was often unreliable. For example, in 1957 customers reported that certain types of diaphragms were not effective in keeping sperm out of the uterus. Instead of being elastic and conforming to the shape of the cervix, these diaphragms were stiff and left gaps through which the sperm could swim. Other problems included contraceptive jelly or ointment that dissolved during sex, thus losing its spermicidal function, and vaginal suppositories that caused skin irritation. Officials lamented that women who used faulty contraceptives and became pregnant were resistant to trying other methods of birth control in the future.[112] Another major issue in expanding access to birth control was supply. Factories manufacturing birth control exhausted the necessary raw materials for production (which then needed to be imported), and birth control went out of stock in stores for long periods of time. Contraceptive ointment, for example, was sold out in Tianjin for half of 1956. Supply issues tended to be more severe in rural areas, and the authorities complained that the selection of

[108] TMA, X0092-C-000429-039.
[109] TMA, X0092-C-000429-039; CCSL, SA201700000409; LMA, 14–16.
[110] TMA, X0092-Y-000123-007. [111] TMA, X0092-C-000429-039.
[112] LMA, 14–16.

birth control options was relatively limited outside of Shanghai and Guangzhou.[113] Finally, despite mandatory training, the staff selling birth control was not always knowledgeable about its use and could not correctly advise customers. Lack of affordable birth control options only further compounded these issues of quality and supply.[114]

As with contraceptives, access to birth control procedures, such as IUD insertions, abortions, and sterilizations, also varied greatly according to location, occupation, and class. While surgical records from the 1950s are rare and particularly difficult to access in China, the available records suggest that at least some individuals were having abortions and sterilizations at this time. As the population continued to grow and grain production lagged, birth control became a national imperative. Consequently, legal restrictions on access to abortion and sterilization surgery were repeatedly relaxed. Under certain conditions, men could now undergo sterilization surgery. Moreover, by 1957 (later in other cities) medical fees for abortion and sterilization were being subsidized in Shanghai.[115] As in the early 1950s, women demanding sterilization surgery needed their husband's permission as well as local health department approval to undergo surgery. In Shanghai, only doctors at designated public hospitals were allowed to perform abortions and sterilizations, whereas in Tianjin, doctors at both public and private medical facilities were permitted to perform these procedures.[116]

Other than female cadres and the dangerously ill, the first people to obtain access to birth control and contraceptive surgeries were those the government felt could contribute most to national productivity, namely workers and their family members. The results of the 1955 *New Women of China* survey mentioned earlier indicated that demand for birth control was relatively high among workers, yet it is unclear what role this played in the national government's decision to grant workers priority access to contraception. Internal government records and other literature revealed that the party was most concerned with the number of hours women workers could labor following a pregnancy.[117] Indeed, a 1958 article in *Zhejiang ribao* warned female workers at the Fuhua Silk Factory to use birth control when returning home to the countryside during the spring festival. The article cautioned that the risk of getting pregnant was greatest in the countryside due to ignorance about birth control and that production levels fall when women get pregnant and take maternity

[113] LMA, 14–16. [114] LMA, 14–16.
[115] SMA, B112-4-118-82; TMA, X0196-C-001315-002.
[116] SMA, B242-1-560; TMA, X0191-C-000058.
[117] People's Republic of China Ministry of Health Education Office, *Jiezhi*, n.p.

leave.[118] In terms of wealth, workers were far from the richest people in Mao's China and yet their superior class status in traditional Marxist terms and their critical role in production gave them privileged access to birth control.

In 1957, the State Council gave all workers and work unit staff in large cities like Shanghai and Tianjin permission to undergo abortions or sterilizations if giving birth would be detrimental to their health. The actual implementation of this policy, however, was left up to individual city governments, which worked with varying degrees of efficiency.[119] When workers were told that they would not receive paid leave following surgery because this type of treatment did not qualify for labor insurance (*laodong baoxian*), many argued that they could not handle the financial burden contraceptive surgery entailed. Ultimately, the national government agreed to give two weeks of paid leave for those who had surgery and to pay for their medical expenses to encourage birth planning.[120] That same year, the State Council also legalized abortions or sterilizations for healthy urban workers and staff but on the condition that all medical fees be paid out of pocket.[121]

Despite a slight loosening of restrictions on birth control surgery, abortions still made up a minute percentage of total pregnancies in the late 1950s. In the first quarter of 1958, in the medium-sized city of Hangzhou, for which there are no accurate population figures, 2,065 women had abortions.[122] Similarly, according to a six-year study in Shandong of 6,779 pregnant women, only 3.68 percent or 250 individuals sought abortion or sterilization surgery. The primary reason cited for undergoing abortion was financial difficulty (*jingji kunnan*), and office staff comprised the majority (56 percent) of those seeking abortions. Housewives (*jiating zhufu*) comprised another 23.2 percent, and the remaining 20.8 percent was made up of teachers, students, farmers, and medical staff.[123] Most of the women undergoing abortions were between twenty-five and twenty-nine years old and already had at least three children, whereas women undergoing sterilization had more than five children.[124] Abortion rates increased to 5.3 percent in 1958 and 8.4

118 Chen Yifang, "Chunjie huijia yao zhuyi biyun" (Pay Attention to Contraception When Returning Home for Spring Festival), *Zhejiang Daily*, February 14, 1958.

119 Scharping, *Birth Control*, 45. 120 SMA, B112-4-118-82.

121 TMA, X0044-Y-000378-013. 122 HMA, 087-003-0218.

123 At this time, the term *jiating zhufu* (housewife) included women who worked part-time for their neighborhood committees and did not have stable work units.

124 Chen Xiyi, Li Huaying, Sun Shusan, and Wang Yimin, "Dian xiyin rengong liuchanshu 250 li fenxi" (An Analysis of 250 Cases of Electrically Induced Abortion) *Shandong yikan* (Shandong Journal of Medicine) 1 (1964): 20–22.

percent in 1962, and the researchers attributed these trends to concomitant birth planning campaigns. Otherwise, abortion and sterilization rates remained relatively low into the early 1960s.

Anecdotal evidence further illuminates the disparities in access to contraception and abortion. The story of Wang Xu, one of my interviewees, offers an illustrative example. Born in 1931 in Nanjing, Wang was eighty-six years old when I met her in 2017. Shortly after the founding of the PRC and the establishment of the 1950 Marriage Law requiring both parties' consent for matrimony, Wang and her husband had a free love marriage. While still living in Nanjing, the couple had three children. At that time, Wang worked in the Office of Economic Planning while her husband had a post in another government office. In 1956, Wang's husband was relocated to a new position, and the couple moved to Shanghai with their three children. Wang immediately noticed a large cultural and intellectual gap between Nanjing and Shanghai – Shanghai was much more open, and birth control was more commonplace. In 1957, the couple had a fourth child, and in 1958 when Wang discovered she was pregnant with a fifth child, she told her husband that it was too much. They both agreed that it would be too difficult to raise and educate five children, so Wang went to the hospital and had a surgical abortion. Afterward, the couple tried using condoms to prevent pregnancy but found them to be a nuisance, so Wang had an IUD inserted, which she had for more than a decade. Whereas most foreign IUDs were made of plastic and had strings that dangled into the vagina for easier removal, Chinese IUDs were stainless steel rings, which often caused heavy menstrual bleeding and were intended to be tamper resistant.[125] Many of Wang's friends experienced problems with their IUDs, including infections, bleeding, and ineffectiveness in preventing pregnancy. Fortunately for Wang, she encountered none of these issues. She said that had she not left Nanjing her life course would have differed and she probably would have had five or six children. She was grateful for the abortion and for the IUD because these things allowed her to be a better mother and to live a happier life.[126]

As a point of comparison with the previous story, consider the account of an interviewee whose mother, Luo, though similar to Wang in many ways, had a very different experience with contraception. Luo was about the same age as Wang and also a Shanghai resident but a resident of the

[125] Susan Greenhalgh, "The Social Construction of Population Science: An Intellectual, Institutional, and Political History of Twentieth-Century Demography," *Comparative Studies in Society and History* 38, no. 1: 28.

[126] Interview with author, Shanghai, January 12, 2017.

suburban district of Baoshan. Unlike Wang, though, Luo was destitute and uneducated. When I asked my interviewee if her mother had had access to birth control in the 1950s, she looked deeply hurt. Her mother had given birth to seven children and abandoned four of them because she was too poor to take care of them. There had been nothing in the way of birth control or abortion, and frankly, she had not even known that these were options for some people.[127] In this case, although Luo lived in Shanghai, her class and low education level – and likely her home's distance from the city center – deprived her of access to the types of services Wang had enjoyed during the same period. When viewed in tandem, these cases demonstrate well the extent of healthcare disparities in 1950s urban China.

Infidelity, Birth Control, and Abortion

In addition to demographic factors, what other determinants contributed to the likelihood of using contraception or undergoing an abortion? Extramarital affairs, widespread to the point that city governments intervened, seem to have been a less documented but common reason for using birth control or undergoing an abortion.[128] This was due in no small part to the fact that although not technically illegal, local officials punished those who committed adultery, and out-of-wedlock pregnancies provided the most indicting evidence of marital infidelity.[129] In fact, one of my interviewees said he was sure that couples having extramarital sex at that time were using birth control but that no one would ever openly admit it.[130] This is not to say that contraception was used in every case of extramarital sex – as many unplanned births attest – but rather that it was perhaps used more in these instances than previously imagined.[131] Due to political sensitivity, individual cases of adultery and contraception use or abortion are difficult to uncover, as the records are mostly sealed. However, I have identified several particularly illuminating cases that highlight the close correlation between birth control use, abortion, and premarital or extramarital affairs.

Court records from a case in Poyang county, Jiangxi illustrate well the connection between infidelity and abortion. In the first case, Yu Chengmei, a 36-year-old husband and father, was having an affair with

[127] Interview with author, Shanghai, January 25, 2017.
[128] TMA, X0053-C-000737-096.
[129] Hangzhou Municipal Archive (HMA), 087-003-0362; SJTUA, Z1-9-222.
[130] Interview with author, Tianjin, September 17, 2016.
[131] ECNUA, As 0358-015-033; ECNUA, En 029-078-018.

a widow named Hu Yumei. Both individuals had the class label of "middle peasant." In June 1955, Hu realized that she was three months pregnant. Not wanting her to have the baby, Yu repeatedly visited a fifty-one-year-old woman named Hong in the neighboring village, begging her to help perform an abortion. Finally, Hong conceded and agreed to help, admitting to having previously assisted in fourteen other abortions. Relying on traditional methods for inducing abortion, Hong inserted an herbal concoction into Hu's vagina. Over the next few days, Hu experienced violent vaginal bleeding, and the pregnancy was aborted. The bleeding, however, never stopped and by the time Hu was brought to the hospital, her pulse had slackened and her body temperature was dropping. Not long after, Hu died from blood loss. When the authorities discovered what had happened, Yu and Hong were arrested for murder. Ultimately, Yu was sentenced to two years in prison while Hong received a seven-year sentence.[132]

Although Yu, whose idea it was to abort the pregnancy, received little criticism in the official case record, the court listed extensive reasons for punishing Hong. The record stated that she had sought personal profit from offering abortions and that she had maimed pregnant women and endangered the lives of children. Moreover, the court accused Hong of sustaining evil practices from the pre-1949 period, when a "feudal" marriage system and poverty had led women to seek wrongful abortions.[133] The court declared that land reform and the 1950 Marriage Law pronouncing marriage a free choice were intended to correct some of these backward practices, yet enduring feudal practices and incorrigible individuals like Hong were to blame for out-of-wedlock pregnancies. While Yu played the most active role in the case (it is unclear whether Hu even wanted the abortion), Hong suffered the harshest consequences and her crimes were framed in terms of "feudal thinking." Perhaps it is not a surprise that Hong suffered the gravest punishment, as the flexible, one-size-fits-all political category of "feudal" practices had long been associated with women. Nowhere in the file is there an assessment of the legality of Hu's abortion, an interesting omission that marks this case as unique from similar ones during the Republican period. While abortion was punishable by law in rural Jiangxi at this time Hu's death seems to have been the main reason for pressing charges against Yu

[132] SJTUA, Z1–3-407.

[133] Wang Zheng has shown how socialist feminists imbued the political term "feudalism" with gendered meanings so that it came to encompass a range of ideas including sexism, patriarchy, and misogyny. Wang Zheng, *Finding Women in the State: A Socialist Feminist Revolution in the People's Republic of China, 1949–1964* (Berkeley: University of California Press, 2017), 102.

and Hong. Had Hu survived the procedure, perhaps the abortion would have gone unnoticed.[134]

The second case demonstrating the correlation between out-of-wedlock pregnancy and abortion is that of Yao, a young man in the Donggou Brigade of Jilin province. Although he was raised in a poor peasant family, Yao was able to attend medical school, became a party member, and was appointed as a doctor of internal medicine in the small city of Taiyuan. In 1951, however, Yao was accused of assaulting (*jianwu*) and impregnating Li, one of the nurses with whom he worked.[135] The case file did not explain the details of the situation but ultimately Yao performed an abortion on the pregnant Li, who died as a result of the surgery. Whether the abortion was done at Li's request is unclear. In fact, it is uncertain what role Li played at all in the case. What is apparent is that Yao's gender and privileged position gave him access to the knowledge and resources to perform the abortion. In China at that time, doctors did not have a high social status but they had information at their disposal. Regardless, the procedure cost Li her life and commenced a downward spiral for Yao into poverty, delinquency, and persecution. Whether real or fabricated by his enemies, Yao's charges – adultery, embezzlement, murder, stealing hospital equipment, attempting to sell his starving niece into prostitution, and criticizing the party – were ultimately withdrawn in 1984. Li's case, on the other hand, was not revisited and she was denied any agency even after death; her voice could not be heard in the archival record.[136]

Contraception also seems to have been a more likely option in unsanctioned relationships. For example, in 1958 a married Beijing bus driver named Zheng Xiaoming initiated an affair with his female colleague, Xu Lu. According to a political confession, Xu and Zheng had sex constantly, often as much as three times a day. Zheng assured Xu that she would not get pregnant because he always used a condom that he carried with him for this purpose. Presumably, Zheng washed out the condom after each use and treated it with talcum powder so he could reuse it. The relationship only ended on November 30, 1965 when the couple came under fire for licentiousness and hooligan-like behavior.[137] As in the

[134] SJTUA, Z1-3-407.

[135] Yao was initially accused of having "improper relations" (*bu zhengdang de guanxi*) with Li, a common euphemism for extramarital sex, but the court ruled that Yao had assaulted Li. As Chapter 5 reveals, the language surrounding permissible sex evolved with the changing political context, making it difficult to ascertain whether Li consented to intercourse.

[136] ECNUA, En 0351-150-012.

[137] Stanford University Cadre Archive (SUCA), Box 33.

previous abortion case, the desired goal of preventing conception was achieved, but in this case both parties benefited from the ability to regulate their fertility and conceal their extramarital relationship.

If these cases are at all representative – and there are many more like them – fear of being caught having sex outside of marriage seems to have been a common motivation for using contraception or resorting to abortion. That said, the likelihood of contraception or abortion appearing in the archive in relation to premarital sex or adultery is also high since such relationships – and sometimes unsanctioned abortions – were considered criminal. Nevertheless, the staggering number of cases of affairs linked to abortions suggests a more substantial link. In all of these cases, the individuals involved sought to take circumstances into their own hands. More often than not, the stakes were higher for women, and naturalized ideas about gender shaped legal adjudication.

Conclusion

Initially, access to contraceptives was severely limited, but grain shortages, mass starvation, and labor inefficiency produced a gradual loosening of these restrictions, with burdens falling unevenly on men and women. Rather than seeking to enhance individual reproductive decision-making, party leaders looked to birth planning as a way to modernize society, deepen political governance, and optimize (women) workers' labor potential. Despite these ambitious goals, birth control practices in 1950s China differed noticeably according to class, location, and education level, a trend that continued even after the One Child Policy's implementation.

For China, the 1950s marked the beginning of a slow and messy transition from haphazard, unsystematic regulation of reproduction to attempted hegemonic population control. In reality, the state's growing attention to reproduction resulted in a disproportionately large focus on women's bodies. As we will see in Chapter 4, from the perspectives of both individuals and the state, the 1960s would resolve some earlier issues while creating new ones.

4 "Birth Planning Has Many Benefits": Weaving Family Planning into the Fabric of Everyday Life, 1959–1965

The Great Leap Forward is often remembered for the historic famine it produced. The population of China stood at 672,070,000 in 1959, but the Great Famine (1959–1962) – also known as the three years of difficulty (*sannian kunnan shiqi*) – caused an estimated 18 to 30 million deaths.[1] Despite widespread starvation and the staggering death toll of the Great Leap Forward, the national population increased steadily through the 1960s due to high fertility and reduced infant and child mortality.[2] In fact, the only time China's national population (as opposed to the population growth rate) actually decreased between 1949 and 1981 was in the years 1960 and 1961.[3] By 1966, the national population had swelled to 742,060,000, of which 18 percent (133,130,000 people) lived in urban areas.[4]

Though some scholars have argued that official efforts to counter population growth were abandoned during the Great Leap, overlooked evidence suggests that that was not entirely the case.[5] Indeed, women in major cities continued to have voluntary abortions and sterilizations. As during the late 1950s, some high-ranking cadre women who did not have time for more children were granted official permission to undergo abortions, but the party stipulated that a woman could only have an abortion for this reason once every three years.[6] Non-cadre women with four or more children and economic needs could also petition for and

[1] National Birth Planning Committee Integrated Planning Division, *Chinese Birth Planning Statistical Yearbook*, 1.

[2] Kaufman et al., "Family Planning Policy and Practice in China: A Study of Four Rural Counties," *Population and Development Review* 15.4 (1989): 708.

[3] National Birth Planning Committee Integrated Planning Division, *Chinese Birth Planning Statistical Yearbook*, 1.

[4] Judith Banister, *China's Changing Population* (Stanford: Stanford University Press, 1991), 332.

[5] Thomas Scharping, *Birth Control in China, 1949–2000: Population Policy and Demographic Development* (London: RoutledgeCurzon, 2003), 47.

[6] Jung Chang, *Wild Swans: Three Daughters of China* (New York: Touchstone, 2003), 393

undergo sterilization surgery, as one of my interviewees did.[7] In cities like Shanghai, contraceptive use continued to grow, but finding new channels for accessing birth control was more difficult during this period.[8]

Following the catastrophe of the Great Leap Forward, the party took a less ambiguous stance on birth control. Seeking to promote the ideological and material need for birth control, the CCP developed new mechanisms to extend state control over sexuality. Shanghai was at the forefront of these efforts, with its campaigns providing a national model for implementing birth planning. Effectively paving the way for "hard," or coercive, birth control implementation in future decades, local officials began testing more extensive "soft" tactics – cultural productions, focus groups, and exhibits of contraceptives – to encourage birth planning.[9]

Although these fragmented efforts were slightly more systematic and localized than in the 1950s, resource shortages, contradictory state directives, and individual resistance to birth control presented challenges to the consolidation of state power over reproduction. Moreover, the conflicting opinions of officials, medical practitioners, and patients regarding the efficacy of traditional medicine in family planning further complicated the situation. In this context, contraceptive practices involved ongoing negotiation among diverse actors: provincial and local birth planning authorities, as well as individuals and their families.

Birth Planning as Art and Entertainment

The food shortages associated with the Great Leap Forward provided greater impetus to promote the voluntary delaying of marriage and childbearing. Foreshadowing the renewed national emphasis on family planning after the Great Leap, as early as the late 1950s some cities, such as Shanghai, Tianjin, and even Luoyang, had already created birth planning small groups, but they lacked the funding and support to make much of an impact.[10] In 1963, the Central Committee formally announced that late marriage and birth planning should be studied and implemented in urban China. A few months later in early 1964, the Birth Planning Office of the State Council was established and similar offices were formed in certain provinces and cities, beginning the process of

[7] Interview with author, Shanghai, December 20, 2016.
[8] Kohama, "Jihua shengyu de kaiduan," 118.
[9] Susan Greenhalgh and Edwin Winckler make the distinction between soft and hard birth control policy tactics in *Governing China's Population.*
[10] *Luoyang shizhi* (Luoyang Gazetteer), October 15, 2009, http://www.lydqw.com/DB/BookContent.aspx?BookID=200904080002&Content=Digital.

institutionalizing family planning.[11] As part of this broader ideological campaign, provincial and municipal Departments of Public Health produced cultural works designed to weave birth planning into the local cultural fabric. These works included films, songs, plays, and exhibits, each of which was accompanied by discussion groups and lectures.

The methods used to promote birth planning mimicked and foreshadowed those employed in other Maoist campaigns. Jennifer Altehenger has argued that Mao-era legal propaganda sought to affirm the correct interpretation of new state directives by linking certain policies to the moral and political categories of right and wrong. Similarly, cultural workers promulgating family planning sought not only to reverse the earlier verdict on birth control (for those who were not aware that the official policy had changed) but also to render the new birth planning directives legible to the masses.[12] Like Altehenger, Brian DeMare and Denise Ho have also made important observations about state tools of popular mobilization that are relevant to understanding birth planning campaigns. DeMare argues of the Land Reform era that state-sponsored literature and art forms provided "scripts" for enacting state-directed political campaigns, giving the masses a vocabulary and set of fictional scenarios to reenact in real life.[13] Not so differently, Ho posits that Maoist exhibitions – museums, work unit exhibits, and commissioned posters and pamphlets, among others – could both modernize and mobilize, introducing the masses to the vocabulary and slogans of revolution and curating a specific political narrative that legitimated the CCP.[14] The birth planning propaganda of the 1960s ignited revolution in its own way: urging mass participation in family planning, providing narratives for promoting birth planning in different contexts, and laying the foundation for the formalization of birth planning discussion groups and films under the One Child Policy.

Following the Central Committee decree to promote family planning, mandatory classes about birth planning and hygiene, arranged by gender and marital status, became increasingly common in workplaces across much of urban China. In what Foucault described as the "incitement to discourse" through which normative sexuality was constructed and legitimized, workers met in groups to discuss the benefits of birth planning, to

[11] White, *China's Longest Campaign*, 59.

[12] Jennifer Altehenger, *Legal Lessons: Popularizing Laws in the People's Republic of China, 1949–1989* (Cambridge, MA: Harvard University Press, 2018), 13–14.

[13] Brian Demare, *Land Wars: The Story of China's Agrarian Revolution* (Stanford: Stanford University Press, 2019), 98.

[14] Denise Ho, *Curating Revolution: Politics on Display in Mao's China* (Cambridge: Cambridge University Press, 2017), 13.

express their fears about using birth control, and to provide feedback on contraceptives they had tried.[15] Moreover, local departments of health were tasked with producing birth control guides and exhibits. In 1963, for example, Jiangsu province's Department of Health produced 167,000 copies of birth control guides and posters, as well as broadcasts, exhibits, slide shows, and blackboard bulletins about birth control viewed by 2,557,627 people.[16]

Provincial-level Departments of Public Health (*sheng weisheng ting*) also ordered that films promoting birth planning be screened in both the cities and the countryside, with particular emphasis on more crowded areas.[17] Such films sought to introduce the basics of sex education, as well as "scientific" family planning methods, including abortion and male and female sterilization.[18] Likewise, the films discouraged couples from using dangerous methods of birth control, namely homemade abortifacients and home abortion surgeries.[19]

Each participating province's and city's Department of Public Health created a unique and comprehensive set of directions for the screening of birth planning films. While some cities had already issued these instructions in the late 1950s, perhaps because of limited access to birth control products, film screenings only seem to have become common in the 1960s when curbing population growth became a greater priority.[20] In Guangdong province, during screenings of birth planning films, male and female audience members were to be organized into separate sections or on separate floors of local theaters for viewing. According to the regulations, children and foreigners were not permitted to watch. Circulation of the films was also strictly prohibited, especially in areas where many ethnic minorities lived.[21] Perhaps officials feared that the possibility of state-led family planning would spark further social unrest among marginalized ethnic groups already dissatisfied with Communist Party rule.

Organizing film screenings involved collaboration between a number of entities. In Tianjin, birth planning films were advertised in the *Jiankang bao* (Health Times) and then viewings were scheduled at various local factories and enterprises and in residential areas. The Women's

[15] TMA, X0032-C-000153; Michel Foucault, *The History of Sexuality, Vol. 1: An Introduction* (New York: Pantheon Books, 1978), 33.

[16] Huo Xuanji, "Dayuejin zhihou de jihua shengyu, 1962–1966" (Family Planning Policy after the Great Leap Forward, 1962–1966) (Master's thesis, Nanjing University, 2015), 36.

[17] Kohama, "From 'Criminal Abortion' to 'Birth Planning'" 346; LMA, 14–16.

[18] GMA, 307-1-353-94~94. [19] LMA, 14–16.

[20] Interview with author, Shanghai, August 10, 2016. [21] GMA, 307-1-353-94~94.

Figure 4.1 *"Biyun shuang"* (Advertisement for contraceptive cream), 1957.
Source: Ni juedui mei jianguo 50 nian qian wuhan jietou biyun guanggao (Birth control advertisements on the streets of Wuhan fifty years ago you have never seen before). *Sohu*, May 6, 2016. https://www.sohu.com/a/73608709_199944.

Federation, trade unions, factories, and other local organizations also arranged exhibitions of contraceptives, lectures, and contraceptive sales stations as a complement to the birth control films.[22] In one instance, the Tianjin Foreign Trade Committee (*waimao dangwei*) held a birth control exhibition that occupied a space of fifty-six square meters and consisted of 124 billboards explaining the benefits of delayed marriage, birth control, abortion, IUD insertion, and sterilization.[23] Similar arrangements for film viewings and accompanying events were made in Shanghai, Luoyang, and other cities.[24] In Wuhan, billboards advertising specific contraceptive products even appeared on street corners (Figure 4.1).[25]

[22] TMA, X0092-C−000429−038; TMA, X0032-C-000153.
[23] TMA, X0033-Y-000203.
[24] CCSL, SA201700000409; ECNUA, Acu 0357-013-022; LMA, 14–16; Qingdao Municipal Archive (QDMA), C0056–001-00379.
[25] Ni juedui mei jianguo 50 nian qian wuhan jietou biyun guanggao (Birth control advertisements on the streets of Wuhan fifty years ago you have never seen before), *Sohu*, May 6, 2016, https://www.sohu.com/a/73608709_199944.

Yet, overt references to sexuality and the mechanics of reproduction were not universally welcomed. One 70-year-old man from Shanghai mentioned having seen a birth planning film in 1964 when he was twenty years old, which was also the legal marriage age at that time. Being of age, he and his fellow workers were forced to watch the film, though neither the men nor the women could bear to look at the screen. After the screening, a cadre asked the viewers whether they had sex lives (*xing shenghuo*); no one would respond and the young women looked especially uncomfortable.[26] Similarly, while the city-wide birth control exhibits were extremely well attended, especially those in populous areas like Beijing and Shanghai, some cadre reports confessed that viewers were reluctant to engage with birth planning propaganda.[27] In Hangzhou, for example, some older residents reportedly turned bright red with embarrassment upon viewing the birth planning exhibits. To the annoyance of parents and other spectators, children and teenagers would repeatedly follow the adults into the birth planning exhibits, where the youths would view the contraceptives with relish (*jinjinyouwei*), making an already awkward scenario even more uncomfortable.[28]

Even without the presence of curious children, birth planning work was sometimes considered taboo. At the Changhua Cotton Cloth Factory in Shanghai, for example, birth planning advocates hung birth control posters around their factory, pasting them on the walls of the women's restroom, in the women's dormitory, and in the factory entrance, yet according to factory reports, most women workers refused to look at the posters because they felt uncomfortable doing so. Only through repeated thought meetings did they come around to the idea of publicly viewing birth planning posters.[29] Over the next decade, this gradual transition also occurred at the macro level, with repeated public articulations of sexuality making a once more private topic thoroughly public.

In an effort to reach a broad audience of both literate and illiterate people, local work units and birth planning commissions also produced songs, plays, booklets, picture-story books (*lianhuanhua*), and posters (Figure 4.2) promoting the benefits of late marriage and birth planning.[30] Many of these works described similar situations: parents with traditional views tried to convince their teenage children to marry early but the

[26] The legal marriage age was raised to 18 for women and 20 for men in 1950. Interview with author, Shanghai, August 10, 2016.
[27] CCSL, SA201700000409.
[28] CUHKA, "Zhejiang sheng zai jieyu gongzuo zhong de yixie pianxiang" (Some Deviations in Birth Control Work in Zhejiang Province).
[29] CCSL, SA201700000409.
[30] ECNUA, Acu 0357-030-026; ECNUA, Acu 0357-030-002.

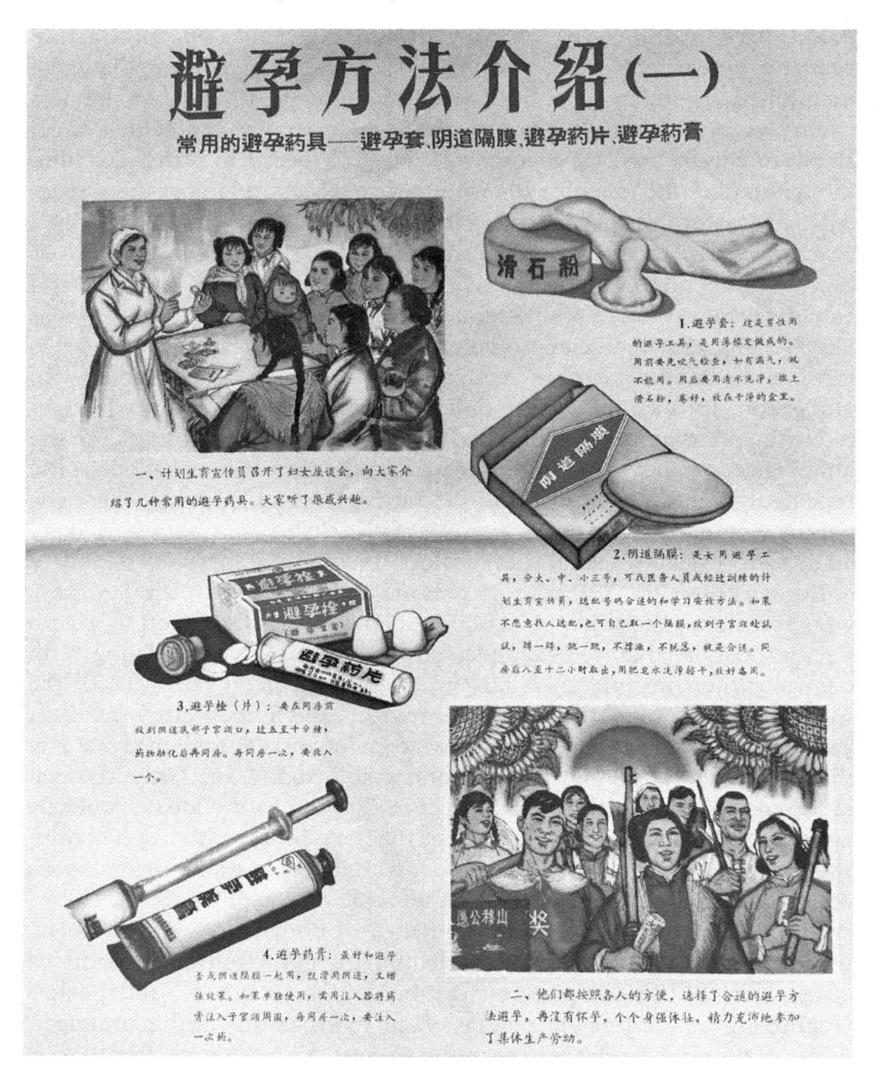

Figure 4.2 Birth planning poster introducing different birth control methods, 1966.
Source: Shandong Provincial Birth Planning Work Committee, Shandong Province Department of Hygiene, “Rengong liuchuan” (Abortion), poster, 1966.

youths wished to postpone marriage in accordance with the party's late marriage campaign. This caused problems at home, but ultimately all parties agreed that marrying later was in the young peoples' best interest. The youths argued that they would be overwhelmed and exhausted working or studying and raising children, that their bodies were not fully developed, and that early marriage was backward. In other works, young adult friends debated the benefits and drawbacks of early marriage. Three universal assumptions undergirded these works of propaganda: that marriage is a precondition for sexuality and childbearing, that all couples who marry have children, and that all newlyweds have children immediately. The efficacy of cultural works in influencing personal reproductive decisions, I suspect, relied largely on a shared commitment to these ideas, and for many young women, a commitment to postponing the burdens of motherhood and married life. One ditty from Shanxi province advocating delayed marriage is as follows:

"The Benefits of Late Marriage"
(Mother Is Not Confused Ditty)

MOTHER: This year I am 55 and I need to find my son a wife.
I have no money to do this, so I worry.

MOTHER: My oldest daughter is named Zhang Chunxiu. This year she is 19.
She is not married, this is really confusing. Ayo!
She is not married, this is really confusing.

MOTHER: We just held a meeting calling Chunxiu to take the lead in implementing late marriage. Mother is angry! Ayo! Mother is angry.

DAUGHTER: The party proposed implementing late marriage. Chunxiu will take the lead and not fall behind. She took a written pledge. Ayo! She took a written pledge.

DAUGHTER: I heard mother from the beginning, so long as you speak clearly and with reason.
Mother, she is not confused. Ayo! Mother, she is not confused.

DAUGHTER: Mother, you look here. This is my pledge.
Guess what the circumstances are (for signing the pledge). Ayo! You guess.

MOTHER: No need to look or to guess, in order to give your brother a wife.
You have no way of marrying later. Ayo! You have no way of marrying later.

DAUGHTER: These days marriage is one's own decision. Marriage as a business deal should be abolished. Mother, you are very confused! Ayo! Mother, you are very confused!

MOTHER: I understand that marriage is a free choice, but getting married is like wearing clothes. No matter what you still have to wear them. Mother is not confused. Ayo! Mother is not confused.

DAUGHTER: Older brother is 20 and I am 19. Our bodies are not fully developed yet.
There is no benefit to worrying about marriage. Ayo! Mother, you are really confused!

MOTHER: Men marry, women marry; this is handed down from our ancestors. I was only 15 when I married.
Who wouldn't praise me for being a good wife? Ayo! I am not confused!

DAUGHTER: In those days, that was the social system. Having children early (these days) is a crime. It wastes one's youth. Ayo! Mother, you are really confused!

MOTHER: Early childbearing brings early happiness and prevents the issue of having no one to take your place when you get old.
Productive labor involves suffering. Ayo! I am not confused!

DAUGHTER: If early childbearing brings early happiness, why didn't Big Brother and Big Sister do it?
As soon as mother mentioned it, her tears flowed like two rivers. Ayo! As soon as mother mentioned it, her tears flowed like two rivers.

MOTHER: You must never speak of Big Sister and Big Brother.[31] As soon as it was mentioned, I wanted to cry.
You cannot control whether you endure calamities and suffer hardships. Ayo! Do you all blame me?

DAUGHTER: Early childbearing is not merely about suffering hardships. Production and studying are both delayed.
Mother, you are very confused. Ayo! Mother, you are very confused.

MOTHER: You only have to speak clearly and with reason. Others will listen (to your opinion) and be convinced.
I am not confused at all. Ayo! I am not confused at all.

MOTHER: Your marriage is your own decision, age 28 or 25.
I will not be so troublesome again. Ayo! I will not be so troublesome again.

DAUGHTER: Mother really is a good mother, agreeing to take the lead in delaying marriage.

[31] It would seem that Chunxiu's older siblings also disobeyed their mother's order to marry and have children at a young age.

MOTHER: Chunxiu really is a good daughter, taking the lead in implementing late marriage.

DAUGHTER: Mother is not confused. Ayo! Mother is not confused.

MOTHER: I am not confused. Ayo! Mother is not confused.[32]

Playing into the stereotype of older women as irrational and superstitious – the embodiment of pre-Communist China – the storyline centered around a daughter trying to convince her middle-aged mother to align her views with those of the new society. Whereas her blubbering mother harbored a "feudal" preference for early marriage, the daughter was armed with clarity and scientific ideas about physiology, which allowed her to calmly persuade her mother of the value of delaying marriage. According to this narrative, under the guidance of the Communist Party and its modern ideology, objective reason ultimately prevailed over subjective traditions grounded in ignorance and emotion.

A play produced and performed in Tianjin by the Tianjin Food Factory Amateur Art Troupe in 1963, though set at a factory rather than in the countryside, contains similar themes about overcoming the traditional desire for early marriage to enable greater production levels. The play, however, was more explicit about the effects of early marriage on maternal health and the advantages of family planning. It also sought to counter the enduring preference for boys and emphasized that large families limit a young mother's ability to participate in critical political meetings. The play, set in the summer of 1957, focused on three young women. The eldest, Lizhu, was twenty-six years old and already married. Twenty-two-year-old Xiujuan put off marriage in order to work and study. The youngest, Chunmei, who had just turned eighteen, wanted to marry early because eighteen was the minimum marriage age for women. Her comrades warned her that marrying early would negatively impact her work and study, while having children early would be hard on her immature body. They urged her to wait until age twenty-six to get married and age twenty-eight to have her first child, like her friends Xiujuan and Lizhu.

Chunmei did not listen and got married. Five years later, Chunmei had three children and was pregnant with the fourth. She was incredibly busy with strenuous household duties, and her productivity levels at work were low. She was also frequently absent from work. Moreover, her

[32] ECNUA, Acu 0357-030-043.

household was noisy and chaotic, she missed political meetings, and she was perpetually exhausted. Meanwhile, Xiujuan was still not married and her mother nagged her to hurry up and have a child so that she could hold her grandson. Xiujuan responded that the party had called on her and other young people to take the lead in delaying marriage. As Chunmei argued with her husband about what to do with so many children, the birth planning committee told Chunmei that, like the economy, pregnancies must be planned too. This was a reference to Chairman Mao's 1957 speech to the Enlarged Third Plenary Session of the Eighth Central Committee of the CCP, in which he argued that unmitigated population growth was at odds with a socialist planned economy, so childbearing should be planned as well.[33] The play continued, arguing that overpopulation was bad for production and that the best solution was sterilization surgery. This was a radical departure from ten years earlier when a larger population was seen as the key to increasing production rather than in opposition to it. The birth planning committee told Chunmei that it would be easy to get sterilized after she gave birth to her fourth child and that men and women contribute equally in the new society so there was no need to try for more sons. Finally, Chunmei was sterilized and her decision was honored as a birth planning victory. She also helped her production group achieve record production levels, and Chunmei was deemed a model for other young women.[34] Like the ditty earlier, this predictable play promoted delayed marriage and birth planning in response to two central concerns of the CCP, increasing worker productivity and preserving maternal health (likely so as not to overburden the fragile healthcare system).[35]

Other works of propaganda offered visual representations of these themes. Examples of drawings and posters portraying the benefits of family planning were numerous and could be found throughout much of China in the early 1960s. The poster "*Jihua shengyu, yifeng yisu*" (Plan Births, Change the Customs) is one such example produced in Tianjin in 1963 (Figure 4.3).[36] The four sections illustrate the four primary benefits of practicing birth control: greater production, improved work and study,

[33] White, *China's Longest Campaign*, 60. [34] TMA, X0032-C-000153-18.
[35] GPA, 233-2-267-33-39; BMA, 100-001-00897.
[36] "Jihua shengyu, yifeng yisu" (Plan Births, Change the Customs), 1963, "Zhe xie jianzheng le jihua shengyu de haibao..." (Posters Attesting to Birth Planning..." *Shishe shishi de boke* (The Collecting Historical Events Blog), March 24, 2016, http://blog.sina.com.cn/s/blog_e39346e40102wej2.html.

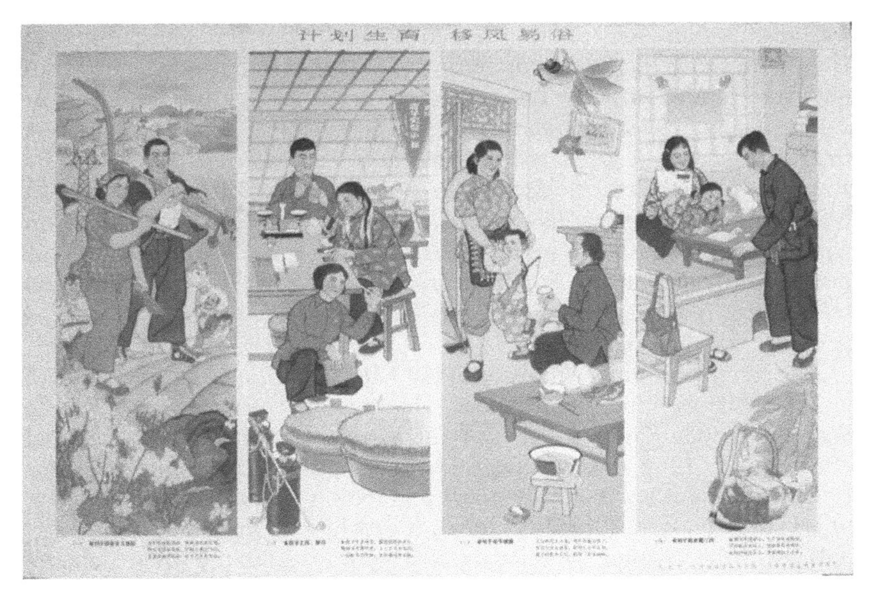

Figure 4.3 "*Jihua shengyu, yifeng yisu*" (Plan births, change the customs), 1963.
Source: US National Library of Medicine.

enriched health, and more time for educating and raising the next generation. The family members are depicted with plump, ruddy faces, smiling and enjoying hard work, abundant food, and family time. The subtext suggests that in contrast to the pre-Communist years, under the Communist regime women can labor in the fields and conduct scientific research alongside men, even while raising children and caring for the elderly.

In the early 1960s, similar posters were printed as far away as Guangdong and Xinjiang provinces. One poster from Guangdong, entitled "*A Li de fannao*" (A Li's Troubles), depicts a young woman nicknamed A Li, who is struggling with too many children and exhausting responsibilities (Figure 4.4).[37] A Li is pictured attempting to feed, bathe, and clothe her five small children. She is shown tilling the fields,

[37] "A Li de fannao" (A Li's Troubles), 1964, "Zhe xie jianzheng le jihua shengyu de haibao…" (Posters Attesting to Birth Planning…" *Shishe shishi de boke* (The Collecting Historical Events Blog), March 24, 2016, http://blog.sina.com.cn/s/blog_e39346e40102wej2.html.

washing clothes, and bathing naked babies under the scorching sun. Even with the help of a grandparent, A Li struggles to meet the needs of her large family. In each frame of the poster, A Li looks increasingly exhausted and overwhelmed until she discovers birth control. In the final frame, she is depicted without her children. Instead, A Li is standing alongside her husband in their lush fields, the implication being that birth control has not only given her more time to focus on agricultural production but has also enriched her marriage.[38] This poster tacitly affirms the importance of conjugal love, or at least marital harmony, while reinforcing the idea that what is good for the family is good for the nation.

A poster promoting birth planning in Xinjiang offers a final example of visual birth planning propaganda. This poster, "*Jihua shengyu haochu duo*" (Birth Planning Has Many Benefits), printed in Xinjiang's capital of Urumqi in 1964, contains text in both Simplified Chinese and Uyghur script to make it legible to the local population (Figure 4.5).[39] Xinjiang province in western China is known for its large population of individuals from the Uyghur Muslim minority group. Like the other posters, this one framed the benefits of birth planning in terms of improving health and productivity. Even though the figures pictured in the poster are phenotypically indistinguishable from Han Chinese, the propaganda messages have been tailored slightly to fit the particular nationalistic goals of the CCP in minority regions. The six frames, from top left to bottom right, highlight the benefits of birth planning: strengthening socialism, expanding production and study among the masses, raising and training "red" successors, planning family life, protecting maternal and child health, and bringing health and prosperity to the people.

Similar messages can be found in contemporaneous birth planning posters from other regions of China, yet these ideas take on additional layers of meaning in the context of China's so-called borderland regions.[40] Given the Communist Party's emphasis on quelling social

[38] "Zhe xie jianzheng le jihua shengyu de haibao…" (Posters Attesting to Birth Planning…) *Shishe shishi de boke* (The Collecting Historical Events Blog), March 24, 2018, http://blog.sina.com.cn/s/blog_e39346e40102wej2.html; unfortunately, the poor resolution of this image makes it nearly impossible to analyze the accompanying text.

[39] "Jihua shengyu haochu duo" (Birth Planning Has Many Benefits), 1964; "Zhe xie jianzheng le jihua shengyu de haibao…" (Posters Attesting to Birth Planning…) *Shishe shishi de boke* (The Collecting Historical Events Blog), March 24, 2016, http://blog.sina.com.cn/s/blog_e39346e40102wej2.html.

[40] For more on the history of ethnic classification in the PRC, see Thomas Mullaney, *Coming to Terms with the Nation: Ethnic Classification in Modern China* (Berkeley: University of California Press, 2010).

Figure 4.4 “*A Li de fannao*” (A Li’s troubles), 1964.
Source: “Zhe xie jianzheng le jihua shengyu de haibao…” (Posters Attesting to Birth Planning…” *Shishe shishi de boke* (The Collecting Historical Events Blog), March 24, 2016. http://blog.sina.com.cn/s/blog_e39346e40102wej2.html.

Figure 4.5 *“Jihua shengyu haochu duo”* (Birth planning has many benefits), 1964.
Source: “Zhe xie jianzheng le jihua shengyu de haibao…” (Posters Attesting to Birth Planning…” *Shishe shishi de boke* (The Collecting Historical Events Blog), March 24, 2016. http://blog.sina.com.cn/s/blog_e39346e40102wej2.html.

unrest and bringing ethnic minorities into the national fold, the connection between citizenship and hygiene practices is particularly critical. The implication is that birth planning, as well as the particular vision of society it entails, is part and parcel of citizenship in the modern Chinese nation. In other words, overcoming ethnic differences and obtaining the same rights as Han Chinese involve practicing family planning. Just as this message is racialized, it is also gendered. In contrast to the posters from Tianjin and Guangdong, which seem to be directed entirely at a female audience, the image of an athletic-looking man throwing a shotput in the final frame suggests an attempt to appeal to masculinity. The message seems to be that while women can attain better health, raise healthier, smarter children, and be more productive through birth planning, men, particularly Uyghur men, can bring honor, prosperity, and strength to the nation/ethnic group (*minzu*).

When I interviewed a forty-four-year-old Uyghur academic about her and her mother's perceptions of birth planning in China, she said that neither she nor her mother agreed with this type of state-mandated family planning. Born and raised in Korla, Xinjiang, my interviewee (we'll call her Alim) is the daughter of a water engineer and an elementary school teacher. Alim taught Mandarin to Uyghur elementary school students in Xinjiang for ten years, and after obtaining her master's degree in linguistics, she began working at the Institute of Linguistics at the Chinese Academy of Social Sciences in Urumqi. In her words, "deliver[ing] a baby should be a family's decision, not a government ['s]." In direct contrast to the poster's claim that fewer children meant healthier mothers, Alim felt that having too few children was actually bad for a woman's health, although she did not say why.[41] Evidently, she did not find the abundant birth planning propaganda she encountered to be persuasive, but it is also possible that this was a result of a lessening emphasis on family planning during Alim's young adulthood.[42]

Despite Alim's reaction to birth planning propaganda, it is possible that other women responded differently to the state's messages, particularly in the moment (as opposed to recalling events from much earlier). A rare set of letters between two sisters in the early 1960s sheds some

[41] Interview with author, email, 4/24-4/25/19.

[42] Alim's interview took place in 2019 during a period of heightened ethnic tensions in Xinjiang. It is likely that concerns about the government's current treatment of Uyghurs colored her perception of state-mandated birth planning in the past.

light on the issue of whether the intended audiences of state propaganda related to its content. Both sisters were originally from Shanghai but were living apart at this time. In a letter from July 1963, Ximao, the older sister, urged her younger sister, Zhenyuan, who was living with her husband and infant in Changsha, Hunan, to practice birth control. Ximao advised Zhenyuan not to become pregnant again until her baby turns three, meaning that she must resolutely practice family planning for the next three years. Ximao warned her sister that if she did have another child, it would further deplete the family's already limited financial resources and impact her health and work.[43] It is possible that Ximao was simply parroting what she had seen in state propaganda, but I suspect given the personal nature of the letters, that she was also disclosing her genuine fears for her sister's wellbeing, particularly because Zhenyuan was going through a difficult time. Ximao instructed her sister to buy condoms at the pharmacy and use them every time she had sex, not allowing even one slip-up. Ximao urged Zhenyuan to act with perseverance, patience, and understanding in convincing her husband to use birth control (the assumption being that the husband would be reluctant to use condoms) and cautioned that becoming angry and giving up on birth control would only lead to failure in this endeavor. From these letters, it would seem that the propaganda's message – that practicing birth control promotes maternal health and enables mothers to focus on their own work – spoke to individual concerns, ones that also emerged in my interviews. Yet, at the individual level the greatest motivating factor for using birth control appears to have been self-preservation rather than a desire to serve the state.

A theme related to birth control as a survival strategy that warrants further discussion but is rarely mentioned in birth planning propaganda is the practical issue of childcare. One of the great draws of socialism is the promise of access to free childcare services for all. Yet, a variety of sources from factory work reports to personal letters reveal that sufficient access to childcare in the late 1950s and early 1960s posed a very real problem for parents, specifically mothers. Workers at the Baoji Leather Shoe Factory in Shanghai, for example, were living on meagre wages and lamented that they could not afford a nanny to watch their children while the parents were at work, especially if one spouse had to return home to the countryside.[44] In other cases, childcare was offered for factory workers, but each year so many new children needed care that there

[43] Zhang Letian and Yan Yunxiang, *Personal Letters between Lu Qingsheng and Jiang Zhenyuan, 1961–1986* (Leiden: Brill, 2018), 338–340.
[44] CCSL, SA201700000409.

were not enough nannies to watch over all of them.[45] In Luoyang, a directive from the Henan Provincial Department of Health mimicked these concerns, stating that there was not enough organized childcare to support all of the young children in the area.[46] Likewise, in the previously mentioned private exchange of letters between two sisters, the older sister advised her younger sister to send her newborn baby to live with its grandparents in the event that she could not obtain childcare. Otherwise, she would run the risk of falling behind on her work.[47] If this issue was so pressing, particularly for mothers bearing the double burden of being mothers and workers, why was this topic never mentioned in propaganda materials promoting birth planning?

Perhaps the topic was elided because acknowledging the realities of childcare would be seen as recognition of the fact that not all socialist ideals were being realized. Moreover, this omission might be attributed to the assumption that women were inherently responsible for childcare until the state could finance it.[48] In lieu of such social services, individual efforts like late marriage, condom use, and sterilization had to stand in for where the state fell short of its promises. This also suggests that while cultural productions and propaganda materials broadly couched the need for birth control in terms of ideological commitment to the party, the slogans and promotional materials that spoke to concrete problems were probably most persuasive.

Not so differently from the state-sponsored cultural productions of the Cultural Revolution period, local government bureaus and work units composed songs, dramas, and posters promoting late marriage and birth planning to dislodge traditional preferences for early marriage and large families. The call to have fewer children also dovetailed with the notion that males and females could contribute equally to the New China so there was no need to try for more sons. That the audiences these works targeted were largely female suggests that either women were primarily blamed for encouraging early marriage or that women were believed to be the only ones capable of stemming the tide of early marriage. More realistically, since marriage necessarily led to childbearing, women – who had more to lose from early marriage and less to gain from it – were more likely to support delayed marriage and family planning. Just as with contraception, then, the burden of stabilizing population growth at the level of the individual family unit fell more heavily on women than on men, thus partially undermining the claim that delayed marriage promoted

[45] Ibid. [46] LMA, 14–16. [47] Zhang and Yan, *Personal Letters*, 338–340.

[48] Harriet Evans, "Past, Perfect or Imperfect: Changing Images of the Ideal Wife," in *Chinese Femininities/Chinese Masculinities: A Reader*, eds. Susan Brownell and Jeffrey N. Wasserstrom (Berkeley: University of California Press, 2002), 339.

Figure 4.6 Spectators view posters promoting the One Child Policy, 1980s.
Source: “Shengyu xuanchuan haibao: jihua shengyu kouhao ying yushijujin,” *Zhongguo ribao*, April 11, 2016. http://cn.chinadaily.com.cn/2016-04/11/content_24446988.htm.

gender equality. As trite as these works of birth planning propaganda may seem to the contemporary reader, the themes discussed in these pieces spoke directly to widespread concerns among the Chinese populace.[49]

The trend of promoting family planning through art continued after the death of Chairman Mao (Figures 4.6 and 4.7), as evidenced by the publication of the Compilation of Birth Planning Literature and Art Propaganda Materials (*Jihua shengyu wenyi xuanchuan cailiao huibian)* in late 1976 under Mao’s successor, Hua Guofeng.[50] This book aggregated songs, short plays (*xiao huaju)*, and cross-talk skits related to birth planning from communes, hospitals, mines, and other work units across China. In many ways, these works echoed the themes of earlier cultural works.[51] Perhaps not surprisingly, films and posters promoting birth

[49] BMA, 100-001-00897.
[50] *Jihua shengyu wenyi xuanchuan cailiao huibian* (Compilation of Birth Planning Literature and Art Propaganda Materials) (Beijing: Renmin weisheng chubanshe, 1976).
[51] Evincing the malleability of Maoist doctrine, these materials also included references to contemporaneous political campaigns: the “Criticize Lin Biao, Criticize Confucius” movement, resisting revisionism and separatism, and condemning the Gang of Four

Figure 4.7 Spectators view a film promoting the One Child Policy, 1984.
Source: "35 Years of Family Planning," *Sina*, November 3, 2015, http://slide.news.sina.com.cn/j/slide_1_45272_90810.html/d/8#p=8.

planning are still a feature of Chinese society today and have evolved along with the state's changing political agenda.

One Step Forward, Two Steps Back

In addition to producing birth planning art and entertainment, through what other mechanisms did the state seek to deepen its control over sexuality and reproduction? Improved and more precise recordkeeping was an increasingly important tool for quantifying, categorizing, and constructing "correct" reproductive practices. Abortion records in the 1950s were scattered and unsystematic except in the case of court records of "illegal" abortions, acts punished at the local level for not meeting the qualifications for abortion under national law. By the 1960s, however, recordkeeping with respect to pregnancy and birth control use was becoming increasingly meticulous and widespread, at least in cities.

(blamed for the Cultural Revolution); *Jihua shengyu wenyi xuanchuan cailiao huibian* (Compilation of Birth Planning Literature and Art Propaganda Materials) (Beijing: Renmin weisheng chubanshe, 1976).

According to the official Luoyang city gazetteer, 267 abortions and 860 IUDs insertions were performed in Luoyang in 1963, one of the earliest years for which that city has medical records.[52] In terms of integrating birth planning and labor, each work unit was expected to keep precise records calculating how many abortions, vasectomies, tubal ligations, and IUD insertions were performed.[53] Work units were asked to report the number of births each month and encourage women with large families to have an IUD insertion or sterilization to prevent having too many children. As with other campaigns in China, more aggressive recordkeeping meant that work units in theory could single out individuals for punishment who failed to comply with birth planning goals. However, some work units failed to report their rates of birth control use, thus making accurate statistics more difficult to obtain. Additionally, even in the early 1960s, small cities and rural areas had minimal records related to changes in individual household size.

Work units and birth planning offices also adopted more intrusive tactics for encouraging contraception. Spearheading the birth planning campaign, by the late 1950s, Shanghai had already begun establishing neighborhood committees in each *lilong* (lane neighborhood). These local networks promoted women's literacy and employment alongside birth planning.[54] Propaganda workers went door-to-door preaching the benefits of birth planning and allaying individual concerns about birth control.[55] By the early 1960s, the trend of establishing and expanding neighborhood birth planning offices had also taken root in Tianjin and Luoyang.[56] In Luoyang's Jianxi district, for example, the number of propaganda workers at the Zhengzhou birth planning office, most or all of whom were women, increased from twelve to forty-one, and reportedly, of 298 women of childbearing age, 257 were convinced to use some form of contraception. Those who agreed to undergo abortion or sterilization were offered help with house chores, subsidies, and even gifts of fruit.[57]

Despite what might, from the perspective of state actors, be considered successes in promoting a modern health regime, family planning was still not widespread in the early 1960s, and in some places, it had barely made a dent. On the one hand, some official birth planning reports bragged

[52] *Luoyang shizhi* (Luoyang Gazetteer), October 15, 2009, http://www.lydqw.com/DB/BookContent.aspx?BookID=200904080002&Content=Digital; medical recordkeeping in Luoyang began in the late 1950s.
[53] TMA, X0032-C-000153
[54] Kohama, "Jihua shengyu de kaiduan," 117; CCSL, SA201700000409.
[55] CCSL, SA201700000409. [56] LMA, 120; TMA, 00094-001-000011-0006.
[57] LMA, 120.

that family planning and late marriage were now known in every household (*jiayu huxiao*). This claim was undoubtedly hyperbolic, as many interviewees attested that they had not heard of birth planning at that time. On the other hand, the same reports conceded that there were numerous obstacles to implementing the birth planning agenda and that birth rates were still rising in some work units.[58]

Even at this early stage in the birth planning project when the state had a consistent policy of voluntary contraception, there were already reports of coercion.[59] Employees who resisted risked being accused of "thought obstacles" (*sixiang zhang'ai*) or "incorrect thought responses" (*bu zhengque sixiang fanying*), which were addressed with more focus groups and "thought education."[60] Ironically, there was a direct correlation between family size and absences from factory or commune work meetings about birth control. In many cases, those individuals who, in the eyes of the authorities, most needed birth control were least likely to learn about it because they were busy taking care of their children.[61] In Beijing and Jiangsu province, women who did not want to have abortions or sterilizations reported being forced to do so.[62] Likewise, in some cases, doctors inserted IUDs or performed abortions without their patients' consent.[63] In other cases, work units offered individuals the choice between aborting out-of-wedlock pregnancies and losing their jobs. This was the case for Zhou Yan, a female worker at the North Station branch of the National Transport Guild in Shanghai, who began having an affair with her male colleague. Zhou, aged thirty-two and originally from Funing in Jiangsu province, became pregnant, and the affair was discovered. Because the couple was not married, she was pressured into having an abortion, which she ultimately did. She was accused of violating the marriage law and sentenced to thought reform.[64] Similar cases

[58] GMA, 231-1-29-44�44. [59] GMA, 317-1-147-8�11; BMA, 002-020-00379.

[60] CUHKA, "Liaoning biyun xuanchuan gongzuo zhong pengdao de qunzhong sixiang zhangai" (Ideological Obstacles of the Masses Encountered During Liaoning Birth Control Propaganda Work); TMA, X0065-C—000366-004.

[61] GMA, 233-2-267-33-39; BMA, 100-001-00897.

[62] Huo, "Dayuejin zhihou de jihua shengyu, 1962–1966" (Family Planning Policy after the Great Leap Forward, 1962–1966), 56.

[63] BMA, 002-020-00391.

[64] SMA, C41-1-247-57. Aminda Smith shows that thought reform was originally conceived of as a way to refashion the mindsets of the "dangerous classes" – thieves, beggar, and prostitutes – who held "vacillating loyalties, disruptive tendencies that sowed discord and chaos, and a parasitic unwillingness to labor." The idea was that through political training these wayward elements of society could be remolded into productive members of society, as in cases of women who underwent abortions. Yet, the 1957 institutionalization of reform through labor acknowledged that sometimes

took place in other major cities like Beijing, where unmarried women workers were forced to abort their pregnancies or risk losing their jobs.[65]

Some couples, particularly those in major cities like Shanghai and Tianjin, supported using contraception or undergoing contraceptive surgeries, yet birth planning teams all reported encountering some degree of resistance to birth control from couples, individuals, and even medical personnel.[66] Several older doctors, for example, argued that abortion was unethical and recalled a saying from only a few years earlier in the 1950s: "Abortion: the disadvantages are great, the benefits are few." Their concerns were partially addressed in terms of improving the safety of abortions, but this occurred amid a rising abortion rate.[67]

From the perspective of potential birth control users, reactions to contraception and birth control surgeries were deeply gendered, though rarely were men alone in perpetuating the patriarchal status quo.[68] Many couples were open to using birth control or undergoing sterilization but only after having at least one son. Female interviewees in Shanghai, Tianjin, and Luoyang, particularly those who had moved to the city later in life, told me that at that time women without sons were seen as failures and mocked by other women. Only with a son can the patriarchal family line continue, and in many cases, husbands and wives would have done anything to have at least one son, including resisting birth control.[69] In Xicheng district of Beijing, for example, women went as far as lying to newly hired birth planning propaganda staff, saying that they were already using birth control when they were not. Forceful health

thought reform was not enough and that truly incorrigible elements needed to undergo forced labor. In many cases, males who engaged in sex with sent-down youth and facilitated abortion were perceived as being beyond reform. Aminda M. Smith, *Thought Reform and China's Dangerous Classes: Reeducation, Resistance, and the People*. Lanham: Rowman & Littlefield, 2013.

[65] BMA, 002-020-00391.

[66] Kohama, "The Beginning of Birth Planning," 123–124; interview with author, Tianjin, July 2, 2019.

[67] Huo, "Dayuejin zhihou de jihua shengyu, 1962–1966" (Family Planning Policy after the Great Leap Forward, 1962–1966), 60.

[68] Other scholars of gender, such as Judith Stacey and Delia Davin, have shown that women were sometimes complicit in upholding patriarchal practices during the Mao era. Harriet Evans coined the term "patchy patriarchy" to refer to this "uneven reconfiguration of ideas and practices centering on … assumptions about marriage, reproduction, family, kinship, and female virtue." Judith Stacey, *Patriarchy and Socialist Revolution in China* (Berkeley: University of California Press, 1983); Delia Davin, *Woman-Work: Patriarchy and the Party in Revolutionary China* (Oxford: Oxford University Press, 1976); Harriet Evans, *Beijing from Below: Stories of Marginal Lives in the Capital's Center* (Durham: Duke University Press, 2020), 219.

[69] Interview with author, Luoyang, November 19, 2016; interview with author, Luoyang, November 14, 2016; interview with author, Shanghai, August 23, 2016; interview with author, Tianjin, February 13, 2017.

inspectors later uncovered these falsehoods.[70] In other cases, in-laws, especially mothers-in-law, who derived status from the birth of a grandson, opposed the use of birth control and the termination of a pregnancy through abortion, revealing that the issue of whether to use contraception was sometimes viewed as a familial decision.[71] Many women also feared that using contraceptives would negatively affect their marital lives, cause pain or illness, or result in sterilization.[72] Betraying certain assumptions about male sexual pleasure, these women seemed to think that their husbands would not be sexually satisfied if they used contraception.

Their concerns were often warranted, as some men actively resisted using condoms.[73] According to reports and interviews from Shanghai, Tianjin, and Luoyang, one of the most common reasons for not wanting to use birth control devices was that men found them troublesome (*mafan*) and uncomfortable.[74] Some complained that the process of washing, storing, and reusing condoms was simply unfeasible.[75] Others refused to use condoms on the basis of reduced sensation and pleasure. In fact, one fifty-eight-year-old man in Tianjin told me that he and his wife have long used the unreliable withdrawal method, rather than condoms, to preserve the feeling of flesh on flesh (*rou ai rou de ganjue*).[76] Still others mocked their wives relentlessly for bringing home condoms until they gave up the cause of promoting condom use.[77] Even when work units began distributing condoms free of charge to employees, few couples would use them.[78] My interviewees reported almost unanimously that men hated using condoms for these reasons and would rather risk unwanted pregnancy than bother with this type of protection.[79]

In fact, the issue of men not liking condoms was so well known that it was even depicted in official propaganda promoting the benefits of

[70] BMA, 002-020-00379.

[71] BMA, 002-020-00391; Tina Phillips Johnson, *Childbirth in Republican China: Delivering Modernity* (Lanham: Lexington Books, 2011), xvii.

[72] BMA, 002-020-00379; LMA, 99; TMA, 00023-002-000434-0009; LMA. 120; Kohama, "The Beginning of Birth Planning," 123.

[73] Male resistance to using condoms continues to be an issue today; Sarah Mellors, "The Trouble with Rubbers: A History of Condoms in Modern China," *Nan Nü: Men, Women and Gender in China* 22, no. 1: (2020): 150–178.

[74] BMA, 002-020-00379; BMA, 100-001-00897; CCSL, SA201700000409.

[75] BMA, 100-001-00897.

[76] Interview with author, Tianjin, February 13, 2017.

[77] CCSL, SA201700000409.

[78] Interview with author, Shanghai, January 12, 2017; interview with author, Luoyang, August 2, 2015; interview with author, Shanghai, December 22, 2017; interview with author, Tianjin, February 13, 2017.

[79] Men's resistance to using condoms may also have been a product of parental pressure to produce more children and/or a male heir.

避孕要坚持使用可靠方法

1.王小云，她有五个孩子，天天忙不过来。自从保健所告訴她用阴茎套避孕后，一年沒有怀孕。

2.她的爱人嫌使用阴茎套麻烦，总不太願意。一天，他听說有个偏方可以避孕，就抄下来給小云看，劝她吃药。

3.小云到药舖买了药，連吃兩付，以为这下不会再生孩子了。

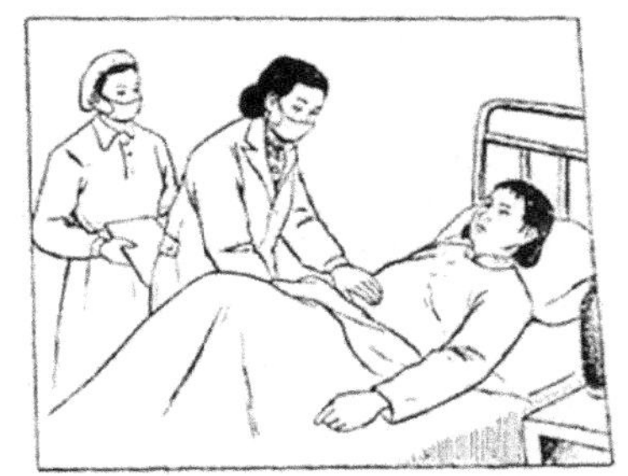

4.过了几个月，小云又怀孕了。大夫对她說：这次生产后，只有坚持使用可靠方法，才不会怀孕。

Figure 4.8 Birth planning cartoon: "*Biyun yao jianchi shiyong kekao fang fa*" (When using contraception, one must adhere to a reliable method), 1958.
Source: The Education Institute of the Beijing Public Hygiene Bureau, Beijing Science and Technology Popularization Association, eds. Rural Birth Planning Album (Beijing: Beijing chubanshe, 1958).

contraception. Take the following cartoon, for example (Figure 4.8).[80] The text reads: When Using Contraception, One Must Adhere to a Reliable Method

[80] "Biyun yao jianchi shiyong kekao fangfa" (When Using Contraception, One Must Adhere to a Reliable Method), Beijingshi gonggong weishengju weisheng jiaoyusuo yu beijingshi kexue jishu puji xiehui (Hygiene Education Institute of the Beijing Public Hygiene Bureau and Beijing Science and Technology Popularization Association), *Nongcun jihua shengyu huace* (Rural Birth Planning Album) (Beijing: Beijing Publishers, 1958), n.p.

1. Wang Xiaoyun had five children and was too busy every day. Since she was advised at the health clinic to use condoms, she had not been pregnant for a year.
2. Her husband said that condoms were too troublesome and generally did not use them willingly. One day he heard about a folk prescription for contraception. He copied it down and gave it to Xiaoyun, convincing her to buy the medicine.
3. Xiaoyun went to the pharmacy to buy the medicine and took two pills, thinking that she would not get pregnant again.
4. After a few months, Xiaoyun became pregnant once more. The doctor said to her: after this birth, only stick to reliable birth control methods, and then you will not get pregnant.[81]

The cartoon acknowledged that not only did men find condoms troublesome, but they would do just about anything to avoid wearing them. In this case, the husband even unknowingly convinced his wife to consume questionable folk prescriptions as contraception – a method addressed in greater detail later in the chapter.

One particularly inventive method factory administrators in Shanghai deployed to encourage condom use was holiday cards. According to a variety of sources, rates of worker pregnancy spiked during the Chinese New Year when workers returned to their natal villages to celebrate the holiday, a problem that resulted in thousands of sick days and reduced worker productivity across the board. In order to prevent this problem, labor union leaders at the Huachang Cotton Cloth Factory gave all women workers a new condom to take home for the Spring Festival. To ensure that the condoms were not simply ignored or forgotten, the factory sent each woman worker two New Year's cards. The first wished her and her family a happy new year. The second reminded her to practice birth control for two reasons: (1) to guarantee that she could compete in her factory's labor competition and (2) to ensure maternal health and familial happiness. Women were seen as responsible for combatting male resistance to condom use, and a primary justification for using condoms was improving worker productivity.

Although birth planning propaganda almost exclusively targeted women workers, one case stands out for its focus on male workers. The

[81] Beijingshi gonggong weishengju weisheng jiaoyusuo yu beijingshi kexue jishu puji xiehui (Hygiene Education Institute of the Beijing Public Hygiene Bureau and Beijing Science and Technology Popularization Association), *Nongcun jihua shengyu huace* (Rural Birth Planning Album) (Beijing: Beijing chubanshe, 1958), n.p.

holiday card approach was so successful in reducing worker pregnancies at Huachang Cotton Cloth Factory during the Spring Festival, this method was even recommended for use at Shanghai factories employing majority male workers.[82] The Baoji Leather Shoe Factory, for instance, even went so far as to send holiday cards to male workers and then follow up with home visits to ensure that workers spending the holiday in Shanghai were actually practicing birth control. According to one report, as a result of this program, the majority of male workers at the Baoji Factory ended up using condoms.[83]

Some interviewees told me said that condoms were available early on even in rural contexts and that men were willing to use them.[84] Demographer Thomas Scharping also argues that condoms were the most common form of contraception used in China during the early 1960s, and indeed, condom use emerged in surprising circumstances.[85] In 1964, in a case most likely from rural Shanxi, a man called Dong Xing was charged with raping a woman named Chen Lan multiple times. The case stands out in that prior to committing each rape Dong purchased and used a condom *(baoxiantao)* to ensure that Chen would not become pregnant. In a 1965 report on the case, Chen said that her rapist had gotten the condom from his fourth aunt (*sigu*) but that using birth control was his own idea.[86] The case was exposed as part of the Four Cleanups Movement, a socialist education campaign Mao launched in 1963 to weed out so-called "reactionary" elements. Because of the nature of this campaign, it is unclear whether this was an actual case of rape or a case of consensual sex that was later deemed rape as a political move. If the intercourse was consensual, that may have accounted for the premeditation and Dong's advance procurement of contraception.

This case and similar ones aside, the general reluctance to use condoms even when they were made available reveals an underlying power differential between men and women with the condom as the site of the struggle.[87] Men also resisted birth planning lectures and family planning in general because they felt that birth control did not have anything to do with them.[88] While most interviewees, male and female, argued that family planning was the responsibility of both men and women, women confided that in reality birth planning was always by default the woman's responsibility.[89]

82 CCSL, SA201700000409. 83 Ibid.
84 Interview with author, Luoyang, August 2, 2015.
85 Scharping, *Birth Control in China*, 182. 86 ECNUA, B 022-010-035.
87 Zheng Tiantian, *Ethnographies of Prostitution in Contemporary China* (London: Palgrave Macmillan), 8.
88 GMA, 233-2-267-33-39.
89 Interview with author, Shanghai, August 31, 2016; February 5, 2017.

Male resistance to condom use can be found in many parts of the world at many points in history, yet men arguing that they have nothing to do with family size and birth control – a claim I encountered several times during my interviews – is not universal.[90] In contrast to China, some studies of birth control in the West argue that for hundreds of years men were primarily responsible for contraceptive use, as knowledge about birth control and the ability to control one's fertility were construed as evidence of masculinity.[91] In fact, the condom was the most popular form of contraception in the United States in the 1950s, and sales only decreased in the 1960s following the invention of oral birth control for women.[92] Male resistance to condom use in China can be attributed to several factors, including culturally specific notions of masculinity, the widely held belief that contraception belongs in the female domain, and fears of reduced sexual pleasure.[93] In this context, women were often forced to work around their husbands' inflexibility.

In addition to conflicting responses to birth planning propaganda, structural issues also posed unexpected challenges for the emerging birth planning apparatus. As in the 1950s, lack of hygienic conditions, limited medical expertise, resource shortages, and overpriced yet unreliable birth control products plagued efforts to promote birth control. Although issues with medical quality appear to have been widespread, they were even more likely to occur in rural areas, which did not receive state funding and therefore had fewer doctors and more antiquated medical equipment. For these reasons, the state first introduced complex contraceptive procedures like IUD insertions, surgical abortions, and sterilizations in the cities rather than in the countryside. Similarly, more sophisticated birth control methods like uterine caps, which require a doctor's precise assessment and fitting, were mainly made available in

[90] Iris Lopez, *Matters of Choice: Puerto Rican Women's Struggle for Reproductive Freedom* (New Brunswick: Rutgers University Press, 2008), 59, 122, 149; Atina Grossman, *Reforming Sex: The German Movement for Birth Control and Abortion Reform, 1920–1950* (New York: Oxford University Press, 1995), 68.

[91] Kate Fisher, *Birth Control, Sex, and Marriage in Britain, 1918–1960* (Oxford: Oxford University Press, 2006), 194, 229; Kate Fisher, "The Delivery of Birth Control Advice," in *Oral History, Health and Welfare*, eds. Joanna Bornat et al. (London: Routledge, 2000), 266.

[92] Andrea Tone, "Making Room for Rubbers: Gender, Technology, and Birth Control Before the Pill," *History and Technology* 18, no. 1 (2010), 67.

[93] My research suggests that unlike in some parts of the West, the ability to procure and use condoms was not viewed as a sign of masculinity. Mellors, "The Trouble with Rubbers": 178. Historically, in China, as Chapter 2 explains, it was also believed that male health depended on obtaining *yin* from sexual intercourse with a woman.

cities. To the extent that any birth control existed in the countryside, the state emphasized the sale of condoms there.[94]

Problems with advocating contraception began with the training of medical workers. A 1964 internal reference (*Neibu cankao*) report noted the dearth of information about contraception even among physicians. The report claimed that of all medical personnel, new medical school graduates and older doctors, knew the least about contraception and contraceptive surgeries as neither group had much training in these areas. To gauge contraception knowledge among medical staff, the Xuanwu District Department of Public Health in Beijing conducted a workshop with 126 doctors and midwives. When asked questions about correct birth control practices, the doctors and midwives provided a wide variety (*wuhua bamen*) of answers, most of which were incorrect. For example, when asked in which part of the body a vasectomy took place, some responded "in the scrotum" (which is the correct answer) but others argued that it took place in the abdomen. In another case, some workshop participants responded that contraception (*biyun*) is when "yin and yang are in disagreement (*buhe*)," a line of thinking found in some strands of TCM. While other respondents knew that this was not the correct answer, they could not explain why. Finally, when asked to calculate the rhythm method's safe period – the period during a woman's monthly cycle when she is least likely to become pregnant from intercourse – some doctors and midwives said that the ovulation period was safest, when this is in fact the window in which women are most susceptible to pregnancy. The workshop's results showed that even in one of China's most developed cities, knowledge about contraception was not widespread among medical personnel.[95]

The follow-up report on the workshop argued that confusion and debate about what constituted effective birth control were present in the medical field as a whole. There was even disagreement among TCM practitioners about the medical theory behind birth control. Some practitioners of TCM believed contraception was linked to the balance of *yin* and *yang*, while others said that that argument was more consistent with Daoist metaphysical theory than with TCM.[96]

Against this backdrop, it is not difficult to imagine that medical accidents abounded. In Beijing between 1963 and 1964, for example, large numbers of errors were made in performing abortions, sterilizations, and insertions.[97] According to internal reports, medical malpractice in the area of birth planning resulted in damaged reproductive organs,

[94] TMA, X0092-Y—000123—007. [95] BMA, 002-020-00379.
[96] BMA, 002-020-00379. [97] BMA, 135-001-01472.

disability, and even death.[98] In some abortion and sterilization cases, improper application of anesthesia resulted in patient death. In other cases, doctors accidentally left medical gauze or surgical tools inside of the abdomens of women having abortions or sterilization surgery, leading to severe pelvic inflammation. A report in Zhejiang province showed that tubal ligations frequently were ineffective in preventing further pregnancies.[99] In other cases, sterilization left the patient's bladder permanently damaged and IUD insertions perforated the uterus leading to heavy bleeding and the ring getting stuck in the wall of the abdominal cavity. For example, a young woman named Wang Xiuqin decided to have sterilization surgery in 1960. During the procedure, the doctor hit an artery, causing heavy internal bleeding, shock, and eventually death.[100] In several mid-term (16–23 weeks) abortions involving the use of the drug Rivanol to induce premature labor, the doctor mismeasured the dosage or did not test the patient for allergies, leading to death. In 1963, for instance, a woman in Luoyang undergoing a mid-term abortion because she felt she could not take care of another child died from an overdose of Rivanol. The doctor apparently administered more than fifty times the dose, resulting in cardiac arrest and death. A similar case had occurred the day before but the patient was transferred to another hospital and saved.[101] Infections and uterine abscesses due to unhygienic surgical conditions and excessive, unmonitored blood loss were also common.[102] In some cases, abortion surgery failed to terminate the pregnancy, meaning that the woman still gave birth to a baby, or in worse cases, gave birth to a disabled and disfigured child.

While vasectomies were far less common than tubal ligations and abortions, mistakes occurred in their execution as well. In some cases, misuse of local anesthetics or overly large surgical incisions caused tissue necrosis, organ failure, and testicular damage. In other instances, the surgical wounds bled so much that a second, or even a third, surgery needed to be performed.[103] Most commonly, the surgeries were simply performed incorrectly, missing the vas deferens altogether and thus not having the desired effect of sterilization. The error was typically discovered when the patients' wives unexpectedly became pregnant.[104]

According to a number of reports, these medical errors were the result of sloppy surgical practices, poorly trained medical personnel, and a general lack of understanding about the importance of sterile hospital

[98] ZPA, J165-003-068-217.
[99] ZPA, J115-003-067-030; ZPA, J115-003-068-029; ZPA, J115-003-068-005.
[100] ECNUA, En 0351-032-012. [101] LMA, 80. [102] ZPA, J115-003-068-160.
[103] LMA, 129. [104] BMA, 135-001-01472.

environments. While most cases of contraceptive surgery did not result in serious problems, enough did to cause concern and distrust of the medical system. Indeed, people who had undergone IUD insertions or sterilization surgeries were quick to report their experiences to friends and colleagues. At the same time, there was limited access to first-rate healthcare in much of China, so it is understandable why individuals might be reluctant to go under the knife, given the circumstances. Problems with ineffective birth control and contraceptive surgeries account in part for the reason the population of China continued to grow rapidly during these years.[105]

An additional problem that was a holdover from the 1950s was the high cost and limited supply of contraceptives. In 1963, the Tianjin Economic Committee reported that local factories such as the Yutai Rubber Factory and Yutai Latex Factory had produced their first condoms. However, production costs were high, raw materials were insufficient, and factories were largely unprepared for this type of production.[106] At this time, most condoms in Tianjin were either imported or purchased from factories in Shanghai and Guangzhou. With a child-bearing population of 1.4 million (700,000 couples), the city of Tianjin reported sales of 646,000 condoms in March 1963 and 126,000 in the first half of April that same year.[107] The city ambitiously planned to produce 6 million condoms in the next six months, allowing for around eight condoms per couple.[108]

In 1963, the central government also ordered the production of 2 million contraceptive suppositories, but supply and quality proved problematic. At this time, Beijing claimed that a portion of the city's population used suppositories, and Shanghai also boasted high sales of suppositories. However, a report from Shanghai lamented that 130,230 of the 1,538,900 suppositories in storage waiting to be sold had deteriorated and were no longer usable, amounting to a 123,300-yuan loss.[109] The city faced similar problems with cervical caps, as well as with acetic acid and glycerin to be used as spermicides, all of which degraded in storage.[110] Tianjin residents also reported that suppositories were sold out in their city. Of those who had purchased them, the responses were mixed. Some users said they were effective in preventing pregnancy, while others said they were not. Tianjin sought to also produce suppositories with

[105] National Birth Planning Committee Integrated Planning Division, *Chinese Birth Planning Statistical Yearbook*, 1.
[106] TMA, X0110-D-000192-005.
[107] TMA, X0110-D-000192-005.
[108] TMA, X0110-D-000192–004.
[109] SMA, B 123-5-167-126.
[110] SMA, B 123-5-167-126.

help from Beijing, but it is unclear if these products were any more effective in preventing pregnancies than their predecessors.[111]

In Tianjin and elsewhere, cost was also an impediment to adopting birth control or undergoing a contraceptive procedure. Seeking to alleviate this issue, in 1962, the Tianjin Municipal Department of Public Health made vasectomies, tubal ligations, abortions, and IUD insertions free (through work unit reimbursement) to workers with labor insurance and their family members. As a result, 303,990 IUD insertions and 123,760 abortions were performed between 1963 and 1964.[112] Similarly, in 1964, the city of Guangzhou significantly lowered the prices of all contraceptive surgeries for cadres, workers, and their families to make these procedures appealing and affordable. Tubal ligation surgeries decreased from 5 *yuan* to 2 *yuan*, simultaneous tubal ligation and abortion decreased from 8 *yuan* to 3 *yuan*, abortion from 3 *yuan* to 1 *yuan*, vasectomies from 3 *yuan* to 1 *yuan*, and IUD insertion from 1.5 *yuan* to free.[113] In addition, women undergoing IUD insertions could be reimbursed for presurgery examinations, but they had to foot the bill for hospital registration fees and the cost of the actual IUD out of pocket. Cadres, workers, and their families undergoing sterilization, however, would be reimbursed for the cost of the presurgery exam, hospital registration fees, and any additional fees, thus incentivizing sterilization over temporary birth control, a trend that would continue for decades.[114]

Another major impediment to promoting birth planning seems to have been a widespread lack of awareness about changing policies toward birth control, abortion, and sterilization, both at the national and local levels. Internal reports *(Neibu cankao)* bemoaned the fact that many cadres were not clear about the exact meaning of birth planning and did not know the difference between this policy and Malthusian population theory, which Mao had deemed "bourgeois" and "capitalist" only a few years earlier. Some cadres even asserted that having children was a fundamental principle of Marxism and that using birth control was anti-Marxist.[115] At this time, terms like "Malthusian" and "Marxist" were exceedingly malleable. Cadres were right in feeling confused about the difference between birth planning and Malthusianism because there was no clear distinction and the so-called fundamental premises of

[111] TMA, X0110-D-000192–005.

[112] Huo, "Dayuejin zhihou de jihua shengyu, 1962–1966" (Family Planning Policy after the Great Leap Forward, 1962–1966), 41–42.

[113] The average net income for an urban household in 1964 was 102.3 yuan; "Per Capita Annual Income and Expenditure Urban and Rural Households," All China Data Center, chinadataonline.org.

[114] GMA, 317-1-122-96�97.

[115] BMA, 002-020-00379.

Chinese Marxism changed frequently in CCP rhetoric. Even as some provincial and local cadres deemed birth control in opposition to Marxism, others argued that contraception had always aligned with socialist values. Ideology, in these instances, was strategically adapted to changing sociopolitical circumstances.

This same confusion about frequently changing policies was even more magnified at the grassroots level. While some of the individuals I interviewed were aware that contraception was available in major cities during the early 1960s, almost none of them knew that for large swaths of the urban population the cost of surgeries and IUD insertions could be reimbursed. Moreover, many, especially less well-educated urbanites, still thought that Mao's official policy toward population was "*duozi duofu*" (more sons, more happiness).[116] Even local officials were confused. In 1962, for instance, the Henan Province Department of Hygiene had to reissue the 1957 guidelines for abortion and sterilization because so many work units were unclear about the policy.[117] Relatedly, in Hangzhou, court judges asked why abortions were suddenly being encouraged when in the recent past they had been labeled as dangerous and illegal.[118]

Issues with producing and popularizing contraceptives, prevalent medical mishaps, and confusion about changing policies presented serious challenges to early birth planning. Despite reports touting the success of these efforts, in reality, policy implementation was a protracted and messy process.

Old Wine in a New Bottle (*xinping jiujiu*)

The precarious position of TCM in the birth planning movement also demonstrates well the tension between the lofty rhetoric of state family planning reports and practical challenges to policy implementation. Although TCM was deployed at various times as part of official efforts to promote family planning, it also repeatedly challenged the state biopolitical apparatus. In the 1950s, China had 500,000 doctors of traditional medicine and only 50,000 doctors of Western medicine. Moreover, until the late 1960s, rural access to Western medicines was extremely limited, while herbal medicines were far cheaper than their Western counterparts.[119] Seeking to capitalize on the popularity, accessibility, and affordability of TCM and to reinforce the notion that China

[116] Interview with author, Shanghai, June 8, 2016; LMA, 99. [117] LMA, 62.

[118] CUHKA, "Zhejiang sheng zai jieyu gongzuo zhong de yixie pianxiang" (Some Deviations in Birth Control Work in Zhejiang Province).

[119] Fang Xiaoping, "Barefoot Doctors and the Provision of Rural Health Care," in *Medical Transitions in Twentieth-Century China*, eds. Bridie Andrews and Mary Brown Bullock (Bloomington: Indiana University Press, 2014), 273.

had a rich medical heritage unique from the West, the Ministry of Health collected recipes for herbal contraception from TCM practitioners. Although there was no consensus about the herbs' value as contraceptives even among TCM practitioners, between 1956 and 1957, these formulas were circulated for the first time in provincial and municipal newspapers, as well as in the magazine *Women of China*.[120] The decision to circulate herbal contraceptive recipes in newspapers and magazines read by educated Chinese was particularly ironic since these recipes were largely associated with the illiterate underclasses during the Republican era.[121] Local government organs, like the Luoyang Municipal Department of Public Health, also instructed officials to include recipes for traditional Chinese abortifacients in official birth control propaganda.[122]

In response to the popularity of herbal contraceptives, in 1957 researchers at Peking Union Medical College and other institutions also began testing the efficacy and safety of such herbal recipes. Many women who consumed these formulas reported debilitating side effects, including severe pain and hemorrhaging. In one case, twenty party cadres developed symptoms like full-body swelling, uterine hemorrhaging, and blistering of the tongue after consuming contraceptive powder from a local TCM clinic in Henan province. The powder was later found to contain ground-up leeches and mercury chloride (calomel), a common but toxic ingredient in traditional herbal contraception.[123] Meanwhile, researchers also worked to develop a "five flavors abortion pill," an herbal abortifacient for mass consumption, but this project was eventually abandoned when no real breakthroughs were made.[124] Many instances of negative side effects associated with herbal contraceptives led the central government to officially condemn these methods in 1962.[125]

However, these traditional recipes reemerged in official publications only a few years later. According to one barefoot doctor's manual – a medical guide for minimally trained healthcare workers delivering medical services in rural China – there were several well-known recipes for homemade herbal contraceptives. These herbal remedies, like the ones promulgated in 1956 and 1957, were likely taken from the *Bencao*

[120] Tien, "Sterilization," 227.
[121] Important news articles were also read aloud over the loudspeaker system within each work unit.
[122] LMA, 14–16.
[123] Tien, "Sterilization, Oral Contraception, and Population Control in China," *Population Studies* 18, no. 3, 232.
[124] Scharping, *Birth Control*, 182.
[125] Tien, "Sterilization," 232.

gangmu (Compendium of Materia Medica), one of the most influential medical texts in imperial China. The *Bencao gangmu* contains more than thirty different herbs and medicinal plants that can be made into abortifacients or cause sterilization. Although the barefoot doctors did not formally begin work until 1968, their methods, like those of TCM doctors, stemmed from much earlier medical practices and suggested that homemade contraceptives transcended the rural-urban divide.[126] A barefoot doctor's manual from 1977 recommended that, for five months, women consume nine tender, 5-inch stalks of *P. massoniana* (Chinese red pine) and one *liang* of white stipa roots after each period. This method was an effective form of contraception for three years. Alternatively, a woman could consume the juices of *C. japonica* (Japanese bamboo fern), *D. auranticocaulis* (medicinal lotus), and *P. polyphylla* (Herb Paris). Taken three times a day during menstruation, this formula could serve as a contraceptive for eight months. Other herbal contraceptives included wine mixed with the flowers and roots of Herb Paris, which was effective for a year. Lastly, the manual suggested that in the case of a pregnancy in the first trimester, black bamboo mixed with white wine and sugar was an effective way of inducing abortion. For women who were not pregnant, this concoction could prevent conception.[127]

There is some evidence that methods like this worked, as in a case in which a woman consistently drank tea boiled with the herb *hemazi*, permanently ending her menstrual cycle and thus preventing pregnancy.[128] Other sources suggested that women wanting to miscarry consume safflower, rice wine, and herbal remedies to induce bleeding and abort fetuses.[129] One hospital noted that each year multiple women were admitted after consuming abortifacients made from blister beetles, a practice that often led to death.

Limited records from this period suggest that not only were women using traditional herbal abortifacients, but in some cases they were using them together with or instead of Western family planning techniques, much as had been done in cities during the Republican period. Moreover, the use of these methods was not exclusive to uneducated,

[126] Scharping, *Birth Control*, 176.

[127] Marvin E. Weisberg and John R. Graham, *A Barefoot Doctor's Manual: A Guide to Traditional Chinese and Modern Medicine* (Cloudburst Press, 1977), 61.

[128] Hua Han, "Under the Shadow of the Collective Good: An Ethnographic Analysis of Fertility Control in Xiaoshan, Zhejiang Province, China," *Modern China* 33, no. 3 (2007): 328.

[129] Huang Yuchuan, *Zhonggong jieyu yundong* (Chinese Communist Party's Birth Control Movement) (Hong Kong: Union Research, 1967), 22.

rural women. Take the case of Liu Shijun from Xicheng district in Beijing for example. Liu was a thirty-one-year-old Sichuanese mother of two, a boy aged twelve and a girl aged six. In 1960, she began working at the Erlong Road service center, but in 1962 she had to return home due to illness. Her husband was in the military, and in 1961 she successfully consumed safflower to abort a pregnancy. In 1962, she again consumed safflower to induce abortion, but this time she also jumped from a window to ensure that the miscarriage was complete (deliberate self-harm was not uncommon among women desperate to avoid giving birth). She became pregnant again in 1964 and went to see her former colleague Wu at the service center. Liu asked, "Is having a sterilization painful?" She said that she had been using an IUD for the last two years and had not checked to see if she was pregnant again. Wu went to the hospital on Liu's behalf and asked a doctor if he could perform an abortion on Liu. Liu said that she had already used safflower to abort two pregnancies without a hitch. If she got an abortion in the hospital she would have to stay overnight and there would be no one to take care of her two children. On April 19, 1964, Liu consumed alcohol infused with safflower, but her chest started burning severely. She visited the hospital twice over the next twenty-four hours when her temperature dropped dramatically. She was eventually transferred to the Beijing Number Two Hospital, where she died that afternoon.[130] For Liu, dire circumstances, ineffective Western contraception, and repeated herbal abortions eventually cost her her life.

Similar themes emerged a few years later in cases from rural Poyang county and neighboring counties in Jiangxi province. While relying solely on abortion, women and couples experimented with whatever medicine was available to them. Often couples made several attempts to terminate their pregnancies before attaining the desired goal, and few of the techniques they employed depended strictly on Western medicine. In a case from 1974, a young woman became pregnant out of wedlock and her lover dug up herbs to enable her to abort the fetus.[131] In another case from 1968, a married woman having an affair with a neighbor became pregnant and consumed abortifacient herbs. The abortifacient did not work, so her lover took her to a local hospital for a surgical abortion. That method, too, was unsuccessful, so the woman again inserted herbs into her vagina to induce abortion. Although the final attempt allowed her to abort, the woman developed a high fever coupled with intense pain and died soon after.[132] In a third case, a young woman developed a

[130] BMA, 002-020-00391. [131] JTUA, Z1–11-21. [132] JTUA, Z1–10-657.

relationship with the local party secretary who was twenty years her senior. When the young woman discovered that she was pregnant, the couple tried four times to induce an abortion by consuming Yunnan *baiyao* (a coagulant), musk, and other herbs, but they failed every time. Ultimately, the young woman was able to undergo a surgical abortion, which terminated the pregnancy, but this was a last resort.[133] Indeed, women experiencing unwanted pregnancies relied on whatever methods of abortion they knew about.

When neither surgical nor herbal abortions were available, women resorted to their own methods grounded in local practice. In her impressive ethnography of birth control and abortion in rural and urban areas of Xiaoshan county, Zhejiang province (now part of the city of Hangzhou), Hua Han reveals the creative and horrifying methods women used to limit family size. Han's research focuses on the Lai lineage, the women of which for many years engaged heavily in handicraft spinning and weaving. Before the 1970s, almost every family in the township of Xiaoshan had a large wooden loom at home. Some women desperate not to give birth pulled the bar beaters of their family looms into their lower abdomens to induce abortions.[134] A rural peasant woman named Ying, for example, born in 1924, had six children, two of whom died at birth leaving four living children. After a fifth child was born in 1957, she prolonged breastfeeding to prevent herself from becoming pregnant again. When she noticed her stomach growing bigger once more, she hit herself with the loom beater in an attempt to abort. However, she was unsuccessful.[135] In other cases, women resorted to jumping or performing heavy physical activity to induce miscarriage.[136]

Cases like these reveal that the guiding force in individual medical decision-making was often simply pragmatism. Acting out of self-preservation, women used whatever method of birth control they had access to – though they almost always consumed abortifacients or had surgical abortions, rather than using prophylactics. Still, experiences with contraception continued to vary greatly, and some women used traditional Chinese abortifacients and Western contraceptives in conjunction. Access to Western-style birth control also did not preclude women from using folk medicine or TCM. This aligns with demographer Sripati Chandrasekhar's observation during his 1958 visit to China that many

[133] JTUA, Z1-11-123; for more on sent-down youth and the Sent-Down Youth Movement, see Chapter 5.
[134] Han, "Under the Shadow of the Collective Good," 330.
[135] Han, "Under the Shadow of the Collective Good," 331.
[136] Ibid., 322–323; Zheng, *Ethnographies of Prostitution*, 37.

women preferred traditional Chinese herbal abortifacients over Western surgical abortions even if the former could be more dangerous.[137]

Conclusion

The devastating human toll of the Great Leap Forward forced the central government to once again address the question of population control. This time, provincial and municipal authorities deployed a wider array of tactics to shift public opinion in favor of birth control and prepare medical personnel to carry out the birth planning agenda. The use of plays and posters to promote family planning in the 1960s inaugurated a trend that lasted for decades. Group conversations and cultural activities were used to challenge the traditional preference for early marriage and sons, to some effect. By tailoring propaganda materials to the concerns of local communities, the state sought to solidify its role in regulating reproduction. Whether as a result of this campaign or not, birth rates dropped significantly in Shanghai and Luoyang.[138]

Other official efforts, however, faced more obvious challenges. Provincial and municipal governments sought to standardize contraceptive information, train medical professionals in family planning, and hold individual work units responsible for employee birth control use. Yet, limited resources and lack of coordination proved to be significant impediments. Ultimately, confusion about birth control, individual opposition to it, and conflicting ideas about the efficacy of traditional medicine posed a genuine challenge to these efforts. For the aforementioned reasons, promoting family planning was not a straightforward, top-down endeavor. Rather, because birth control intersected with so many disparate aspects of life – state-society relations, gender dynamics, and medicine, to name a few – promoting birth planning involved intense negotiation among diverse actors.

[137] UOT, box 19, folder 43.
[138] Kohama, "The Beginning of Birth Planning," 125; LMA, 99.

5 Controlling Sex and Reproduction across the Urban–Rural Divide, 1966–1979

In 1966, Chairman Mao launched the Cultural Revolution (1966–1976), a political movement intended to destroy the ossifying bureaucratic class and purge the party-state of "capitalist roaders" (those believed to be harboring capitalist loyalties).[1] Through the Cultural Revolution, Mao sought to reignite popular support for the Communist cause in the wake of the failed Great Leap Forward, further consolidate his power within the Party, and prevent "revisionism" (as in the case of the Soviet Union, where Stalin's policies were rolled back by his more moderate successor).[2] Fears of stagnation in the pursuit of socialism also inspired millions of young people to participate in factional battles. The Cultural Revolution resulted in tremendous violence, hundreds of thousands if not millions of deaths, and unprecedented social dislocation. In this fraught environment, any act or idea perceived as running counter to Mao's policies – including birth control or abortion at times – could result in punishment. Although concerns about economic development and food shortages had generated high-level endorsement of birth planning in the early 1960s, in reality, birth control and abortion continued to be perceived as politically suspect among some members of the rural population.

In the early years of the Cultural Revolution, Mao exhorted millions of Red Guards – middle school and high school age students – to travel the country in coed bands igniting class struggle (an experience called *chuanlian* in Chinese). For these young people, many of whom had never left their hometowns, this period offered a rare opportunity to travel and have unsupervised interaction with the opposite sex. In 1968, in part to curb the wanton violence of the Cultural Revolution, Mao accelerated the Sent-Down Youth Movement (1955–1980), a program that

[1] Yiching Wu, *The Cultural Revolution at the Margins: Chinese Socialism in Crisis* (Cambridge: Harvard University Press, 2014), 20.

[2] Roderick MacFarquhar and Michael Schoenhals, *Mao's Last Revolution* (Cambridge, MA: Harvard University Press, 2006), 8–9.

dispatched urban youth to rural areas to "learn from the peasants." During this movement, millions of youth were sent to the hinterland to serve on production brigades and in construction corps.

Historian Jeremy Brown and political scientist Nara Dillon locate the roots of the pronounced urban–rural divide in contemporary China in the policies of the Mao era, arguing that uneven policies during this period deepened disparities between the cities and the countryside.[3] Yet, historians Miriam Gross and Sigrid Schmalzer have also highlighted the critical role that sent-down youth and grassroots medicine and science played in bridging the urban–rural divide.[4]

From the perspective of reproduction, the convergence of the city and the countryside brought on by these mass movements created new and unprecedented problems that deepened state biopolitical power while also exposing the tensions among national directives, local policy implementation, and grassroots sexual realities. On the one hand, local officials limited the discussion of birth control among unmarried individuals, used mechanisms like the court system to monitor and police reproductive practices, and improved recordkeeping with respect to family planning. On the other hand, people devised new ways of defying the government, and inconsistent policies provided space for individual maneuvering and co-opting of state-sanctioned contraceptives in contexts for which they were not intended.

Cultures of Sex and Birth Control

Records acknowledging birth control use or abortion among unmarried couples during the height of the Cultural Revolution between 1966 and 1968 are few and far between. The dearth of materials might be attributed to a number of different factors: state silencing of topics related to sex during this period, political turmoil that made family planning more difficult, or close guarding of birth planning files by contemporary Chinese authorities. In contrast, abortion records among unmarried youth from the early 1970s are quite numerous, even more plentiful than

[3] Jeremy Brown, *City Versus Countryside in Mao's China: Negotiating the Divide* (Cambridge: Cambridge University Press, 2012), 1; Nara Dillon, *Radical Inequalities: China's Revolutionary Welfare State in Comparative Perspective* (Cambridge: Harvard University East Asia Center, 2015), 3.

[4] Miriam Gross, *Farewell to the God of Plague: Chairman Mao's Campaign to Deworm China* (Berkeley: University of California Press, 2016), 2–3; Sigrid Schmalzer, *Red Revolution, Green Revolution: Scientific Farming in Socialist China* (Chicago: University of Chicago Press, 2016), 92.

those from the years immediately preceding the advent of the Cultural Revolution.

Scholars of gender and sexuality in twentieth-century China have long debated whether the state's role in sexual matters changed dramatically with the start of the Cultural Revolution in 1966. Mayfair Yang has stated that "there was a dearth of both public and private discussions of sex during the Cultural Revolution."[5] Harriet Evans elaborates that publications on sex and birth control were available in the early PRC in the 1950s and early 1960s but that they became scarce with the start of the Cultural Revolution.[6] Emily Honig notes that two conflicting narratives appear in Cultural Revolution memoirs – tales of sexual repression and examples of widespread sexual violence and promiscuity. She concludes from these paradoxical accounts that although the Cultural Revolution was sexually repressive, it involved the "continual negotiation of sex and sexuality," in which the role of the state in silencing sexuality was not usually obvious.[7]

Diaries, memoirs, court records, film, literature, and interviews reveal that one's experience with sex and contraception during the Cultural Revolution and the Sent-Down Youth Movement varied greatly based on individual circumstances: whether an individual was old enough to embark on journeys with other Red Guards between 1966 and 1968, whether he or she was dispatched to the countryside for reeducation, and how much time was spent away from home.

Emily Honig rightly argues that one's experience with sex during the Cultural Revolution was largely dictated by the institution or "sexual climate" a person was in.[8] In general, sex seems to have rarely been discussed in some spaces and yet it pervaded all aspects of political life, as sexual transgressors were a primary target of Cultural Revolution violence and the punishments doled out to them were deeply gendered. In his memoir, author Zhu Xiao Di recalls that as a youth during the early Cultural Revolution, he learned about sex largely through reading big character posters (*da zi bao*) and public accusations of counterrevolutionary behavior, including engaging in extramarital relations.[9] Similarly,

[5] Mayfair Yang, "From Gender Erasure to Gender Difference: State Feminism, Consumer Sexuality, and Women's Public Sphere in China," in Mayfair Mei-hui Yang (ed.), *Spaces of Their Own: Women's Public Sphere in Transnational China* (Minneapolis: University of Minnesota Press, 1999), 44.

[6] Evans, *Women and Sexuality in China*, 8.

[7] Emily Honig, "Socialist Sex: The Cultural Revolution Revisited," *Modern China* 29.2 (2003), 154, 171.

[8] Honig, "Socialist Sex," 171.

[9] Zhu Xiao Di, *Thirty Years in a Red House: A Memoir of Childhood and Youth in Communist China* (Amherst: University of Massachusetts Press, 1998), 53.

novelist Yu Hua remembers the way a Cultural Revolution poster featuring a cartoon of an adulterous couple aroused his interest.[10] Michael Schoenhals explains that "sex featured often and not very discreetly in big character posters" but was often framed as evidence of "revisionism" or other Maoist political offenses.[11] If the purpose of exposing sexual transgressions was to reinforce the ideals of premarital chastity and marital fidelity, public pronouncements of lewd behavior also ensured that discussions of sexual behavior were given a certain, if irregular, prominence.

As for the role of sexuality in print culture, publications on sex were not explicitly banned by the state but people self-silenced for fear of being accused of being insufficiently "red." Those found reading "bourgeois" books – foreign literature, books published before 1949, and books with any reference to love or sex – would be forced to confess their errors and punished accordingly.[12] Something as banal as singing love songs or writing love notes could also be grounds for political punishment.[13] At the same time, Red Guards burned some but not all forbidden books. In fact, there are numerous examples of the ways in which young people worked around this issue. In some memoirs, young people broke into Red Guard strongholds and stole banned books that had yet to be burned. In other cases, Red Guards looking to make some quick money sold confiscated books on the black market.[14] Many memoirs tell of young people secretly reading *shou chaoben*, hand-copied versions of forbidden "yellow" texts that were circulated underground.[15]

Those from historically wealthier and better-educated families had a much higher chance than their peers of obtaining access to these types of materials either before or during the Cultural Revolution. In one case, the daughter of an elite Guomindang family had even read the *Kama Sutra* in high school, a book that her father had hidden from the authorities in his library.[16] Similarly, in the semi-autobiographical novel by Dai Sijie, *Balzac and the Little Chinese Seamstress*, two teenage boys from Beijing, Ma and Luo, find foreign books stashed away in a fellow sent-

[10] Yu Hua, *China in Ten Words*, translated by Allan H. Barr (New York: Pantheon Books, 2011), 58.

[11] Michael Schoenhals, "Sex in Big-Character Posters from China's Cultural Revolution: Gendering the Class Enemy," in *Gender and Mass Dictatorship: Global Perspectives*, eds. Jie-Hyun Lim and Karen Petrone (Basingstoke: Palgrave Macmillan, 2011), 250.

[12] Interview with author, Tianjin, February 14, 2017.

[13] Fan Shen, *Gang of One* (Lincoln: Bison Books, 2006), 156; JTUA, Z1-10-842.

[14] Jung Chang, *Wild Swans: Three Daughters of China* (New York: Touchstone, 2003), 368.

[15] Honig, "Socialist Sex," 148; Anchee Min, *Red Azalea* (New York: Anchor Books, 1994), 75; Bai Ge, *1966–1976: Zhongguo baixing shenghuo shilu* (1966–1976: Record of the Life of China's Ordinary People) (Beijing: Jingguan jiaoyu chubanshe, 1993), 283.

[16] Shen, *Gang of One*, 270.

down youth's suitcase, which they surreptitiously read along with their friend, a local seamstress.[17] Some of these books contained nude images of women, which would have fallen into the political category of pornography at that time and been severely punished. Similar stories abound in other Cultural Revolution memoirs.

Discussion of sex was not limited to illicit books and was far less taboo in more rural contexts. According to memoirs of sent-down youth, peasants often made lewd jokes and exchanged dirty stories, habits that rubbed off on relocated urban youth.[18] At the same time, they learned about intercourse from watching dogs and pigs mate.[19] To the chagrin of sent-down youth, male peasants often wore crotch-less pants in the fields and sometimes even worked in the nude. Similarly, some women went topless, except for young women, who wore a cloth over their breasts.[20] All of this came as a shock to many modest sent-down youth when urban and rural sex cultures collided during the 1960s and 1970s.

If information on sex in general was difficult to come by in some places, then what about information about birth control in particular? While official publications on birth control were scarce during the peak years of the Cultural Revolution (1966–1968), these books became increasingly common beginning in 1969. However, books about birth control use promoted family planning only within the context of marriage, and their target audiences were married couples. In fact, some people reported only obtaining official information on birth control for the first time when registering their marriages; unmarried people relied on married friends to share the secrets of contraception with them.[21] Not only was it difficult for unmarried people to acquire family planning materials through official channels, but as with Western novels, being caught with such literature as an unmarried person might result in censure for bourgeois behavior.

Sex and Birth Control in Practice

During the Cultural Revolution, Red Guards' professed attitudes toward sex and their actual behavior were often at odds. Many Red Guards saw

[17] Dai Sijie, *Balzac and the Little Chinese Seamstress: A Novel*, Ina Rilke, trans. (New York: Knopf, 2001), 52.

[18] Shen, *Gang of One*, 145; Gao Yuan, *Born Red: A Chronicle of the Cultural Revolution* (Stanford: Stanford University Press, 1987), 19.

[19] Min, *Red Azalea,* 71; Rae Yang, *Spider Eaters: A Memoir* (Berkeley: University of California Press, 1997), 262; interview with author, Shanghai, December 22, 2017; and Honig, "Socialist Sex," 156.

[20] Shen, *Gang of One*, 82; Honig, "Socialist Sex," 156.

[21] Carl Djerassi, *The Politics of Contraception* (New York: W.W. Norton, 1979), 189.

themselves as the righteous protectors of Chinese socialism, and yet they at times engaged in the most bourgeois of acts: premarital sex. Red Guards in major cities like Shanghai, Beijing, Guangzhou, Chengdu, and Changsha who became disheartened with the Cultural Revolution instead turned to play and romance to fill the void.[22] They roamed the city streets horsing around, reading love stories, and flirting with strangers, as depicted in the film "In the Heat of the Sun" (*Yangguang canlan de rizi*).[23] By engaging in what the government labeled "individual problems" (*geren wenti*), these youths resisted the revolution and gave voice to their grievances.[24] The same tendency toward romance can be seen among Red Guards who traveled on China's transportation system free of charge spreading the spirit of revolution. Some male Red Guards even admitted that they viewed *chuanlian* as an opportunity to assault girls, and certainly not all Red Guard sex was consensual.[25]

In *Hawthorn Tree Forever,* a novel by Ai Mi that later was turned into a film by Zhang Yimou, the main character's best friend participates in *chuanlian,* traveling the country with other revolutionary youth. In the process, she becomes involved with a male Red Guard from her school. Ultimately, after the two have sex, the girl, who has no prior sexual experience, realizes she is pregnant and secretly has a surgical abortion at the hospital. The abortion is traumatic and embarrassing. Though this story is fictional, it reflects at least in part the reality of the era. In her memoir *Wild Swans,* Jung Chang recalls that a classmate of hers went traveling with her fellow Red Guards and became pregnant. As a result, her father beat her and her peers gossiped about her until she killed herself out of shame.[26] According to some accounts, pregnancies among Red Guards were so common that the national birth rate, which had been in decline, rebounded in 1968 and 1969.[27]

In contrast, in her memoir *Spider Eaters,* Rae Yang mentions the common charges of sex among Red Guards but argues that she and her peers never engaged in such acts because of their taboo nature.[28] On the contrary, Red Guards were notorious for punishing and torturing individuals charged with rape and extramarital affairs.[29] It is important to

[22] Li Bingkui, *Kuanglan yu qianliu: Zhongguo qingnian de xinglian yu hunyin, 1966–1976* (Raging Waves and Undercurrents: Sexuality and Marriage among Chinese Youth, 1966–1976) (Beijing: Shehui kexue wenxian chubanshe, 2015).

[23] *Yangguang canlan de rizi* is a film that was released in 1994 based on Wang Shuo's short story "Dongwu xiongmeng" (Ferocious Animals). The setting is Beijing during the Cultural Revolution, and the main character, a teenage boy named Ma Xiaojun, spends his time fighting rival gangs and chasing girls.

[24] Li, *Raging Waves and Undercurrents.*

[25] Ibid.; Honig, "Socialist Sex," 155.

[26] Chang, *Wild Swans,* 317.

[27] Li, *Raging Waves and Undercurrents,* 210.

[28] Yang, *Spider Eaters,* 193.

[29] Zhu, *Thirty Years,* 43; Yang, *Spider Eaters,* 151.

note that there was little evidence of laws banning extramarital affairs outright but that accusations of sexual crimes were based on informal or "unwritten" rules under the authority of local leadership.[30]

If premarital sex was somewhat common among Red Guards, it seems to have been a much larger problem among urban youth sent down to the countryside. The first group of youth was transferred to the countryside as early as 1955, but the bulk of "educated" youth were sent down between 1968 and the late 1970s.[31] In total, more than 17 million youth, or ten percent of the urban population, were sent to the countryside to remote places such as Heilongjiang, Yunnan, Inner Mongolia, and Guizhou.[32] Between 1962 and 1979, the majority of sent-down youth came from China's three centrally administrated cities: Shanghai (1,259,200), Beijing (636,300), and Tianjin (465,100).[33] Luoyang did dispatch sent-down youth to the countryside, but the numbers were insignificant compared to bigger cities.

One account of the lives of sent-down youth is particularly illuminating with respect to sexuality and premarital intercourse. In the novel mentioned earlier, *Balzac and the Little Chinese Seamstress*, two teenage boys from Beijing, Ma and Luo, are sent to rural Sichuan in 1971 for reeducation. Luo falls for a young seamstress and she becomes pregnant with his child. Because the law forbids marriage until age twenty and having an abortion typically requires a marriage certificate, Ma trades a gynecologist a copy of a forbidden French book for a secret surgical abortion.[34]

Though fictional, this story illustrates a number of noteworthy trends among sent-down youth. During the Sent-Down Youth Movement, rates of "illegal cohabitation," premarital sex, and abortion among sent-down youth rose dramatically.[35] In his memoir, *Gang of One*, former sent-down youth Fan Shen reveals how sent-down youth exchanged sex for favors. In one instance, a girl referred to as "Big Quilt" exchanged sex with her brigade leader for the opportunity to leave the countryside early to attend nursing school. When Big Quilt became pregnant by the brigade leader, she was also allowed to have an abortion. Other female

[30] Honig, "Socialist Sex," 153.

[31] Michel Bonnin, *The Lost Generation: The Rustification of China's Educated Youth (1968–1980)*, Krystyna Horko, trans. (Hong Kong: Chinese University Press, 2013).

[32] Liu Xiaomeng, *Zhongguo zhiqing koushushi* (The Oral Histories of Chinese Educated Youth) (Beijing: Zhongguo shehui kexue chubanshe, 2004), 1.

[33] Jin Dalu and Lin Shengbao, eds., *Shanghai zhishi qingnian shangshan xiaxiang yundong jishilu*, 1968–1981 (Chronicle of Shanghai Rusticated Youth During the Sent-Down Youth Movement, 1968–1981) (Shanghai: Shanghai shudian chubanshe, 2014), 1.

[34] Dai, *Balzac*, 184.

[35] Li, *Raging Waves and Undercurrents*.

sent-down youth similarly exchanged sex for transfers to better positions and exclusion from hard labor. It was also common for premarital pregnancy to result in a quick marriage.[36] In *Gang of One*, Fan's friend Smoking Devil, a sent-down youth from Beijing, gets a local village girl pregnant. The two make amends by agreeing to marry, whereby Smoking Devil gives up his urban residence permit (*hukou*) and foregoes any chance of ever returning to the city.[37]

Other sources reveal a different dimension of unplanned pregnancy. Two women I interviewed, one in her fifties and one age seventy-five, were both from Tianjin, poor, and relatively uneducated. They argued that during the Cultural Revolution, there were lots of premarital relationships. In most cases, rather than marrying the baby's father, if a girl became pregnant she would "throw away" (*reng*) the child since abortions were rare at that time.[38] Similarly, in *Wild Swans*, villagers find a dead baby that presumably was abandoned.[39] Several interviews affirmed the validity of these accounts, stating that during the Cultural Revolution countless sent-down youth and Red Guards on *chuanlian* had premarital sex.[40] According to one 57-year-old man from Shanghai, no one wanted to raise a baby without a residence permit, which was denied to children born out of wedlock, so the young mothers secretly gave birth to these babies (*sishengzi*) in the countryside and gave them away to local families.[41] State policies limiting movement created conditions that put women in a double bind – they could either keep their out-of-wedlock babies, who would then face life without the residence permit essential for obtaining housing, education, and medical care, or the mothers could give up or "throw away" their babies, all of which were emotionally traumatic courses of action. In other cases, unmarried women tried to drown their babies or had dangerous, sometimes fatal, abortions administered by amateur practitioners or local doctors.[42] According to two former sent-down youths from Tianjin, getting pregnant out of wedlock and keeping the baby was more shameful at that time than having an abortion, so unmarried young women during the Cultural Revolution underwent abortions to avoid losing face (*diu mianzi*)[43].

Relationships between sent-down youth or sent-down youth and locals that resulted in forbidden pregnancies seem to have been very common, but the consequences varied significantly. Emily Honig and Zhao

[36] BMA, 100-001-00897. [37] Shen, *Gang of One*, 107.
[38] Interview with author, Tianjin, February 13, 2017; Honig, "Socialist Sex," 153.
[39] Chang, *Wild Swans*, 437. [40] Interview with author, Shanghai, December 10, 2016.
[41] Interview with author, Shanghai, December 10, 2016.
[42] Interview with author, Shanghai, December 10, 2016.
[43] Interview with author, Tianjin, June 27, 2019.

Xiaojian note that in seeking to punish sexual misconduct in the countryside, local authorities targeted powerless rural men and charged them on dubious grounds with violating female sent-down youth. At the same time, local officials deliberately overlooked the sexual transgressions of male sent-down youth with local women.[44] A series of typically inaccessible court records from rural Jiangxi similarly suggests that the outcome of sexual relationships (regardless of consent) and the resultant pregnancies were closely linked to the status of the couple involved.

The case of Cheng Xuan, a man who came from a peasant family that farmed a small plot of rented land in rural Jiangxi, is illustrative. Although Cheng only had a junior high school education, he served first as a village clerk, then as a socialist educator for his work team, and eventually as a junior high school teacher. At age forty, he met Fang Lingling, a sent-down youth from Shanghai. The two began sleeping together, and Fang became pregnant. Cheng asked other people to help him procure an abortifacient, but the abortion was unsuccessful. When news of the affair got out, Cheng, although dismissed from his job, stole a letter of introduction from his work unit and brought Fang to a hotel, where the couple "illegally" shared a room by posing as husband and wife. Finally, Cheng took Fang to the commune health clinic, where he found a doctor willing to perform an abortion.[45] In this case, Cheng's position provided him with the resources to escape scrutiny in the commune and attain an abortion for Fang.

In another case, a sent-down youth from Shanghai developed a relationship with the local party secretary, a college-educated man from Shanghai who was twenty years her senior. When the young woman discovered that she was pregnant, the couple experimented with *baiyao,* musk, and other Chinese herbal abortifacients to no avail. Finally, the young woman was able to use her urban *hukou* to return home to Shanghai where she had a surgical abortion.[46] Around the same time, a female sent-down youth called Cao, also from Shanghai, developed a relationship with the head of her work unit. The couple met secretly many times and when Cao discovered she was pregnant she consumed *Shidishui*, or "Ten Drops," a Chinese patent medicine used to cool the body (in TCM, heat is associated with pregnancy).[47] When the medication failed to induce an abortion and Cao's pregnancy was discovered,

[44] Honig and Zhao, *Across the Great Divide*, 95. [45] JTUA, Z1–11-22.

[46] JTUA, Z1–11-123.

[47] In the 1970s, rural use of TCM patent medicines increased steadily due to their ubiquity and convenience; Fang, "Barefoot Doctors," 275.

her work unit permitted her to have a surgical abortion "to prevent the spread of her negative influence" to her peers.[48]

In all of these cases, the young women were permitted to have abortions either at a commune clinic in the countryside or at an urban hospital. During that period, it was common for sent-down youth who became pregnant in the countryside to return to the city to have abortions. Emily Honig also found that sent-down youth working in the Jiangsu countryside went to Nanjing for abortions if they could not obtain them locally.[49] In general, young women without connections to the city – especially, women with rural *hukou* – and those who developed relationships with less prominent figures in their communes did not fare as well as the young women in the above cases. The fates of these women were closely linked to the statuses of the men they were involved with. Men with seniority, access to greater resources, and higher levels of education could offer their lovers more flexibility in terms of access to abortions. At the same time, it is plausible that men in senior positions, nearly all of whom were married, had greater incentive to help their partners attain abortions because they had reputations and careers to protect. Whether acting out of patriarchal self-interest or altruism, in each of the above cases the male lover was arrested and sent to jail.

Not all sent-down youths shared these types of experiences. Others were stationed in very different "sexual climates" and therefore had different experiences with sexuality. Construction corps, for example, were much more tightly regulated than village production brigades.[50] I interviewed a 70-year-old couple born and raised in Tianjin. In 1970, the husband was sent to Inner Mongolia and the wife to Heilongjiang in frigid northern China as part of construction corps. According to the couple, not only was there no premarital sex but apparently men and women rarely interacted. The wife charged that anyone who had premarital sex during the Cultural Revolution was immoral; no one in her work unit had abortions or threw out babies. She became very upset when I even suggested that such a thing was possible.[51] Another interviewee, a fifty-eight-year-old man also born and raised in Tianjin, was also sent to a construction corps in Heilongjiang in 1970. As far as he knew there were no premarital sex and no forbidden pregnancies. No one abandoned babies or had secret abortions. As the other interviewees had said, men

[48] JTUA, Z1-10-883.
[49] Honig, "Socialist Sex," 172; Emily Honig and Xiaojian Zhao, *Across the Great Divide: The Sent-Down Youth Movement in Mao's China, 1968–1980* (Cambridge: Cambridge University Press, 2019), 107.
[50] Honig, "Socialist Sex," 171.
[51] Interview with author, Tianjin, February 15, 2017.

and women were kept completely separate in single-sex brigades, so there was little opportunity for any type of relationship to develop.[52] In *Spider Eaters*, Rae Yang tells a similar story of her construction corps in rural Heilongjiang. She compares herself and her fellow sent-down youth to ascetic monks and nuns because of their spartan lifestyles and abstinence.[53]

In addition to differences in "sexual climate," conflicting official campaigns as well as the timeframe in which youths underwent reeducation in the countryside were critical in shaping attitudes toward sex and romance. In the early 1970s, even as the CCP promoted "wanhun" (late or delayed marriage) and "jihua shengyu" (birth planning) in the countryside and condemned youth caught flirting or reading provocative books, the slogan "take root in the rural areas" (*zhagen nongcun*) became popular.[54] This expression referred to the notion that educated youth should marry and settle down permanently in the villages where they were being rusticated to show enduring support for rural development. In particular, female educated youth were encouraged to marry local peasants or fellow educated youth, thus giving up their urban *hukou* and stemming the tide of rusticated youth returning to the cities (due to illness and the pursuit of higher education and new jobs).[55]

Similar themes emerge in *Mao's Lost Children: Stories of the Rusticated Youth of China's Cultural Revolution*, a collection of accounts of the lives of sent-down youth at Daling Farm (later converted into a militia regiment) on Hainan Island. By 1973, there were more than 110,000 reeducated youth, mostly from Guangzhou, living on Hainan Island.[56] In the late 1960s, the expression "being rooted in Hainan" referred to committing oneself to the revolutionary cause. However, by the early 1970s, that same slogan referred to getting married and starting a family on the island.[57]

The campaign to permanently settle in the countryside (*chadui luohu*) was fraught with contradictions. Some youth faced pressure to settle down in the countryside, and at times authority figures went so far as to play matchmaker for the sent-down youth. In the case of a youth called Huang Rong'er in Hainan, the deputy political commissar of the regiment even offered to help Huang, the son of a senior government official,

[52] Interview with author, Tianjin, February 13, 2017. [53] Yang, *Spider Eaters*, 233.
[54] Bai, *1966–1976*, 283.
[55] Liu Xiaomeng, *Zhongguo zhiqingshi: da chao* (A History of China's Sent-Down Youth: The Main Wave) (Beijing: Zhongguo shehui kexue chubanshe, 1998), 319.
[56] Ou Nianzhong and Liang Yongkang, eds., *Mao's Lost Children: Stories of the Rusticated Youth of China's Cultural Revolution*, Laura Maynard, trans. (Portland: Merwin Asia, 2015), xiii.
[57] Ou and Liang, *Mao's Lost Children*, 256.

settle down with another rusticated youth to set an example for other youth.[58] Similarly, another sent-down youth how from Guangzhou, Fang Jinqi, recalled that she met her husband during the movement to put down roots and was encouraged to marry him.[59] However, Chen Hongguang, a sent-down youth stationed as a medic and laborer in a militia regiment in Hainan, explained that although he developed feelings for a fellow sent-down youth and was encouraged to put down roots, he feared that showing romantic affection could lead to charges of depravity. Ultimately the pair dated but chose not to remain together so as not to give up their right to eventually return to the city and enjoy a higher standard of living.[60] I interviewed a couple in Tianjin, where the husband was from rural Heilongjiang and the wife was a sent-down youth from Tianjin. The couple was assigned to the same army brigade in Heilongjiang, where they were training to fight the Soviet Union. The pair dated and fell in love in the context of the push for sent-down youth to marry in the countryside, but some people did not believe they should get married. They feared that the woman would return to the city permanently after the movement ended and the couple would be permanently separated (the policy forbidding sent-down youth who married in the countryside from moving their families to the city was later reversed). Despite these contradictory sentiments, the realities of rural life – lack of supervision, access to superior housing for married couples, sheer loneliness, and pressure to support the Sent-Down Youth Movement – contributed to a rapid rise in the marriage rate among sent-down youth in the late 1970s. The number of married sent-down youth increased from 480,000 in 1974 to 861,000 in 1977.[61]

Indeed, the "sexual climate" in which a person lived and worked during this period, as well as the time frame in which reeducation occurred, dictated the degree of sexual latitude individuals had and the likelihood of them engaging in sexual relations. While some Red Guards and sent-down youth were sexually active, others lived in sexually repressive environments with little contact with the opposite sex. At the same time, opportunities for premarital sex evidently created a greater demand for abortions in the countryside, as out-of-wedlock pregnancies were condemned just as much as, if not more than, abortions.

Out-of-Wedlock Sex and Abortion in the Eyes of the Law

In 1973, after increasing reports of "harm to sent-down youth," the State Council issued a directive calling for local officials to identify and punish

[58] Ibid., 245. [59] Ibid., 256. [60] Ibid., 251.
[61] Liu, *A History of China's Sent-Down Youth,* 319.

individuals who either had romantic relationships with unmarried female sent-down youth or assaulted them sexually (as we will see, the distinction was often blurry). An additional directive stipulated that cases of rape would be strongly punished, as in the case of two officials who were executed on charges of sexually abusing sent-down youth.[62] Because one of the offenders was charged with *jianwu* (sexual violation or assault), provincial governments interpreted this to mean that all cases of *jianwu* would be treated as seriously as cases of rape, and any case involving a sexual relationship with a female sent-down youth, regardless of consent, would fall under this rubric.[63] This heightened attention to sexual behavior in the early 1970s is responsible for the ballooning supply of archival records mentioning sex among sent-down youth.[64] All this suggests that relationships among sent-down youth and between sent-down youth and locals were an ongoing issue since at least 1968, with these incidents only coming to light after 1973 when the central government called for stricter sexual policing.

Court records from rural Jiangxi illustrate the growing range and depth of state surveillance in the late 1960s and early 1970s. Criminal charges brought against unmarried individuals engaging in sex and the language used to justify penalties in these cases evinced the authorities' intensifying role in determining what constituted "orthodox" sexual behavior. In every one of the cases, a female educated youth was sent from the city to the countryside, where she began having sexual relations with a local man. In almost every case, the male was significantly older and had some education or authority even if he was from a poor peasant background. The court records often claimed that the male "baited" (*you'er*) or "seduced" (*youhuo* or *tiaoxi)* the female youth with flowery and deceiving words (*huayan qiaoyu*).[65] Official accounts explicitly framed these relationships in terms of sexual violation or assault (*jianwu*).[66] This language paints female youth as passive and denies them agency while possibly misconstruing the nature of the intercourse. Perhaps this was a product of the broader denial of female sexual desire or an effort to reinforce the trope of female sexual purity. In her memoir *Red Azalea,* Anchee Min describes the heartbreaking case of a fellow sent-down youth named Little Green. Little Green, the eighteen-year-old daughter of urban intellectuals, was caught having sex in a field with a young soldier.

[62] Emily Honig and Xiaojian Zhao, *Across the Great Divide: The Sent-Down Youth Movement in Mao's China, 1968–1980* (Cambridge: Cambridge University Press, 2019), 99.

[63] Honig and Zhao, *Across the Great Divide*, 100. [64] Ibid., 95. [65] Z1-10-847.

[66] The term "jianwu" is used in reference to sexual relationships with female sent-down youth, regardless of consent, in court records from Jiangxi, Heilongjiang, Shanxi, and other places; Honig and Zhao, *Across the Great Divide*, 95.

When Little Green's brigade leader accused the man of rape, Little Green did not defend him although the act likely was consensual. It seems she wanted to preserve some degree of personal dignity and protect her reputation, as girls who had premarital sexual contact with boys were scorned, ridiculed, and much worse. At the same time, female sent-down youth wishing to avoid blame for "inappropriate" sexual behavior could file charges of rape against their lovers. In the case of Little Green, the young man was given the death penalty, and Little Green, now a social pariah, went mad from guilt.[67]

Many of the circumstances in which sent-down youth engaged in sexual relationships suggest that there may have been consent. Often couples had sex many times over the span of several years before being caught and punished.[68] Take, for example, the case of a female sent-down youth named Yu Meilan, who developed a relationship with a twenty-seven-year-old middle peasant named Lin Ziyi. According to the security bureau report, Lin brought Yu gifts of pork, sugar, and sesame seeds to "seduce" her. The couple met countless times and when other sent-down youth returned to Shanghai to visit relatives Yu stayed behind to be with her lover. When Yu discovered that she was pregnant, Lin bought her an abortifacient, but when that failed he took her to the local hospital for a surgical abortion. Because the pregnancy was too far along, the doctor refused to perform the surgery. Lin was subsequently charged with sexual assault (*jianwu*) and given a five-year sentence.[69] Even in cases where a couple was engaged to be married, the man was still charged with rape when he had sex with his fiancée.[70] These cases suggest that charges were based less on concrete evidence and testimonials than on the whim of local authorities. Moreover, such accusations of rape likely stemmed from the moralistic and classist assumption that sex between an uneducated older peasant and a young urban girl was only possible under duress.

Gendered cultural norms also played a significant role in dictating how individuals responded to accusations of sexual indecency. The state's assessment of whether a relationship fit with so-called societal values and expectations for the ideal family unit was critical in determining legality. In these cases, intercourse simply for pleasure, rather than for perpetuating the family line in marriage, was deemed unorthodox.

In addition to these more ambiguous cases, straightforward cases of coerced sex (*qiangjian*) also abounded.[71] Numerous memoirs and court records recall instances of heterosexual and homosexual rape either

[67] Min, *Red Azalea*, 56. [68] JTUA, Z1-10-883; JTUA, Z1-11-123.
[69] Ibid., Z1-10-930. [70] Ibid., Z1-10-929.
[71] Liu, *A History of China's Sent-Down Youth*, 263–264.

committed by villagers or cadres onto sent-down youth or by sent-down youth onto other sent-down youth.[72] The lack of formal supervision in rural areas made sent-down youth particularly vulnerable to sexual violence with few channels for recourse until the State Council released directives addressing this issue. According to a State Council report of violence against sent-down youth, incomplete national statistics reveal that between 1969 and 1973, 23,000 cases of abuse of sent-down youth were reported, of which 70 percent were cases of raped or seduced female sent-down youth.[73]

Because rates of rape, consensual premarital sex, and unregistered cohabitation of couples in the countryside were so high, many people assumed that female sent-down youth were no longer virgins after returning from the countryside.[74] In fact, in 1974 the central government decreed that contraceptives such as oral birth control, condoms, and cervical caps be distributed free in the countryside, in particular among sent-down youth.[75] However, distribution of these products likely varied greatly by region according to local government preferences and infrastructure. The Department of Gynecology and Obstetrics within the Guangdong Province Maternal and Child Health Center (*Guangdong sheng fuyou baojian yuan*) even went so far as to conduct a survey of the menstrual schedules of female sent-down youth. The survey collected data on the menstrual cycles of 3,125 sent-down youth dispatched from the cities of Guangzhou and Foshan to work on tea farms between 1969 and 1974. The study focused on the age at which most girls had their first period and the number of days between each period before and after being sent down. The survey's ostensible goal was to "attend to the physiological characteristics of female sent-down youth," that is to determine if the stress of working and living in the countryside had any negative physiological consequences, such as amenorrhea.[76] I suspect, however, that the study also served the purpose of legitimizing regular

[72] JTUA, Z1–10-929; "Nü zhiqing koushu wenge shiqi liangxing guanxi beican jingli rang ren zhenjing" (Female Sent Down Youths' Shocking Oral Histories of Tragic Sexual Experiences During the Cultural Revolution), *Liushu yaofeng de boke* (Shaking Willow Blog), June 8, 2015, http://blog.sina.com.cn/s/blog_443bf8ae0102voa4.html.

[73] It should be noted that these figures include accusations of rape in instances where rape did not, in fact, occur; "Nü zhiqing koushu wenge shiqi liangxing guanxi beican jingli rang ren zhenjing" (Female Sent Down Youths' Shocking Oral Histories of Tragic Sexual Experiences during the Cultural Revolution), *Liushu yaofeng de boke* (Shaking Willow Blog), June 8, 2015, http://blog.sina.com.cn/s/blog_443bf8ae0102voa4.html.

[74] Yang, *Spider Eaters,* 248; Honig, "Socialist Sex," 162; Ma Bo, *Blood Red Sunset: A Memoir of the Chinese Cultural Revolution,* Howard Goldblatt trans. (New York: Penguin Books, 1996), 174.

[75] SMA, B123–8-1051. [76] GMA, 512-A1.6-8-21.

health inspections and menstrual reporting, thus deepening the state's knowledge of individual sexual health and providing consistent information regarding the likelihood of premarital pregnancy. Menstrual tracking in the early 1970s not only paved the way for stricter government control over reproductive health under the One Child Policy but also served as a means of preventing unreported, and potentially dangerous, abortions in the countryside.

Despite this increased attention to young women's physiology and sexual experiences, court records from this period charging males with helping female sent-down youth undergo abortions made little or no mention of whether the women consented or took any initiative in the matter. In fact, in almost every case only the man was arrested and charged with assisting in the abortion but the woman appears to have only undergone "thought reform." Moreover, in only half of the abortion cases from Poyang county was the female youth's name listed in the court record (otherwise she was simply referred to as "woman"), while the male's full name, including nicknames, was given in every case.[77] It is possible that because men were perceived as dominant, it was virtually inconceivable that a woman might pursue an abortion of her own volition. Conversely, the intention might have been to protect the reputations of urban young women involved in abortion cases at the expense of their rural male lovers.

Official explanations for charging individuals with having premarital/extramarital sex or undergoing abortions were typically framed in terms of ideological crimes and personal moral failings because neither sex out of wedlock nor abortions were actually against the law. For example, many court records charged men who facilitated their lovers' abortions with disturbing the social order, negatively influencing society, espousing bourgeois ideologies, and failing to thoroughly study Marxist-Leninist-Maoist teachings.[78] Such accusations tied personal decisions to the fate of society as a whole while conflating sexual transgressions with ideological commitment. Official court records also charged that sexual relationships were efforts to undermine reeducation in the countryside, class struggle, and Chairman Mao's great strategic plan, all of which were considered counterrevolutionary acts.[79] Given the emphasis on productivity, the harsh realities of life in the countryside, and the "feminization" of agriculture work during the collective period, it is not surprising that impeding a woman's labor efforts was considered a very serious crime.[80]

[77] Unnamed female victims are referred to as *nüfang*, meaning woman.
[78] JTUA, Z1-10-884. [79] Ibid., Z1-10-883, Z1-10-928.
[80] Women played a dominant role in agricultural work during the era of collectivization; Hershatter, *The Gender of Memory*, 220.

In addition, helping a lover obtain an abortion was sometimes interpreted as evidence of shirking personal responsibility for one's actions.[81] Some case records argued that by engaging in sexual intercourse, men enacted physical and emotional damage on young female educated youths. In the case of abortions, the male defendant was often accused of harming or destroying the young woman's body (*shenti shoudao cuican*).[82] However, the impact on the woman was rarely the central focus of the court records and at no point was it evident what role she played in the affair (unless she died, which would have made the charges more severe). These cases evince the dual mechanisms of formal and informal sanction in place, whereby men received the brunt of the legal punishment, but women were often ostracized socially.

The Rise of the Barefoot Doctors and the Evolving Role of the State

Based on data from the Ministry of Health, Thomas Scharping estimates that abortion rates nationwide nearly doubled from 13.3 percent in 1971 to 22.3 percent in 1975.[83] Yet, he approximates that the national abortion rate was only 6.5 percent in 1965 on the eve of the Cultural Revolution.[84] In her ethnographic study of women in rural Shaanxi, Gail Hershatter found that abortions were already well known in the countryside in the late 1960s and some of her interviewees had undergone these procedures at a local hospital.[85] One way to account for the dramatic increase in abortions during the late 1960s and early 1970s is the accelerated deployment of barefoot doctors – paramedics, who were often sent-down youth – to the countryside beginning in 1968.[86]

The rise of the barefoot doctors was part and parcel of the systematic intensification of state control over reproduction. Relying on a combination of Western, Chinese, and folk medicine, barefoot doctors not only delivered a wide range of critical medical services to places with little to no health infrastructure, but they also served as vectors for disseminating information about contraception and abortion.[87] In her study of a village in Liaoning province in the late 1960s and 1970s, Masako Kohama found that female barefoot doctors there adopted a "gender-sensitive"

[81] JTUA, Z1-10-884, Z1-11-21. [82] Ibid., Z1-10-884.
[83] Scharping, *Birth Control in China*, 121. [84] Ibid., 121.
[85] Hershatter, *The Gender of Memory*, 206–207.
[86] White, *China's Longest Campaign*, 54.
[87] Fang, "Barefoot Doctors," 271. China's rural healthcare system had three tiers: the county, commune, and brigade levels. Barefoot doctors were members of the middle tier: commune production brigades. Fang, "Barefoot Doctors," 268.

approach to birth planning mobilization. Armed with more than just rudimentary medical training, these medical workers successfully earned the trust of village women and played an instrumental role in convincing them to adopt family planning measures.[88] Although Kohama asserts that her study is hardly representative even of rural Liaoning, it is safe to say that barefoot doctors served as mediators between top-down policies implemented at the provincial and commune levels and local receptors (Figure 5.1).

The upsurge in publications of encyclopedic medical guides also facilitated the spread of state medicine into rural areas.[89] An examination of four barefoot doctor guides published during roughly the same period – *Rural Healthcare Handbook* (1968), *Popular Handbook for Rural Healthcare* (1969), *"Barefoot Doctor" Training Materials* (1970), and *Rural Doctor Handbook* (1971) – reveals that each contained a chapter dedicated solely to family planning. The introductions to these medical handbooks state that the contents were specifically designed to guide sent-down youth and middle school, high school, and college graduates in their efforts to bring healthcare to the countryside.[90] All four texts contained descriptions of birth control techniques, including condoms, diaphragms, IUDs, oral contraceptives, contraceptive ointments, and the rhythm method. They also mentioned surgeries for abortion and sterilization.[91]

Despite superficial similarities, these handbooks were highly inconsistent. Because each edition was compiled and published locally by region or by city, the books privileged different types of family planning strategies. While some guides contained diagrams and step-by-step guides to performing contraceptive surgeries and IUD insertions, others merely introduced these procedures with little explanation, indicating that not all of the information in the guidebooks was intended to be put into practice. The 1968, 1970, and 1971 editions all devoted considerable space to the details of inserting and removing IUDs, performing female

[88] Masako Kohama, "Zhongguo nongcun jihua shengyu de puji – yi 1960–1970 niandai Q cun wei li" (The Popularization of Birth Planning in Rural China – The Case of Q Village, 1960s–1970s) *Jindai zhongguo funü shi yanjiu* 19 (2011): 190.

[89] Fang Xiaoping, *Barefoot Doctors and Western Medicine in China* (Rochester: University of Rochester Press, 2012), 59.

[90] *Nongcun yiliao weisheng shouce* (Rural Healthcare Handbook) (Shanghai: Shanghai kexue jishu chubanshe, 1968), 1; *Nongcun yiliao weisheng puji shouce* (Popular Handbook for Rural Healthcare) (Shanghai: Shanghai "nongcun yiliao weisheng puji shouce" bianxie zu, 1969), 1.

[91] *Nongcun yiliao weisheng puji shouce* (Rural Healthcare Handbook), 346; "'Chijiao yisheng' peixun jiaocai" ("Barefoot Doctor" Training Materials) (Beijing: Renmin weisheng chubanshe, 1970), 254–257; *Nongcun yisheng shouce* (Rural Doctor Handbook) (Beijing: Renmin weisheng chubanshe, 1971), 660–680.

Figure 5.1 Birth planning poster: *"Chijiao yisheng xuanchuan jihua shengyu haochu, gei sheyuan tigong mianfei biyun yaoju"* (A barefoot doctor disseminates the benefits of birth planning; the commune provides free contraceptives), 1960s.
Source: US National Library of Medicine.

and male sterilizations, and conducting surgical abortions. However, the volume from 1969 did not discuss these procedures in detail.[92] Based on that text alone, it would have been highly unlikely that a medic with limited training could have performed a successful abortion or sterilization surgery.

Upon closer scrutiny, other inconsistencies appear in these medical guides. While the party had officially discouraged using traditional herbal remedies for family planning in 1962 in response to numerous reports of negative and even fatal reactions to the formulas, some barefoot doctor manuals from the 1970s explicitly promoted these types of traditional contraception methods. Barefoot doctor's manuals published in 1974 and 1977, for example, provided herbal recipes for contraception, abortion, and sterilization.[93] In Luoyang, guidelines for medical workers, including barefoot doctors, suggested that attention be paid to effective methods grounded in Chinese herbal medicine, folk practices, and acupuncture.[94] At the same time, other health guides from this period completely elided the topic of herbal abortifacients and contraceptives, likely because they were thought to be dangerous and unreliable.

One account from a female sent-down youth, Han Moumou, from Tianjin illustrates the diverse types of information barefoot doctors disseminated. According to Han, when she was sent to the Anhui countryside in 1968, she started sleeping with a male sent-down youth from Shanghai. When she told him she was concerned about getting pregnant, he mentioned that a barefoot doctor had told him to eat raw soybeans to prevent conception. When Han found herself three months pregnant, her lover told her that a barefoot doctor had taught him how to perform an abortion. Using a method common for late-term abortions, the young man inserted a tube of saline water attached to a bottle into Han's vagina.[95] After four or five hours, the fetus finally emerged.

[92] "Directions for performing a tubal ligation," *Nongcun yiliao weisheng shouce* (Rural Healthcare Handbook), 679; Directions for performing a vasectomy, *Nongcun yiliao weisheng shouce* (Rural Healthcare Handbook), 677; "Directions for performing an abortion (uterine dilation and curettage)," *Nongcun yiliao weisheng shouce* (Rural Healthcare Handbook) (1971), 675; "Directions for performing abortions and sterilizations," *Nongcun yiliao weisheng puji shouce* (Popular Handbook for Rural Healthcare), 346.

[93] U.S. Department of Health, Education, and Welfare Public Health Service, *A Barefoot Doctor's Manual (Translation of a Chinese Instruction to Certain Chinese Health Personnel)* (John E. Fogarty International Center for Advanced Health Studies, 1974), 173–175; Weisberg, Marvin E. and John R. Graham. *A Barefoot Doctor's Manual: A Guide to Traditional Chinese and Modern Medicine (The American Translation of the Official Chinese Paramedical Manual* (Cloudburst Press, 1977), 61–62.

[94] LMA, B118. [95] Rigdon, "Abortion Law," 548.

Although Han fainted from the pain, she ultimately survived to tell the tale.[96]

Even as some health workers were promoting abortions in the countryside either using TCM formulas or biomedical technologies, unmarried people were being punished for undergoing and performing abortions. Although the barefoot doctor guides made no mention of the fact that these medicines and procedures were reserved for married couples, that seems to have been the underlying assumption. In the eyes of the authorities, then, there was no tension between promoting abortions as birth control among married couples and punishing instances of abortion among unmarried couples. Moreover, decreasing population growth took precedence over female health as women were encouraged to use family planning methods only recently deemed too dangerous for public consumption.

Despite very real inconsistencies in medical discourse and practice, the state continued to systematize and standardize birth planning. In 1971, the State Council issued a directive calling for the establishment of local birth planning offices and small groups.[97] At the same time, greater emphasis was placed on subsidizing family planning through free birth control supplies and reimbursements for medical procedures.[98] As a complement to barefoot doctors, the government sent birth control teams into the countryside to monitor fertility and appointed "sister-in-law team leaders," rural woman cadres, and brigade leaders, to serve as the "backbone" of birth planning implementation in the countryside.[99] Over the course of the 1970s, women leaders' responsibilities expanded from mobilizing resources and personnel for birth planning and distributing contraceptives and information about family planning to monitoring the menstrual cycles of women of childbearing age and disseminating birth targets.[100] As early as 1970, a reporting system that compiled county, municipal, and provincial levels birth planning information was in place in some provinces.[101] In 1971, the policy of "later, longer, fewer" (*wan, xi, shao*) – which encouraged later marriage, longer spacing between children, and fewer children per couple – was adopted.[102] Under this policy, rural couples were only allowed to have three

[96] Wang Nanfang, "1950 niandai zhongguo jietou lugu de biyun guanggao" (Explicit Contraceptive Advertisements on the Streets of China in the 1950s), *Sina* (blog), September 7, 2015, http://blog.sina.com.cn/s/blog_4ac5b19f0102vzxm.html?tj=2.

[97] White, *China's Longest Campaign*, 59.

[98] Ibid.

[99] Zheng, *Ethnographies*, 46, 84; White, *China's Longest Campaign*, 85.

[100] White, *China's Longest Campaign*, 85–86.

[101] Ibid., 87.

[102] Kaufman et al., "Family Planning," 725.

children.[103] By 1973, specific birth targets were being disseminated throughout the whole nation as part of the national economic plan, and by 1974 governments down to the county level were being assigned specific annual targets for population growth.[104] As a precursor to later policies mandating that only couples with birth permits have children, in the 1970s some communes and brigades were already allocating birth permits to individual couples permitted to have a baby.[105] In 1978, the Central Committee further tightened birth restrictions under the slogan "one is best, two at most," thus setting the stage for more stringent fertility limitation in the 1980s.[106]

Another factor that facilitated more effective reproductive policing was the shift toward detailed and elaborate recordkeeping in the 1970s. Tong Lam shows that between the late Qing dynasty and the Mao era China underwent a paradigm shift from seeking truth from Confucian values to privileging empirical social facts as the basis for governance.[107] Building on this foundation, Arunabh Ghosh chronicles China's "crisis in counting," or the quest for reliable statistical data in the early years of the PRC.[108] Changes in recordkeeping were part of the larger epistemological move toward conceptualizing the people within China's borders as a "population" and viewing individual health statistics as integral to statecraft. In practice, this transition involved teaching medical teams how to collect accurate statistical data and determine what constituted a useful statistic.

In her book on the campaign to eradicate snail fever in Maoist China, Miriam Gross charts the process through which state governance and statistics became intertwined in the countryside. According to Gross, in the late 1950s when grassroots groups realized that they lacked the baseline data necessary to evaluate the effect of the anti-snail fever campaign, they began collecting data such as the sex, age, occupation, and disease stage of snail fever patients. However, because there were no set forms, statistics were inconsistent and difficult to compare. In fact, standardized medical forms were not deemed useful until after the 1950s.[109] The lack of emphasis on recordkeeping was due in part to

[103] Susan Greenhalgh, "Controlling Births and Bodies in Village China," *American Ethnologist* 21, no. 1 (1994): 6; For more on the campaign associated with *wan, xi, shao* in the 1970s, see chapter 6.

[104] White, *China's Longest Campaign,* 87.

[105] White, *China's Longest Campaign,* 87.

[106] Greenhalgh, *Just One Child,* 86–87.

[107] Tong Lam, *A Passion for Facts: Social Surveys and the Construction of the Chinese Nation State, 1900–1949* (Berkeley: University of California Press, 2011), 3–4.

[108] Arunabh Ghosh, *Making It Count: Statistics and Statecraft in the Early People's Republic of China* (Princeton: Princeton University Press, 2020), 2–3.

[109] Gross, *Farewell to the God of Plague,* 214.

the fact that Mao had once deemed this practice a bourgeois waste of time.[110]

A similar transition from imprecise or nonexistent recordkeeping to the methodical and invasive documenting of all aspects of sexual health is evident with respect to birth planning. In the 1950s and 1960s, the standard forms in individual official dossiers only contained categories like name, age, class background, education level, work hours, and work attendance rate.[111] Similarly, individual dossiers contained minimal information about reproduction other than the name of the person's spouse and the number of living children they had. By the 1970s, however, these files included precise details regarding reproduction and family planning. A new section titled either "late marriage and birth planning" (*wanhun jihua shengyu*) or "birth planning situation" (*jihua shengyu qingkuang*) was added to the forms and included information like the number of children a person had, as well as what type of contraception that person and his or her spouse were using.[112] Some forms were more detailed than others, which likely produced the same problem of inconsistent and incomparable statistics as in Gross' study. The most comprehensive records featured a chart with boxes to be filled in regarding "number of children that met birth planning conditions," "number of IUD insertions and removals," "rate of successful birth control use," "number of male or female sterilizations," "number of abortions," and "use of oral contraceptives."[113] These details were juxtaposed with information about individual work productivity, highlighting the centrality of family planning to meeting national labor goals.

Like the training of barefoot doctors, improved recordkeeping played a critical role in facilitating the "legibility" of the countryside.[114] For example, birth planning records for Wenshui county, Shanxi organized family planning statistics for the year 1976 by village. For each village, the aggregate numbers of male and female sterilizations, abortions, IUD insertions, and children born that met birth planning conditions were delineated.[115] The villages were also ranked in terms of family planning rate and ability to meet birth planning targets. This process created accountability to the state at the individual, village, and county levels,

[110] Ibid., 216.
[111] The Maoist state created and maintained individual files for each citizen.
[112] ECNUA, Ai 0358-024-003; ECNUA, Ai 0358-024-008; ECNUA, Ai 0358-024-001.
[113] ECNUA, As 0358-099-040; ECNUA, Ai 0358-024-001; ENUA, Ai 0358-024-009.
[114] Gross, *Farewell to the God of Plague*, 40, 210.
[115] "Jieyu cuoshi luoshi qingkuang paidui gongbu" (Village Ranking in Terms of Implementation of Birth Control Measures), 1976.

with statistics offering seemingly irrefutable evidence of one's productivity in implementing birth planning, or lack thereof.

As for Wenshui's performance, the county's statistics were largely representative of the birth planning ratios apparent in other parts of rural China. In 1976, 588 women in Wenshui underwent sterilization, whereas only eighteen men were sterilized, highlighting the tendency for women to bear the responsibility for sterilization. Of 31,604 eligible women (there is no corresponding statistic for men), 4,305 women had IUDs inserted and another 759 had abortions.[116] These statistics not only illustrate the growing pervasiveness of rural birth planning but also reveal that public discussion of birth control practices both at the individual and collective levels became normalized during the 1970s. These trends likely eased the transition to the One Child Policy, when more uniform reproductive monitoring became standard.

Conclusion

The period from 1966 until the implementation of the One Child Policy in 1979 bore witness to some of twentieth-century China's most turbulent years. Schools were closed, millions of people were persecuted and killed for being "class enemies," and families were torn apart through repeated political campaigns. To make matters worse, the Sent-Down Youth Movement created what has been referred to as a "lost generation" of people, many of whom were denied the opportunity to attend college and instead were required to perform manual labor under grueling conditions.[117]

From the perspective of sex and reproduction, the Cultural Revolution and the Sent-Down Youth Movement expanded opportunities for sexual contact among male and female youth in unprecedented ways, exposed sent-down youth to overt discussions of sexuality, and disseminated knowledge about abortion to the countryside through barefoot doctors. These movements also inadvertently facilitated the normalization of abortion by increasing rural access to this service and the number of people forced to resort to this procedure. The conflicting nature of state policies is best exemplified by the fact that even as family planning, including abortion, became mandatory in cities, couples who became

[116] ECNUA, As 0358-099–038.

[117] That being said, other sent-down youth made the best of their circumstances, and some even attended college when the university entrance exams were restored in the late 1970s. Bonnin, *The Lost Generation*, xvii-xviii; Honig and Zhao, *Across the Great Divide*, 127–129.

pregnant out of wedlock were being punished for undergoing abortion in the countryside.

Despite these inconsistencies, the effects of escalating attention to reproduction vis-à-vis the creation of a rural birth planning infrastructure were also reflected at the statistical level. If the central government's goal was to decrease unplanned births, this objective was partially achieved but within a broader context of continual population growth in absolute terms. Indeed, the population ballooned from 742,060,000 in 1966 to 970,920,000 in 1979, but the population growth rate dropped from 22.7 to 13.3 percent during the same timeframe.[118]

[118] National Birth Planning Committee Integrated Planning Division (*Guojia jihua shengyu weiyuanhui zonghe jihua si*), *Chinese Birth Planning Statistical Yearbook* (Quanguo jihua shengyu tongji ziliao huibian) (N.p.: n.p., 1983), 1.

6 The Rise and Demise of the One Child Policy, 1979–2015

In late 1979, when leaders determined that the population growth rate was not declining rapidly enough to achieve national targets, the CCP replaced the "one is best, two at most" fertility policy – which rewarded families with one child and penalized those with more than two – with the infamous One Child Policy.[1] This policy, as the name suggests, permitted only one child per couple with consequences for violations, ranging from fines to mandatory abortion or sterilization. Initially, the One Child Policy not only applied to the Han majority but even extended to China's fifty-five officially recognized minority groups. In 1984, restrictions were relaxed in some places in response to rural resistance. Even with only about 35.4 percent of the population falling under the original policy, the name "One Child Policy" endured.[2] From its inception, the One Child Policy was controversial both inside and outside of China.

Many have asked how this course of action came to be considered the best solution to China's population concerns. In the context of post–World War II decolonization, the social sciences emerged as a way to repackage colonial knowledge as politically neutral information within a changing world order.[3] Between the mid-1940s and the mid-1950s, the field of demography shifted from an effort to interpret historical fertility patterns to a basis for policy decisions that supported the burgeoning "population establishment" – the network of scholars, activists, and politicians who advocated a decline in fertility through population planning programs.[4] The dominant line of thinking, "demographic transition theory," contended that fertility decline was a benchmark of

[1] White, *China's Longest Campaign*, 65.

[2] Gu Baochang, Wang Feng, Guo Zhigang, and Zhang Erli, "China's Local and National Fertility Policies at the End of the Twentieth Century," *Population and Development Review* 33, no. 1 (2007), 138.

[3] John DiMoia, "Counting One's Allies": The Mobilization of Demography, Population, and Family Planning in East Asia, late 1920s–Present," *East Asian Science, Technology and Society* 10 (2016), 358.

[4] Connelly, *Fatal Misconception*, 155.

socioeconomic modernization – a growing obsession among social scientists – and that a large population was an impediment to economic development.[5] Conversely, it was believed that decreased fertility levels resulting from aggressive birth control activism could foster rapid economic modernization within developing societies. Although this was a bastardization of the original demographic transition theory – which viewed socioeconomic development as a precondition for decreased fertility – this altered model became the dominant framework for understanding poverty alleviation in the developing world.[6]

In contrast to Mao, who had believed that a large workforce was essential for economic growth, Mao's successor Deng Xiaoping, an avowed technocrat and adherent to demographic transition theory, argued that the "quality," rather than the size, of the population was most important for achieving economic development.[7] Given this historical background and the fact that Deng launched the post-Mao economic reforms in 1978, it is not particularly surprising that China turned to such extreme population measures in the late 1970s. Yet, in *Just One Child: Science and Policy in Deng's China*, Susan Greenhalgh reveals that rather than being developed by demographers, as one would expect, the One Child Policy was the brainchild of policy entrepreneur, Song Jian, and a group of missile scientists. The group claimed its methods were objective and scientific when in reality demographic predictions were made on the basis of political ideology. Nonetheless, the CCP used the mantle of "modern science" to legitimize itself and its One Child Policy.[8]

The questionable tactics used to dramatically reduce population growth in China have triggered Western accusations of coerced abortion and sterilization, as well as pervasive female infanticide. Whereas the official party line argues that the One Child Policy prevented 400 million births, suggesting a sharp decline in population growth post-1979, demographers have shown that three-fourths of the fertility decline since 1970 occurred *prior* to the policy's enactment. In fact, they argue, most of the post-1980 fertility decline was due to improved socioeconomic conditions rather than policy enforcement – a product of the

[5] Michael E. Latham, *Modernization as Ideology: American Social Science and "Nation Building" in the Kennedy Era* (Chapel Hill: University of North Carolina Press, 2000), 23.

[6] Simon Szreter, "The Idea of Demographic Transition and the Study of Fertility Change: A Critical Intellectual History," *Population and Development Review* 19, no. 4 (1993), 669–672; Dennis Hodgson, "Demography as Social Science and Policy Science," *Population and Development Review* 9, no. 1 (1983): 11.

[7] Technically Hua Guofeng was Mao's successor, but he was only in office for two years.

[8] Susan Greenhalgh, *Just One Child: Science and Policy in Deng's China* (Berkeley: University of California Press, 2008), 48–50.

demographic transition that typically follows industrial development.[9] As the most ambitious social engineering project to date, the policy has been a topic of global interest since the 1980s and innumerable publications in the social sciences, public health, and the popular press have debated the policy's merits. Rather than aiming for a comprehensive analysis of the One Child Policy, this chapter highlights several underexplored themes that are useful for understanding this period, including local reception of the policy and the challenge of introducing sex education.[10]

Given the current lack of access to archival documents on the One Child Policy – in recent years these documents were effectively purged from official Chinese archives – this chapter draws on oral histories, ethnographic and sociological studies, and fiction, to reflect on the thirty-six-year lifespan of the One Child Policy. Most scholarship to date has argued that urban couples were indeed limited to one child per couple unless they met specific requirements.[11] While some studies have shown that policy enforcement waxed and waned in the countryside, it is unclear to what extent enforcement differed in cities of different sizes at different administrative levels.

This research demonstrates that even within cities, socioeconomic and rural–urban disparities played a critical role in determining the ways in which the policy was enforced and received. Among wealthier urbanites who were raised in major cities, particularly Shanghai, the policy was carried out with greater ease because by the 1980s a new model of childrearing had overtaken the more "traditional" model emphasizing larger families. In other words, as many of my interviewees suggested, middle-class, urban families were more receptive to the One Child Policy because they already believed that providing a child with the best possible education and opportunities was more important than having additional heirs. Moreover, long-term residents of cities no longer relied on additional sons for farm labor and in fact found supporting multiple offspring to be expensive and burdensome. Residents of the countryside and less economically developed cities like Luoyang, in contrast, were more resistant to fertility limitations because they had less exposure to the newer urban middle-class standard of childrearing. Furthermore,

[9] Martin King Whyte, Wang Feng, and Yong Cai, "Challenging Myths about China's One-Child Policy," *The China Journal* 74 (2015): 144.

[10] For a detailed examination of various aspects of the One Child Policy, see Elisabeth Croll, Delia Davin, and Penny Kane, eds., *China's One-Child Family Policy* (London: Macmillan, 1985).

[11] Karen Hardee-Cleaveland and Judith Banister, "Fertility Policy and Implementation in China, 1986–88," *Population and Development Review* 14, no. 2 (1988): 273; Greenhalgh, "Controlling Births and Bodies," 14.

individuals from poorer families and those who were raised in rural areas were more likely to view additional children as an important source of labor. This disparity, in turn, shaped the way the policy was enforced in Shanghai, Tianjin, and Luoyang. In the long term, the One Child Policy not only exacerbated the historical preference for boys, but it launched a renewed interest in eugenics, as parents felt pressure to "optimize" the qualities of their one and only child, and official rhetoric explicitly emphasized the "quality" of the population.

The Partial Transition from Reactive to Proactive Population Control

A vital aspect of deepening state control over reproduction was an attempt to shift from reactive birth control methods, like abortion, to proactive birth planning. IUDs, oral contraceptives, and sterilization surgeries played key roles in official plans to enact this shift at the national level during the 1970s and the One Child Policy era. However, not all of these methods proved particularly influential in the long term due to a combination of uneven policy enforcement and lukewarm reception. In addition, inconsistent government policies regarding traditional medicine enabled the use of herbal abortifacients to endure.

IUDs

IUD use within the context of marriage became more widespread throughout the 1970s, and insertions reached record numbers – 16.74 percent – in 1975 (although annual IUD insertions would briefly exceed this number in the 1980s).[12] Many interviewees said this was the first type of birth control they used, and they did so starting in the early 1970s.[13] The state encouraged and then mandated that mothers have an IUD inserted after their first birth and sterilization after their second birth.[14] IUDs, however, elicited different responses from different acceptors.[15] An interviewee in her early forties who had moved from a

[12] Scharping, *Birth Control in China*, 121.

[13] Interview with author, Luoyang, November 16, 2016; interview with author, Tianjin, September 17, 2016; interview with author, Shanghai, August 30, 2016.

[14] Interviews with author, Luoyang, November 14, 2016.

[15] Not so differently from my interviewees, feminist activists and scholars of reproduction have variously argued that the IUD is oppressive and liberating. On the one hand, writing about the IUD's early years in the 1960s, Betsy Hartmann and Andrea Tone have argued that the IUD was a method for controlling population at the expense of

village just outside Luoyang to the city to work in the 2010s told me that although she already had two children, when the doctor performed the IUD insertion after her second birth, she screamed out "What the heck are you doing?" (*ni gan ma*) because it was not her decision.[16] According to an older interviewee from Luoyang who had her only child in the 1980s, "Men always wanted more children – if a couple only had daughters the husband might rip the IUD out of his wife, which could destroy her uterus. Alternatively, women with only daughters who hoped for another chance to have a son might also rip out their IUDs or insert wires into their vaginas to remove their IUDs by hand if there was no professional to help them. This was very dangerous and could lead to death."[17] Interviewees in Shanghai affirmed that in the past the only safe way to remove IUDs was with professional assistance but that doctors were often unwilling to help women remove their mandatory IUDs.[18]

As with many other aspects of family planning, access to IUDs was not uniform. Even as some women sought to secretly remove their IUDs, others could not obtain them. According to one 77-year-old man from Luoyang:

> One big problem in the 1970s was a shortage of IUDs especially in more backward parts of the countryside (*luohou de difang*). People seeking birth control would visit different clinics looking for IUDs, but in many cases the clinics had run out. People would try to get jobs in more urban areas in part because urban residents had much better access to IUDs.[19]

poor, uneducated, non-white, and non-Western women. On the other hand, Ruth Dixon-Mueller and Gloria Feldt argued that the IUD is politically neutral and an important tool for women's reproductive liberation. Acknowledging both of these threads, Michelle Murphy and Chikako Takeshita suggest that whether the IUD was perceived as oppressive or emancipatory depended on the context in which it was being deployed. Often the same technology that denoted women's reproductive freedom in the Global North was used coercively to solve the "population crisis" in the Global South. Betsy Hartmann, *Reproductive Rights and Wrongs: The Global Politics of Birth Control* (Boston: South End Press, 1995); Andrea Tone, "Violence by Design: Contraceptive Technology and the Invasion of the Female Body," in *Lethal Imagination: Violence and Brutality in American History*, ed. Michael A. Bellesiles (New York: New York University Press, 1999); Ruth Dixon-Mueller, *Population Policy and Women's Rights: Transforming Reproductive Choice* (Westport: Praeger, 1993); Gloria Feldt, *The War on Choice: The Right-Wing Attack on Women's Rights and How to Fight Back* (New York: Bantam Books, 2004); Michelle Murphy, *Seizing the Means of Reproduction: Entanglements of Feminism, Health, and Technoscience* (Durham: Duke University Press, 2012); Chikako Takeshita, *The Global Biopolitics of the IUD: How Science Constructs Contraceptive Users and Women's Bodies* (Cambridge: MIT Press, 2013).

[16] Interview with author, Luoyang, July 10, 2019. [17] Ibid., November 14, 2016.

[18] Interview with author, Shanghai, December 22, 2016.

[19] Interview with author, Luoyang, November 16, 2016.

In fact, one senior family planning official said that as of 1965 the national supply of IUDs could meet just 8 percent of the demand but that the supply of IUDs expanded gradually throughout the 1970s.[20] In this way, even those people who wanted to limit the size of their families were left to fend for themselves without state support.

The combination of IUD shortages, high rates of failure among contraceptive users, and an increase in the number of women of childbearing age contributed to a rise in the birth rate in the mid-1970s.[21] Although they were intended for use up to twenty years, more than 30 percent of these IUDs either failed or were expelled from the body within two years of insertion.[22] High birth control failure rates had another consequence: an upswing in abortion rates. Joan Kaufman et al. have shown that even in the late 1980s, a large proportion of abortions were performed as a follow-up to contraceptive failure resulting in unintended pregnancy.[23] A 1985 fertility survey showed that IUDs had a failure rate of 8 to 14 percent, while other fertility surveys in the late 1980s indicated a 29 percent failure rate among IUD users.[24]

"The Pill"

During the late Republican period and the early years of the People's Republic, Tianjin's Huifu Pharmaceutical Factory produced a type of oral contraceptive, which was discontinued in 1958 after users reported abdominal pain. It is likely that early oral contraceptives were ineffective, and yet Tianjin vowed to renew production in 1963, which it eventually did.[25] In 1967, mass production of the female pill began and expanded in 1969 when production of oral contraceptives was included in the national economic plan.[26]

In the process of developing the oral contraceptive formulas most widely used today, researchers experimented with a variety of different methods and formulas. In 1971, researchers even began developing an

[20] Scharping, *Birth Control in China*, 181.
[21] White, *China's Longest Campaign*, 138. Chinese IUDs were certainly not the only IUDs to have problems. In the mid-1970s, thousands of American women with IUDs experienced infections resulting in septic abortion, permanent infertility, and even death. Takeshita, *The Global Biopolitics of the IUD*, 6.
[22] Scharping, *Birth Control in China*, 107.
[23] Kaufman et al. also argued that abortion and sterilization were widely used as forms of contraception. Kaufman et al., "Family Planning Policy and Practice in China: A Study of Four Rural Counties," *Population and Development Review* 15, no. 4 (1989), 725.
[24] Scharping, *Birth Control in China*, 107.
[25] TMA, X0110-D-000192–005.
[26] Scharping, *Birth Control in China*, 182.

oral contraceptive for men derived from cottonseed oil.[27] The inspiration to use cottonseed oil as a contraceptive emerged in 1969 when the Chinese Academy of Science sent a team to study an outbreak of fever, malaise, and burning sensations among peasants in Hebei province.[28] The symptoms were eventually linked to cottonseed oil, which contains a compound called gossypol. While peasants had traditionally boiled the cottonseed before pressing it, which rendered the gossypol inactive, under the commune system cottonseed was pressed cold, resulting in the outbreak. Studies of Chinese rats demonstrated that doses of gossypol caused male infertility in two to four weeks, but that healthy sperm production returned gradually after the treatment ceased. On these grounds, the male pill containing gossypol was approved for use in China in 1972, and it even inspired human clinical trials through the World Health Organization (WHO) in the 1980s.[29] Yet, the WHO trials concluded that gossypol is toxic, and therefore the pill was not approved for broader use. Even within China, the male pill never caught on, and although it is not totally clear why, one Chinese doctor explained that "Men are not very enthusiastic (about taking birth control)."[30]

At the same time, researchers developed "the Chinese vacation pill" (literally, the pill for visiting relatives, or *tanqinyao*). Also called Anordrin, *tanqinyao* is a postcoital pill developed for married couples who live apart for extensive periods and only meet once or twice a year, generally for periods of about four weeks. Something like contemporary Western emergency contraception (i.e. "Plan B"), Anordrin blocks the production of progesterone, thus preventing the implantation of a fertilized egg in the uterus. Anordrin should be taken immediately after sex and then again the following morning. This contraceptive method is recommended for couples who have frequent sex during a short period of time because the pill is less effective when used sporadically. Since the dose of steroid each pill contains is near or exceeds the recommended monthly maximum for hormone consumption in the United States, 200 mg, this type of pill was never approved for American use. Nonetheless, Anordrin was formally approved for public use in China in 1974 and is still available today.[31]

[27] Wang et al., *Dangdai zhongguo de weisheng shiye* (Public Hygiene Undertakings in Modern China), 243.
[28] Djerassi, *The Politics of Contraception*, 203.
[29] G. M. H. Waites, C. Wang, and P. D. Griffin, "Gossypol: Reasons for Its Failure to Be Accepted as a Safe, Reversible Male Antifertility Drug," *International Journal of Andrology* 21, no. 1 (1998): 8–9.
[30] Djerassi, *The Politics of Contraception*, 202–204.
[31] Djerassi, *The Politics of Contraception*, 202–204.

Based on studies conducted throughout the 1960s and '70s, Chinese researchers eventually developed four different types of oral hormonal contraceptives in various doses: compound 18 (*shiba jia*) short-term oral contraceptive made of methyl-norgestrienone, ethinyl estradiol (*guici-chun*), oral contraceptive one (*yi hao*), and oral contraceptive two (*er hao*).[32] Significant challenges regarding the manufacturing of oral contraceptives, however, initially impeded their mass production. In the manufacturing of compound 18 tablets, for example, workers reported negative side effects associated with the process of coating the pills in sugar. On the one hand, male workers suffered from swollen breasts and impotence due to excessive exposure to estrogen. On the other hand, female workers experienced abnormal menstrual cycles, vomiting, and dizziness, symptoms typically associated with the first trimester of pregnancy. Despite months of treatment, a portion of the workers suffering from adverse health effects never recovered.[33]

In seeking to develop oral contraceptives with a safer production process, Shanghai Pharmaceutical Factory Number 7 began working on the "Chinese paper pill." This oral birth control consisted of medicated sheets each containing twenty-two squares, one for each day. The production process was safer for workers, the medicine's structure was light, small, and easy to ship and store, and the product simple and inexpensive to produce.[34] While the daily version of this pill never caught on in China, a "paper pill" that only needs to be consumed every thirty days eventually became more common.[35]

Still pursuing a safe way to manufacture compound 18 tablets while protecting workers, a pharmaceutical factory in Beijing began trial production of polyethylene glycol 6000 in May 1972. Polyethylene glycol 6000 was first tested on white mice and dogs and then underwent human trials when the substance was declared harmless. The Shanghai Municipal Bureau of Health approved the medicinal specifications for polyethylene glycol 6000 and agreed to aim for production. In 1973, the Tianjin Municipal Bureau of Health approved the use of polyethylene glycol 6000 as the excipient in birth control tablets in lieu of coating the pills in sugar, the process of which had been dangerous to workers.[36] The idea to change to production of polyethylene glycol 6000 was in fact inspired by pharmaceutical literature from the United States, Britain,

[32] GMA, 296-A2.2-32-57. [33] BMA, 135-002-00654.

[34] Djerassi, *The Politics of Contraception*, 201.

[35] Nicole Smith, "Some Surprising Insights on Birth Control and Contraception Practices in China," *Article Myriad*, December 7, 2011, http://www.articlemyriad.com/birth-control-contraception-china/.

[36] BMA, 135-002-00654.

and Japan. Following the switch to production of polyethylene glycol 6000, workers in the oral contraceptive factory reported no adverse side effects.[37]

Thus, production of compound 18 took off. According to a 1974 report from the Beijing Pharmaceutical Factory Revolutionary Committee, in 1970 Beijing produced 600,000 tablets of compound 18, and in 1971 this number increased to 111.3 million. Similarly, in 1972 a Shanghai factory produced 98.05 million tablets, and in 1973 a total of 303.6 million tablets of compound 18 were produced to meet rising demand.[38] In 1974, a nationwide total of 14,949,700 doses of oral birth control pills had been produced, consisting of two different doses of oral contraceptive one and two of oral contraceptive two, as well as compound 18 and ethinyl estradiol.[39] By 1974, oral contraceptives were available to some degree in nearly every province, centrally governed municipality, and autonomous region and were distributed free of charge.[40] Oral contraceptives made of different combinations and doses of hormones were distributed to different provinces. And yet initially, oral contraceptives seem mainly to have been sold in major cities, namely Beijing, Shanghai, and Guangzhou.[41]

Oral contraceptives never became the most common method of birth control in China for several reasons. First, for many years the supply was not great enough to serve anyone other than urbanites. Second, beginning in the late 1980s, obtaining oral contraceptives required users to pay a deposit, as this method was not specifically regulated under the One Child Policy and users needed to prove their willingness to consistently take the pills.[42] Third, surveys showed that oral contraceptives even in the mid and late 1980s had failure rates of 27 to 33 percent.[43] A seventy-three-year-old woman from Shanghai told me that once she had briefly considered taking oral birth control tablets but that she decided against it because so many women who used it ended up becoming pregnant unintentionally.[44] Finally, many women fear that oral contraceptives will permanently alter their hormones, impeding future conception. Interviewees almost unanimously cited the fact that birth control is "unhealthy" and "unnatural" as a primary reason not to use it.[45] Given

[37] BMA, 135-002-00654. [38] Ibid. [39] GMA, 296-A2.2-32-57. [40] Ibid.

[41] Ibid.; Anibal Faundes and Tapani Luukkainen, "Health and Family Planning Services in the Chinese People's Republic," *Studies in Family Planning* 3, no. 7 (1972): 174–175.

[42] Scharping, *Birth Control in China*, 108. [43] Ibid., 107.

[44] Interview with author, Shanghai, December 22, 2017.

[45] Interview with author, Xiamen, June 13, 2019; interview with author, Luoyang, July 10, 2019; interview with author, Tianjin, July 2, 2019; interview with author, Tianjin, June 27, 2019.

this background, it is not surprising that oral contraceptive use in China remained between 3 and 6 percent in the 1980s and early 1990s, whereas IUD acceptors constituted 30 to 35 percent of contraceptive users during the same timeframe.[46]

Sterilization

Like IUD insertions, sterilization surgeries became increasingly common in the 1970s, in part because in some places they were mandated for couples with at least two children. Kaufman et al. argue that 88 percent of sterilizations took place after 1971 when Premier Zhou Enlai officially endorsed the principle of "later, longer, fewer" (*wan, xi, shao*).[47] However, different parts of China had different timelines for peaks in sterilization. Gail Hershatter notes in her oral histories of women in rural Shaanxi that 1971 was the first year tubal ligations became available in a number of villages and "many women actively sought them out."[48] According to Tyrene White, the earliest mass sterilization campaign took place between 1973 and 1975 and was followed by another sterilization campaign between 1979 and 1980.[49] In the countryside, these campaigns were enacted by mobile medical teams as they passed through particular villages, whereas in the city a woman could demand a sterilization surgery at the local hospital at any time.[50] In a study of four rural counties in Fujian and Heilongjiang provinces, Kaufman et al. reported that "high tides" of female sterilization occurred in one county in Heilongjiang between 1979 and 1980 and in another in 1981, whereas two counties in Fujian witnessed peaks in sterilization rates from 1979 to 1980 and in 1983, respectively.[51] Peaks in IUD insertions and sterilizations often corresponded to "shock attacks" or "crash drives" (*tuji*) – periods of intense birth planning campaign activity that emphasized rapid results. For example, in Hebei mobile medical "shock teams" performed 1.1 million contraceptive procedures in 1972 and 1.98 million in 1973.[52] While the vast majority of sterilized individuals across China were women, in the 1970s the state made a brief but concerted effort to promote greater gender equality by encouraging men to undergo

[46] Scharping, *Birth Control*, 114. [47] Kaufman et al., "Family Planning," 725.
[48] Hershatter, *The Gender of Memory*, 207. [49] White, *China's Longest Campaign*, 135.
[50] Kohama, "The Popularization of Birth Planning in Rural China," 200.
[51] Kaufman et al., "Family Planning," 721–723.
[52] White, *China's Longest Campaign*, 108.

vasectomies. Nationwide, approximately 170 million IUD insertions and sterilization surgeries were performed between 1971 and 1979.[53]

Given the diversity of experiences with sterilization, at times these procedures were welcomed and appreciated, and at other times they were deeply resented and viewed as unwelcome intrusions of state power.[54] One 74-year-woman told me that her uncle *(shushu)* was sterilized in the 1970s. She said that the procedure was quick and simple, only taking ten minutes. However, afterward, he became very ill, developing an infection and a high fever.[55] Although male sterilization rates rose throughout the 1980s in response to more stringent and coercive population policy implementation, tubal ligations continued to be three to four times more common than vasectomies.[56] One 76-year-old man from Luoyang refused to have this procedure because he feared it would lead to weight gain. He said that like plump eunuchs in imperial times and neutered cats, men who get sterilized become obese. For this reason, even though his coworker was granted a reward for voluntarily undergoing sterilization in the 1970s, my interviewee refused to do so.[57]

A number of female interviewees who had children in the late 1970s and early 1980s said that they also were never sterilized but instead had long-term IUDs inserted. While mass sterilization drives were common in the countryside, some urban residents of childbearing age in Shanghai, Tianjin, and Luoyang were not forced to undergo this surgery because the government trusted urban women not to surreptitiously remove their IUDs.[58] Similarly, couples who were in their 50s in the late 1970s and early 1980s typically were not forced to insert IUDs or undergo sterilization because they were assumed to be past reproducing age. However, because the suburbs of these cities were often in reality rural areas (even if they technically fell within the city's jurisdiction), residents of the suburbs were still at the mercy of mobile sterilization teams.[59] These differential sterilization policies even within the context of a given city can be attributed to the fact that although cities like Shanghai and Tianjin boasted some of the country's highest levels of birth planning, city

[53] Leo F. Goodstadt, "China's One-Child Family: Policy and Public Response," *Population and Development Review* 8, no. 1 (1982), 46.

[54] Interview with author, Shanghai, August 31, 2016; interview with author, Shanghai, December 10, 2016; interview with author, Shanghai, December 12, 2016.

[55] Interview with author, Luoyang, July 7, 2019.

[56] Scharping, *Birth Control,* 114.

[57] Interview with author, Luoyang, July 7, 2019.

[58] Interview with author, Shanghai, June 20, 2019; interview with author, Tianjin, June 27, 2019; interview with author, Luoyang, July 10, 2019; interview with author, Luoyang, July 11, 2019.

[59] *Luoyang shizhi* (Luoyang Gazetteer), October 15, 2009, http://www.lydqw.com/DB/BookContent.aspx?BookID=200904080002&Content=Digital.

suburbs still had substantially higher birth rates than city centers. Indeed, in 1978 Tianjin's suburbs had twice the birth rate of the city's central districts.[60]

Yet, everyone I interviewed agreed unanimously that coerced IUD insertion, abortion, and sterilization did not become a major problem until the 1980s.[61] Several men and women I interviewed in Shanghai admitted that they were sterilized as part of sterilization drives or compelled to undergo IUD insertions immediately after the birth of their first child.[62] I heard similar stories elsewhere, though sterilization and IUD insertions – voluntary or coerced – seem to have become widespread earlier in Shanghai than in Tianjin and Luoyang. As Gail Hershatter observes in her study of gendered memories of the Maoist campaigns, many people I interviewed could not remember whether the One Child Policy was implemented in the late 1970s or the early 1980s, a phenomenon I attribute to old age, differences in local implementation rates and individual circumstances, and the fact that during the 1970s the central government passed a series of increasingly stringent family planning policies, making it difficult to keep track of which policy corresponded to which year.

Abortions and Abortifacients

In the early 2000s, medical ethicist Nie Jing-Bao interviewed hundreds of Chinese women about their experiences with abortion. He found that the two most common reasons for undergoing this procedure were premarital sex, which will be discussed later, and being forced to adhere to the national family planning policy.[63] Nie's findings also revealed that attitudes toward abortion vary greatly across China with one-third of his interviewees viewing abortion as unethical.[64]

Statistically, abortions increased steadily in the late 1970s and early 1980s and remained at over 41.5 percent of live births through 1995. Mimicking the peaks in IUD insertions and sterilizations during periods of particularly stringent policy enforcement, abortion rates spiked first in

[60] Goodstadt, "China's One-Child Family," 43.
[61] Interview with author, Luoyang, August 2, 2015; interview with author, Shanghai, December 10, 2016; Connelly, *Fatal Misconception*, 346.
[62] Interviews with author, Shanghai, December 10, 2016.
[63] Nie Jing-Bao, *Behind the Silence: Chinese Voices on Abortion* (Lanham: Rowman & Littlefield Publishers, 2005), 96.
[64] Nie, *Behind the Silence*, 131.

1983 (69.8 percent) and again in 1991 (62.4), each time in response to the availability of the previous year's census figures.[65]

Generally speaking, abortion rates diverged across the rural–urban divide. According to Thomas Scharping's calculations, abortion rates during the 1980s were significantly higher in urban areas with lower fertility. However, in the early 1990s, abortion rates in the countryside outpaced urban ones when authorities in rural areas with previously low abortion rates and high fertility starting using abortion as a "crash instrument" of birth planning.[66] For example, Scharping estimates that in 1988, 51 percent of births in Henan, the province where Luoyang is located, were outside of the plan, a statistic that induced a crackdown on out-of-plan births; by 1992, this number had decreased to 35.2 percent.[67]

Abortion rates also differed by age group. By 1988, nearly 17 percent of Chinese women had undergone at least one abortion and another 8 percent had experienced more than one abortion. Women aged thirty-five to forty-four were particularly affected by the timing of the abortion crackdowns with 50 to 75 percent having undergone at least one abortion (Nie puts the number at 67 percent).[68] Shanghai had far and away the most abortions throughout the 1990s, with particularly high rates of abortion among unmarried teenage girls, a trend that continues today.[69] Indeed, in 1994, Shanghai had an astonishing 287 abortions per 100 live births.[70]

As mentioned earlier, abortions were also used in the case of failed contraceptives that resulted in pregnancy. According to official data, in 1982 48 percent of abortions were due to contraceptive failure; by 1990 this number had reached 70 percent and was largely due to ineffective IUDs.[71] Most cases of abortion involved either surgery or a medically induced termination of the pregnancy, and as a later section of this chapter will show, the likelihood of abortion often correlated to the sex of the baby.

Despite their marginal place in official abortion discourses and statistics, abortifacients of all types have continued to play a role in Chinese reproductive culture. Matthew Sommer has argued that despite various campaigns to end the use of herbal abortifacients, these practices endured even after the implementation of the One Child Policy.

[65] Scharping, *Birth Control in China,* 121–122; for more detailed information on how these statistics were calculated and the challenges involved, see Scharping, *Birth Control in China,* 120–125.

[66] Scharping, *Birth Control in China,* 125.

[67] Ibid., 234.

[68] Ibid., 125; Nie, *Behind the Silence,* 96–97.

[69] Scharping, *Birth Control in China,* 125.

[70] Ibid., 125.

[71] Ibid., 125.

Indeed, medical reports from Beijing, Gansu, Guangdong, Guizhou, Hebei, Hong Kong, Hubei, Jiangxi, Qinghai, Shaanxi, Shandong, Tianjin, and Yunnan all mentioned attempts – typically among unmarried women – to induce abortion using various decoctions made of herbs, insects, and roots.[72] One hospital in Shandong, for example, reported eighty-eight cases between 1989 and 1996 of poisoning from consuming ground-up mylabris – a type of toxic blister beetle – to induce abortion. Another hospital in Shandong reported forty-two such cases between 1997 and 2001. The active ingredient in blister beetles can cause severe burns and even death but rarely terminates pregnancy.[73]

Other kinds of herbal abortifacient use can be found in cases from the late 1970s through the 2000s. In 1981, a woman surnamed Yang, who was a twenty-six-year-old worker at a Shanghai Plastics Factory, discovered that she was pregnant and inserted a root called "local ox knee" (*tu niuxi*) into her cervix. Twenty-four hours later, Yang experienced spells of coldness and fever, and even after undergoing dilation and curettage at the hospital, she passed away from complications related to the ox knee. In other cases, unmarried women secretly inserted motherwort herb (*yimu cao*), white leadwort root (*baihua dan*), or trichosanthes root (*tianhua fen*) into their vaginas to induce abortion, but all of the reported cases resulted in death.[74] Still, it is less likely that nonfatal cases were reported, thus skewing the data toward fatal cases of herbal abortion.

In some places, state-run medical facilities even employed related methods, seeking to subject herbal abortion formals to rigorous scientific testing. For example, in 1979, Henan province began testing the use of herbs for inducing late-term abortion.[75] This involved either grinding up the root of *yuanhua* (lilac daphne), a small yellow flower that grows in northern China, and inserting it into the cervix to induce abortion or extracting a powder from the root of *tianhua* (trichosanthes root),

[72] Sommer, "Abortion in Late Imperial China," 146; Xun Xianwen, "banmao zhongdu siwang erli" (Two Cases of Death from Mylabris Poisoning), *Zhongguo fayixue zazhi* (Chinese Journal of Forensic Medicine) 3 (1990): 156; Chen Jinhua, "Yong banmao duotai yinqi zhongdu siwang" (Using Mylabris to Induce Abortion Leads to Fatal Poisoning), *Xingshi jishu* (Forensic Science and Technology) 5 (1980): 37–38.

[73] Sommer, "Abortion in Late Imperial China," 146.

[74] Yao Jisheng, Zhang Taiyun, and Li Yanji, "32 li duotai siwang an fenxi" (An Analysis of 32 Cases of Fatal Abortion), *Xingshi jishu* (Forensic Science and Technology) 5 (1982): 14; Zhang Cun, "Baihua dan duotai baixiezheng jixing shen gongneng shuaijie siwang yi li baogao" (A Case of Death by Septicemia and Kidney Failure from Use of *Baihua dan* as an Abortifacient), *Guangxi zhongyiyao* (Guangxi Journal of Traditional Chinese Medicine) 1 (1986): n.p.

[75] *Luoyang shizhi* (Luoyang Gazetteer), October 15, 2009, http://www.lydqw.com/DB/BookContent.aspx?BookID=200904080002&Content=Digital.

another plant widely used in abortions, and injecting it into the patient to trigger abortion.[76] While the former method with its efficiency and high rate of efficacy was used extensively in Luoyang in the late 1970s, the latter method was discontinued in some parts of China because it caused nausea and weakness.[77]

Clearly, use of herbal abortifacients was not confined to unauthorized spaces. Each year to this day, numerous academic papers are published discussing the benefits and drawbacks to using herbal abortifacient methods that have been refined through clinical trials. More recent testing of herbal abortion methods suggests that the methods themselves are not always dangerous or ineffective and that with some fine-tuning these approaches could be deemed viable. This is not entirely surprising, given the long history of herbal abortifacient use worldwide. However, the majority of women utilizing herbal abortifacients in China during earlier periods were not doing so under professional supervision, and as reports on the fatal consequences of such methods suggest, these abortion techniques as generally practiced were unsafe and unreliable.

Reports also indicate that in the 1980s and beyond women were still practicing other types of abortion via traditional, non-herbal abortion methods and the misuse of potent Western pharmaceuticals. According to one medical report, thirty-two women between 1990 and 1993 underwent abortion through massage (*anmo*) , moxibustion, and acupuncture (*zhenjiu*) with relatively high rates of success – 84.3 percent.[78] Another recurring theme in abortion records from this period, as in earlier ones, was overdosing on antimalarial drugs (rural abuse of Western medicine in general accelerated beginning in the 1970s).[79] One study of fatal abortions found that between 1972 and 1981 eighteen women had died from consuming various combinations of quinine and chloroquine to induce abortion.[80] Other reports support the claim that these practices could be found elsewhere.[81]

[76] Rigdon, "Abortion Law," 548–549.

[77] *Luoyang shizhi* (Luoyang Gazetteer), October 15, 2009, http://www.lydqw.com/DB/BookContent.aspx?BookID=200904080002&Content=Digital.

[78] Li Ming, "Anmo liuchan 32 jingyan jieshao" (Introducing the Experience of 32 Abortions Through Massage), *Anmo yu daoyin* (Chinese Manipulation & Qi Gong Therapy) 4 (1993): n.p.

[79] Fang Xiaoping attributes this trend to increased access to affordable Western drugs, unlimited prescription of medications, and the practice of self-medication; Fang, "Barefoot Doctors," 276.

[80] Yao, Zhang, and Li, "An Analysis of 32 Cases of Fatal Abortion," n.p.

[81] Pan Zhengzhong and Feng Guozhen, "Weihun xianyu suo yinqi de" (What Premarital Pregnancy Gives Rise To), *Shehui* (Society) 2 (1986): 21.

The vast majority of individuals using the aforementioned methods, rather than relying on doctor-administered surgical or medically induced (with mifepristone and misoprostol) abortion methods, were young and unmarried women.[82] Often these women were ashamed that they had engaged in premarital sex and that they had become pregnant out of wedlock, conduct that was still considered immoral and taboo in some places. Furthermore, they feared legal repercussions as premarital sex was still technically classified as a type of "hooliganism."[83] Therefore, these young women sought to secretly remedy their situations and avoid having unauthorized children. According to a Chinese news article from 1986, 27.9 percent of abortions that year in Beijing were performed on unmarried women, often those who engaged in intercourse with their fiancés but could not get formal permission to marry due to age or work restrictions. Similarly, high abortion rates among unmarried women were reported in other major cities like Tianjin.[84]

While one might hypothesize that women in cities were using safer abortion methods while women in poorer, more rural areas were engaging in traditional or alternative abortion practices, in reality the line between urban and rural women was not so fixed. The influx of rural young women to urban factories in the 1990s and 2000s further blurred the rural–urban medical divide, and records show that cases of herbal abortifacient use took place in both rural and urban environments. A Uyghur woman who had lived in the capital of Xinjiang province for many years said she knew of pregnant women who used either traditional Uyghur medicine or Chinese herbal medicine to abort unwanted or unsanctioned pregnancies. She argued that these methods were typically effective during the first three months of pregnancy and that as long as the abortion took place when the embryo was less than forty days old, according to Islamic law, abortion was permitted.[85] Still, many cases of herbal abortifacient use were associated with women with little wealth or education, but validating this claim requires further investigation.

Interviews with pharmacists in 2019 suggest that in recent years the "Morning After Pill" and over-the-counter medications that induce abortion have largely supplanted herbal abortifacients.[86] On the plus

[82] Wei Xia, Shouzhang She, and Taihing Lam, "Medical versus Surgical Abortion Methods for Pregnancy in China: A Cost-Minimization Analysis," *Gynecologic and Obstetric Investigation* 72 (2011): 257.

[83] Burkitt, "Sex in China."

[84] Rigdon, "Abortion Law and Practice in China," 549–550.

[85] Interview with author, email, April 25, 2019.

[86] Interview with author, Luoyang, July 8, 2019; interview with author, Luoyang, July 10, 2019.

side, these pills have undergone government testing and are much safer than untested herbal abortifacients. Yet, in reality both types of medicines, when taken frequently, enable a reliance on abortifacients as birth control, particularly among young women engaging in premarital sex. That is not to say that all young people rely on abortion rather than prophylactics – indeed some use condoms or have IUDs inserted – but abortion remains a common alternative.[87]

Compliance, Collusion, and Resistance

In 1979, when the One Child Policy was implemented, the national population stood at 975,428,000 with 184,959,000 people living in cities and 129,401,000 living in towns. The other 661,068,036 people still lived in the countryside. Nationwide, according to official statistics, 79.8 percent of people were already practicing birth control, the highest rates of which corresponded to major urban centers. Indeed, official statistics suggest that Shanghai had a staggering contraception rate of 97.3 percent, while 85.7 percent of people were practicing contraception in Tianjin.[88] Although precise statistics for Luoyang are unavailable, the contraception rate in 1979 for all of Henan province, where Luoyang is located, was 85.9 percent. From this, it can be inferred that the contraception rate was slightly higher for Luoyang proper, as birth planning was more strictly carried out in cities than in rural areas.[89]

Part of the codification of the One Child Policy involved setting strict birth planning targets for local cadres to achieve and supporting those efforts with monetary rewards and penalties, preferential access to housing and healthcare for those with only one child, and even higher production quotas for those who violated the policy.[90] Work units were charged with policing their employees, and women of childbearing age were required to have checkups (*yunjian*) every three months to check for unsanctioned pregnancies.[91] Urban couples accepted being limited to one child for fear of themselves or their relatives losing their jobs or being

[87] Interview with author, Luoyang, July 8, 2019; interview with author, Luoyang, July 10, 2019.
[88] National Birth Planning Committee Integrated Planning Division, *Chinese Birth Planning Statistical Yearbook*, 28.
[89] National Birth Planning Committee Integrated Planning Division, *Chinese Birth Planning Statistical Yearbook*, 30.
[90] White, *China's Longest Campaign*, 105.
[91] Interview with author, Luoyang, August 2, 2015; interview with author, Luoyang, July 10, 2019.

forced to pay high fines.[92] This comprehensive system of financial incentives and penalties built on an earlier program established in the mid-1970s. The extent of the fines and benefits, however, depended on locality. Abortions and sterilizations were free of charge by 1971 and individuals undergoing these procedures could enjoy paid leave, but a number of my interviewees claimed they had no knowledge of this policy at the time.[93] In 1973, the Ministry of Health also issued a document outlining standardized vacation allowances for birth control procedures.[94] Nevertheless, relatively few women would have enjoyed access to these benefits, as they were only valid for full-time urban employees in the state sector.[95]

The initial program of penalties for having too many children was also subject to regional disparities. Interviewees in Shanghai and Luoyang said that in the mid-1970s they knew people who had paid fines (*fakuan*) for having too many children.[96] Fear of losing one's job was one of the greatest motivating factors behind couples' decisions to comply with the policy.[97] In addition, although resisting the policy was tempting, they knew they could not survive without the government benefits allocated to one-child families.[98] In general, couples in Shanghai and Tianjin seemed more willing to accept the limitations of the One Child Policy than their counterparts in Luoyang. In fact, I did not encounter a single person who had violated the One Child Policy in the first two cities.

In Luoyang, a number of interviewees found violating the policy and potentially facing punishment to be worth the risk. One interviewee said that in the early 1980s her brother and his wife, who were working at a state enterprise and were the parents of a little girl, had a second child without permission, hoping the child would be a boy. The baby turned

[92] Hardee-Cleaveland and Banister, "Fertility Policy and Implementation in China, 267; interview with author, Shanghai, December 10, 2016; interview with author, Shanghai, December 12, 2016; interview with author, Shanghai, August 23, 2016.

[93] Wang et al., *Dangdai zhongguo de weisheng shiye* (Public Hygiene Undertakings in Modern China), 235; interview with author, Shanghai, November 7, 2016; interview with author, Shanghai, December 12, 2017.

[94] White, *China's Longest Campaign,* 103.

[95] Dillon, *Radical Inequalities,* 3; According to Nara Dillon, rural residents and urbanites working in the largely female collective sector were denied access to critical labor insurance benefits, such as family planning subsidies and post-surgery vacation allowances.

[96] Interview with author, Luoyang, August 2, 2015; interview with author, Shanghai, February 10, 2017; White, *China's Longest Campaign,* 104.

[97] Hardee-Cleaveland and Banister, "Fertility Policy and Implementation in China, 267; interview with author, Shanghai, December 10, 2016; interview with author, Shanghai, December 12, 2016; interview with author, Shanghai, August 23, 2016.

[98] Interview with author, Tianjin, June 27, 2019.

out to be a girl and the couple was fined 700 *yuan*, even though they only made several hundred *yuan* annually. Still not deterred, two years later, the wife gave birth to another baby, but it too was a girl. Consequently, the husband's work unit took away the family's housing and a year's salary. My interviewee suggested that had her brother and his wife been rural residents, perhaps the policy would not have been so harshly enforced, as rural couples typically faced milder penalties for family planning violations.[99] A fifty-year-old pharmacist in Luoyang also told me that after the birth of her first child in the late 1970s, she was not forced to have an IUD inserted. In the mid-1980s, she violated the One Child Policy by having a second child. Although she was permitted to keep her job, she and her husband were forced to pay the prohibitive sum of several thousand *yuan* in fines.[100]

Yet, two other interviewees' experiences in Luoyang during the late 1970s and early 1980s suggest that not all policy violations were treated so harshly. A seventy-four-year-old woman from Luoyang told me that she had two daughters in the 1970s. Because she and her husband wanted to have a son, the wife was able to avoid having an IUD inserted after the birth of the second child. (It was encouraged but not required until 1979.) She finally gave birth to a son in 1979, a violation of the policy "one is best, two at most." Even though both husband and wife had urban *hukou*, they were allowed to keep their jobs on the condition that they paid a fine for violating the policy. At that point, having achieved her goal of having a son, my interviewee voluntarily agreed to undergo sterilization.[101] Similarly, another Luoyang resident with urban *hukou* told me that she gave birth to a daughter in the late '70s, had an IUD inserted and removed, and then had a son in 1980, after which she chose to be sterilized. The woman did not lose her job for having a second child and was not required to have an abortion even though the policy called for such "remedial measures" (*bujiu cuoshi*) in cases of unsanctioned pregnancy.[102] These anecdotes demonstrate that in practice the so-called One Child Policy was relatively flexible and was adapted to local circumstances.[103] Because Henan province is located

99 Interview with author, Luoyang, August 2, 2015.
100 Interview with author, Luoyang, July 10, 2019.
101 Interview with author, Luoyang, August 7, 2019.
102 Interview with author, Luoyang, July 11, 2019; *Luoyang shizhi* (Luoyang Gazetteer), October 15, 2009, http://www.lydqw.com/DB/BookContent.aspx?BookID=200904080002&Content=Digital.
103 Gu Baochang, Wang Feng, Guo Zhigang, and Zhang Erli, "China's Local and National Fertility Policies at the End of the Twentieth Century," *Population and Development Review* 33, no. 1 (2007): 138.

in the less economically developed region of central China and Luoyang is not the provincial capital, beginning in 1984 couples whose first child was a girl were allowed to have a second child after a certain time interval.[104]

Under the One Child Policy, couples who only had one child received healthcare subsidies (*baojian fei*), retirement funds, priority housing, and larger grain allotments.[105] One couple I interviewed said they received 5 *yuan* a month throughout the early 1980s from the Tianjin government as incentive not to have a second child.[106] Conversely, couples who had more children than permitted (*chaosheng*) were forced to pay an "excess-child fee" (*duo zinü fei*), which typically consisted of 10 percent of each parent's salary for the next fourteen years. The exact terms of the sanctions were determined at the provincial rather than the national level and therefore were not uniform.[107]

In 1984, the policy was relaxed slightly, and exceptions were made for Han and minority people in certain situations.[108] Urban couples were permitted to have a second child if their first child was disabled and unable to perform "normal" amounts of labor, in the case of remarriage where only one spouse had a child from a previous marriage, and if a couple raised their first child to adulthood and unexpectedly became pregnant again. The specific conditions for determining eligibility for a second child were outlined at the provincial level and thus varied geographically.

Perhaps more surprising than stories of resistance to the One Child Policy were accounts of couples that fully supported the mandate for personal reasons (as opposed to for the benefit of the nation). For some couples, the policy simply affirmed personal convictions that smaller

[104] Gu et al., "China's Local and National Fertility Policies," 138. By 1989, similar policies had been enacted in eighteen provinces, as well as less developed areas in Jiangsu and Sichuan; White, *China's Longest Campaign*, 167.

[105] ECNUA, Ai 0358-032-015.

[106] In reality, the amount of compensation may have been greater. Interview with author, Tianjin, February 15, 2017.

[107] Scharping, *Birth Control*, 137; White, *China's Longest Campaign*, 105.

[108] Although China's minority groups have long been permitted to have two children per couple – three if the parents have rural *hukou* – the government has recently accelerated efforts to diminish the Uyghur population. In the last few years, the Chinese government has spent millions of dollars on birth control campaigns, mandating that Uyghur women insert IUDs and undergo abortion and sterilization surgeries. Women with more than two children are also being saddled with oppressive fines. If those charged with violating the family planning policy cannot pay their fines, they risk being sent to detention camps. "China Forces Birth Control on Uighurs to Suppress Population," *Associated Press*, June 29, 2020, https://apnews.com/269b3de1af34e17c1941a514f78d764c.

families are more economical. A fifty-five-year-old retired factory worker from Tianjin told me that life was stressful and the pressure was so great that she had never wanted to have more than one child in the first place. Her daughter was born in 1990, and at that point few of her friends wanted to have more than one child because of the cost, time, and energy required to raise them. She said in particular because her daughter wanted to wear stylish clothes and go to college; she was grateful that she only had one child.[109] Her point that multiple children were difficult to raise and educate reminded me of an interviewee from Shanghai who, after having a daughter in 1972, actively sought out sterilization because she and her husband did not want to risk additional pregnancies. Instead, they wanted to focus all of their money and energy on their one daughter, who ended up becoming highly educated and now lives abroad.[110] I had similarly interviewed a retired party cadre in Shanghai whose wife gave birth to their first child, a girl, in the early 1960s and then chose to stop having children because the couple was too busy to raise more.[111] I encountered these types of stories the most in Shanghai, where systematic birth planning measures and the One Child Policy were first implemented.

Other scholars have shown that enforcement of the policy was more uneven in the countryside than in the cities but that there was also greater resistance to family planning. As in the city, in 1984, certain rural couples were permitted to have a second child. Reasons for permitting rural couples to do so included all of the previous reasons plus additional ones: having a first child who was a girl, both parents being only children, and facing special hardships, among others.[112] Numerous ethnographic studies of the response to birth planning in rural China show that peasants primarily desired more children to guarantee support in old age.[113] Given the patrilocal structure of most Chinese communities, couples desired at least one son because daughters married out of the family, leaving their biological parents to fend for themselves in old

[109] Interview with author, Tianjin, June 27, 2019.
[110] Interview with author, Shanghai, February 15, 2017.
[111] Interview with author, Shanghai, August 10, 2016.
[112] Wang et al., *Dangdai zhongguo de weisheng shiye* (Public Hygiene Undertakings in Modern China), 70; Luoyang renkou he jihua shengyu weiyuanhui (Luoyang Population and Birth Planning Committee), *Luoyangshi renkou he jihua shengyu zhi, 1985–2014* (The Chronicle of Population and Family Planning of Luoyang, 1985–2014) (Luoyang: Luoyang shi renkou he jihua shengyu weiyuanhui, 2015), 27.
[113] Jeffrey Wasserstrom, "Resistance to the One-Child Family," *Modern China* 10, no. 3 (1984): 361; Wasserstrom reveals that, rather than being based solely on prejudice, the preference for male babies was grounded in patrilocal marriage patterns.

age.[114] In addition, the symbolic importance of sons for carrying on the family line in a patrilineal society and the social pressure to have a son perpetuated a preference for boys.

Due in part to these realities, policy enforcement differed by region and even by county. Karen Hardee-Cleaveland and Judith Banister, John Aird, and Steven Mosher all have argued that "remedial measures" – forced abortion or sterilization – were common in cases of unauthorized pregnancies.[115] Similarly, Ma Jian's novel about the excesses of the One Child Policy, *The Dark Road,* depicts the grotesque violence inflicted upon rural women with unauthorized pregnancies and the ways in which family planning officials forcibly performed late-term abortions and sterilizations.[116] In contrast, Kaufman et al. found that in some counties in rural Fujian and Heilongjiang, sympathetic local cadres, who were well aware of the practical need for more children did not force women with unauthorized pregnancies to abort. Instead, these women were fined for second or higher-order births. In other cases, couples were given up to fourteen years to pay off their fines or not forced to pay at all because cadres understood the villagers' limited economic means.[117] One man in his early thirties from rural Henan province told me that his parents had given birth to six daughters in the 1980s in pursuit of a son. Once the mother gave birth to a seventh child, a boy, the family stopped trying for more children. Because the parents were poor farmers and local cadres understood their desire for a son, the family did not have to pay any fines.[118] At other times, peasants and cadres colluded to fight the policy; village cadres either turned a blind eye to early marriages and early childbirth, or they permitted the illegal buying and selling of birth permits. In addition, some cadres hid unauthorized births or inflated the contraception rates in their jurisdictions when reporting to higher authorities. In some instances, cadres did not even take birth planning targets seriously if these measures were not used to evaluate cadre performance.[119]

[114] Huang Shu-min, *The Spiral Road: Change in a Chinese Village through the Eyes of a Communist Party Leader* (Boulder: Westview Press, 1998), 180.

[115] Hardee-Cleaveland and Banister, "Fertility Policy and Implementation in China," 258; John Shields Aird, *Slaughter of the Innocents: Coercive Birth Control in China* (Washington, DC: AEI Press, 1990), *32*; Steven Mosher, *Broken Earth: The Rural Chinese* (New York: The Free Press, 1983), 254.

[116] Ma Jian, *The Dark Road: A Novel*, trans. Flora Drew (New York: Penguin Press, 2013), 7.

[117] Kaufman et al., "Family Planning Policy and Practice in China," 720; Hardee-Cleaveland and Banister, "Fertility Policy and Implementation in China," 255.

[118] Interview with author, Luoyang, July 4, 2019.

[119] White, *China's Longest Campaign*, 183, 192.

Evidence also suggests that clever villagers drew on their own resourcefulness to resist the policy. One common resistance strategy was secretly and illegally removing an inserted IUD, a procedure that was dangerous and could even result in death.[120] According to other studies and some of my interviewees, women without a son were significantly more likely to find a way to remove their IUDs. In Mo Yan's novel *Frog*, for example, the narrator's wife Renmei, a woman living in Northern Gaomi Township, Shandong province, secretly had her IUD removed in an attempt to produce a son.[121] According to anthropologist Huang Shu-min's interviews from Lin village in rural Fujian, a woman could pay a mere 10 *yuan* to an "illegal midwife" to remove an IUD, and the frequency with which this occurred affirmed many cadres' beliefs that villagers would not practice contraception unless forced to do so.[122] Women secretly removing their IUDs became such a major problem that in April 1981, the Ministry of Justice ruled that unauthorized IUD removals would be prosecuted as instances of fraud and bodily harm, and in cases where the consequences were fatal, manslaughter. By the 1990s, compulsory regular gynecological exams to confirm that IUD acceptors were still using their IUDs had become standard in some places.[123]

Other resistance strategies included evasion and confrontation. Women might run away or hide from birth planning work teams, wait to conceive until after biannual examinations, and then give birth in their natal villages, or conceive during a holiday break and then give birth while working away from home.[124] *The Dark Road,* for example, portrays a rural husband and wife who flee their village and become migrant workers in a polluted town in Guangdong so they can evade family planning authorities and have a second child – although they already have a daughter, they try desperately for a son to carry on the family name.[125] Despite the fact that cases of policy violation in pursuit of a male heir were most common in the 1980s, a woman in her thirties I interviewed in Luoyang who had moved from a village just outside the city told me how she hoped her second child would be a boy since her first child was a girl. She said that people in the village would look down on her and talk behind her back if she did not have a son, which is a great loss of face.[126] In extreme cases of evasion, family planning authorities

[120] Wasserstrom, "Resistance to the One-Child Family," 361.
[121] Mo Yan, *Wa* (Frog) (Shanghai: Shanghai wenyi chubanshe (Shanghai Literature and Art Press), 2009), 76.
[122] Huang, *The Spiral Road,* 181. [123] Scharping, *Birth Control,* 106–107.
[124] Huang, *The Spiral Road,* 182; White, *China's Longest Campaign,* 173–174.
[125] Ma, *The Dark Road,* 30. [126] Interview with author, July 10, 2019.

might arrest policy violators and even demolish their homes. As for confrontation, some peasants who were unhappy with strict family planning policies physically attacked local cadres attempting to collect taxes or enforce birth planning. In addition, sometimes villagers damaged the property of cadres as retaliation or resorted to arson.[127]

Strategies of resistance well documented in the Western media were abandoning daughters, putting them up for adoption, or committing infanticide. Kay Ann Johnson shows that parents were often heartbroken over having to give up their daughters and only did so out of fear of unendurable physical and financial punishments.[128] In some instances, couples hid their unauthorized children and secretly raised them. Often children were quietly put up for local adoption or given to relatives, but the adoptions were never formally registered. Parents would simply leave their daughters in public places or on doorsteps in the hope that other people might take them in. Less frequently, daughters were adopted overseas. In the 1990s and early 2000s, over 120,000 Chinese children were adopted internationally.[129] As for infanticide, or more commonly, gendercide (female infanticide), this practice re-emerged in the 1980s in response to the One Child Policy. Gendercide was the combined byproduct of son preference, maltreatment of women who only had daughters, the need for male labor to support rural households, and fear of punishment for policy violation.[130] Based on countless interviews with rural Chinese women, the author Xinran graphically depicts gendercide in her book *Message from an Unknown Chinese Mother: Stories of Loss and Love*. She relates stories of widespread gendercide through smothering, abandonment outdoors in winter, and drowning during the height of the One Child Policy.[131] Sometimes the mothers would feel so guilty after killing their baby girls that they would commit suicide.[132] Officially, infanticide was widely condemned and in some cases, perpetrators were sentenced to prison terms.[133] Yet, rather than addressing the specific issue of gendercide, the policy was relaxed to allow rural couples with one daughter to try for a second child.[134]

127 White, *China's Longest Campaign*, 193–197.
128 Kay Ann Johnson, *China's Hidden Children: Abandonment, Adoption, and the Human Costs of the One-Child Policy* (Chicago: University of Chicago Press, 2016), 18.
129 Johnson, *China's Hidden Children*, 11.
130 Elisabeth Croll, Delia Davin, and Penny Kane, eds., *China's One Child Family Policy* (London: Macmillan, 1985), 62; White, *China's Longest Campaign*, 201.
131 Xinran, *Message from an Unknown Chinese Mother: Stories of Loss and Love*, trans. Nicky Harman (New York: Scribner, 2010), 68, 76, 81.
132 Xinran, *Message from an Unknown Chinese Mother*, 121.
133 Wasserstrom, "Resistance to the One-Child Family," 356.
134 White, *China's Longest Campaign*, 200.

A final method of resistance that is also relatively well known globally is sex-selective abortion. In 1979, China produced its first ultrasound machine capable of fetal sex determination, and by 1987 there were 13,000 ultrasound machines nationwide.[135] Amid rising concerns about sex-selective abortion, in September 1986 the National Commission for Family Planning and the Ministry of Health prohibited prenatal diagnosis at the request of the mother, except when used by authorized hospitals to diagnose certain hereditary diseases. Individuals or clinics that violated this ban were made liable to penalties, and the ban was repeatedly affirmed in the late 1980s, early 1990s, and early 2000s.[136] Nevertheless, the sex ratio continued to shift in favor of male babies. According to the official statistics of the All-China Women's Federation, nationwide in 1987 there were 106.32 boys for every 100 girls. In some provinces, according to these statistics, the gender disparity was more pronounced, as in Anhui province where the ratio of boys to girls was 110.28:100, and in Shaanxi, where the ratio was 109.28:100 in 1987.[137] While disconcerting, Chinese officials at first argued that a gender imbalance had existed in China for much of the twentieth century, so the skewed gender ratio was nothing new.[138] Yet, the reality was that decollectivization in the 1980s made household productivity the most important factor in raising rural families' income. Therefore, families desired sons to maximize revenue from their newly privatized land.[139] Not surprisingly, the national census from 1990 revealed that there were 114 male births for every 100 female births, with the largest gender imbalances (about 117:100) found in Guangxi and Zhejiang provinces.[140] At this point, officials stopped denying the link between the One Child Policy and the gender ratio crisis. Indeed, the 2010 census indicated that the national sex ratio had reached an alarming 120 males for every 100 females, with a gender ratio as distorted as 150:100 in some parts of Guangdong.[141]

[135] White, *China's Longest Campaign*, 202.

[136] Nie Jing-bao, "Non-Medical Sex-Selective Abortion in China: Ethical and Public Policy Issues in the Context of 40 Million Missing Females," *British Medical Bulletin* 98 (2011): 13.

[137] Zhonghua quanguo funü lianhehui yanjiusuo (All China Women's Federation Research Institute), *Zhongguo funü tongji ziliao, 1949–1989* (Statistical Data on Chinese Women, 1949–1989) (Beijing: Zhongguo tongji chubanshe (Chinese Statistical Press), 1991), 25.

[138] All China Women's Federation Research Institute, *Zhongguo funü tongji ziliao, 1949–1989* (Statistical Data on Chinese Women, 1949–1989), 24–25.

[139] Wasserstrom, "Resistance to the One-Child Family," 363.

[140] Barbara Miller, "Female-Selective Abortion in Asia: Patterns, Policies, and Debates," *American Anthropologist* 103, no. 4 (2001): 1084-1085.

[141] Nie, "Non-Medical Sex-Selective Abortion in China," 9.

Tyrene White astutely observes that through strategies such as sex-selective abortion, parents "rejected the state's claim of ideological hegemony and sovereignty over the production of offspring but adapted its principles of social engineering to reengineer the shape of their own households."[142] In other words, even as people resisted total state control over reproduction, they adopted a similar logic and applied it to their own families.

More broadly, this phenomenon has resulted in approximately 40.9 million "surplus men" in China, who will not be able to find wives, and as of 2010, a deficit of over 100 million girls worldwide due to related factors in other parts of Asia and Eastern Europe.[143] From this trend, Mara Hvistendahl and others have forecasted that "a world full of men" will bring heightened levels of violence, crime, prostitution, child marriage, and other social ills.[144]

And yet, my interviews indicate that Chinese attitudes toward sons and daughters, at least in cities, are not as homogeneous as they appear in Western media. I interviewed two men in Shanghai, one aged sixty and the other aged sixty-nine, each of whom had one daughter born in the 1980s. Both men enthusiastically agreed that, in the context of the One Child Policy, they did not prefer a son over a daughter, and claimed that son preference is only a major problem in the countryside.[145] In the city, where having more children is not useful for increasing household income, daughters and sons have the same value. Other interviewees even stated that girls were preferred over boys because in practice daughters were more loyal to their natal families than sons and more likely to care for their parents in old age.[146] In addition, when a couple is married, the husband's family is expected to buy the couple a home, which can be prohibitively expensive in Chinese cities, so it costs less to have a daughter.[147] Other interviewees said that the ideal family consists of two

[142] White, *China's Longest Campaign*, 207.

[143] Nie, "Non-Medical Sex-Selective Abortion in China," 8.

[144] Mara Hvistendahl, *Unnatural Selection: Choosing Boys Over Girls, and the Consequences of a World Full of Men* (New York: Public Affairs, 2011), 237.

[145] This finding is consistent with the results of Vanessa Fong's study of the first generation of children raised under the One Child Policy. Fong found that parents provided their sole child with the same financial resources and care, regardless of gender; Vanessa Fong, *Only Hope: Coming of Age Under China's One-Child Policy* (Stanford: Stanford University Press, 2004), 107.

[146] Interview with author, Luoyang, November 17, 2016; interview with author, Luoyang, July 10, 2019.

[147] Interview with author, Shanghai, June 20, 2019; interview with author, Luoyang, July 10, 2019; interview with author, Tianjin, June 26, 2019. Leta Hong Fincher's work illustrates how male gender bias undergirds the expectation that parents will purchase a home for their sons. Not only are parents more likely to buy an apartment for a son than

children, a boy and a girl, not just one or the other. The son will carry on the family name, while the daughter will help care for the parents in old age.[148] One couple who had their sole daughter in the 1980s told me that through changes in the economy, the roll-back of the social welfare system, and the One Child Policy, the idea of having one child – male or female – had become thoroughly normalized.[149] Indeed, anthropologist Yan Yunxiang observed that rural policy violations decreased sharply beginning in the 1990s, in part because new parents at that point were part of a generation that was accustomed to birth planning and valued individual happiness and material comforts more than their parents did.[150] Nevertheless, several men in their sixties from Tianjin and Shanghai who each only had a daughter confessed that they wished they had a son to carry on the family line but not so much as to violate the One Child Policy or commit infanticide.[151] These anecdotes suggest that attitudes toward daughters vary greatly and that reproductive decisions today are shaped as much if not more by practical concerns – like having support in old age and being able to buy a home for an adult child – than by gender bias.[152]

Making Better Babies: Eugenics in Post-Mao China

In his analysis of scholarship on the global dynamics of eugenics, Frank Dikotter writes, "Far from being a politically conservative and

a daughter, but women are excluded from the property deeds of 80 percent of marital homes, thus denying women the opportunity to benefit from the lucrative real estate market. Fincher, *Leftover Women* 13, 56–59.

[148] Interview with author, Shanghai, June 17, 2019. In the case that a couple has a daughter and a son, sometimes the son is still given preferential treatment over the daughter; Harriet Evans, *The Subject of Gender: Daughters and Mothers in Urban China* (Lanham: Rowman & Littlefield Publishers, 2008), 129-131.

[149] Interview with author, Tianjin, June 27, 2019.

[150] Yan Yunxiang, *Private Life Under Socialism: Love, Intimacy, and Family Change in a Chinese Village, 1949-1999* (Stanford: Stanford University Press, 2003), 208–210.

[151] Interview with author, Shanghai, June 19, 2019; interview with author, Tianjin, June 25, 2019. The two men I interviewed in Shanghai were both from Subei, a region in northern Jiangsu province. The two interviewees were barely literate and performed jobs such as selling vegetables and hauling garbage, common positions for Subei people living in Shanghai. Historically, Subei people were associated with poverty, ignorance, and dirtiness, and therefore, faced ethnic discrimination. Emily Honig, "Migrant Culture in Shanghai: In Search a Subei Identity," in *Shanghai Sojourners*, ed. Frederic Wakeman Jr. and Yeh Wen-hsin (Berkeley: University of California Press, 1992), 239.

[152] Susan Greenhalgh and Jiali Li similarly argue that culture is not static and therefore gender ideologies also change over time. Though Chinese gender values in the 1970s through the 1990s appear on the surface to resemble those of the past, closer analysis reveals important differences. Susan Greenhalgh and Jiali Li, "Engendering Reproductive Policy and Practice in Peasant China: For a Feminist Demography of Reproduction," *Signs* 20, no. 3 (1995): 610.

scientifically spurious set of beliefs that remained confined to the Nazi era, eugenics belonged to the political vocabulary of virtually every significant modernizing force between the two world wars."[153] Indeed, from the late nineteenth century through the 1970s, eugenics was the international language of scientific modernity and today it continues to quietly shape such diverse fields as public health, psychiatry, and social services.[154]

Following World War II and the Holocaust, overtly eugenic language in much of the world was reframed as "social welfare" or "family planning," meaning that individuals from dysgenic groups were encouraged or even forced not to reproduce to reduce their "burden" on society.[155] In China, however, the term for eugenics used in the late nineteenth and early twentieth centuries, *yousheng*, never gained the same negative connotation it did elsewhere. In fact, this term was widely used in official rhetoric during the Republican period and again from the 1970s onward, and yet this topic has received little academic coverage. For example, the slogan "*yousheng youyu*" (bear and rear better children) appeared frequently in 1980s birth planning propaganda.[156] In 1982, the State Council and Central Committee of the CCP issued a joint statement calling for the dissemination of information about "scientific" birth control, administration of premarital and prenatal checkups, improving the safety and reliability of contraceptive procedures, and increasing the "quality" (*suzhi*) of the population. Measures of population quality included infant mortality rate, overall population mortality rate, average life span, and rate of illness.[157]

One aspect of this eugenic program involved reaffirming the policy that marriage between people related within several generations was prohibited because intermarriage within families increased the likelihood of congenital diseases. According to a law promulgated in 1982, couples related within three generations, as well as those suffering from previously untreatable illnesses, such as mental illness or tuberculosis, were prohibited from marrying.[158] While this may seem like a radical departure from earlier practices, in fact marriage laws introduced in 1945 and

[153] Frank Dikotter, "Race Culture: Recent Perspectives on the History of Eugenics," *American Historical Review* 103, no. 2 (1998): 467.
[154] Dikotter, "Race Culture," 467. [155] Ibid., 469.
[156] Wang et al., *Dangdai zhongguo de weisheng shiye* (Public Hygiene Undertakings in Modern China), 247.
[157] Deng, Ma, and Wu, *Dangdai zhongguo de jihua shengyu shiye* (The Contemporary Chinese Birth Planning Project), 206.
[158] Wang et al., *Dangdai zhongguo de weisheng shiye* (Public Hygiene Undertakings in Modern China), 251.

1950 also forbid people with certain illnesses from marrying.[159] The 1950 Marriage Law even prohibited marriage between "a man and a woman who are lineal relatives by blood or collateral relatives by blood (up to the fifth degree of relationship) as determined by custom."[160] The 1982 law simply built on this foundation.

Beginning in 1980, to realize the goal of a "better quality" population, major cities like Beijing, Shanghai, and Tianjin started establishing premarital health clinics and popularizing premarital health examinations. As premarital testing became more commonplace in China, some provinces even made it mandatory for obtaining a marriage certificate. Between 3 and 5 million people were found to have congenital mental impairment. Official rhetoric claimed that people with mental disabilities, deformities, "abnormal or defective" sex organs, or chromosomal disorders presented "an obstacle to birth planning."[161] Therefore, couples with genetic diseases were encouraged not to have children, and pregnant couples with genetic diseases were encouraged to voluntarily abort.[162]

At first, some provinces introduced more stringent eugenic policies than others, but eventually a more uniform policy was passed at the national level. In 1988, Gansu province passed China's first law prohibiting mentally handicapped people from having children, and a similar law was soon enacted in Liaoning province. Laws passed in 1992 in Zhejiang and Henan provinces mandated that if one partner in a married couple suffered from a chronic mental disorder, he or she should be sterilized.[163] Finally, at the tenth National People's Conference in late 1994, the central government passed the Maternal and Infant Health Law, which made premarital health examinations compulsory and stipulated that if one person in a married couple has a serious hereditary disease, venereal disease, mental disorder, or contagious disorder, he or she "should" undergo sterilization to prevent "inferior births."[164]

159 Chung, *Struggle for National Survival*, 161.

160 The original text reads: "Jinzhi jiehun de tiaojian wei: 1, Wei zhixi xueqin, huo wei tongbao de xiongdi meimei he tong fu yi mu huo tong mu yi fu de xiongdi meimei zhe; qita wudai nei de pangxi xueqin jian jinzhi jiehun de wenti, cong xiguan." Huo, "Dayuejin zhihou de jihua shengyu, 1962–1966" (Family Planning Policy after the Great Leap Forward, 1962–1966), 54.

161 Wang et al., *Dangdai zhongguo de weisheng shiye* (Public Hygiene Undertakings in Modern China), 254.

162 Wang et al., *Dangdai zhongguo de weisheng shiye* (Public Hygiene Undertakings in Modern China), 254; Deng, Ma, and Wu, *Dangdai zhongguo de jihua shengyu shiye* (The Contemporary Chinese Birth Planning Project), 209.

163 Dikotter, *Imperfect Conceptions*, 173.

164 Population Council, "The New Chinese Law on Maternal and Infant Health Care," *Population and Development Review* 21, no. 3 (1995): 699.

Figure 6.1 Birth planning clinic poster: "*Guojia mianfei biqian yousheng xiangmu*" (Free national prenatal eugenics project), 2015.
Source: Photograph by author.

In 2003, mandatory premarital health checks were phased out. A birth planning official and gynecologist in Luoyang informed me that since premarital health examinations are no longer required for marriage registration, many young people are simply not having them. The doctor attributed this trend to the fact that few people want to share information about their personal lives or sexual behavior.[165] In addition, these examinations were highly intrusive and could potentially destroy a match, so it makes sense why young people would not voluntarily subject themselves to this type of treatment.

However, the continuing salience of eugenic thought in contemporary Chinese policy was still evident when I visited a birth planning clinic in Luoyang in August 2015. Upon entering the clinic, visitors were greeted by a large pink billboard hanging from the ceiling that said "Free National Prenatal Eugenics Project" (*guojia mianfei yunqian yousheng xiangmu*) (Figure 6.1).[166]

The walls were lined with brightly colored posters depicting happy families and illustrating the correct steps to be taken as part of the "three

[165] Interview with author, Luoyang, August 2, 2015.
[166] "Guojia mianfei yunqian yousheng xiangmu" (Free National Prenatal Eugenics Project), Luoyang, 2015.

Figure 6.2 Birth planning clinic poster: "Jihua shengyu youzhi fuwu san da gongcheng" (The three big projects of top-quality birth planning service), 2015.
Source: Photograph by author.

big projects" (*san da gongcheng*): (1) high-quality birth control service, (2) birth deformity intervention, and (3) genital tract infection intervention (Figure 6.2).[167] The posters demonstrated correct contraceptive practices, as well as methods for preventing, diagnosing, and addressing the transmission of genetic diseases and uterine infections that can lead to premature birth or miscarriage. Most controversially, the posters demonstrated how to test for and intervene (via abortion) in the case of congenital deformities. The "three big projects" initiative has been in place since at least 2001, and its expansion is part of an ongoing nationwide effort to improve the quality of the population as a whole.[168] As in

[167] "The Three Big Projects of Top Quality Birth Planning Service" (jihua shengyu youzhi fuqu san da gongcheng), Luoyang, 2015.

[168] Zhu Yu, "Woguo jiang shishi jihua shengyu shengzhi jiankang youzhi fuwu san da gongcheng (My Country Will Implement Three Major Projects for High-Quality Birth Planning and Reproductive Health Services). *Guangming ribao* (Guangming Daily), June 7, 2001, https://www.gmw.cn/01gmrb/2001-06/07/05-12E1300CFCC7501B48256A640004088A.htm.

Luoyang, billboards promoting "quality" and eugenic births can be found on display in many clinics and hospitals across China.

Whatever the perceived societal benefit of this and related projects, the preoccupation with high-quality babies in contemporary Chinese cities – as measured by physical appearance, cognitive ability, and genetic pedigree – cannot be denied. In a situation in which an increasingly privatized system is replacing the state's prevision of welfare and health services, what might have been a more marginal discourse has become mainstream.

The Challenge of Sex Education

Another aspect of the One Child Policy era reproductive reforms was introducing premarital sex counseling. During the Mao era, information about sex and birth control was only disseminated to married couples. As part of the initiative to produce higher-quality births, the Maternal and Infant Health Law stipulated that Chinese young people be offered guidance on sexual hygiene and birth control strategies in addition to premarital health examinations. Sex education had never been institutionalized in the PRC, but this marked a step in that direction. Nevertheless, throughout the 1990s implementation of sex education programs in secondary schools and universities was slow and unsystematic.[169] Further compounding this issue was the fact that the predominant approach to sex education preached sexual morality through abstinence, rather than "safe sex," for preventing pregnancy and disease transmission.[170] Young people were simply told to control their sexual impulses, which they were warned could be dangerous, and to stay away from degenerate publications like pornography.[171] Such rhetoric may appear familiar because, as Harriet Evans has shown, many of the discourses on sexuality promoted in the 1980s and early 1990s simply replicated those advocated in the 1950s.[172]

Just before mandatory premarital health examinations ended in 2003, the government enacted a law making sex education compulsory in schools. An article published in *The Lancet* in 2004 reported that progress was slow on this front and that some teachers were reluctant to use sex

[169] Alessandra Aresu, "Sex Education in Modern and Contemporary China: Interrupted Debates across the Last Century," *International Journal of Educational Development* 29 (2009): 537.

[170] Aresu, "Sex Education in Modern and Contemporary China," 538.

[171] Emily Honig and Gail Hershatter, *Personal Voices: Chinese Women in the 1980's* (Stanford: Stanford University Press, 1988), 61.

[172] Evans, "Defining Difference," 365.

education textbooks, which had been introduced for the first time in 2002.[173] Similarly, some parents were resistant to their children learning about sex, arguing that young people will learn through experience at the appropriate time.[174] There have been several recent cases in which members of the public became angry about sex education. In a case from 2017, a mother in Zhejiang took issue with schools teaching sex education when her second grader obtained access to a sixth-grade sex education textbook. As a result of her protest, at least one local school recalled the textbook.[175] The mother also argued that the textbook's images, which even included references to homosexuality, were far too graphic (Fig. 6.3).[176] Sex education books, even those that promoted a strictly heteronormative vision of Chinese society, provoked similar responses among parents in Guangdong and Guangxi.[177] In another case from 2015, the decision to install free condom machines on Zhejiang University's campus sparked fears that the school was encouraging (premarital) sex among students.[178] Given these responses to measures promoting sexual wellness, it is not entirely surprising that no more than 57 percent of Chinese high school and college students are estimated to have been exposed to some form of sex education. Although sex education tends to be more common in urban areas than rural ones, a survey by the Shanghai Municipal Government showed that even in one of China's largest cities, Shanghai, only 15 percent of high school students had received some form of sex education from either teachers or parents.[179]

The central government ultimately deemed sex education imperative for a number of reasons. First, studies have shown that many young

[173] Jonathon Watts, "China Sex Education Lags behind Sexual Activity," *The Lancet* 363, April 10, 2004, http://www.thelancet.com/pdfs/journals/lancet/PIIS0140673604159941.pdf.

[174] Hu Jiawei, "Why It's Time for Chinese Educators to Open Up about Sex," *Sixth Tone*, June 19, 2017, http://www.sixthtone.com/news/1000361/why-its-time-for-chinese-educators-to-open-up-about-sex.

[175] Jiayun Feng, "Controversy Over Sex-Ed Textbook," *SupChina*, March 6, 2017, https://supchina.com/2017/03/06/controversy-sex-ed-textbook.

[176] "Xiaofang huiying xiaoxue xing jiaoyu keben zhengyi: jiang zejie tui xiangguan kecheng" (School Responds to Textbook Disputes in Primary School Sex Education: Will Select Opportunities to Promote Related Courses), *Zhongguo xinwen wang* (China News), March 7, 2017, http://www.chinanews.com/sh/2017/03-07/8167055.shtml (accessed May 30, 2018).

[177] Aresu, "Sex Education in Modern and Contemporary China," 539.

[178] "China's Campus Condom Giveaway Both Protects and Offends," *Global Times*, November 29, 2015, http://www.globaltimes.cn/content/955525.shtml.

[179] Jonathon Watts, "China Sex Education Lags Behind Sexual Activity," *The Lancet* 363, April 10, 2004, http://www.thelancet.com/pdfs/journals/lancet/PIIS0140673604159941.pdf.

Figure 6.3 A sex education textbook from Zhejiang province, 2017.
Source: "Xiaofang huiying xiaoxue xing jiaoyu keben zhengyi: jiang zejie tui xiangguan kecheng" (School Responds to Textbook Disputes in Primary School Sex Education: Will Select Opportunities to Promote Related Courses), *Zhongguo xinwen wang* (China News), March 7, 2017, http://www.chinanews.com/sh/2017/03-07/8167055.shtml (accessed May 30, 2018).

people are not knowledgeable about sexual harassment and therefore cannot protect themselves from it.[180] Indeed, sociologist Liu Dalin confirmed in his broad study of sexuality that the number of rape cases in China increased in the 1980s and 1990s.[181] Sex education was introduced in some places in the 1980s for this reason, yet reports show that the scope of these reforms was limited.[182] Numerous interviewees and friends who married in the 1980s and early 1990s told me that they simply knew nothing about sex or sexual hygiene until marriage.[183] Second, sexually transmitted diseases are on the rise because young people do not know to use protection. HIV infections, for example, are

180 Hu, "Why It's Time for Chinese Educators to Open Up about Sex."
181 Aresu, "Sex Education in Modern and Contemporary China," 536.
182 Harriet Evans, *Women and Sexuality in China*, 35.
183 Interviews with author, Tianjin, February 13, 2017; interview with author, Shanghai, February 10, 2017.

increasing among young people with the annual growth rate at about 35 percent for people between ages fifteen and twenty-four.[184] Similarly, syphilis is still a problem as nearly 500,000 new cases were reported in China in 2014.[185] Third, China is experiencing an uptick in unwanted pregnancies, and abortions are common among young women who have no knowledge about sex or contraception.[186] According to surveys conducted by sociologist Li Yinhe and official government organs, more than 70 percent of young people have had premarital sex – up from 15 percent in 1989 – and many young women in China use abortion as their primary form of birth control.[187] While official statistics estimate that over 13 million abortions are performed annually, 62 percent among women ages twenty to twenty-nine, experts argue that this is a "vast underestimation" because it overlooks nonsurgical (i.e., medicinal) abortions and those carried out in unlicensed clinics.[188] According to Qi Rongyi, chief physician of the gynecology and obstetrics department at a hospital in Tianjin, the number of girls under sixteen undergoing abortions at her hospital is increasing 30 percent annually.[189] Zhao Jing, the founder of an internet-based sex education company, notably stated that many women "think having an abortion is like taking a nap" because advertisements claim to offer "painless abortions." Therefore, young women underestimate the seriousness of these procedures.[190]

[184] James Griffiths, Nanlin Fang, and Serenitie Wang, "China's Lack of Sex Education Is Putting Millions of Young People at Risk," *CNN*, December 6, 2016, https://www.cnn.com/2016/11/30/health/china-sex-education-world-aids-day.

[185] Laurie Burkitt, "Sex in China: Abortion, Infection and Lack of Education," *The Wall Street Journal*, December 8, 2015, https://blogs.wsj.com/chinarealtime/2015/12/08/sex-in-china-abortion-infection-and-lack-of-education/.

[186] Griffiths, Fang, and Wang, "China's Lack of Sex Education is Putting Millions of Young People at Risk"; "China's Campus Condom Giveaway Both Protects and Offends," *Global Times*, November 29, 2015, http://www.globaltimes.cn/content/955525.shtml.

[187] Alyssa Abkowitz, "More and More Chinese People Are Having Pre-Marital Sex," *The Wall Street Journal*, April 16, 2015, https://blogs.wsj.com/chinarealtime/2015/04/16/more-and-more-chinese-people-are-having-pre-marital-sex/.

[188] Griffiths, Fang, and Wang, "China's Lack of Sex Education is Putting Millions of Young People at Risk"; Yang Wanli, "High Abortion Rate Triggers Fears for Young Women," *China Daily*, January 27, 2015, http://www.chinadaily.com.cn/china/2015-01/27/content_19412949.htm.

[189] Yang Wanli, "High Abortion Rate Triggers Fears for Young Women," *China Daily*, January 27, 2015, http://www.chinadaily.com.cn/china/2015-01/27/content_19412949.htm.

[190] Griffiths, Fang, and Wang, "China's Lack of Sex Education Is Putting Millions of Young People at Risk"; Yang Wanli, "High Abortion Rate Triggers Fears for Young Women," *China Daily*, January 27, 2015, http://www.chinadaily.com.cn/china/2015-01/27/content_19412949.htm; Langchao gongzuoshi (Wave Studio), "Zhongguo dajie shang weishenme dou you rengong liuchan guanggao?" (Why Do Chinese Streets All

Even though the central government employs approximately 700,000 full-and part-time workers for dispensing contraceptives nationwide, sex educators, who are concerned about unsettling phenomena related to lack of sex education and the government's delayed ability to address these issues, have taken matters into their own hands. Some have set up their own sex education apps, such as Yummy and Buzz and Bloom (*mifeng lanhua*), which provide sexual hygiene tips via the messaging app, WeChat.[191] Others have organized sex education meetups and classes for students.[192] Educators and activists have praised the rapid progress China has made in embracing sex education but agree that there is still much more work to be done.[193]

Conclusion

The One Child Policy will long be remembered as the most extreme attempt to expedite economic growth through a program of nationwide IUD insertions, sterilizations, and abortions. In seeking to interpret the implications of this monumental state undertaking, scholars and journalists have examined the One Child Policy from many different angles. Those scholars writing about the 1980s and 1990s have shed light on rural resistance to birth limitations and the precipitous increase in sex-selective abortion and female infanticide during those years. Other scholars have analyzed the One Child Policy in terms of the shrinking labor force, lack of old-age support, rising rates of kidnapping and sex trafficking, and other social issues. In addition, journalist Mei Fong has shown how the uneven age distribution in contemporary China has produced a generation of "little emperors" – stereotyped as self-centered, spoiled, and weak – who in reality face formidable pressure from their parents to become educated, marry, and purchase a home.[194]

Adding to the conversation, this chapter has highlighted the relationship between wealth disparities and the implementation and reception of

Have Advertisements for Abortion?), *Huxiu*, June 11, 2018, https://www.huxiu.com/article/247901.html.

[191] Griffiths, Fang, and Wang, "China's Lack of Sex Education Is Putting Millions of Young People at Risk"; Yang, "High Abortion Rate Triggers Fears for Young Women."

[192] Sarah O'Meara, "Workshop Teaches Children How to Guard against Sexual Abuse," *Sixth Tone*, July 5, 2016, http://www.sixthtone.com/news/1034/workshop-teaches-children-how-guard-against-sexual-abuse.

[193] Hua Shengdun, "Sex Education in China Evolving," *China Daily USA*, April 16, 2015, http://usa.chinadaily.com.cn/china/2015-04/06/content_20010305.htm.

[194] Mei Fong, *One Child: The Story of China's Most Radical Experiment* (Boston: Houghton Mifflin Harcourt, 2016), 95.

the One Child Policy.[195] Compared to Shanghai and Tianjin, where a new model of childrearing had become the norm, in Luoyang families still generally supported having more children. For them, having heirs to carry on the bloodline and generate household income outweighed the importance of offering their children a prestigious education and the accompanying professional opportunities. Moreover, the fact that the threat of dismissal from work was less frequently enforced in Luoyang may have fostered greater temptation to violate the policy, hence the government's emphasis on sterilization in less economically developed regions. In short, the way the policy was implemented and how it was received varied from place to place, and even from one household to another.

Against this backdrop, the demand that couples have only one child, government promotion of "quality" births, and the passage of the eugenic Maternal and Infant Health Law also inspired an increased emphasis on bearing children with "good" genes. These concerns, as well as climbing rates of sexual harassment and rape, abortion among unmarried women, and HIV/AIDS infections, stimulated national efforts to introduce sex education. Dovetailing with the need for more uniform access to sex education is the continued use of abortion as a primary birth control method and reliance on dangerous herbal abortion techniques. Despite some improvements in these areas, abortion rates among young women remain high and detractors continue to criticize compulsory sex education in schools, suggesting that these issues will be particularly difficult to tackle.

[195] Delia Davin, Elisabeth Croll, Margery Wolf, and Penny Kane have also analyzed the influence of socioeconomic and rural–urban differentials on gender roles, women's social status, and reproduction in twentieth-century China. Delia Davin, *Woman-Work: Patriarchy and the Party in Revolutionary China* (Oxford: Oxford University Press, 1976); Elisabeth Croll, *Feminism and Socialism in China* (Abingdon: Routledge, 1978); Margery Wolf, *Revolution Postponed: Women in Contemporary China* (Stanford: Stanford University Press, 1985); Penny Kane, *The Second Billion: Population and Family Planning in China* (Ringwood: Penguin Books, 1987).

Epilogue: Birth Control and Abortion in the *Longue Durée*, 1911–2021

In 2015, the One Child Policy – what has become emblematic of technocratic efforts to demographically engineer modernity – was formally replaced with a Two Child Policy to be implemented in 2016. Then, in response to census results indicating that the birth rate had declined steeply, in 2021 the policy was again relaxed, and a Three Child Policy was enacted.[1] With more than 18 percent of the population over sixty, the central government is now encouraging larger families to support the country's graying population and supplement the dwindling workforce, trends resulting from the One Child Policy.[2] As with the One Child Policy when it was initially introduced, at first glance this policy reform appears to mark a sharp break with the previous era. However, as Chapter 6 has shown, since the 1980s exceptions were made for a second child in a variety of circumstances with as much as two-thirds of couples being eligible for two children. With that in mind, what can be garnered from examining birth control practices since the early twentieth century?

Taking a long view of the history of sex and reproduction in modern China reveals critical continuities from the Republican period through the Mao era and into the reform era (1978–present). Many of the same discourses that gained credence during the late Qing and Republican eras – discourses concerned with modernity and national stature, health and labor productivity, women's bodies and family structure, and the role of the state in engineering the population – continually shaped state policies. Time and again, these longstanding themes were adapted to specific political and local contexts, yet socioeconomic and political factors, more so than concerns about women's wellbeing, continually dominated the national conversation about birth control and abortion.

[1] Keith Zhai, "China Three-Child Policy Aims to Rejuvenate Aging Population," *Wall Street Journal,* May 31, 2021, https://www.wsj.com/articles/china-to-ease-limits-on-births-allowing-couples-to-have-three-children-11622447583.

[2] "Population Distribution in China in 2019, by Broad Age Group," *Statista,* https://www.statista.com/statistics/251524/population-distribution-by-age-group-in-china/.

An analysis of reproduction during the twentieth and early twenty-first centuries also suggests that contemporary state policies and individual contraceptive practices owe much to those of earlier periods. Although state power over reproduction did gradually expand and intensify, bringing private life under government authority to an unprecedented degree, these efforts built on a foundation established much earlier. In fact, the legal framework the Communists inherited from the Qing and Nationalist governments played a critical role in paving the way for Mao-era sexual policing and the One Child Policy's implementation. In both the Republican era and the People's Republic, government measures promoting certain reproductive practices and restricting others were challenged and negotiated, producing unforeseen and deeply gendered consequences. Perhaps the reform era and the end of the One Child Policy, then, did not mark paradigm shifts as much as points along a trajectory of gradual change. Examining sexuality and reproduction in the *longue durée* illuminates a number of important historical continuities. For the sake of simplicity, I have divided them into four broad categories – sexuality and the law, fertility culture, gender, and medicine.

Sexuality and the Law

The family unit has long been viewed as the bedrock of Chinese society. During the late imperial period, the patriarchal extended family unit was envisaged to be a microcosm of the state: Harmonious, morally upright families would produce a just, Confucian society. Even within the New Culture reforms of the Republican era in which the ideal of the *xiao jiating* (small family or nuclear family) emerged – a model later adopted by the Communist Party to denote a break with the traditional family structure – the family unit remained essential to political governance and social organization.[3] In the reform era, the family unit continues to be an important mechanism for maintaining social stability. For instance, in response to mounting reports of elder neglect, the Communist Party is now appealing to "traditional" Confucian values like filial piety to encourage familial support for the ballooning elderly population. Campaigns calling for a return to so-called family values expose the essential role family organization plays in the CCP's visions of governance.

Like the instrumentalization of the family unit as a tool for managing society, the Chinese state has also long regulated "unorthodox" sexual

[3] Glosser, *Chinese Visions of Family and State*, 24.

behavior. During the Qing dynasty, a new category of crime (*jian*, meaning illicit sex) was developed because sex outside of marriage (excluding sex with concubines) was perceived as a threat to the social order and fixed gender roles.[4] Unmarried men, called *guanggun* ("bare branches" or "rootless rascals"), were viewed as morally and politically deviant, being prone to preying upon chaste women (and boys), engaging in criminal behavior, and flouting social norms.[5] At the same time, infidelity was considered a crime but one that only applied to women, whose chastity was a prized virtue. As part of the shift toward a more modern legal framework, lawmakers in the mid-Republican period sought to apply the Qing criminalization of adultery more evenly to men and women, so rather than simply charging women with adultery, beginning in 1935 men could also be charged with this crime.[6] To appease activists calling for gender equality, sexual policing would, at least in theory, be applied uniformly to male and female adulterers. In short, even the premodern Chinese state was invested in patrolling the boundaries of normative sexual behavior.

Examining sexual policing in the long term reveals that the execution of laws dictating which forms of sexual intercourse were permitted remained much the same throughout the twentieth century. Indeed, extramarital relationships continued to be treated as crimes in the Mao era and beyond.[7] The same was true for premarital sex, which until 1997, was categorized as an illegal act of "hooliganism."[8] This legal policing of premarital sex continued throughout the Mao era and even into the reform period. While the degree and severity of punishment for unsanctioned sex varied throughout this timeframe, reaching its zenith in the Mao era, the basic principle remained the same. Even today, although infidelity is commonplace and has even become an integral part of homosocial business and government culture, it still runs the risk of producing legal trouble.[9] In a 2011 case of "wife swapping," the perpetrators were sentenced to three and a half years in jail. These sentences

[4] Matthew Sommer, *Sex, Law, and Society in Late Imperial China* (Stanford: Stanford University Press), 30.
[5] Sommer, *Sex, Law, and Society*, 98.
[6] Tran, "Sex and Equality in Republican China: The Debate over the Adultery Law," 214.
[7] Shao-Chuan Leng, "The Role of Law in the People's Republic of China as Reflecting Mao Tse-Tung's Influence," *Journal of Criminal Law and Criminology*, 68, no. 3 (1977): 368.
[8] Burkitt, "Sex in China."
[9] Harriet Zurndorfer, "Polygamy and Masculinity in China: Past and Present," in, *Changing Chinese Masculinities: From Imperial Pillars of State to Global Real Men*, eds. Kam Louie, Derek Hird, and Geng Song (Hong Kong: Hong Kong University Press, 2016), 14.

were lighter than what they might have been in the 1970s and 1980s but were consequential nonetheless.[10] As in earlier periods, the contemporary state's ability to police sexuality is certainly not absolute or uniform, but the threat of punishment is always lurking in the background. In this way, adultery and other forms of "illicit" or nonnormative sex were continually policed from late imperial times to the present, revealing that the state had a relatively large degree of involvement in private life even prior to the Mao era and the One Child Policy.

Other efforts to safeguard the conjugal family at the expense of alternative sexual practices include recent campaigns to shame educated single women into prioritizing marriage. In 2007, the All-China Women's Federation began promoting the expression "leftover women" (*shengnü*) – a derogatory term used to describe unmarried urban professional women aged twenty-seven (later, age twenty-five) or older.[11] As urban women obtain higher levels of education, they increasingly postpone marriage and childbearing, sometimes indefinitely. The "leftover women" campaign seeks to redirect women's energy away from achieving professional goals toward marrying and having healthy babies.[12] Sociologist Leta Hong Fincher links the "leftover women" propaganda to the state's desire for social stability. In light of the fact that China currently has at least 30 million more men than women – a consequence of sex-selective abortions under the One Child Policy – the refusal of "high-quality" women to marry is seen as breeding social disorder because restless single men are more prone to violence and crime than their married counterparts. Moreover, by refusing to have children, such "leftover women" are denying the state access to their "superior" genes, genes that would ostensibly improve the "quality" of the population and contribute to national economic development.[13] The "leftover women" campaign further argues that if women focus on their educations and careers but then do have children later in life, the children will be more prone to birth defects. In fact, rather than addressing public health crises like air pollution, state media blame older mothers for the growing numbers of babies born with birth defects.[14]

The law works in tandem with the "leftover women" campaign to limit women's options outside of marriage. In 2013, for instance, the city of Wuhan proposed a draft regulation charging single mothers onerous

[10] Burkitt, "Sex in China."
[11] Leta Hong Fincher, *Leftover Women: The Resurgence of Gender Inequality in China* (London: Zed Books, 2014), 13.
[12] Fincher, *Leftover Women*, 44. [13] Ibid., 53. [14] Fincher, *Leftover Women*, 57.

fines for out-of-wedlock pregnancies.[15] Relatedly, according to national law, only married Chinese women can freeze their eggs for future use, an action increasingly common among women pursuing higher education and demanding careers. In 2020, a second law was proposed to reinforce the original one – the new law would explicitly ban single women from accessing egg-freezing services.[16] Even today, state-sponsored campaigns and the law work in concert to preserve the heteronormative, conjugal family unit.

Also related to family organization as the basis for political stability is the persistent support for eugenics between the Republican period and the present. In the interwar period (and even earlier in some parts of the United States), eugenic laws that banned the "unfit" from reproducing and sometimes even mandated sterilization were passed in places like the United States, Japan, Switzerland, Sweden, Denmark, Mexico, and Germany.[17] The global fascination with eugenics in the late nineteenth and early twentieth centuries spoke to elite Chinese reformers concerned with strengthening the nation.[18] Building on a much longer history of prenatal education for producing smarter, healthier babies, eugenics aligned with emerging ideas about racial fitness and nation building. The preoccupation with making better babies endured through the Mao era when health campaigns sought to improve maternal and infant health, lower infant mortality rates, and prevent those deemed unfit from bearing children. Although the explicit goal of emphasizing the "quality" of births over the quantity only emerged in the 1970s and early 1980s, similar sentiments had been expressed by some since the early twentieth century. In fact, the eugenic slogan "*yousheng, youyu*" (superior births, superior education) espoused in government rhetoric since the 1980s was taken directly from the Counseling Center for Birth Control (*Shengyu jieyu zixunbu*), one of China's first organizations promoting birth control education. Established by two professors, Lei Jieqiong at Yanjing University and Chen Da of Qinghua University, during the Republican period, the center published a Population Column in the newspaper *Peiping Chenbao* (Beijing Morning News). In the 1930s,

15 Ibid., 45.

16 Zhang Wanqing, "Proposed Ban on Single Women Freezing Eggs Gets Chilly Reception," *Sixth Tone*, May 26, 2020, http://www.sixthtone.com/news/1005711/proposed-ban-on-single-women-freezing-eggs-gets-chilly-reception.

17 Chung, *Struggle for National Survival*, 16; Dikotter, "Race Culture," 468; Connelly, *Fatal Misconception*, 80.

18 Although overtly eugenic laws were only passed in some places, as Matthew Connelly demonstrates, support for the international eugenics movement sprung up around the world.

the center advocated "*shaosheng, yousheng, youyu,*" meaning "fewer births, superior births, superior education."[19] Many of the principles first endorsed by Lei and Chen would become central to the CCP's eugenic policies.

Following World War II, eugenics fell out of favor in many parts of the world due to its association with the Nazis. Yet, even during the 1960s and '70s, involuntary sterilization – often framed as a social welfare measure necessary to alleviate poverty – targeted the working class, the disabled, and racial and ethnic minorities. During that timeframe, forced sterilizations continued (and in some cases even accelerated) in places like the continental United States, Puerto Rico, Scandinavia, Japan, and India.[20] In one of the most overt examples of the persistence of eugenics, Japan's Eugenic Protection Law, which "legalized abortion, sterilization, and birth control for eugenic purposes," was only rolled backed in 1996 under international pressure.[21]

As for China, despite regime changes and shifting political priorities, overtly eugenic laws have been in existence since the Republican period. Premarital health examinations and a ban on reproduction among the "unfit" were first proposed under the Nationalists. In 1950, the Communist Party affirmed these ideas by prohibiting marriages between people with hereditary illnesses. Mandatory premarital health examinations under the One Child Policy and the 1994 Maternal and Infant Health Law merely upheld and extended these policies. In the context of the One Child Policy, it became even more critical to parents that they do everything in their power – including aborting fetuses that tested positive for congenital issues – to ensure that their sole child was born as healthy as possible. Even with the switch to the Two Child Policy (and then the Three Child Policy), as of yet, few urban parents are voluntarily having multiple children, meaning that the emphasis on perfecting one's one and only child will likely continue. Eugenic laws and the normalization of eugenic rhetoric in Chinese medical circles today are indebted to the eugenic policies of earlier periods.

[19] Lei Jieqiong, "Huainian Yang Chongrui yishi" (Remembering Dr. Yang Chongrui) in *Yang Chongrui Boshi, Danchen bai nian jinian* (Dr. Yang Chongrui, 100 Years Memorial Since Her Birth), ed. Yan Renying (Beijing: Beijing Medical University and China Union Medical College, 1990), 1.

[20] Connelly, *Fatal Misconception*, 10; Roberts, *Killing the Black Body,* 90; Rebecca Jane Williams, "Storming the Citadels of Poverty: Family Planning in India, 1975–1977," *Journal of Asian Studies* 73, no. 2 (2014): 484.

[21] Takeuchi-Demirci, *Contraceptive Diplomacy,* 215.

Fertility Culture

Since at least the fall of the Qing dynasty, attitudes toward childbearing in China have varied greatly. Demographers and feminist scholars have debated the extent to which families practiced abortion, infanticide, or "early stopping" in imperial times.[22] While some scholars contend that couples with limited resources actively sought to limit births, others argue that large families with many sons were always the traditional ideal. Still, the fact that this debate exists at all suggests that there is evidence of many different types of fertility cultures and practices. In the Republican period, some women, most conspicuously the urban working class and prostitutes, used *tiaojingyao*, herbal abortifacients, or surgical abortions to regulate their fertility. Similarly, during the Mao era, some women actively sought out birth control for financial, medical, and social reasons, while others did everything in their power to avoid contraception. Even during the One Child Policy era with the relatively unified state message that family planning is good for individual families and the nation, some couples wanted to have several children whereas others were content with just one.

Since the 1980s, a new type of fertility culture has been emerging in urban China, but it certainly is not universal.[23] The idea that having more than one child is not feasible in today's China is a theme that emerged almost universally in my interviews with parents and grandparents. Interviewees with children in their late twenties and early thirties said that their grown children can only afford to have one child because raising and educating a child is so expensive.[24] Grandparents also understood that times had changed and that even with a secure job and help at home, raising a child with a bright future requires an enormous supply of resources. A number of interviewees had even adjusted their expectations for when a young person should marry, now believing that it is normal to wait until one's early thirties to marry and have a child.[25] Young parents also elaborated the reasons for not wanting to have a second child: To be successful, a child will eventually need a house, a car, and a college education (ideally, abroad), all of which are incredibly expensive. For this generation of parents, being able to provide a higher living standard for one child is more important than having many children.

[22] Lee and Wang, *One Quarter of Humanity*, 7–8; Sommer, "Abortion in Late Imperial China," 99; Bray, *Technology and Gender*, 323; Wolf and Engelen, "Fertility and Fertility Control," 134. See note 166 for an overview of this debate.

[23] Yan, *Private Life under Socialism*, 205.

[24] Interview with author, Tianjin, July 1, 2019.

[25] Interview with author, Tianjin, June 29, 2019.

An interview I conducted with a 39-year-old woman in Luoyang in 2019 clearly illustrates these sentiments. The woman, the manager at an electronics company and the mother of a pudgy nine-year-old boy, said that she would not have a second child despite the change in state policy and the fact that she herself is an only child. She explained that her job was very stressful and she was exhausted from working and taking her son to and from school and daycare. Moreover, she and her husband were saving for their son's college education and would not want to care for a baby now that their first child was already so big.[26] Nothing could persuade her to have a second child at this point, given the high cost associated with raising the first.

This new middle-class fertility culture emphasizing the value of having an only child has not simply replaced older ideas about fertility. Rather, this is just one of many strands in the ever-growing range of popular ideas about childbearing in China. In fact, although this is a marginal view, some interviewees said that it was acceptable to never marry or have kids because times have changed.[27] Indeed, China does not possess one monolithic fertility culture, and new ideas are continually being added to this collection.

What is particularly noteworthy is that few people I interviewed who endorsed the continuation of single-child families attributed this decision to official policy. Rather, they interpreted their behavior as being a product of changing economic policies and social norms. This explanation further reinforces the prediction that convincing middle-class urban couples to have a second (let alone a third) child will not be an easy sell. Economic incentives to produce more children could be a possible solution, as in the case of a Jiangsu fiber optics company offering preferential consideration for promotions to employees who elect to have more children.[28] Similarly, some provincial governments are offering bonuses, such as extended maternity leave and 200,000-*yuan* rewards, to couples who voluntarily have a second child, a tactic taken from the One Child Policy era when single-child families received financial benefits.[29] Yet, memories of the One Child Policy era have barely begun to

[26] Interview with author, Luoyang, July 8, 2019.

[27] Interview with author, Tianjin, June 29, 2019.

[28] Xue Yujie, "Jiangsu Company Rewards Employees for Having More Kids," *Sixth Tone*, April 3, 2019, http://www.sixthtone.com/news/1003803/jiangsu-company-rewards-employees-for-having-more-kids.

[29] "Shanxi: 2016 nian qi shishi liang hai zhengce, nüfang sheng er hai jiangli 60 tian jiaqi" (Shanxi: Since the Implementation of the Two Child Policy in 2016, Women Who Have a Second Child Will Receive a 60-Day Leave), *Minnang wang* (Southern Fujian Network), January 20, 2016, http://www.mnw.cn/news/shehui/1086933.html; "Zhege difang wei le guli sheng er tai, zuiduo jiangli 20 wan, ke haishi qi dao shenme

fade, and events like the recent charging of couple a prohibitive 320,000 *yuan* ($45,000) fine for having a third child have kept those recollections fresh.[30] Despite potential perks for having additional children, in an increasingly competitive world, it seems unlikely that the desire to provide one's child with the highest quality of life and access to a superior education will go out of style among China's middle class.

Gender

Another enduring theme in China's modern reproductive history has been the uneven and gendered burden of fertility control. From Republican times (and much earlier) to the present, it has consistently been the responsibility of women to either prevent conception or prevent childbirth through abortion. Women also were and continue to be statistically more likely to have sterilization surgeries than men, even though tubal ligations are more invasive than vasectomies. According to China's National Population and Family Planning Commission, in 1971 42.6 percent more women than men were sterilized. In 2015, an astounding 723.7 percent more women were sterilized than men.[31] The emphasis on female sterilization can be attributed in part to perceptions about health and the body. For example, some men fear that a cut to the body will result in a critical loss of *qi*, which in turn will lead to impotence. Yet, the most significant factors seem to be the deeply rooted belief that women should bear the burden of family planning and the party's willingness to appease men's patriarchal demands. For these reasons, men only undergo vasectomies when forced to by the state (typically during targeted campaigns), if they are cadres seeking to prove their loyalty to the party, or when their wives are too sick to survive this type of procedure.[32] Although rates of female sterilizations among Han women are dropping nationwide, annual sterilization quotas are still in place in some areas of China. In particular, as of 2017, mothers with two daughters – women who might want to try for a son outside of the policy – were the

xiaoguo" (In order to Encourage the Birth of Second Children, This Place is Rewarding Up to 200,000 Yuan, But It's Having No Effect), *Sina*, May 4, 2020, https://k.sina.cn/article_6426234852_17f088fe400100pynd.html?from=baby.

[30] "Guangdong yi fuqi chaosheng bei zhengshou 32 wan yuan shehui fuyang fei" (A Couple in Guangdong was Levied a 320,000 Yuan Excess Child Fee), *Sina*, June 11, 2020, http://gd.sina.com.cn/news/2020-06-11/detail-iircuyvi7858914.shtml.

[31] Miao Xin and Liu Chang, "Chinese Women Bear the Major Burden of Contraception," *Sixth Tone*, March 8, 2018, https://twitter.com/SixthTone.

[32] Huang, *The Spiral Road*, 181.

primary targets for sterilization.[33] A similar emphasis on female sterilization is also evident in the forced family planning programs recently launched in Xinjiang to restrict childbearing among ethnic Uyghurs. Sterilization rates among Uyghur women in Xinjiang increased sevenfold between 2016 and 2018.[34]

The issue of gender inequality with respect to birth control is further compounded by the persistent dislike of condoms among Chinese men, many of whom argue that condoms significantly reduce the sexual experience and that birth control is the sole responsibility of women.[35] Rather than forcing their reluctant partners to use condoms, in the Republican and early Mao era, women were instructed to insert vinegar-covered cotton balls in their vaginas as suppositories or wash vigorously with soapy water after coitus.[36] In the early 2000s, some women were also advised to douche with soap or vinegar and take the "morning after pill" if their husbands refused to use condoms.[37] Zheng Tiantian has even argued that in the context of the commercial sex industry, male patrons today perceive rejecting condoms as masculine and liberating.[38] Certainly not all men reject condoms or believe that birth control is solely a female responsibility, but low condom-use statistics among Chinese youth do suggest that, compared with condom use in other East Asian countries, Chinese men are particularly averse to this form of contraception.[39]

[33] Meng Zhao and Danni Fu, "Sterilization Quotas Endure in Two-Child Policy Era," *Sixth Tone*, February 22, 2017, http://www.sixthtone.com/news/1964/sterilization-quotas-endure-in-two-child-policy-era.

[34] "China Forces Birth Control on Uighurs to Suppress Population," *Associated Press*, June 29, 2020, https://apnews.com/269b3de1af34e17c1941a514f78d764c.

[35] Sarah Mellors, "The Trouble with Rubbers: A History of Condoms in Modern China," *Nan Nü: Men, Women and Gender in China* 22, no. 1 (2020): 178.

[36] Shandong weisheng ting (Shandong Department of Hygiene), *Jieyu xuanchuan shouce* (Birth Control Propaganda Handbook) (Jinan: Shandong People's Publishing House, 1958), 25–26.

[37] Zheng, *Ethnographies of Prostitution*, 51. [38] Ibid., 8.

[39] Although there are no precise statistics for nationwide condom use in China today, Thomas Scharping estimates that in 1992 only 1.5 percent of married, reproductive-age women nationwide relied on condoms. More recently, a 2004 study of undergraduates at nineteen universities in East China found that 16.1 percent of students had had sexual intercourse. Of these, 21.8 percent did not know how to use a condom at all and almost 70 percent reported not knowing how to use a condom correctly. In 1998 (as well as today), Japan boasted a 78-percent condom use rate due to historically limited access to other forms of birth control, such as the pill. Similarly, a 2017 study found that condoms are the most popular form of contraception among Korean women. Scharping, *Birth Control*, 114; Lijun Tang, Rucheng Chen, Danqin Huang, Haocheng Wu, Hong Yan, Shiyue Li, and Kathryn L. Braun, "Prevalence of Condom Use and Associated Factors among Chinese Female Undergraduate Students in Wuhan, China," *AIDS Care* 25, no. 14 (2013): 517; Tiana A. E. Norgren, *Abortion Before Birth Control: The Politics of*

A final example of the enduring role of gender in determining reproductive practices is the phenomenon of sex-selective abortions. The rise in sex-selective abortions in China is well documented, but what it sometimes overlooked is the fact that often mothers themselves seek these procedures to improve their own status, providing further evidence of the pervasiveness of patriarchal values.[40] Although sex-selective abortion only emerged in the One Child Policy era, in fact, women in China had long been seeking help in guaranteeing that their unborn babies would be male. Certain aspects of *taijiao*, or fetal education, for example, were believed to help ensure that a fetus would be male.[41] Prior to 1949 and to some extent afterward, pregnant women would seek out the advice of a fortune-teller to determine fetal sex. Such practices re-emerged in the post-Mao period alongside more technologically advanced methods like prenatal screening.[42] A man from Shanghai in his sixties told me that couples wanting a male baby should try to conceive five days after the woman's period ends to guarantee that they have a boy.[43] In the age of web marketing, the preference for male babies among a subset of the population can even be seen in internet advertisements. In 2018, after the implementation of the Two Child Policy, the Chinese internet mega-retailor, *Taobao*, advertised an alkaline pill for mothers with a daughter hoping to conceive a son as their second child (Figure E.1).[44] An alkaline environment is believed to be more conducive to conceiving a baby boy than a baby girl.[45] Although this advertisement and others promoting related products were criticized and removed from the internet, they speak to the perceived social capital associated with sons.

Reproduction in Postwar Japan (Princeton: Princeton University Press, 2001), 8; Kim Min Jeong, "The Contraceptive Trend in Korea," *Maturitas* 100 (2017): 173.

40 Hvistendahl, *Unnatural Selection*, 37.

41 Ann Anagnost, "Family Violence and Magical Violence: The Woman as Victim in China's One-Child Family Policy," *Women and Language* 11, no. 2 (1988): 4.

42 Anagnost, "Family Violence," 3.

43 Interview with author, Shanghai, February 10, 2017.

44 Wang Kaiqiang, "Shengle nü'er zenme ban? Taobao yao ni chi yao bao shengnan, xingbie qishi jinri hai zai?" (What Can Be Done If You Have a Daughter? Taobao Wants You to Take Medicine to Guarantee That You Give Birth to a Boy; Does Gender Discrimination Still Exist Today?), *Sina*, April 29, 2018, http://k.sina.com.cn/article_5334137897_13df07c29001009vfz.html.

45 Zhang Yiling, "Taobao guanggao cheng shingle nü'er zenme ban, Jiangsu fulian zazhi huyu daoqian" (Jiangsu Women's Federation Magazine Calls for an Apology Regarding Taobao Advertisement Entitled 'What To Do If You Have A Daughter?') *Sina*, April 27, 2018, http://news.sina.com.cn/s/2018-04-27/doc-ifztkpip4325744.shtml.

Figure E.1 Advertisement on *Taobao*: "Shengle nü'er zenme ban? Er tai yong jian yunbao" (What can be done if you have a daughter? Take an alkaline pill for your second child), 2018.
Source: Wang Kaiqiang, "Shengle nü'er zenme ban? Taobao yao ni chi yao bao shengnan, xingbie qishi jinri hai zai?" (What Can Be Done if You Have a Daughter? Taobao Wants You to Take Medicine to Guarantee That You Give Birth to a Boy; Does Gender Discrimination Still Exist Today?), *Sina*, April 29, 2018, http://k.sina.com.cn/article_5334137897_13df07c29001009vfz.html.

Medicine

The medical pluralism and syncretism apparent in China today also have long histories. In the early twentieth century, Western and traditional medicine were not distinctly defined categories, and medical practitioners and consumers turned to both medical systems in addressing the issue of fertility regulation. Republican-era advertising also drew on the language and semiotics of both medical traditions to sell products that blurred the line between contraception and abortifacients. Although TCM became more empirical and Western medicines more widely available during the Mao era, Western contraceptive and abortion methods never fully supplanted traditional ones. Even in the post-Mao era, birth control practices remain diverse and imbued with specific cultural meanings. *Tiaojingyao*, and *tongjingyao*, for example, are still commonly available in China today. In addition, Western and traditional abortion and contraceptive techniques have been synthesized into new methods, such as an injection that induces abortion from medicinal roots. Although they look quite different from their predecessors in the early twentieth century, as in the Republican and Mao eras, both Western medicine and TCM still coexist today in the Chinese medical marketplace, a phenomenon that can increasingly be found in other parts of the world.

A final and important continuity related to medicine is the theme of abortion as contraception. As this book has shown, abortion was the most well-recorded form of fertility control in the Republican period, and abortion rates have remained high since the 1970s despite increased access to condoms and other prophylactics.[46] The taboo nature of pre- and extramarital sex, gendered family planning responsibilities, the limited cultural stigma associated with abortion, and a persistent lack of general knowledge about safe and effective prophylactics among unmarried women have contributed to the enduring reliance on abortion. These factors are not all that different from the ones that undergirded women's decisions to undergo abortion in the Republican era. Whether this trend will reverse itself with the introduction of more systematic and comprehensive sex education and the loosening of family planning restrictions remains to be seen.

What these historical resonances show is that an eye to the past is useful for interpreting the present, and even for imagining the future. As the One Child Policy fades into the past, other historical continuities and ruptures with respect to sexuality and the law, fertility culture, gender, and medicine may become evident. More open archival access may someday also shed light on the less understood aspects of contraception and reproduction in twentieth-century China. To what extent future contraceptive practices will continue to draw on historical paradigms, as well as the position the One Child Policy era and its precursors will occupy in the popular historical imagination, are as of yet unknown.

[46] Nie Jing-Bao, *Behind the Silence*, 96.

Appendix: Interviews

Interview Date	Interview Location	Interviewee Information
August 2, 2015	Luoyang	Husband and wife – both in their late 50s
June 8, 2016	Shanghai	Two men – one in his 50s and one in his 70s
June 12, 2016	Ningde	Woman – aged 70
August 10, 2016	Shanghai	Man – aged 70
August 11, 2016	Shanghai	Woman in her late 50s
August 23, 2016	Shanghai	Woman in her mid-50s
August 30, 2016	Shanghai	Five women – all in their 60s
August 31, 2016	Shanghai	Woman – aged 46
September 17, 2016	Tianjin	Man – aged 70
October 23, 2016	Beijing	Woman – aged 85
November 7, 2016	Shanghai	Man – aged 73
November 14, 2016	Luoyang	Woman – aged 52
November 16, 2016	Luoyang	Man – aged 77
November 17, 2016	Luoyang	Two men – both aged 76
November 21, 2016	Luoyang	Woman – aged 77
December 10, 2016	Shanghai	Five men – all in their late 50s to early 60s
December 20, 2016	Shanghai	Two women – one aged 67 and one aged 84
December 22, 2016	Shanghai	Two men – one aged 65 and one aged 76
December 22, 2016	Shanghai	Woman – aged 73
December 24, 2016	Shanghai	Husband and wife both aged 74
January 12, 2017	Shanghai	Woman – in her 60s
January 12, 2017	Shanghai	Woman – aged 86
January 25, 2017	Shanghai	Two women – one aged 62 and one in her late 80s
February 5, 2017	Shanghai	One man – aged 64 – and one woman – aged 66
February 10, 2017	Shanghai	Two men in their late 60s
February 10, 2017	Shanghai	Man – in his 60s
February 13, 2017	Tianjin	Two women – one in her late 50s and one aged 75
February 13, 2017	Tianjin	Man – aged 69
February 13–15, 2017	Tianjin	Man – aged 58
February 14, 2017	Tianjin	Man – aged 63
February 14, 2017	Tianjin	Man – aged 74

(*cont.*)

Interview Date	Interview Location	Interviewee Information
February 14, 2017	Tianjin	Mother – late 70s – and daughter – late 50s
February 15, 2017	Tianjin	Husband and wife – both aged 70
February 15, 2017	Tianjin	Woman – in her early 70s
April 24, 2019	Email	Uyghur woman – aged 44
June 13, 2019	Xiamen	Woman – aged 40
June 17, 19, 2019	Shanghai	Man – aged 65, woman – aged 58
June 19, 2019	Shanghai	Man – aged 63
June 20, 2019	Shanghai	Man – aged 69, man – aged 60
June 21, 2019	Shanghai	Woman – aged 84
June 25, 2019	Tianjin	Man – aged 52, man – aged 54
June 26, 2019	Tianjin	Man – aged 90
June 26, 2019	Tianjin	Woman – aged 54
June 27, 2019	Tianjin	Woman – aged 55
June 27, 2019	Tianjin	Husband and wife – aged 66
June 29, 2019	Tianjin	Woman – aged 61
July 1, 2019	Tianjin	Man – aged 91, man – aged 84
July 2, 2019	Tianjin	Woman – aged 81
July 4, 2019	Luoyang	Husband and wife – aged 80
July 8, 2019	Luoyang	Woman – aged 39
July 10, 2019	Luoyang	Woman – aged 50
July 10, 2019	Luoyang	Two women – one in late 30s, one in early 40s
July 10, 2019	Luoyang	Woman – aged 49
July 10, 2019	Luoyang	Woman – in her early 50s
July 11, 2019	Luoyang	Woman – aged 70

Glossary

Anmo	按摩
Anquanqi biyunfa	安全期避孕法
Baihua dan	白花丹
Baiyao	白药
Bencao gangmu	本草纲目
Biren	避妊
Biyun	避孕
Baoxiantao	保险套
Buhe	不合
Buyao	补药
Bu zhengque sixiang fanying	不正确思想放映
Cai Yuanpei	蔡元培
Chadui luohu	插队落户
Chenjiu	陈旧
Chuanlian	串连
Chunyao	春药
Da zi bao	大字报
Dandiao	单调
Datai	打胎
Dataiyao	打胎药
Diu mianzi	丢面子
Dongfang zazhi	东方杂志
Duotai	堕胎
Duozi duofu	多子多福
Fakuan	罚款
Fengjian zhuyi	封建主义
Funü shijie	妇女世界
Funü zazhi	妇女杂志
Geren wenti	个人问题
Guangdong sheng fuyou baojian yuan	广东省妇幼保健院
Guanggun	光棍

Guitoutao	龟头套
Guojia mianfei yunqian yousheng xiangmu	国家免费孕前优生项目
He-Yin Zhen	何殷震
Hinin	避妊
Huayan qiaoyu	花言巧语
Hukou	户口
Huamei wanbao chenkan	华美晚报晨刊
Hu Shi	胡适
Hutong	胡同
Jiabuxi	加布西
Jian	奸
Jiankang bao	健康报
Jianwu	奸污
Jiating zhufu	家庭主妇
Jiayu huxiao	家喻户晓
Jiefang ribao	解放日报
Jieyu	节育
Jieyu biyunfa	节欲避孕法
Jihua shengyu	计划生育
Jihua shengyu wenyi xuanchuan cailiao huibian	计划生育文艺宣传材料汇编
Jindai funü	近代妇女
Jing	精
Jingji kunnan	经济困难
Jinjinyouwei	津津有味
Jinzhi jiehun de tiaojian wei: 1, Wei zhixi xueqin, huo wei tongbao de xiongdi meimei he tong fu yi mu huo tong mu yi fu de xiongdi meimei zhe; qita wudai nei de pangxi xueqin jian jinzhi jiehun de wenti, cong xiguan.	禁止结婚的条件为：1，为直系血亲，或为同胞的兄弟姊妹和同父异母或同母异父的兄弟姊妹者；其他五代内的旁系血亲间禁止结婚的问题，从习惯。
Kang Youwei	康有为
Laodong baoxian	劳动保险
Liang Qichao	梁启超
Liangqi xianmu	良妻贤母
Lianhuanhua	连环画
Lu Xun	鲁迅
Luobo zhuang de dongxi	萝卜状的东西

Luohou de defang	落后的地方
Mafan	麻烦
Mama	嬷嬷
Mama tang	嬷嬷堂
Mifeng lanhua	蜜蜂兰花
Ming zhenliao	明诊疗
Neibu cankao	内部参考
Nichu jingfa	溺除精法
Ninshin seigen	妊娠制限
Niunai putao	牛奶葡萄
Pan Guangdan	潘光旦
Qi	气
Qi'er	弃儿
Qipao yaofen	起泡药粉
Ren duo liliang da	人多力量大
Reng	扔
Rengong liuchan	人工流产
Rou ai rou de ganjue	肉挨肉的感觉
Rouren shuchang buyi pohuai	柔韧舒畅不易破坏
Ruyidai	如意袋
San da gongcheng	三大工程
Sanji seigen	產児制限
Sannian kunnan shiqi	三年困难时期
Shaosheng, yousheng, youyu	少生，优生，优育
Shaying tang	杀婴堂
Shenbao	申报
Sheng weisheng ting	省卫生厅
Shengnü	剩女
Shengyu jieyu zixunbu	生育节育咨询部
Shengyu jiezhi	生育节制
Shengyu kongzhi	生育控制
Shenjing shuairuo de bing	神经衰弱的病
Shenti shoudao cuican	身体受到摧残
Shidishui	十滴水
Shou chaoben	手抄本
Shushu	叔叔
Si shengzi	私生子
Sigu	四姑
Sixiang zhang'ai	思想障碍
Ta de you	她的友
Tanqinyao	探亲药

Taobao	淘宝
Taijiao	胎教
Tiaojingyao	调经药
Tianhua fen	天花粉
Tingyundan	停孕丹
Tiaoxi	调戏
Tiwai paijingfa	体外排精法
Tongjingyao	通经药
Tufa	土法
Tuji	突击
Tu niuxi	土牛膝
Waimao dangwei	外贸党委
Wanhun	晚婚
Wan, xi, shao	晚，希，少
Weisheng	卫生
Wuhua bamen	五花八门
Xiao jiating	小家庭
Xin funü yuekan	新妇女月刊
Xin Tianjin Huabao	新天津画报
Xing	性
Xing shenghuo	性生活
Xinping jiujiu	新瓶旧酒
Yang	阳
Yang Chao Buwei	杨步伟
Yang Chongrui	杨崇瑞
Yindaosai	阴道塞
Yixun	医讯
Yangguang canlan de rizi	阳光灿烂的日子
Yangsheng	养生
Ye Dehui	叶德辉
Yijing	遗精
Yimu cao	益母草
Yin	阴
Yinjingtao	阴茎套
You wenhua de ren	有文化的人
You'er	诱饵
Youhuo	诱惑
Yousheng	优生
Yousheng, youyu	优生，优育
Yunjian	孕检
Yusei	优生

Zhagen nongcun	扎根农村
Zhang Jingsheng	张竞生
Zhang Xichen	章锡琛
Zhenjiu	针灸
Zhejiang ribai	浙江日报
Zhidi meiruan jingjiu naiyong	质地美软经久耐用
Zhiyu liangyou	制育良友
Zhongguo funü	中国妇女
Zhonghua minguo wan sui	中华民国万岁
Zhou Jianren	周建人
Zhuitai	坠胎

References

Libraries and Archives

Beijing Municipal Archives (BMA)
Chinese University of Hong Kong Archives (CUHKA)
Columbia University C.V. Starr East Asian Library
East China Normal University Archives (ECNUA)
Fudan University Contemporary China Social Life Data and Research Center (CCSL)
Guangdong Provincial Archives (GPA)
Guangzhou Municipal Archives (GMA)
Hangzhou Municipal Archives (HMA)
Harvard-Yenching Library
Luoyang Municipal Archives (LMA)
National Library of China
Princeton University Rare Books and Special Collections
Qingdao Municipal Archives (QMA)
Shanghai Jiao Tong University Archives (SJTUA)
Shanghai Library
Shanghai Municipal Archives (SMA)
Stanford University Cadre Archive (SUCA)
Stanford University East Asia Library
Tianjin Municipal Archives (TMA)
University of Toledo Archives
Wellcome Library
Zhejiang Provincial Archives (ZPA)

Theses and Dissertations

Callahan, Karen Lee. “Dangerous Devices, Mysterious Times: Men, Women, and Birth Control in Early Twentieth-Century Japan.” PhD diss., University of California, Berkeley, 2004.

Cunningham, Maura Elizabeth. “Shanghai's Wandering Ones: Child Welfare in a Global City, 1900–1953.” PhD diss., University of California, Irvine, 2014.

David, Mirela. "Free Love, Marriage, and Eugenics: Global and Local Debates on Sex, Birth Control, Venereal Disease and Population in 1920s–1930s China." PhD diss., New York University, 2014.

Huo, Xuanji 霍炫吉. "Dayuejin zhihou de jihua shengyu, 1962–1966" 大跃进之后的计划生育 (Family Planning Policy after the Great Leap Forward, 1962–1966). Master's thesis, Nanjing University, 2015.

Ma, Ling. "Gender, Law, and Society: Abortion in Early Twentieth Century China." PhD diss., State University of New York, Buffalo, 2016.

Yu, Lianshi 俞莲实. "Minguo shiqi chengshi shengyu jiezhi yundong de yanjiu: Yi Beijing, Shanghai, Nanjing wei zhongdian" 民国时期城市生育节制运动的研究—以北京，上海，南京为重点 (The Birth Control Movement in Republican Cities: A Focus on Beijing, Shanghai and Nanjing). PhD diss., Fudan University, 2008.

Primary and Secondary Sources

"A Women's Health Class in 1955." Everyday Life in Maoist China. https://everydaylifeinmaoschina.wordpress.com/2015/10/02/a-womens-health-class-in-1955/ (accessed June 1, 2018).

Abkowitz, Alyssa. "More and More Chinese People Are Having Pre-marital Sex." *Wall Street Journal*, April 16, 2015. https://blogs.wsj.com/chinarealtime/2015/04/16/more-and-more-chinese-people-are-having-pre-marital-sex/.

Achan, Jane et al. "Quinine, an Old Anti-Malarial Drug in a Modern World: Role in the Treatment of Malaria." *Malaria Journal* 10, no. 144 (2011): 1–12.

Aird, John Shields. *Slaughter of the Innocents: Coercive Birth Control in China*. Washington, DC: AEI Press, 1990.

Almond, Douglas, Hongbin Lin, and Shuang Zhang. "Land Reform and Sex Selection in China." National Bureau of Economic Research, last modified November 2017. www.nber.org/papers/w19153.pdf.

Altehenger, Jennifer. *Legal Lessons: Popularizing Laws in the People's Republic of China, 1949–1989*. Cambridge, MA: Harvard University Press, 2018.

Anagnost, Ann. "Family Violence and Magical Violence: The Woman as Victim in China's One-Child Family Policy." *Women and Language* 11, no. 2 (1988): 16–22.

Andrews, Bridie. *The Making of Modern Chinese Medicine, 1850–1960*. Honolulu: University of Hawaii Press, 2014.

Aresu, Alessandra. "Sex Education in Modern and Contemporary China: Interrupted Debates across the Last Century." *International Journal of Educational Development* 29, no. 5 (2009): 532–541.

Avdeev, Alexandre, Alain Blum, and Irina Troitskaya. "The History of Abortion Statistics in Russia and the USSR from 1900 to 1991." *Population* (English Edition) 7 (1995): 39–66.

Bai, Ge 白戈. *1966–1976: Zhongguo baixing shenghuo shilu* 1966–1976 中国百姓生活 实录(1966–1976: Record of the Life of China's Ordinary People). Beijing: Jingguan jiaoyu chubanshe, 1993.

Banister, Judith. *China's Changing Population*. Stanford: Stanford University Press, 1991.

Baum, Emily. "Health by the Bottle: The Dr. Williams' Medicine Company and the Commodification of Well-Being." In *Liangyou, Kaleidoscopic Modernity and the Shanghai Global Metropolis, 1926–1945*, edited by Paul G. Pickowicz, Kuiyi Shen, and Yingjin Zhang. Leiden: Brill, 2013.

"Healthy Minds, Compliant Citizens: The Politics of 'Mental Hygiene' in Republican China, 1928–1937." *Twentieth-Century China* 42, no. 3 (2017): 215–233.

The Invention of Madness: State, Society, and the Insane in Modern China. Chicago: University of Chicago Press, 2018.

"Beijing you bushao jiguan ganbu yaoqiu biyun he rengong liuchan" 北京有不少机关干部要求 避孕和人工流产 (Many Government Officials in Beijing Demand Birth Control and Abortion). Neibu cankao 内部参考 (1955).

Beijingshi gonggong weishengju weisheng jiaoyusuo yu beijingshi kexue jishu puji xiehui 北京 市公共卫生局卫生教育所与北京市科学技术普及协会 (Hygiene Education Institute of the Beijing Public Hygiene Bureau and Beijing Science and Technology Popularization Association). *Nongcun jihua shengyu huace* 农村计划生育画册 (Rural Birth Planning Album) Beijing: Beijing chubanshe, 1958.

Bonnin, Michel. *The Lost Generation: The Rustification of China's Educated Youth (1968–1980)*. Krystyna Horko, trans. Hong Kong: Chinese University Press, 2013.

Bray, Francesca. *Technology and Gender: Fabrics of Power in Late Imperial China.* Berkeley: University of California Press, 1997.

Brown, Jeremy. *City versus Countryside in Mao's China: Negotiating the Divide.* Cambridge: Cambridge University Press, 2012.

Burkitt, Laurie. "Sex in China: Abortion, Infection and Lack of Education." *Wall Street Journal*, December 8, 2015. https://blogs.wsj.com/chinarealtime/2015/12/08/sex-in-china-abortion-infection-and-lack-of-education/.

Butler, Judith. *Gender Trouble: Feminism and the Subversion of Identity*. New York: Routledge, 1990.

Chang, Jung. *Wild Swans: Three Daughters of China*. New York: Touchstone, 2003.

Chen, Jinhua 陈金华. "Yong banmao duotai yinqi zhongdu siwang" 用斑蝥堕胎引起中毒死亡 (Using Mylabris to Induce Abortion Leads to Fatal Poisoning). *Xingshi jishu* 刑事技术 (Forensic Science and Technology) 5 (1980): 37–38.

Chen, Xiyi, Li Huaying, Sun Shusan, and Wang Yimin 陈希夷， 李华英，孙树三， 王逸民. "Dian xiyin rengong liuchanshu 250 li fenxi" 电吸引人工流产术250例分析 (An Analysis of 250 Cases of Electrically-Induced Abortion). *Shandong yikan* 山东医刊 (Shandong Journal of Medicine) 1 (1964): 20–22.

Chen, Yifang 陈怡芳. "Chunjie huijia yao zhuyi biyun" 春节回家要注意避孕 (Pay Attention to Contraception When Returning Home for Spring Festival). *Zhejiang ribao* 浙江日报(Zhejiang Daily), February 14, 1958.

Cheng, Hu 城虎. "Jingju qudi shaonü kouchui ruyidai" 警局取締少女口吹如意袋 (Authorities Prohibit Young Girls from Inflating Condoms." *Jipu* 吉普36 (1946): n.p.

Chiang, Howard. *After Eunuchs: Science, Medicine, and the Transformation of Sex in Modern China*. New York: Columbia University Press, 2018.

"Chijiao yisheng" peixun jiaocai" 赤脚医生"培训教材 ("Barefoot Doctor" Training Materials). Beijing: Renmin weisheng chubanshe, 1970.

"China Forces Birth Control on Uighurs to Suppress Population." *Associated Press*, June 29, 2020. https://apnews.com/269b3de1af34e17c1941a514f78d764c.

"China's Campus Condom Giveaway Both Protects and Offends." *Global Times*, November 29, 2015. www.globaltimes.cn/content/955525.shtml.

"Chulemi Contraceptive Cream." Inside Red China. http://radfilms.com/China_1957_Birth_Control_Vaginal_Foam.html (accessed June 1, 2018).

"Chunyao an jieshu qifeng" 春藥案結束啟封 (Aphrodisiac Case Closed). *Shenbao* 申報, July 28, 1930.

Chung, Yuehtsen Juliette. *Struggle for National Survival: Chinese Eugenics in a Transnational Context, 1896–1945*. New York: Routledge, 2002.

Cochran, Sherman. "Marketing Medicine and Advertising Dreams in China, 1900–1950." In *Becoming Chinese: Passages to Modernity and Beyond*, edited by Wen-hsin Yeh, 62–97. Berkeley: University of California Press, 2000.

Connelly, Matthew. *Fatal Misconception: The Struggle to Control World Population*. Cambridge: Harvard University Press, 2008.

Croll, Elisabeth. *Feminism and Socialism in China*. Abingdon: Routledge, 1978.

Croll, Elisabeth, Delia Davin, and Penny Kane, eds. *China's One-Child Family Policy*. London: Macmillan, 1985.

Dai, Sijie. *Balzac and the Little Chinese Seamstress: A Novel*. Ina Rilke, trans. New York: Knopf, 2001.

David, Mirela. "Bertrand Russell and Ellen Key in China: Individualism, Free Love, and Eugenics in the May Fourth Era." In *Sexuality in China: Histories of Power and Pleasure*, edited by Howard Chiang, 76–98. Seattle: University of Washington Press, 2018.

"Female Gynecologists and Their Birth Control Clinics: Eugenics in Practice in 1920s–1930s China." *Canadian Bulletin of Medical History* 35, no. 1 (2018): 1–31.

"'The Task Is Hers:' Going Global, Margaret Sanger's Visit to China in 1922." *Asian Pacific Perspectives* 14, no. 1 (Fall 2016): 75–99.

Davin, Delia. *Woman-Work: Patriarchy and the Party in Revolutionary China*. Oxford: Oxford University Press, 1976.

Deng, Liqun 邓力群, Ma Hong 马洪, and Wu Heng 武衡, eds. *Dangdai zhongguo de jihua shengyu shiye* 当代中国的计划生育事业 (The Contemporary Chinese Birth Planning Project). Beijing: Dangdai Zhongguo chubanshe, 1992.

Diamant, Neil. *Revolutionizing the Family: Politics, Love, and Divorce in Urban and Rural China, 1949–1968*. Berkeley: University of California, Press, 2000.

Dikotter, Frank. *The Discourse of Race in Modern China*. London: C Hurst & Co, 1992.

Imperfect Conceptions: Medical Knowledge, Birth Defects, and Eugenics in China. New York: Columbia University Press, 1998.

"Race Culture: Recent Perspectives on the History of Eugenics." *American Historical Review* 103, no. 2 (1998): 467–478.

Sex, Culture, and Modernity in China: Medical Science and the Construction of Sexual Identities in the Early Republican Period. Honolulu: University of Hawaii Press, 1995.

Dillon, Nara. *Radical Inequalities: China's Revolutionary Welfare State in Comparative Perspective*. Cambridge: Harvard University East Asia Center, 2015.

Dixon-Mueller, Ruth. *Population Policy and Women's Rights: Transforming Reproductive Choice*. Westport: Praeger, 1993.

Djerassi, Carl. *The Politics of Contraception*. New York: W.W. Norton, 1979.

Dong, Pingmei 董平美. "Shengyu jiezhi de lilun he shiji" 生育節制的理論和實際 (The Theory and Practice of Birth Control). *Dongfang zazhi* 東方雜誌 (East Asian Miscellany) 33, no. 7: 55–61.

"Duzhe dui 'Xin Zhongguo funü' kandai 'Biyun fangfa' yiwen de fangying" 读者对《新中国妇 女》刊戴《避孕方法》一文的反映 (Readers' Responses to the Article 'Birth Control Methods' in *New Women of China* magazine). Neibu cankao 内部参考 (1955).

Eaton, A. W. "Feminist Philosophy of Art." *Philosophy Compass* 3 (2008): 873–893.

Ehrlich, Paul R. *The Population Bomb*. New York: Sierra Club/Ballantine Books, 1968.

Evans, Harriet. *Beijing from Below: Stories of Marginal Lives in the Capital's Center*. Durham: Duke University Press, 2020.

"Defining Difference: The "Scientific" Construction of Sexuality and Gender in the People's Republic of China." *Signs* 20, no. 2 (1995): 357–394.

"Past, Perfect or Imperfect: Changing Images of the Ideal Wife." In *Chinese Femininities/Chinese Masculinities: A Reader*, edited by Susan Brownell and Jeffrey N. Wasserstrom, 335–360. Berkeley: University of California Press, 2002.

The Subject of Gender: Daughters and Mothers in Urban China. Lanham: Rowman & Littlefield Publishers, 2008.

Women and Sexuality in China: Dominant Discourses of Female Sexuality and Gender Since 1949. Cambridge: Polity Press, 1997.

Fan, Shen. *Gang of One*. Lincoln: Bison Books, 2006.

Fang, Xiaoping. "Barefoot Doctors and the Provision of Rural Health Care." In *Medical Transitions in Twentieth-Century China*, edited by Bridie Andrews and Mary Brown Bullock, 267–282. Bloomington: Indiana University Press, 2014.

Barefoot Doctors and Western Medicine in China. Rochester: University of Rochester Press, 2012.

Faundes, Anibal and Tapani Luukkainen. "Health and Family Planning Services in the Chinese People's Republic," *Studies in Family Planning* 3, no. 7 (1972): 165–176.

"Fei budeyi buyao zuo rengong liuchan" (Do Not Have an Abortion as a Last Resort). *Qingdao ribao* (Qingdao Daily), March 12, 1957.

Fei, Siyen. "Writing for Justice: An Activist Beginning of the Cult of Female Chastity in Late Imperial China." *Journal of Asian Studies* 71 (2012): 991-1012.

Feldt, Gloria. *The War on Choice: The Right-Wing Attack on Women's Rights and How to Fight Back*. New York: Bantam Books, 2004.

Feng, Jiayun. "Controversy Over Sex-Ed Textbook." *SupChina*, March 6, 2017. https://supchina.com/2017/03/06/controversy-sex-ed-textbook.

Fincher, Leta Hong. *Leftover Women: The Resurgence of Gender Inequality in China*. London: Zed Books, 2014.

Fisher, Kate. *Birth Control, Sex, and Marriage in Britain, 1918–1960*. Oxford: Oxford University Press, 2006.

"The Delivery of Birth Control Advice in South Wales between the Wars." In *Oral History, Health and Welfare*, edited by Joanna Bornat et al., 251–270. London: Routledge, 2000.

Fong, Mei. *One Child: The Story of China's Most Radical Experiment*. Boston: Houghton Mifflin Harcourt, 2016.

Fong, Vanessa. *Only Hope: Coming of Age Under China's One-Child Policy*. Stanford: Stanford University Press, 2004.

Foucault, Michel. *The History of Sexuality, Vol. 1: An Introduction*. New York: Pantheon Books, 1978.

Furth, Charlotte. *A Flourishing Yin: Gender in China's Medical History: 960–1665*. Berkeley: University of California Press, 1999.

Gao, Yuan. *Born Red: A Chronicle of the Cultural Revolution*. Stanford: Stanford University Press, 1987.

Ghosh, Arunabh. *Making It Count: Statistics and Statecraft in the Early People's Republic of China*. Princeton: Princeton University Press, 2020.

Glosser, Susan. *Chinese Visions of Family and State, 1915–1953*. Berkeley: University of California Press, 2003.

Gong, Jin 公瑾. "Guanyu deguo de qingpo jueyu lu (ouzhou tongxun)" 關於德國的強迫絕育律 (歐洲通訊) (About the Law of Forced Sterilization in Germany (European Communication)). *Dongfang zazhi* 東方雜誌 (East Asian Miscellany) 31, no. 9 (1934): 7–10.

Gong, Mu 公木. "Ruyidai bian yang paopao" 如意袋變洋泡泡 (Condoms Become Foreign Balloons). *Guoji xinwen huabao* 國際新聞畫報 (International News Pictorial) 52 (1946): 11.

Greenhalgh, Susan. "Controlling Births and Bodies in Village China." *American Ethnologist* 21, no. 1 (1994): 3–30.

Just One Child: Science and Policy in Deng's China. Berkeley: University of California Press, 2008.

"The Social Construction of Population Science: An Intellectual, Institutional, and Political History of Twentieth-Century Demography." *Comparative Studies in Society and History* 38, no. 1: 26–66.

Greenhalgh, Susan and Jiali Li. "Engendering Reproductive Policy and Practice in Peasant China: For a Feminist Demography of Reproduction." *Signs* 20, no. 3 (1995): 601–641.

Greenhalgh, Susan and Edwin A. Winckler. *Governing China's Population: From Leninist to Neoliberal Biopolitics*. Stanford: Stanford University Press, 2005.

Griffiths, James, Nanlin Fang, and Serenitie Wang. "China's Lack of Sex Education Is Putting Millions of Young People at Risk." *CNN*, December 6, 2016. www.cnn.com/2016/11/30/health/china-sex-education-world-aids-day.

Gross, Miriam. *Farewell to the God of Plague: Chairman Mao's Campaign to Deworm China*. Berkeley: University of California Press, 2016.

Gu 谷. "Yizhou jianping: zaoyun yu jieyu" 一週簡評：早婚與節育 (Weekly Comment: Early Marriage and Birth Control). *Shanghai dangsheng* 上海黨聲 1 (1935): 22.

Gu, Baochang, Wang Feng, Guo Zhigang, and Zhang Erli. "China's Local and National Fertility Policies at the End of the Twentieth Century." *Population and Development Review* 33, no. 1 (2007): 129–147.

Gu, Jiantang 顾鉴塘. "Minguo shiqi renkou yanjiu tanwei" 民国时期人口研究探微 (An Exploration of Population Studies during the Republican Era). *Beijing daxue xuebao: zheshe ban* 北京大学：哲学版 (Beijing University Journal: Philosophy Society Edition) (2001). www.szrmf.com/paper/48916.html.

Gu, Nan 古男. "Changshi tanhua: biyun yu jieyu" 常識談話：生育與墮胎 (Common Sense Conversation: Birth Control and Abortion). *Tielu zhigong* 鐵路職工(Railway Worker) 43, no. 133 (1930): 2–4.

"Guangdong yi fuqi chaosheng bei zhengshou 32 wan yuan shehui fuyang fei" 广东一夫妻超生 被征收32万元社会抚养费 (A Couple in Guangdong was Levied a 320,000 Yuan Excess Child Fee). *Sina*, June 11, 2020. http://gd.sina.com.cn/news/2020-06-11/detail-iircuyvi7858914.shtml.

"Gulou yiyuan zhishi jieyu: yi you sanshi ren" 鼓楼医院指示节育：已有三十人 (Gulou Hospital Provides Birth Control Instruction: Already Served 30 Patients). *Guangxi yikan* 广西医刊 (Guangxi Medical Journal) 12, no. 2 (1935): 10–11.

Guo, Quanqing 郭泉清. *Shiyong biyunfa* 实用避孕法 (Practical Birth Control Methods). Shanghai: Jia zazhi she, 1950.

Guojia jihua shengyu weiyuanhui zonghe jihua si 国家计划生育委员会综合计划司 (National Birth Planning Committee Integrated Planning Division). Quanguo jihua shengyu tongji ziliao huibian 全国计划生育统计资料汇编 (*Chinese Birth Planning Statistical Yearbook*). Guojia jihua shengyu weiyuanhui zonghe jihua si, 1983.

Han, Hua. "Under the Shadow of the Collective Good: An Ethnographic Analysis of Fertility Control in Xiaoshan, Zhejiang Province, China." *Modern China* 33, no. 3 (2007): 320–348.

Hardee-Cleaveland, Karen and Judith Banister. "Fertility Policy and Implementation in China, 1986–88." *Population and Development Review* 14, no. 2 (1988): 245–286.

Harrison, Henrietta. "'A Penny for the Little Chinese': The French Holy Childhood Association in China, 1843–1951." *The American Historical Review* 113, no. 4 (2008): 72–92.

Hartmann, Betsy. *Reproductive Rights and Wrongs: The Global Politics of Birth Control*. Boston: South End Press, 1995.

Hebei sheng weisheng ting (河北省卫生厅). *Jiezhi shengyu wenda* 节制生育问答 (Questions and Answers about Birth Control). Tianjin: Hebei renmin chubanshe, 1962.

Henriot, Christian. *Prostitution and Sexuality in Shanghai: A Social History, 1849–1949*. Translated by Noel Castelino. Cambridge: Cambridge Universit2y Press, 2001.

Hershatter, Gail. *Dangerous Pleasures: Prostitution and Modernity in Twentieth-Century Shanghai*. Berkeley: University of California Press, 1997.

The Gender of Memory: Rural Women and China's Collective Past. Berkeley: University of California Press, 2011.

"Regulating Sex in Shanghai: The Reform of Prostitution in 1920 and 1951." In *Shanghai Sojourners*, edited by Frederic Wakeman Jr. and Yeh Wen-hsin. Berkeley: University of California Press, 1992.

Women in China's Long Twentieth Century. Berkeley: University of California Press, 2007.
Hinrichs, T.J. and Linda L. Barnes, eds. *Chinese Medicine and Healing: An Illustrated History*. Cambridge: Harvard University Press, 2012.
Ho, Denise. *Curating Revolution: Politics on Display in Mao's China*. Cambridge: Cambridge University Press, 2017.
Hodgson, Dennis. "Demography as Social Science and Policy Science." *Population and Development Review* 9, no. 1 (1983): 1–34.
Hong, Li 鴻黎. "Zhencao wenti" 貞操問題 (The Chastity Problem), *Funü zazhi* 婦女雜誌 (Ladies' *Journal)* 2, no. 2 (1941): 29.
Honig, Emily. *Sisters and Strangers: Women in the Shanghai Cotton Mills, 1919–1949*. Stanford: Stanford University Press, 1992.
"Socialist Sex: The Cultural Revolution Revisited." *Modern China* 29, no. 2 (2003): 143–175.
Honig, Emily and Gail Hershatter. *Personal Voices: Chinese Women in the 1980's*. Stanford: Stanford University Press, 1988.
Honig, Emily and Xiaojian Zhao. *Across the Great Divide: The Sent-Down Youth Movement in Mao's China, 1968–1980*. Cambridge: Cambridge University Press, 2019.
Hu, Jiawei. "Why It's Time for Chinese Educators to Open Up about Sex." *Sixth Tone*, June 19, 2017. www.sixthtone.com/news/1000361/why-its-time-for-chinese-educators-toopen-up-about-sex.
Hua, Shengdun. "Sex Education in China Evolving." *China Daily USA*, April 16, 2015. http://usa.chinadaily.com.cn/china/2015-04/06/content_20010305.htm.
Huang, Shu-min. *The Spiral Road: Change in a Chinese Village through the Eyes of a Communist Party Leader*. Boulder: Westview Press, 1998.
Huang, Yuchuan 黄雨川. *Zhonggong jieyu yundong* 中共节育运动 (Chinese Communist Party's Birth Control Movement). Hong Kong: Youlian chubanshe, 1967.
Hui, Mingzeng 惠明贈. "Cong Luo Guifang de duotai shuoqi" 辞駱桂芳的墮胎說起 (Talking about Luo Guifang's Abortion). Wufeng banyue qikan 舞風半月期刊 *(Dance Bimonthly Periodical)* 2, no. 3 (1938): 15.
"Huoshan baofa (liu yuefen de wunü zhang: liu yue san ri (ponü datai)" 火山爆发（六月份的舞　女账）：六月三日（迫女打胎）(Volcanic Eruption: June Dancer's Account: June 3 (A Girl's Forced Abortion). *Wuchang texie* 舞场特写 (Dance Scene) 2 (1939): n.p.
Hvistendahl, Mara. *Unnatural Selection: Choosing Boys over Girls, and the Consequences of a World Full of Men*. New York: Public Affairs, 2011.
"Jiajiale biyun pian" 家家乐避孕片 (Happy Family Birth Control Pills). *Hangzhou ribao* 杭州 日报 (Hangzhou Daily), May 3, 1959.
Jiang, Liu 江流. "Yi ge bei nüedai de nüxing" 一個被虐待的女性 (An Abused Girl). *Xiandai Funü* 現代婦女 (Modern Woman) 13 (1949): 28.
"Jieyu yu duotai shaying" 節育與墮胎殺嬰 (Birth Control and Abortion as Baby Killing). *Yongsheng* 永生 (1936): 80.
Jin, Dalu 金大陆 and Lin Shengbao 林升宝, eds. *Shanghai zhishi qingnian shangshan xiaxiang yundong jishilu, 1968–1981* 上海知识青年上山下乡运动纪事录 (Chronicle of Shanghai Rusticated Youth during the Sent-Down Youth Movement, 1968–1981). Shanghai: Shanghai shudian chubanshe, 2014.

Jiu, Jiu 九九. "Ruyidai junshi shang de gongxian" 如意袋軍事上的貢獻 (The Military's Contribution of Condoms). *Yizhou jian* 一週間13 (1946): 9.

Johnson, Kay Ann. *China's Hidden Children: Abandonment, Adoption, and the Human Costs of the One-Child Policy*. Chicago: University of Chicago Press, 2016.

Women, the Family, and Peasant Revolution. Chicago: University of Chicago Press, 1987.

Johnson, Tina Phillips. *Childbirth in Republican China: Delivering Modernity*. Lanham: Lexington Books, 2011.

Jones, Claire L. *The Business of Birth Control: Contraception and Commerce in Britain before the Sexual Revolution*. Manchester: Manchester University Press, 2020.

Ju, You 鞠有. "Wang Wenlan tunji ruyidai" 王文蘭囤積如意袋 (Wang Wenlan Hoards Condoms). *Yefeng* 野風 (Wild Wind) 2 (1946): n.p.

Kane, Penny. *The Second Billion: Population and Family Planning in China*. Ringwood: Penguin Books, 1987.

Kaufman, Joan, Zhang Zhirong, Qiao Zinjian, and Zhang Yang. "Family Planning Policy and Practice in China: A Study of Four Rural Counties," *Population and Development Review* 15, no. 4 (1989): 707–729.

Ke, Shi 克士. "*Shengyu jiezhi datai he ertong gongyu*" 生育节制打胎和儿童公育 (Birth Control, Abortion, and Childcare). *Dongfang zazhi* 东方杂志 (East Asian Miscellany) 31, no. 21 (1934): 5–6.

"Kedou biyun danfang wuxiao" 蝌蚪避孕单方无效 (Tadpole Birth Control Home Remedy Is Not Effective). *Zhejiang ribao* 浙江日报 (Zhejiang Daily), April 16, 1958.

"Kedou biyun zhengzai shiyan, xianzai bu yao mangmu fuyong" 蝌蚪避孕正在试验，现在不 要盲目服用 (Using Tadpoles as Birth Control is Currently Being Tested, For Now Do Not Blindly Consume Them). *Zhejiang ribao* 浙江日报 (Zhejiang Daily), March 31, 1957.

"Kelian jinü duotai zhiming" 可憐妓女墮胎致命 (Pitiful Prostitute Dies from Abortion), *Shenbao* 申報, September 1, 1933.

King, Michelle T. *Between Birth and Death: Female Infanticide in Nineteenth-Century China*. Stanford: Stanford University Press, 2014.

"Margaret Sanger in Translation: Gender, Class, and Birth Control in 1920s China." *Journal of Women's History* 29, no. 3 (2017): 61–83.

Klausen, Susanne M. *Race, Maternity, and the Politics of Birth Control in South Africa, 1910–39*. London: Palgrave Macmillan, 2004.

Koblitz, Anne Hibner. *Sex and Herbs and Birth Control*. Seattle: Kovalevskaia Fund, 2014.

Kohama, Masako 小浜正子. "Cong 'feifa duotai' dao 'jihua shengyu:' jianguo qianhou xing he shengzhi zhi yanlun kongjian de bianqian" 从"非法堕胎"到"计划生育"—建国前后性和生殖言论空间的变迁 (From "Criminal Abortion" to "Birth Planning:" The Changes of Discursive Space with Regard to Sex and Reproduction before and after 1949). In *Jindai zhongguo chengshi yu dazhong wenhua* 近代中国城市与大众文化, edited by Jiang Jin and Li Deying, 330–355. Beijing: Xinxing chubanshe, 2008.

小浜正子. "Jihua shengyu de kaiduan—1950–1960 niandai de Shanghai" 计划生育的开端—1950–1960年代的上海 (The Beginnings of Birth Planning in

Shanghai in the 1950s and 1960s). *Zhongyang yanjiuyuan jindaishi yanjiusuo jikan* 中央研究院近代史研究所集刊 68 (2010): 97–142.

小浜正子. "Zhongguo nongcun jihua shengyu de puji – yi 1960–1970 niandai Q cun wei li" 中国农村计划生育的普及—以1960–1970年代Q村为例 (The Popularization of Birth Planning in Rural China—The Case of Q Village, 1960s–1970s). *Jindai zhongguo funü shi yanjiu* 近代中国妇女史研究 19 (2011): 173–214.

Lam, Tong. *A Passion for Facts: Social Surveys and the Construction of the Chinese Nation State, 1900–1949*. Berkeley: University of California Press, 2011.

Latham, Michael E. *Modernization as Ideology: American Social Science and "Nation Building" in the Kennedy Era*. Chapel Hill: University of North Carolina Press, 2000.

Lean, Eugenia. "The Modern Elixir: Medicine as a Consumer Item in the Early Twentieth-Century Chinese Press." *UCLA History Journal* 15, no. 0 (1995): 65–92.

Lee, James Z. and Wang Feng, *One Quarter of Humanity: Malthusian Mythology and Chinese Realities, 1700–2000*. Cambridge: Harvard University Press, 1999.

Lei, Jieqiong 雷洁琼. "Huainian Yang Chongrui yishi" 怀念杨崇瑞医师 ("Remembering Dr. Yang Chongrui"). In *Yang Chongrui Boshi, Danchen bai nian jinian* 杨崇瑞博士诞辰百年纪念 (Dr. Yang Chongrui, 100 Years Memorial Since Her Birth), edited by Yan Renying, 1–3. Beijing: Beijing yike daxue, Zhonguo xiehe yike daxue lianhe chubanshe, 1990.

Lei, Sean Hsiang-lin. *Neither Donkey Nor Horse: Medicine in the Struggle over China's Modernity*. Chicago: University of Chicago Press, 2014.

Leng, Shao-Chuan. "The Role of Law in the People's Republic of China as Reflecting Mao Tse-Tung 's Influence," *Journal of Criminal Law and Criminology*, 68, no. 3 (1977): 356–373.

Leung, Angela Ki Che. "Relief Institutions for Children in Nineteenth-Century China." In *Chinese Views of Childhood*, edited by Anne Behnke Kinney. Honolulu: University of Hawai'i Press, 1995.

"Liang yaofang chaohuo yinju chunyao" 两药房抄获淫具春药 (Two Pharmacies Were Searched – Obscene Products and Aphrodisiacs Were Seized). *Shenbao* 申报, March 4， 1937.

Li, Bingkui 李秉奎. *Kuanglan yu qianliu: Zhongguo qingnian de xinglian yu hunyin, 1966–1976* 狂澜与潜流—中国青年的性恋与婚姻， 1966–1976 (Raging Waves and Undercurrents: Sexuality and Marriage among Chinese Youth, 1966–1976). Beijing: Shehui kexue wenxian chubanshe, 2015.

Li, Bozhong 李伯重. "Duotai, biyun, yu jueyu: Song Yuan Ming Qing shiqi Jiang-Zhe diqu de jieyu fangfa ji qi yunyong yu chuanbo" 堕胎，避孕，与绝育：宋元明清时期江浙地区的节育方法及其实用与传播 (Abortion, Contraception, and Sterilization: Fertility Control and Its Dissemination in Jiangsu and Zhejiang during the Song, Yuan, Ming, and Qing Dynasties). In *Hunyin jiating yu renkou xingwei* 婚姻家庭与人口行为 (Marriage, Family, and Population Behavior) edited by Li Zhongqing 李中清, Guo Songyi 郭松义, and Ding Yizhuang 定宜庄, 172–196. Beijing: Beijing daxue chubanshe, 2000.

Li, Ming 李明. "Anmo liuchan 32 jingyan jieshao" 按摩流产32例经验介绍 (Introducing the Experience of 32 Abortions through Massage). *Anmo yu daoyin* 按摩与导引 (Chinese Manipulation & Qi Gong Therapy) 4 (1993): n.p.

Liu, Lydia H. *Translingual Practice: Literature, National Culture, and Translated Modernity – China, 1900–1937*. Stanford: Stanford University Press, 1995.

Liu, Lydia, Rebecca Karl, and Dorothy Ko, eds. *The Birth of Chinese Feminism: Essential Texts in Transnational Theory*. New York: Columbia University Press, 2013.

Liu, Xiaomeng 刘小萌. *Zhongguo zhiqing koushushi* 中国知青口述书 (The Oral Histories of Chinese Educated Youth). Beijing: Zhongguo shehui kexue chubanshe, 2004.

Zhongguo zhiqingshi: da chao 中国知青：大潮 (A History of China's Sent-Down Youth: The Main Wave). Beijing: Zhongguo shehui kexue chubanshe, 1998.

Long, Sao 龍騷. "Dushi de feng" 都市的風 (The Urban Scene). *Shenbao* 申報, May 15, 1933.

Lu, Dachuan 陆大川. "Wo jieza shujing guan de qianqian houhou" 我结扎输精管的前前后后 (Before and after My Vasectomy). *Zhongguo funü* 中国妇女 (New Women of China) 4 (1963): 11.

Lu, Hanchao. *Beyond the Neon Lights: Everyday Shanghai in the Early Twentieth Century*. Berkeley: University of California Press, 1999.

Lu, Shifu 卢施福. "Feifa zhidao jieyu de chawu he weixian" 非法指导节育的差误和危险 (The Errors and Dangers of Illegally Advising on Birth Control). *Shengming yu jiankang* 生命与健康 (Life and Health) 6 (1928): n.p.

Luoyang renkou he jihua shengyu weiyuanhui (Luoyang Population and Birth Planning Committee). *Luoyangshi renkou he jihua shengyu zhi, 1985–2014* 洛阳市人口和计划生育志 (The Chronicle of Population and Family Planning of Luoyang, 1985–2014). Luoyang: Luoyang shi renkou he jihua shengyu weiyuanhui, 2015.

Luoyang shi renkou pucha lingdao xiaozu bangongshe (Office of the Luoyang Population Survey Leading Small Group). *Henan sheng Luoyang shi di sanci renkou pucha shougong huizong ziliao huibian* 河南省洛阳市第三次人口普查手工汇总资料汇编 (The Compiled Materials of the Third Manual Population Survey of Luoyang, Henan). Luoyang: Luoyang shi renkou pucha lingdao xiaozu bangongshe, 1982.

Luoyang shizhi 洛阳市志 (Luoyang Gazetteer), October 15, 2009. www.lydqw.com/DB/BookContent.aspx?BookID=200904080002&Content=Digital.

Ma, Bo. *Blood Red Sunset: A Memoir of the Chinese Cultural Revolution*. Translated by Howard Goldblatt. New York: Penguin Books, 1996.

Ma, Guoliang 馬國亮. *Zai gei nürenmen* 再給女人們 (Again to the Women). Shanghai: Shanghai liangyou tushu yinshua gongsi, 1933.

Ma, Jian, *The Dark Road: A Novel*. Translated by Flora Drew. New York: Penguin Press, 2013.

MacFarquhar, Roderick and Michael Schoenhals. *Mao's Last Revolution*. Cambridge: Harvard University Press, 2006.

Manning, Kimberly Ens. "Marxist Maternalism, Memory, and the Mobilization of Women in the Great Leap Forward." *The China Review* 5, no. 1 (2005): 83–110.

Mao, Xian 毛咸. "Yiyao wenda: da di 365 hao: beiliuxian zhengfu sa zhangjun wen jieyu" 醫藥問答：答第三六五號北流縣政府薩 (Medical Q&A: Answer Number 365: Beiliu County Government's Sa Zhangjun Asks about Birth Control). *Guangxi weisheng xunkan* 廣西衛生旬刊 (Guangxi Hygiene Journal) 3, no. 2 (1935): 18–19.

Mao Zedong zhuzuo zhuanti zhaibian 毛泽东著作专题摘编 (Thematic Excerpts from Mao Zedong's Works). Beijing: Zhongyang wenxian chubanshe, 2003.

McKibbin, Ross. *Classes and Cultures: England, 1918–1950*. Oxford: Oxford University Press, 1998.

McMillan, Joanna. *Sex, Science and Morality in China*. Abingdon-on-Thames: Taylor and Francis, 2006.

Mellors, Sarah. "The Trouble with Rubbers: A History of Condoms in Modern China," *Nan Nü: Men, Women and Gender in China* 22, no. 1 (2020): 150–178.

Miao, Xin and Liu Chang. "Chinese Women Bear the Major Burden of Contraception." *Sixth Tone*, March 8, 2018. https://twitter.com/SixthTone.

Michelle Murphy, *Seizing the Means of Reproduction: Entanglements of Feminism, Health, and Technoscience*. Durham: Duke University Press, 2012.

Miller, Barbara. "Female-Selective Abortion in Asia: Patterns, Policies, and Debates." *American Anthropologist* 103, no. 4 (2001): 1083–1095.

Milwertz, Cecilia Nathansen. *Accepting Population Control: Urban Women and the One-Child Family Policy*. London: Curzon Press, 1997.

Min, Anchee. *Red Azalea*. New York: Anchor Books, 1994.

Mosher, Steven. *Broken Earth: The Rural Chinese*. New York: The Free Press, 1983.

"Mou hongxing duotai sici" 某紅星墮胎四次 (A Certain Celebrity Had Four Abortions). *Yingwu xinwen* 影舞新聞 (Film and Dance News) 1, no. 12 (1935): 5.

Musallam, B.F. *Sex and Society in Islam: Birth Control before the Nineteenth Century*. Cambridge: Cambridge University Press, 1983.

Ng, Michael H. K. *Legal Transplantation in Early Twentieth Century China: Practicing Law in Republican Beijing*. Abingdon: Routledge, 2014.

Ni juedui mei jianguo 50 nian qian wuhan jietou biyun guanggao 你绝对没见过50年前武汉街 头避孕广告 (Birth Control Advertisements on the Streets of Wuhan 50 Years Ago You Have Never Seen before). *Sohu*, May 6, 2016. www.sohu.com/a/73608709_199944.

Nie, Jing-Bao. *Behind the Silence: Chinese Voices on Abortion*. Lanham: Rowman & Littlefield Publishers, 2005.

"Non-Medical Sex-Selective Abortion in China: Ethical and Public Policy Issues in the Context of 40 Million Missing Females." *British Medical Bulletin* 98 (2011): 7–20.

"Nongcun pochan shengzhong, lai Hu duotai rizhong" 農村破產聲中：來滬墮胎日眾 (Amid Rural Bankruptcy, Many Come to Shanghai for Abortion). *Shenbao* 申報, September 25, 1936.

Nongcun yiliao weisheng puji shouce 农村医疗卫生普及手册(Popular Handbook for Rural Healthcare). Shanghai: Shanghai "nongcun yiliao weisheng puji shouce" bianxie zu, 1969.

Nongcun yiliao weisheng shouce 农村医疗卫生手册 (Rural Healthcare Handbook). Shanghai: Shanghai kexue jishu chubanshe, 1968.

Nongcun yisheng shouce 农村医生手册 (Rural Doctor Handbook). Beijing: Renmin weisheng chubanshe, 1971.

Norgren, Tiana A. E. *Abortion before Birth Control: The Politics of Reproduction in Postwar Japan*. Princeton: Princeton University Press, 2001.

"Nü zhiqing koushu wenge shiqi liangxing guanxi beican jingli rang ren zhenjing" 女知青口述 文革时期两性关系悲惨经历让人震惊 (Female Sent Down Youths' Shocking Oral Histories of Tragic Sexual Experiences during the Cultural Revolution). *Liushu yaofeng de boke* 柳树摇风的博客 (Shaking Willow Blog), June 8, 2015. http://blog.sina.com.cn/s/blog_443bf8ae0102voa4.html.

O'Meara, Sarah. "Workshop Teaches Children How to Guard against Sexual Abuse." *Sixth Tone*, July 5, 2016. www.sixthtone.com/news/1034/workshop-teaches-children-how-guard-against-sexual-abuse.

Ou, Nianzhong and Yongkang Liang, eds. *Mao's Lost Children: Stories of the Rusticated Youth of China's Cultural Revolution*. Laura Maynard, trans. Portland: Merwin Asia, 2015.

Pan, Guangdan. "Zhongguo zhi yousheng wenti" (The Problem of Eugenics in China). *Dongfang zazhi* (East Asian Miscellany) 21, no. 22 (1924): 15

Pan, Guangdan 潘光旦. "Yousheng fukan: shengyu jiezhi de jige biaozhun" 優生期刊：生育節制的幾個標準 (Eugenics Supplement: Several Criteria for Birth Control). *Huanian* 華年 4, no. 22 (1935): 431–435.

Pan, Zhengzhong 潘整中 and Guozhen Feng 冯国桢. "Weihun xianyu suo yinqi de" 未婚先孕 所引起的 (What Premarital Pregnancy Gives Rise to). *Shehui* 社会 (Society) 2 (1986): 20–22.

"Per Capita Annual Income and Expenditure Urban and Rural Households." All China Data Center. Chinadataonline.org (accessed April 28, 2015).

"Ping pohuo mimi duku 平破獲秘密毒窟 (Beiping Secret Drug Stash Exposed). *Shenbao* 申報, November 12, 1947.

Population Council. "The New Chinese Law on Maternal and Infant Health Care." *Population Development Review* 21, no. 3 (1995): 698–702.

Qiu, Peipei. *Chinese Comfort Women: Testimonies from Imperial Japan's Sex Slaves*. Oxford: Oxford University Press, 2014.

Ren, Jin 人金. "Weihun fufu de xingxingwei" 未婚婦女的性行為 (Unmarried Couples' Sexual Behavior). *Funü yuekan* 婦女月刊 (Women's Monthly) 6, no. 6 (1948): 59.

Rigdon, Susan M. "Abortion Law and Practice in China: An Overview with Comparisons to the United States," *Social Science Medicine* 42, no. 4 (1996): 543–560.

Roberts, Dorothy. *Killing the Black Body: Race, Reproduction, and the Meaning of Liberty*. New York: Vintage Books, 1997.

Rocha, Leon. "A Small Business of Sexual Enlightenment: Zhang Jingsheng's 'Beauty Bookshop', Shanghai 1927–1929." *British Journal of Chinese Studies* 9, no. 2 (2019): 1–30.

Rocha, Leon Antonio. "Translation and Two 'Chinese Sexologies': *Double Plum* and Sex Histories." In *Sexology and Translation: Cultural and Scientific*

Encounters across the Modern World, edited by Heike Bauer. Philadelphia: Temple University Press, 2015.

"*Xing: The Discourse of Sex and Human Nature in Modern China*." *Gender and History* 22, no. 3 (2010): 603–628.

Rogaski, Ruth. *Hygienic Modernity: Meanings of Health and Disease in Treaty-Port China*. Berkeley: University of California Press, 2004.

Sanger, Margaret. "Birth Control in China and Japan." October 31, 1922. www.nyu.edu/projects/sanger/webedition/app/documents/show.php?sangerDoc=101865xml (accessed May 10, 2018).

Jieyu zhuyi 節育主意 (Birth Control Doctrine). Translated by Chen Haicheng 陳海澂. Shanghai: Shanghai shangwuban, 1928.

Sanger, Margaret 珊格爾夫. "Shengyu zhicai de shenme yu zenyang" 生育制裁的什麼與怎樣 (Birth Control's What and How).Translated by Hu Shi 胡适. *Funü zazhi* 婦女雜誌 (Ladies' Journal) 8, no. 6 (1922): 129.

Santow, Gigi. "Emmenagogues and Abortifacients in the Twentieth Century: An Issue of Ambiguity." In *Regulating Menstruation: Beliefs, Practices, Interpretations*, edited by Etienne Van de Walle, 64–92. Chicago: University of Chicago Press, 2001.

Scharping, Thomas. *Birth Control in China, 1949–2000: Population Policy and Demographic Development*. London: RoutledgeCurzon, 2003.

Scheid, Volker and Sean Hsiang-lin Lei. "The Institutionalization of Chinese Medicine." In *Medical Transitions in Twentieth-Century China*," edited by Bridie Andrews and Mary Brown Bullock, 244–266. Bloomington: University of Indiana Press, 2014.

Scheper-Hughes, Nancy. *Death Without Weeping: The Violence of Everyday Life in Brazil*. Berkeley: University of California Press, 1993.

Schoenhals, Michael. "Sex in Big-Character Posters from China's Cultural Revolution: Gendering the Class Enemy." In *Gender and Mass Dictatorship: Global Perspectives*, Edited by Jie-Hyun Lim and Karen Petrone, 237–257. Basingstoke: Palgrave Macmillan, 2011.

Selezneva, Ekaterina. "Struggling For New Lives: Family and Fertility Policies in the Soviet Union and Modern Russia." *Ideas*. https://ideas.repec.org/p/hit/hitcei/2015-8.html (accessed October 16, 2016).

Shandong weisheng ting 山东卫生厅 (Shandong Department of Hygiene). *Jieyu xuanchuan shouce* 节育宣传手册 (Birth Control Propaganda Handbook). Jinan: Shandong renmin chubanshe, 1958.

Shanghai di er yixue yuan fu chan ke jiaoyanzu 上海第二医学院妇产科教研组 (Obstetrics and Gynecology Teaching and Research Group of Shanghai Number Two Medical College). *Qingnian hunyin weisheng* 青年婚姻卫生 (Youth Marital Hygiene). Shanghai: Shanghai kexue jishu chubanshe, 1958.

Shanghai jieyu yanjiushe 上海節育研究社 (Shanghai Birth Control Research Society). *Shanghai yishi zhoukan* 上海醫事週刊 (Shanghai Medical Weekly) 6, no. 41 (1940): n.p.

"Shanghai tebie shi qudi yinwei yaowu xuanchuan pin zanxing guiding" 上海特別市取締淫藥物宣傳品暫行規定 (Temporary Rules for the Prohibition of Publicizing Obscene Drugs in Shanghai). *Shenbao* 申報, May 4, 1929.

"Shanxi: 2016 nian qi shishi liang hai zhengce, nüfang sheng er hai jiangli 60 tian jiaqi" 山西： 2016年起实施两孩政策 女方生二孩奖励60天假期 (Shanxi:

Since the Implementation of the Two Child Policy in 2016, Women Who Have a Second Child Will Receive a 60-Day Leave). *Minnang wang* 闽南网 (Southern Fujian Network), January 20, 2016. www.mnw.cn/news/shehui/1086933.html.

Shao, Lizi 邵力子. "Wo dui jieyu wenti de yidian yijian" 我对节育问题的一点意见 (My Opinion on Birth Control). *Renmin ribao* 人民日报 (People's Daily), June 26, 1956.

Shapiro, Hugh. "The Puzzle of Spermatorrhea in Republican China." *Positions* 6 (1998): 551–596.

Shapiro, Judith. *Mao's War against Nature: Politics and the Environment in Revolutionary China*. Cambridge: Cambridge University Press, 1999.

Shen, Yubin. "Cultivating China's Cinchona: The Local Developmental State, Global Botanic Networks and Cinchona Cultivation in Yunnan, 1930s–1940s." *Social History of Medicine* (2019): 1–15.

"Shengyu zhicai de shenme yu zenyang" 生育制裁的什麼與怎樣 (The Hows and Whats of Birth Control) *Funü zazhi* 婦女雜誌 (Women's Magazine) 8, no. 6 (1922): 126–131.

"Sheyan: duotai yu jieyu" 社言：墮胎與節育 (Community Statement: Abortion and Birth Control). *Xinghua* 興華 27, no. 31 (1930): 1–3.

Shi, Chengli 史成礼. "Jianguo yilai jihua shengyu gongzuo gaikuang" 建国以来计划生育工作 概况(Summary of Birth Planning Work after the Founding of the PRC). *Xibei renkou* 西北人口 (Northwest Population) (1980): 33–48.

Smith, Aminda M. *Thought Reform and China's Dangerous Classes: Reeducation, Resistance, and the People*. Lanham: Rowman & Littlefield, 2013.

Smith, Nicole. "Some Surprising Insights on Birth Control and Contraception Practices in China." *Article Myriad*. December 7, 2011. www.articlemyriad.com/birth-control contraception-china/.

Sommer, Matthew H. "Abortion in Late Imperial China: Routine Birth Control or Crisis Intervention?" *Late Imperial China* 31, no. 2 (2010): 97–165.

Sommer, Matthew H. *Sex, Law and Society in Late Imperial China*. Stanford: Stanford University Press, 2000.

Song, Hongjian 宋鸿剑. "Jieza shujingguan hui yingxiang jiankang ma" 结扎输精管会影响健 康吗 (Can Undergoing a Vasectomy Influence One's Health). *Zhongguo funü* 中国妇女 (New Women of China) 4 (1963): 10.

Song, Hongjian 宋鸿剑 and Zhao Zhiyi 赵志一. *Biyun changshi* 避孕常识 (General Knowledge about Birth Control). Shanghai: Shanghai weisheng chubanshe, 1957.

Stacey, Judith. *Patriarchy and Socialist Revolution in China*. Berkeley: University of California Press, 1983.

Stevens, Sarah E. "Figuring Modernity: The New Woman and the Modern Girl in Republican China." *NWSA Journal* 15, no. 3 (Fall 2003): 82–103.

Stopes, Marie. *Ertong Ai* 兒童愛 (Wise Parenthood). Shanghai: Guanghua shuju, 1926.

Sun, Yanyu 孙嚴予. *Jieyu yu yousheng* 節育與優生 (From Birth Control to Eugenics). Shanghai: Meilingdeng & Co., 1949.

Szreter, Simon. "The Idea of Demographic Transition and the Study of Fertility Change: A Critical Intellectual History." *Population and Development Review* 19, no. 4 (1993): 659–701.

"Ta de you" 她的友 (Lady's Friend). *Funü shijie* 婦女世界 (Women's World) 19, no. 11 (1931): n.p.

Takeshita, Chikako. *The Global Biopolitics of the IUD: How Science Constructs Contraceptive Users and Women's Bodies*. Cambridge: MIT Press, 2013.

Takeuchi-Demirci, Aiko. *Contraceptive Diplomacy: Reproductive Politics and Imperial Ambitions in the United States and Japan*. Stanford: Stanford University Press, 2018.

Teng, Emma. *Eurasian: Mixed Identities in the United States, China, and Hong Kong, 1842–1943*. Berkeley: University of California Press, 2013.

Theiss, Janet. *Disgraceful Matters: The Politics of Chastity in Eighteenth-Century* China Berkeley: University of California Press, 2004.

Thompson, Malcolm. "Foucault, Fields of Governability, and the Population-Family-Economy Nexus in China." *History and Theory* 51 (2012): 42–62.

Tien, H. Yuan. "Sterilization, Oral Contraception, and Population Control in China." *Population Studies* 18, no. 3 (1965): 215–235.

"Wan, Xi, Shao: How China Meets Its Population Problem." *International Family Planning Perspectives* 6 (1980): 65–73.

Tien, K. H. "Intraamniotic Injection of Ethacridine for Second-Trimester Induction of Labor." *Obstetrics and Gynecology* 61, no. 6 (1983): 733–736.

Tinsman, Heidi. *Partners in Conflict: The Politics of Gender, Sexuality, and Labor in the Chilean Agrarian Reform, 1950–1973*. Durham: Duke University Press, 2002.

Tone, Andrea. *Devices and Desires: A History of Contraceptives in America*. New York: Hill and Wang, 2001.

"Making Room for Rubbers: Gender, Technology, and Birth Control before the Pill." *History and Technology* 18, no. 1 (2010): 51–76.

"Violence by Design: Contraceptive Technology and the Invasion of the Female Body." In *Lethal Imagination: Violence and Brutality in American History*. Edited by Michael A. Bellesiles. New York: New York University Press, 1999.

Tran, Lisa. "Sex and Equality in Republican China: The Debate over the Adultery Law." *Modern China* 35, no. 2 (2009): 191–223.

"Tu, Peilin." Shanghai Local History Office. www.shtong.gov.cn/node2/node2245/node4522/node10080/node10084/node63755/userobject1ai54188.html (accessed February 28, 2018).

Tu, Peilin 屠培林. *Shaying tang* 杀婴堂 (Infanticide Hall). Shanghai: Huadong renmin chubanshe, 1952.

U.S. Department of Health, Education, and Welfare Public Health Service. *A Barefoot Doctor's Manual (Translation of a Chinese Instruction to Certain Chinese Health Personnel)*. Washington, DC: John E. Fogarty International Center for Advanced Health Studies, 1974.

Waites, G.M.H., C. Wang, and P.D. Griffin. "Gossypol: Reasons for Its Failure to be Accepted as a Safe, Reversible Male Antifertility Drug." *International Journal of Andrology* 21, no. 1 (1998): 8–12.

Wang, Chongyi 王崇一et al. *Dangdai zhongguo de weisheng shiye* 当代中国的卫生事业 (Public Hygiene Undertakings in Modern China), vol. 2. Beijing: Zhongguo shehui kexue chubanshe, 1986.

Wang, Feng, Yong Cai, and Baochang Gu. "Population, Policy, and Politics: How Will History Judge China's One-Child Policy?" *Population and Development Review* 38 (2012): 115–129.

Wang, Shengmin 汪声敏. "Tan anquanqi ji shiyanhu shuansai biyunfa" 谈安全期及食盐糊栓塞 避孕法 (Discussing the Safe Period and Salt Paste Suppository Birth Control Methods). *Hangzhou ribao* 杭州日报 (Hangzhou Daily), April 19, 1957.

Wang, Wenbin 王文彬, Zhao Zhiyi 赵志一, and Tan Mingxun 谭铭勋. *Xing de zhishi* 性的知 识 (Knowledge about Sex). Beijing: Renmin weisheng chubanshe, 1956.

Xing de zhishi 性的知 识 (Knowledge about Sex). Beijing: Renmin weisheng chubanshe, 1957.

Xing de zhishi 性的知 识 (Knowledge about Sex). Beijing: Kexue puji chubanshe, 1958.

Xing de zhishi 性的知 识 (Knowledge about Sex). Beijing: Renmin weisheng chubanshe, 1981.

Wang, Y. Yvon. "Whorish Representation: Pornography, Media, and Modernity in Fin-de-siècle Beijing," *Modern China* 40, no. 4 (2014): 351–392.

"Yellow Books in Red China: A Preliminary Examination of Sex in Print in the Early People's Republic," *Twentieth-Century China* 44, no. 1 (2019): 75–97.

Wang, Yanrui 王延瑞. *Shuluanguan jueyushu* 输卵管绝育术 (Fallopian Tube Sterilization Surgery). Beijing: Renmin weisheng chubanshe, 1959.

Wang, Zheng. *Finding Women in the State: A Socialist Feminist Revolution in the People's Republic of China, 1949–1964*. Berkeley: University of California Press, 2017.

Wasserstrom, Jeffrey. "Resistance to the One-Child Family." *Modern China* 10, no. 3 (1984): 345–374.

Watts, Jonathon. "China Sex Education Lags Behind Sexual Activity." *The Lancet*, April 10, 2004. www.thelancet.com/pdfs/journals/lancet/PIIS0140673604159941.pdf.

Weatherhead, L. D. *Controlling Sexual Life (xingshenghuo de kongzhi)*. Shanghai: Youth Association Books (qingnian xiehui shuju), 1936.

"Wei jinü datai, beigao fa juban" 為妓女打胎，被告舉辦 (Abortion for a Prostitute, the Accused Was Detained and Dealt With), *Shenbao* 申報, January 19, 1949.

Wei, Xia, Shouzhang She, and Taihing Lam. "Medical versus Surgical Abortion Methods for Pregnancy in China: A Cost-Minimization Analysis." *Gynecologic and Obstetric Investigation* 72 (2011): 257–263.

Weisberg, Marvin E. and John R. Graham. *A Barefoot Doctor's Manual: A Guide to Traditional Chinese and Modern Medicine* (The American Translation of the Official Chinese Paramedical Manual). N.p.: Cloudburst Press, 1977.

White, Tyrene. *China's Longest Campaign: Birth Planning in the People's Republic, 1949–2005*. Ithaca: Cornell University Press, 2006.

Whyte, Martin King, Wang Feng, and Yong Cai, "Challenging Myths about China's One-Child Policy." *The China Journal* 74 (2015): 144–159.

Williams, Rebecca Jane. "Storming the Citadels of Poverty: Family Planning in India, 1975–1977." *Journal of Asian Studies* 73, no. 2 (2014): 471–492.

Winder, Daniel. *Reproductive Control or a Rational Guide to Matrimonial Happiness*. Cincinnati: n.p., 1855.

Wolf, Arthur P. "Is There Evidence of Birth Control in Late-Imperial China?" *Population and Development Review* 27, no. 1 (2001): 133–154.

Wolf, Arthur P. and Theo Engelen. "Fertility and Fertility Control in Pre-Revolutionary China." *The Journal of Interdisciplinary History* 38, no. 3 (2008): 345–375.

Wolf, Margery. *Revolution Postponed: Women in Contemporary China*. Stanford: Stanford University Press, 1985.

Wu, Yiching. *The Cultural Revolution at the Margins: Chinese Socialism in Crisis*. Cambridge: Harvard University Press, 2014.

Wu, Zelin 吴泽霖. "Yazhou de jieyu wenti" 亞洲的節育問題 (Asia's Birth Control Problem). *Tushu pinglun* 圖書評論 (Book Reviews) 2, no. 6 (1934): 93–94.

Xiao, Feng 萧风. "Fu kedou buneng biyun" 服蝌蚪不能避孕 (Tadpoles Are Not Birth Control). *Hangzhou ribao* 杭州日报 (Hangzhou Daily), July 7, 1957.

"Xiaofang huiying xiaoxue xing jiaoyu keben zhengyi: jiang zejie tui xiangguan kecheng" 校方回应小学性教育课本争议：将择机推相关课程 (School Responds to Textbook Disputes in Primary School Sex Education: Will Select Opportunities to Promote Related Courses). Zhongguo xinwen wang 中国新闻网 (China News), March 7, 2017. http://www.chinanews.com/sh/2017/03-07/8167055.shtml (accessed May 30, 2018).

Xie, Yunshou 谢筠寿. "Duotai zui" 墮胎罪 (The Crime of Abortion). *Yixun* 醫訊 (Medical News) 2, no. 1 (1948): 3.

"Xingbingyuan mimi weiren duotai" 性病院秘密為人墮胎 (STD Hospital Secretly Performs Abortions). *Shenbao* 申報, August 10, 1930.

"Xingjiao zhongduan—tiwai shejing de biyun fa haobu hao" 性交中断—体外射精的避孕法好 不好 (Intercourse Interruption – Is the Withdrawal Method Good or Bad?). *Qingdao ribao* 青岛日报 (Qingdao Daily), December 22, 1957.

Xinran. *Message from an Unknown Chinese Mother: Stories of Loss and Love*. Nicky Harman, trans. New York: Scribner, 2010.

"Xinshui jieji de bei'ai, xian er'nü duo datai jian fudan, chi kuining wan buxing zhongdu si" 薪水階級的悲哀，嫌兒女多打胎減負擔，吃奎寧丸不幸中毒死 (Sorrow of the Working Class, Feared Having too Many Children So Had an Abortion to Reduce the Burden, Consumed Quinine and Died of Poisoning). *Daminbao* 大民報, December 17, 1947.

Xu, Chongwang 许崇望. Shanghai bai'er yaopin wuxian gongsi 上海拜耳藥品無限公司 (Shanghai Bayer Pharmaceutical Company, Ltd.) *Bai'er yiliao xinbao* 拜耳醫療新報 (Bayer Medical News) 12, no. 2 (1938): n.p.

Xu, Wancheng 許晚成. *Zuixin shiyan nannü biyunfa* 最新實驗男女避孕法 (The Newest Experimental Birth Control Methods for Men and Women). Shanghai: Guoguang shudian, 1941.

Xue, Yujie, "Jiangsu Company Rewards Employees for Having More Kids." *Sixth Tone*, April 3, 2019. http://www.sixthtone.com/news/1003803/jiangsu-company-rewards-employees-for-having-more-kids.

Xun, Xianwen 荀显文. "Banmao zhongdu siwang erli" 斑蝥中毒死亡二例 (Two Cases of Death from Mylabris Poisoning). *Zhongguo fayixue zazhi* 中国法医学杂志 (Chinese Journal of Forensic Medicine) 3 (1990): 156.

Yan, Mo. *Wa* (Frog). Shanghai: Shanghai wenyi chubanshe (Shanghai Literature and Art Press), 2009.

Yan, Yukuan 嚴與寬. *Jieyu de lilun yu fangfa* 節育的理論與方法 (Birth Control Theory and Methods). Shanghai: Dadong Shuju, 1933.

Yan, Yunxiang. *Private Life under Socialism: Love, Intimacy, and Family Change in a Chinese Village, 1949–1999*. Stanford: Stanford University Press, 2003.

Yang, Mayfair Mei-hui. "From Gender Erasure to Gender Difference: State Feminism, Consumer Sexuality, and Women's Public Sphere in China." In *Spaces of Their Own: Women's Public Sphere in Transnational China*,edited by Mayfair Mei-hui Yang, 35–67. Minneapolis: University of Minnesota Press, 1999.

Yang, Rae. *Spider Eaters: A Memoir*. Berkeley: University of California Press, 1997.

Yang, Wanli. "High Abortion Rate Triggers Fears for Young Women." *China Daily*, January 27, 2015. http://www.chinadaily.com.cn/china/2015-01/27/content_19412949.htm.

Yao, Jisheng 姚季生, Zhang Taiyun张泰运, and Li Yanji 李延吉. "32 li duotai siwang an fenxi" 32例堕胎死亡案分析 (An Analysis of 32 Cases of Fatal Abortion). *Xingshi jishu* 刑事技术 (Forensic Science and Technology) 5 (1982): 13–18.

Yeung, Alison Sau-Chu. "Fornication in the Late Qing Legal Reforms Moral Teachings and Legal Principles." *Modern China* 29, no. 3 (July 2003): 297–328.

"Youjian weichengnian nüzi bufang fangmian tiqi gongsu" 誘姦未成年女子捕房方面提起公司 (Court Prosecution for Luring an Underaged Girl). *Shenbao* 申報 15, July 1, 1935.

Yu, Hua. *China in Ten Words*. Allan H. Barr, trans. New York: Pantheon Books, 2011.

"Yue yue hong." *Funü shijie* (Women's World) 17, no. 7 (1931): n.p.

Zhai, Keith. "China Three-Child Policy Aims to Rejuvenate Aging Population." *Wall Street Journal,* May 31, 2021. www.wsj.com/articles/china-to-ease-limits-on-births-allowing-couples-to-have-three-children-11622447583.

Zhang, Cun 张存. "Baihua dan duotai baixiezheng jixing shen gongneng shuaijie siwang yi li baogao" 白花丹堕胎致败血症急性肾功能衰竭死亡一例报告 (A Case of Death by Septicemia and Kidney Failure from Use of *Baihua dan* as an Abortifacient). *Guangxi zhongyiyao* 广西中医药 (Guangxi Journal of Traditional Chinese Medicine) 1 (1986): n.p.

Zhang, Everett Yuehong. *The Impotence Epidemic: Men's Medicine and Sexual Desire in Contemporary China*. Durham: Duke University Press, 2015.

Zhang, Min 章泯. *Qi'er* 棄兒 (Abandoned Child). Shanghai: Xin yanju she, 1937.

Zhang, Ruolin 张若麟, ed. *Funü weisheng ji biyun changshi* 妇女卫生及避孕常识 (General Knowledge about Women's Hygiene and Birth Control). Shijiazhuang: Hebei renmin chubanshe, 1957.

Zhang, Yiling 张义凌. "Taobao guanggao cheng shingle nü'er zenme ban, Jiangsu fulian zazhi huyu daoqian" 淘宝广告称生了女儿怎么办 江苏妇联杂志呼吁道歉 (Jiangsu Women's Federation Magazine Calls for an Apology Regarding Taobao Advertisement Entitled 'What To Do If You Have a

Daughter?') *Sina*, April 27, 2018. http://news.sina.com.cn/s/2018-04-27/doc-ifztkpip4325744.shtml.

Zhao, Meng and Danni Fu. "Sterilization Quotas Endure in Two-Child Policy Era." *Sixth Tone*, February 22, 2017. http://www.sixthtone.com/news/1964/sterilization-quotas-endure-in-two-child-policy-era.

"Zhe xie jianzheng le jihua shengyu de haibao…" 这些见证了计划生育的海报… (Posters Attesting to Birth Planning…" *Shishe shishi de boke* 时拾史事的博客 (The Collecting Historical Events Blog), March 24, 2016. http://blog.sina.com.cn/s/blog_e39346e40102wej2.html.

"Zhege difang wei le guli sheng er tai, zuiduo jiangli 20 wan, ke haishi qi dao shenme xiaoguo" 这个地方为了鼓励生二胎，最多奖励20万，可还是没起到什么效果 (In Order to Encourage the Birth of Second Children, This Place Is Rewarding Up to 200,000 Yuan, But It's Having No Effect). *Sina*, May 4, 2020. https://k.sina.cn/article_6426234852_17f088fe400100pynd.html?from=baby.

Zhen, Ni 珍妮. "Duotai he biyun" 墮胎和避孕 (Abortion and Birth Control). *Xin funü yuekan* 新婦女月刊 (New Women's Monthly) 4 (1946): 20–21.

Zheng, Tiantian. *Ethnographies of Prostitution in Contemporary China: Gender Relations, HIV/AIDS, and Nationalism*. New York: Palgrave MacMillan, 2009.

"'Zhongguo funü' zazhe she" 《中国妇女》杂志社 (*Women of China* Magazine Publisher). Zhonghua quanguo funü lianhe hui 中华全国妇女联合会 (All-China Women's Federation). http://www.women.org.cn/zhuanti/www.women.org.cn/quanguofulian/zhishudanwei/funvzazhishe.htm (accessed May 18, 2021).

Zhonghua quanguo funü lianhehui yanjiusuo 中华全国妇女联合会研究所 (All China Women's Federation Research Institute). *Zhongguo funü tongji ziliao, 1949–1989* 中国妇女统计资料，1949–1989 (Statistical Data on Chinese Women, 1949–1989). Beijing: Zhongguo tongji chubanshe, 1991.

Zhonghua renmin gongheguo weisheng bu weisheng jiaoyu suo 中华人民共和国卫生部卫生教 育所 (Bureau of Hygiene Education of the People's Republic of China Ministry of Health). *Biyun qianhou* 避孕前后 (Before and after Birth Control). Tianjin: Kexue puji chubanshe, 1957.

Zhonghua renmin gongheguo weisheng bu weisheng jiaoyu suo 中华人民共和国卫生部卫生教 育所 (Bureau of Hygiene Education of the People's Republic of China Ministry of Health). *Jiezhi shengyu xuanchuan shouce* 节制生育宣传手册 (Birth Control Propaganda Handbook). Beijing: kexue puji chubanshe, 1958.

"Zhongyao biyun danfang" 中药避孕单方 (Chinese Medicine Contraceptive Prescription). *Qingdao ribao* 青岛日报 (Qingdao Daily), July 22, 1956.

Zhou, E'fen 周萼芬. "Biyun wenti da duzhe wen" 避孕問題答讀者問(Answering Readers' Questions about Birth Control). *Xin zhongguo funü* 新中國婦女 (New Women of China) 74 (1955): 26.

Zhou, Jianren 周建人. "Chan'er zhidu gaishu" 產兒制度概述 (A Summary of Childbirth Limitation), *Dongfang Zazhi* 東方雜誌 (East Asian Miscellany) 19, no. 7 (1922): n.p.

Zhu, Xiao Di. *Thirty Years in a Red House: A Memoir of Childhood and Youth in Communist China*. Amherst: University of Massachusetts Press, 1998.

Zhu, Yu 朱玉. "Woguo jiang shishi jihua shengyu shengzhi jiankang youzhi fuwu san da gongcheng 我国将实施计划生育生殖健康服务三大工程 (My

Country Will Implement Three Major Projects for High-Quality Birth Planning and Reproductive Health Services). *Guangming ribao* 光明日报 (Guangming Daily), June 7, 2001. www.gmw.cn/01gmrb/2001-06/07/05-12E1300CFCC7501B48256A640004088A.htm.

Zi, Nan 子南. "Guafu duotai" 寡婦墮胎 (Widow Abortion). *Shenbao* 申報, March 10, 1935.

Zui xin biyunfa 最新避孕法 (The Newest Birth Control Methods). Shanghai: Zhongguo yousheng jiezhi xiehui, 1948.

Zuo, Songfen 左誦芬. "Zhencao, aiqing, hunyin" 貞操，愛情，婚姻 (Chastity, Love, Marriage). *Xiandai funü* 現代婦女 (Modern Woman) 13 (1949): 11–12.

Zurndorfer, Harriet. "Polygamy and Masculinity in China: Past and Present." In *Changing Chinese Masculinities: From Imperial Pillars of State to Global Real Men*, edited by Kam Louie, Derek Hird, and Geng Song. Hong Kong: Hong Kong University Press, 2016.

Index

Milton Keynes UK
Ingram Content Group UK Ltd.
UKHW020627081223
434004UK00008B/73